PRELUDE TO PA

The Indian Muslim
Imperial System of Control 1920-1932

PRELUDE TO PARTITION

The Indian Muslims and the Imperial System of Control 1920-1932

DAVID PAGE

DELHI
OXFORD UNIVERSITY PRESS
CALCUTTA CHENNAI MUMBAI
1999

Oxford University Press, Great Clarendon Street, Oxford OX2 6DP

Oxford New York
Athens Auckland Bangkok Calcutta
Cape Town Chennai Dar es Salaam Delhi
Florence Hong Kong Istanbul Karachi
Kuala Lumpur Madrid Melbourne Mexico City
Mumbai Nairobi Paris Singapore
Taipei Tokyo Toronto

and associates in

Berlin Ibadan

First published 1982
Second impression 1987
Oxford India Paperbacks 1999

ISBN 0 19 564590 1

Printed in India at Saurabh Print-o-Pack, NOIDA
and published by Manzar Khan, Oxford University Press
YMCA Library Building, Jai Singh Road, New Delhi 110 001

To my parents

Contents

MAPS

Introduction to the Paperback Edition

Fifty years of independence have done little to diminish the scale of interest in the events which led to the end of the British Raj and the division of India into two sovereign independent states. The fiftieth anniversary itself produced a welter of commemorative events and publications, both in Britain and in the Subcontinent, much of it celebratory in character, but a good deal of it devoted to the rights and wrongs of Partition, to responsibility for the bloodshed which accompanied it and the unresolved legacy of bitterness between the two successor states. Partition continues to have an impact: in the memories of millions of individuals and families affected by communal slaughter and ethnic cleansing, in the continuing dispute over Kashmir, and in the costly military and nuclear standoff between the two countries which diverts scarce resources away from human development.

Preamble to Prelude

It is now almost twenty five years since *Prelude to Partition* was written—an attempt by a young British scholar to answer the deceptively simple question: why did relations between Hindus and Muslims deteriorate to the point where partition became a necessity? It was undoubtedly a presumptuous and foolhardy quest, as I was told quite firmly by Sir George Abell, private secretary to the last two Viceroys whom I met in his later incarnation as Chief Commissioner of the British Civil Service. He said: 'I was in India for twenty years and I didn't manage to get to the bottom of it and you certainly won't in three!'. His words were still ringing in my ears five years later and do so even today.

The question had become important to me during a year spent at Edwardes College Peshawar in the mid 1960s teaching English and History for the British charity, Voluntary Service Overseas. It was just after the 1965 war between India and Pakistan and the college garden bore witness to hurried and very amateur efforts to create some kind of air raid shelter. Most of the staff and students were still talking about the days the Indian jets came over—to bomb the Pakistan Air force headquarters. The 1965 war lasted only twenty-three days and came to an end as a result of Soviet mediation, but most Pakistanis were proud that they had held their own against their much larger adversary. It was commonly boasted by my students—and by Pakistanis in general—that one Pakistani soldier was worth nine Indians; that Muslims were better fighters than Hindus—the kind of bravado that the experience of Bangladesh was later to silence. For me it was an intriguing introduction to the Subcontinent, its conflicts and its stereotypes, but it raised more questions than it answered.

It was these experiences which prompted me a year later to begin the research which led to the book. As I sat in Peshawar reading about the history of the area, about Mughal rule in India and about the long mutual association of different communities, I became determined to understand how the subcontinent had come to be divided and how the young college students I was teaching had developed such definite views about Indians and Hindus, of whom, almost without exception, they had no personal experience. It was an attempt to explain the contemporary in terms of the historical which took me down a number of blind alleys before I developed a thesis which I thought began to stand up. But in the process I discovered I had hit on a subject of endless interest—not just to me but to Indians and Pakistanis themselves. The more I became associated with South Asia—and when I finished the thesis I began working for the BBC making programmes for South Asian audiences—the more I realized that the battle over its history is far from finished; it is almost as contested today as it was in 1947.

In the relatively prosperous 1960s, the main political contest in Pakistan was between an apparently progressive military dictatorship and the demand for democracy and regional autonomy. It was not about Islam. The country's ruler, Field Marshal Ayub Khan, looked benignly at us every morning from the front page of the Pakistan Times, sporting a suit and tie and encouraging everyone to work hard for the economic development of the country. The fact that Pakistan was a Muslim country was taken for granted. Friday was a half day so that students could go to the mosque, but most of them did not.

Coming from neighbouring Hazara, Ayub Khan was reasonably popular in Peshawar. But the merging of the provinces of West Pakistan into one unit was not. The North West Frontier had its own strong regional identity; Khan Abdul Ghaffar Khan, then in exile in Kabul, and his son Wali Khan exerted a powerful influence over many of the students. Most Pashtoons took the view that in the name of national unity, legitimate regional self-government and expression were being suppressed. Their language and culture, their traditions of hospitality, their links with their Afghan brothers across the border were all of great importance to them. They may have been pleased that Pakistan had held its own against India, but they wanted to hold their own in Pakistan.

A visit to East Pakistan strengthened these reservations. After Peshawar and the deserts and mountains beyond, landing in Dhaka after a flight of a thousand miles took one into a completely different world. They were all Pakistanis, but geographically, ethnically, culturally, linguistically, they were very far apart. And they felt it. Two or three years before the political crisis came to a head, there was a sense of a country run from elsewhere, of a lack of equality, of a highly politicized Bengali culture out of tune with the management of the state.

This was in 1967—twenty years after the foundation of Pakistan—during which time the democratic foundations of the country had more or less collapsed and been replaced by military and bureaucratic government. The two nation theory survived; indeed in many ways it had been reinforced. But what had first been voiced by a democratically elected Muslim League leadership had been appropriated by the new rulers of the state, powerful military and civil service interests.

As I began my research, the most striking contrast for me was between my own experience of Pakistan and much of the writing on Pakistan history. My experience had highlighted the conflicts within Pakistan between nationalism and regionalism, dictatorship and democracy, secularism and Islam, whereas most Pakistani historians seemed to concentrate on the emergence of Muslim nationalism, the central role of Mahommed Ali Jinnah and the importance of the ideology of Pakistan in the construction of the new state. For them, as Ishtiaq Hussain Qureshi has written 'the attitude of the Muslim community towards the idea of Pakistan was the logical consequence of its history'.[1] They argued that the Muslims had always been a distinct community, always wanted to maintain their separate identity, and that Pakistan was the natural if not inevitable crystallization of that desire.

This teleological approach to Pakistani history, though helpful in bolstering the new state's identity, seemed to ignore political complexities. In the first place, it treated the British Raj and the Hindu and Muslim communities as monoliths which they patently were not. It took nationality for granted without showing how it emerged. It took very little account of the differences within the Muslim community in the run up to Partition. It downplayed completely cooperation between Muslim communities and the Raj. In short, it did not deal with the realities of power in early twentieth-century India. It concentrated on periods when the storyline was strong—particularly the period after 1937—and glossed over much of the rest.

If this sense of official history was strongest in Pakistan, writing in India and Britain on the subject of nationalism and partition was similarly affected by the immediacy of events and the self-justification of many of the leading players. In India the official narrative of nationalism laid the blame on the British for creating division and saw Jinnah not as the father of Pakistan but as a collaborator of the Raj. The British, on the other hand, prided themselves on fostering the unity of India and blamed primordial divisions among the Indians for the re-emergence of division and bloodshed in the last days of empire. Such views, as expressed in the memoirs of politicians or civil servants, though valuable as insights into personal or political experience, were not easy sources for an historian trying to work out what actually happened. Indeed, in those days even a reliable chronology was lacking.

By a happy coincidence, as I began my research, the introduction of a new thirty year rule for British government archives meant that the documents of the inter-war period were opened for the first time and it was possible to find out in detail how the process of decolonization had been managed. Ten years later, almost all the British documentation on the run up to the transfer of power in 1947 had been made available. Over the same period, remarkable archival work was also done in India, particularly by the Nehru Memorial Library, to preserve the papers of nationalist leaders, while the Indian National Archives and the different state archives enabled scholars to explore the work of government in the localities over the same period. Pakistan has been slower to open up its archives and many of the key provincial records on political developments before 1947 are still not available. But the papers of Jinnah and the Muslim League have added greatly to knowledge of the Pakistan movement, even if they have not been as extensively consulted.

As a result, a huge amount of new and interesting work has emerged on the last phase of imperial power. Much of this work has concentrated—like my own—on the structure of empire and separatist and nationalist responses to it, with policy makers and leaders the main focus of attention. But other historians—and more recently, anthropologists and feminists as well—have investigated how political movements were understood and interpreted at different levels of society and have greatly extended our understanding of the range of social, cultural and political reactions to British rule, the complexity of nationalism and the human impact of Partition. What follows is a review of some of this recent work which touches on themes investigated in *Prelude to Partition.* It begins by looking at responses to the book and some new interpretations of Muslim separatism and of Jinnah's role in the demand for Pakistan. It then examines the influence of Imperial strategies and structures on successor states. It deals first with recent writing on the development of Pakistani nationalism and its problems accommodating regional forces, notably in Bengal. It then looks at the dominant Nehruvian nationalist narrative in India and the criticism it has faced from the Subaltern school. The review concludes with a discussion of new feminist and anthropological perspectives on Partition and the continuing value of Partition studies for an understanding of contemporary South Asia.

Responses to Prelude

The explanation of Muslim separatism that I put forward in *Prelude to Partition* owed a good deal to newly available British documentation on the inter-war years. Though I sought to balance the British viewpoint by interviewing surviving Indian and Pakistani politicians and their families, the main focus of the book was on the way in which the British Raj attempted to manage the challenge of nationalism in that period. It looked particularly at the development of representative institutions, which during those years provided first partial and later substantial provincial autonomy, and it argued that these very significant constitutional developments should not be seen simply as concessions to Indian nationalism but rather as a means of offsetting the nationalist challenge and perpetuating Imperial control. According to this theory, the way in which political power was devolved—the balancing of rural against urban, of Muslim against non-Muslim, and the encouragement of the provincial at the expense of the national—played a role in shaping the character of politics, whether among the Muslim separatists or the Congress nationalists. Further, it was argued that the matching of power and population—the beginnings of responsible government, however limited the franchise—introduced a new dynamic into politics which sowed the seeds of important political and economic change. In particular, it changed the balance of power within Muslim India, giving new importance to the Muslim majority areas and displacing the old leadership which had come from the traditional Muslim centres of power in North India.

The aspect of the book which attracted most attention was its location of the roots of Punjabi dominance in Pakistan after 1947 in the close political alliance between the Punjabi Muslims and the Raj during the interwar period. The transformation of the military alliance between the Raj and the great landowners and tribal leaders of Punjab into the politically dominant Unionist party and the key role played by its leaders in shaping the destiny of Muslim India under the auspices of the British were seen to foreshadow the emergence of the Punjabi Muslim interest politically and militarily in Pakistan itself.[2] Though most official Pakistani historiography has tended to concentrate on the role of the minority provinces in the demand for Pakistan, *Prelude* shows how the Punjabi Muslims, under the guidance of Mian Fazli Husain, came to lead Muslim India in the complex constitutional negotiations which resulted in the Government of India Act of 1935. It also shows how the demands of the All India Muslim Conference, which was the most influential Muslim organization during the period, were conceded by the Raj as a means of stabilizing its rule in the face of growing Congress opposition. This was in many ways a key period in the emergence of a consolidated Muslim North West, with Sind separated from Bombay, the Frontier transformed into a Governor's province and the Punjab Muslim majority safeguarded by the continuance of separate electorates under the terms of the communal award. By the end of the 1920s it was clear that the Punjabi Muslims were at one with the Raj in not relishing the prospect of a democratic central government dominated by the Congress party. Rather, they were thinking in terms of maximum provincial autonomy, with residuary powers at that level, and only the loosest control from the centre. Here in embryo was the very same battle over the future shape of India which was to dominate the negotiations of the mid 1940s which ultimately led to Partition.

What some critics found more difficult to accept was that this foreshadowed Partition. For them, it was not the Punjabi Muslims who collaborated with the Raj in the inter-war period who were responsible for Partition but the Muslims of the minority provinces, and particularly the United Provinces, who provided the shock troops of the Muslim League in its demand for a separate state. They argued that it was a weakness of the book that it did not deal more thoroughly with the cultural and religious dimension of Muslim separatism, those important underground tributaries of Muslim political thought which burst into the open in the 1940s. As David Lelyveld put it: 'There is a gap between 1932 and the creation of Pakistan in 1947 and no one will understand it without a healthy respect for the power of symbols'.[3]

Others welcomed what the book had to say about the structure of power, seeing it as a more sophisticated version of the old theory of Divide and Rule, but thought that it went too far in trying to explain communalism in these terms. For historians of the Subaltern school, for example, it was a moot point whether politicians instigated the trend towards communalism after 1920 or were simply beneficiaries of it. For them, the popular roots of communalism were to be found not in the constitutional manipulations of the Raj but in the socio-economic changes brought about in Indian society by the impact of colonialism over a much longer period.[4]

In defence of the position put forward in *Prelude*, it was never argued that a structural approach to Muslim politics in the inter-war period offered a total explanation of separatism; it was always intended to complement existing ideological explanations which tended to concentrate either on developments in North India running up to the formation of the Muslim League or the period after 1937. There are some glimpses in the book of the way in which separatist thinking developed within the realities of power opened up by the Reforms—in Iqbal's strong support for a guaranteed Muslim majority in the Punjab or in the alignment of the Ali brothers with the Punjab Unionists on the platform of the Muslim Conference—but the interconnectedness of the intellectual and the political could certainly have been explored more thoroughly.

At the time, I was conscious that my knowledge of Urdu was too limited to do justice to the complexities of Muslim writing on issues of religion and history and law. As a result of reading and of meeting politicians and clerics, I was aware that there was a body of religious and political thought which stressed the separate identity of Muslims, the superiority of their religion and laws and the need to safeguard their culture in a changing world; it was clear that 'Islam in danger' was a potent rallying cry. It was also evident, however, that the Indian Muslim community was much more differentiated socially, economically, culturally, even religiously, than the concentration on Sir Syed Ahmed Khan and the products of Aligarh might lead one to believe. I found it difficult to accept that separatism was inherent in the Muslim condition or that Pakistan was in some sense inevitable; as I saw it, there needed to be a more structured explanation of why disparate Muslim communities came to regard it as a common goal in the 1940s.

In retrospect, in the attempt to illuminate the working of 'previously neglected factors', *Prelude* may have overemphasized the importance of structures. Obviously political structures do not create community or communalism; separate electorates were a means of mediating power which acknowledged existing religious divisions. But I would argue that in the process they also changed perceptions of community, encouraged the consolidation of a Muslim political identity and intensified political competition around communal issues. Moreover, because the Raj was in the process of devolving responsibility to Indians—first at the provincial and subsequently at the national level—the way it handled Muslim politics played an important role in the emergence of an all-India Muslim community and the kind of choices its leaders made. It was in relation to the Imperial structure of power that they had to define themselves. This is not to deny the importance of well-established traditions of Muslim political thought or of the socio-economic forces which shaped communal consciousness in the localities. But if these streams of thought and consciousness fed into the river of all-India politics, the Imperial system was like a series of dams, diverting the waters to left and right to suit its own purposes. Structures may not tell the whole story but they tell an important part of it.

Other interpretations of Muslim separatism.

Paul Brass and Francis Robinson, both specialists in U.P. Muslim politics, debated some of these issues in the 1970s. Brass asserted that despite a strong sense of their own religion there was no automatic reason for Indian Muslims to adopt what he called an ethnic identity, while Robinson argued that Brass underestimated the 'distinct differences between Hindus and Muslims'. Significantly, the two men disagreed most profoundly about the role of the Muslim political elite. Brass took the view that it was important to look at the political elite as an independent variable because skill and quality of leadership varies and this affects political choices. Robinson argued that Brass exaggerated the role of the Muslim political elite in winning support for separatism and underestimated the part played by religious institutions, by widely held religious values and by government interventions. Robinson, whose early work attributed a considerable role to British policy in the development of separatism, has since modified his views to give more importance to inherited traditions of Muslim thought and Islamic culture.[5]

A more recent attempt to delineate the influence of Muslim political thought on the emergence of separatism is Farzana Shaikh's *Community and Consensus in Islam.* In her investigation of reactions by the North Indian Muslim elite to the introduction of notions of representative government in India, Shaikh shows them to have been influenced by a Mughal ruling class culture, anxious to maintain their special status and social distinction, wary of democracy, particularly its emphasis on individual rights, and supporters of separate electorates because they were in keeping with their sense of Muslim community. Her thesis is that attitudes evolved at that time continued to dominate Muslim thinking right up to independence. These included the notion of political power as trust, the dichotomy between Muslim and non-Muslim, the belief that only Muslims should rule over Muslims, all of which she represents as part of a dominant Indo-Muslim tradition which drew on the Mughal inheritance and the common assumptions of a divinely revealed faith. Though she does not underestimate British influences—indeed she goes as far as to say that 'without an official policy which encouraged Muslims to organise politically as Muslims, there might well have been no Muslim representation to speak of'—she argues that the elements which sustained the politics of Muslim representation were also grounded deep in this tradition.[6] In her working out of this thesis, however, she comes very close to adopting the same kind of teleological approach to Muslim separatism which has influenced 'official' Pakistani history. One may sympathize with her rejection of the view that the demand for a separate homeland was 'no more than a bold attempt to play a dangerous hand of cards' without accepting the contention that Jinnah's every move drew upon 'a view of the political community as an extension of religious fellowship' or that the Muslim League somehow embodied that view even in the 1920s when it was more or less moribund.[7] Her analysis provides useful insights into the kind of traditions drawn on by the UP Muslims in resisting Congress dominance and in demanding Pakistan. But the failure to explore the socio-economic context in which those choices were made in the 1940s or to assess them in the light of Partition itself leaves important questions of context and leadership unanswered. As she herself makes clear, the 'dominant Indo-Muslim tradition' was not as fully accepted in the Muslim majority areas, where the arithmetic of democracy was less hostile, and were the urban traditions of UP and even of East Punjab were balanced by the 'ruralism' of folk Islam. In Shaikh's political analysis of the 1920s and 30s, Fazli Husain's 'spectacular gains'—and indeed the victories of 'ruralism' and 'provincialism' in the 1937 elections—are achieved at the expense of the Indo-Muslim tradition,[8] while the achievement of Pakistan is seen as its successful reassertion. She is right to the extent that the ideology of Pakistan has drawn strongly on that tradition, though the realities of power in the new state have been shaped more by the victories of ruralism and provincialism. It was only when those provincial forces were converted to Pakistan that it became a territorial reality, even if the demand was more vociferous elsewhere.

Recent research on the course of the Pakistan movement in the Punjab has tended to reinforce the view advanced in *Prelude* that the creation of Pakistan was as much about the preservation of established political interests as about the implementation of a new vision of society. David Gilmartin's book *Empire and Islam*, which looks at the emergence of the Pakistan movement in the Punjab from the late 1930s, succeeds extraordinarily well in exploring the interplay between *Din* and *Dunya*, religious consciousness and the political world. Gilmartin shows that the emergence of provincial autonomy on a substantially widened franchise after 1937 found even the apparently impregnable Unionists casting around for a new popular justification for their rule. It was this which first pushed Sikunder Hayat into a closer association with Jinnah and the Muslim League, though in the end they fell out because of the contradiction between Sikunder's commitment to the colonial system and the Muslim League bid to replace it.[9] Gilmartin argues that Jinnah's greatest strength lay in his ability to transcend such tensions, 'to direct Muslim politics towards symbolic goals, even as he compromised to build political support'. He shows how Jinnah could at the same time be compromising with the Punjab Unionists, in order to improve his representative status, and encouraging groups like the Punjab Muslim Students federation who had adopted the demand for a separate Muslim state as early as 1937. These students, who were in the forefront of the Muslim League campaign, came mostly from the urban centres of central and eastern Punjab and were inspired by Iqbal, whose idea of a Muslim political community defined by 'the active ... intensely personal... almost mystical commitment of each individual to Islam' transcended not only formal political structures but also the ulema's preoccupation with the *shariat*. According to Gilmartin, it was this idea, conveyed by Iqbal in his last days, which Jinnah incorporated into his vision of Pakistan in the 1940s. However, though Gilmartin sees the success of the Muslim League in the 1946 elections as 'a new public expression of Muslim community... that justified a cultural redefinition of the state', he also acknowledges that, despite the rhetoric, the elections did not transform the structure of local politics. *Din* and *dunya*—exemplary personal ideals and the world of rural politics—had been publicly joined, with pirs and rural magnates playing critical roles. But, as he himself admits, 'for all its outward political trappings and public ideological identification with Pakistani nationalism, the power of the Muslim League rested largely on the same bases as had the Unionist party.'[10] It was a contradiction that was to affect not just the Pakistan movement but the future of the state itself.

Ian Talbot, who has also worked extensively on Punjab Muslim politics, comes to very similar conclusions. In his early work, he explains the collapse of the Unionist citadel largely in terms of power politics. Providing ample evidence of the late conversion of the Unionists to the Muslim League, he shows how in fielding candidates for the 1946 elections the League frequently preferred recent converts from Unionism with substantial vote banks to League activists of longer standing but less influence. Talbot's analysis of the role of *pirs* and *sufis* in support of the Muslim League reinforces the same point. He finds that most of the *pirs* of the older established shrines deserted the Unionist party because of the Muslim League's rise in status in all India politics. Like the landlords, they wanted to protect their local influence by being on the winning side.[11]

More recently, Talbot has sought 'to restore the popular dimension to our perceptions of the Pakistan movement'.[12] In his book *Freedom's Cry,* he reviews some of the literature on Partition and examines different aspects of the mass movement in Punjab, including the role of the crowd and popular perceptions of Mr Jinnah as the embodiment of political sovereignty. In the light of this, he argues that the failure of the Muslim League to bring about a permanent transformation of local politics after 1947 should not be allowed to obscure the existence of mass participation in the movement. However, though there is no doubt that there was a 'groundswell of rural Punjabi support for the Pakistan demand',[13] and that despite Mr Jinnah's predilections, many *pirs* and *sufis* in west Punjab put the message across in millenarian terms, what the masses made of it has yet to be explored. In some ways the shallowness of the Muslim League movement in West Punjab makes that area a less fertile area of enquiry for this kind of research than East Punjab or the traditional heartlands of Muslim influence in North India, where the Pakistan movement found firmest root among the middle class and where pursuit of the Pakistan ideal led to dramatic changes in the pattern of life.

Reinterpreting Mr Jinnah

Though *Prelude* focused largely on the development of Muslim separatism, it also tried to explain the development of all-India politics—whether nationalist or separatist—in terms of the trend towards provincialization introduced by the Reforms. It showed, for example, how national politicians pressing for concessions at the all-India level after 1920 had to deal with a completely different set of political pressures from their predecessors in the pre-war period. The Lucknow Pack of 1916 was not repeatable in 1928 because by then the divisions between provincial politicians and their political opponents were too deep to be papered over at the national level. What the Muslim Conference was demanding of the British to safeguard Muslim majorities and minorities could never be delivered by the Congress without alienating its own supporters and potential supporters among other communities. As Nehru himself put it. 'Whatever offer we make, however high our bid might be, there is alway a third party which can bid higher, and what is more, give substance to its words.'[14]

This was also the dilemma of Mahommed Ali Jinnah, whose attempt to built an alliance for reform at the national level foundered during the same period. Throughout the 1920s, Jinnah's political ambition remained at the all-India level, where for some years he and his liberal allies cooperated with the Congress Swaraj Party in demanding the introduction of political responsibility. However his efforts to forge another Hindu–Muslim pact to pressurize the Raj fell foul of the escalating demands of Muslim political interests in the provinces and their increasingly vociferous Hindu nationalist opponents. By the end of the decade, with the Indian National Congress abandoning efforts to reach new deals because the terms were too high, Jinnah had to admit that no new pact was possible. He had reached the 'parting of the ways' and retired to London to lick his wounds.

Some reviewers found this treatment of Jinnah as a political broker between Muslim provincial interests and the Congress a useful new way of looking at his career, freeing him from the interpretative constraints imposed by his eventual emergence as the father of Pakistan and showing him dealing with the politics of the central assembly or the all-party conferences in his search for power at the all-India level.[15] The distinctive contribution of Ayesha Jalal's work on Jinnah—*The Sole Spokesman*—is that it pursues this idea right up to Partition itself, arguing that until 1947 Pakistan was only a bargaining counter and that what Jinnah really wanted was power at the centre in a union of Pakistan and Hindustan.[16] The novelty of the book—and the controversy it has provoked—stems from the fact that it portrays Jinnah in this last period as a man with an inward mission of his own, one which he could not communicate even to his own followers. As in the inter-war period examined in *Prelude*, Jinnah is shown as an all-India figure working to reconcile and represent disparate Muslim provincial interests and for much of the time facing tough opposition from the powerful chief ministers of Punjab and Bengal. Jalal shows how these interests were constantly raising the stakes in their demands to the British for special treatment, but she argues that Jinnah continued to look for some accommodation at the centre. She portrays the Lahore resolution of 1940 as a serious setback for Jinnah, envisaging as it did the creation of two Muslim federations, abolishing the centre, and leaving the minority province Muslims high and dry. She says Jinnah had to go along with it, but he knew that it was unacceptable to both Congress and the British, and he also knew that the Muslims were not the sole arbiters of their destiny.[17]

Jinnah's acceptance of the Cabinet Mission plan is seen as part of the same strategy. It offered him what Jalal argues he had wanted from the beginning, a chance to find a solution within the unity of India by giving maximum autonomy to the regional units and allowing for a federal government at the centre with limited powers. The plan explicitly rejected Pakistan but the Muslim League Council, under Jinnah's leadership, accepted it. The problem, as everyone knows, was that Congress did not want a weak centre, and Congress, unlike the Muslim League, had the power to resist it. Jalal says the Cabinet mission had forced Jinnah to reveal his hand but in doing so he had shown his own weakness and aroused suspicions among his own supporters. In the end, she argues, it was not a change of heart on his part but pressure from the rest of the Muslim League Council which forced him to go for Direct Action; otherwise he would have been swept aside himself.[18]

Ayesha Jalal's work has brought home the tentative nature of Pakistan as an objective during the 1940s, but she seems to go too far in arguing that Jinnah had a secret agenda of his own which he could not communicate to his followers. Given the diversity of his following, Jinnah had good reason not to define Pakistan too precisely. He needed to maintain a united front in negotiations at the all-India level and precision would have been divisive. But there is no evidence to suggest that he was not working sincerely to obtain the best terms possible for Muslim India. He may well have continued to hope for an all-India agreement, but by 1946 the only kind of central government he was prepared to accept was not one in which he would have enjoyed any substantial power. Moreover, by the time of the Cabinet Mission plan, trust between the League and the Congress had more or less completely broken down.

Anita Inder Singh has shown in her work on Partition that Jinnah entered into negotiations willing to consider the preservation of some sort of centre but most reluctant to see the establishment of either a central legislature or a constituent assembly for India as a whole. In accepting the Cabinet Mission plan, he wished the three zones to be given primacy and the centre to be delegated only those powers which the zonal constituent assemblies were prepared to relinquish. His demand, moreover, for parity with the Congress in the interim government implied a recognition of the sovereignty of the zonal units; it made no sense at all in a united India, where the Muslims were only thirty percent of the population. For these reasons, Singh seems closer to the mark in arguing that by 1946 'Jinnah and the League intended the claim to a sovereign Pakistan to be more than a bargaining counter...' It was, she argues, a tactic which Jinnah played at Simla 'so that both the other parties had to concede Pakistan, before or when power was transferred to Indians.'[19]

Though the argument about what was meant by Pakistan and whether it was a bargaining counter or not will continue, the revelations of the official records on the transfer of power have made it clear that its emergence as a separate Muslim state was a much more hesitant development than the country's official historians would have us believe. For Jinnah, the long drawn out negotiations were a lawyer's attempt to obtain the best deal for his clients in the last days of empire, with a confederal solution on the right terms among his possible options. But there was an obvious conflict between his openness to such a solution and the sanctions developed to pursue that end. It seems extraordinary in retrospect that Jinnah should have argued that Hindus and Muslims constituted two nations and still expected Pakistan to include undivided Punjab and Bengal with their substantial Hindu and Sikh minorities. Yet there is no doubt that he was deeply disappointed with what he called the 'truncated' and 'motheaten' Pakistan he eventually had to accept.

The same paradox seems to lie at the heart of the continuing controversy in Pakistan over Jinnah's famous speech to the constituent assembly on 11 August. Having achieved Pakistan, he seems to be saying clearly in that speech that it is to be a secular state in which religion will be regarded as a private matter. As he put it: 'You are free to go to your mosques and your temples... that has nothing to do with the business of the state.' And in the same spirit he looked forward to a time when 'Hindus would cease to be Hindus and Muslims would cease to be Muslims, not in the religious sense, because that is the personal faith of each individual, but in the political sense as citizens of the state.' Because this flies in the face of subsequent efforts to make Pakistan an Islamic state, it has proved an uncomfortable inheritance. In the early 1980s, Sharif ul Mujahid, the Director of the Quaid i Azam Academy and biographer of Jinnah, even went as far as to say that it represented ' a serious lapse on his part',[20] while Stanley Wolpert in his biography of Jinnah portrays the whole speech to the constituent assembly as a surreal experience: 'What was he talking about? Had he simply forgotten where he was? Had the cyclone of events so disoriented him that he was arguing the opposition's brief? Was he pleading for a united India on the eve of Pakistan?'[21]. Yet all liberal and secular Pakistanis give this speech an absolute centrality in their interpretation of Jinnah—the founder's guarantee, as he put it himself, of 'equality of rights, privileges and obligations irrepective of colour caste or creed'.

It seems clear that until 1947 itself, Jinnah visualized Pakistan in terms of greater autonomy or independence for existing provinces of British India rather than a strict redrawing of boundaries according to religion. As the Pakistani author Saad Khairi has argued in his *Jinnah Reinterpreted*, 'the presence of non-Muslims was an essential part of Jinnah's Pakistan. Their presence was in fact a guarantee of safety for the Muslims left behind in India.'[22] Moreover, even after 1947, though Jinnah had negotiated the separation of Pakistan from India he did not initially abandon the legal and constitutional framework in which he had lived his earlier political life. As late as mid 1947, Jinnah was still investing in shares and property in India[23] and according to Muhammad Ali Chaiwallah, the man who acted as his solicitor in Bombay, he even had a plan to retire to Bombay after being Governor General of Pakistan.[24] He left his house and furniture there, and in 1947 saw nothing illogical in the thought. It was the killings and riots and the exchange of population of Partition itself which set the seal on the new divided subcontinent and left Jinnah with a great sense of bitterness and betrayal.

The Raj and its nationalist successors

Pakistani sensitivity to the suggestion that Jinnah was prepared to consider a confederal solution to the communal problem is not difficult to understand. However in the 1940s when the post-colonial shape of the Subcontinent was being negotiated, the choice was not just between one state and two; there was a great patchwork of princely states and autonomous provinces and a range of different ideas about how India might be governed once the British departed. It was not a foregone conclusion that the British Raj would be succeeded by a unitary Indian government. Indeed, as *Prelude* demonstrates, the whole trend of constitutional development from 1920 onwards had been encouraging a more federal solution. It was as much the Congress vision of itself as the successor of the Raj as the intransigence of Mr Jinnah which stood in the way of that particular resolution of the Muslim problem.

Prelude does not deal with Congress politics in detail, but it does attempt to show how the Congress strategy of the late 1920s was reaction to the systemic pressures introduced by the Montagu-Chelmsford Reforms. The Congress decision at the time of the Nehru report to abandon its earlier commitment to cross-communal alliances, to withdraw the concessions which it had made in the Lucknow Pact and to stake a new claim to be the premier nationalist organization and the natural successor of the Raj, are all seen as responses to the growing communalization of politics under the reformed constitution. Moreover, though the book deals more with the politics of Motilal Nehru than of Jawaharlal, it does suggest that the final shape of the Nehru report reflected the growing ascendancy of Jawaharlal and his political philosophy, his impatience with religion, his contempt for communal politics and his emphasis on the economic rather than the political character of nationalism. It was a vision of India which met the Congress need to transcend the competing demands of different communities and it marked the beginning of a new confrontation between the Congress and the Raj, in which the centrifugalism induced by the constitution had to be matched by a centripetalism on the part of the Congress if it was to hold nationalist forces together and successfully challenge the British in New Delhi.

It was also a watershed for Congress relations with the Muslims. If it was a serious mistake for the British to make the overriding principle of their programme of constitutional reform outmanoeuvring the Congress, it was arguably an equally serious error on the part of the Congress to take the view that the Muslim question was a colonial creation which would disappear with independence. To refuse to think in terms of coalitions, to attempt to undermine the leadership of the community, however conservative it may have been, by means of the mass contact movement, to insist to the end that Congress represented the whole of India may have been necessary for the rhetoric of nationalism and bargaining with the British, but it had serious consequences for India's plural tradition.

It was argued in *Prelude* that the manner in which power was devolved to the provinces without any corresponding devolution at the all-India level encouraged centrifugalism. The trend was discernible after 1920; it became crystal clear after 1937. Muslim separatism was reinforced by the emergence of autonomous Muslim majority provinces and the Congress had to develop new strategies and new mechanisms to keep the nationalist movement united. Robin Moore's very thorough exploration of the British role in the making of the 1935 Act and the eventual transfer of power reinforces the importance of these themes. In his view, the introduction of provincial autonomy without central responsibility set the Congress a new challenge in its bid to succeed the Raj. In order to maintain the coherence of the national movement, it had to set up a unitary party structure to control the Congress provincial governments. As Moore expresses it: 'Instead of the Congress provincial ministries operating as autonomous governments within a federal structure, they accepted the Congress working committee as the legitimate directorate of a unitary government. The monolithic Congress stood in the place that the unitary Raj had vacated.'[25] Moore sees this as the beginning of a new 'unitarianism' in the Congress which seriously affects its relations with the Muslims and the princes.[26] The Muslim mass contract movement in the United Provinces alienated the Muslim leadership in the Congress provinces, while the Congress call in 1938 for the same democratic rights for states' peoples as for the rest of India, changed attitudes towards the viability of the proposed federal centre. As the Aga Khan put it in 1940, just one month before the Lahore resolution was passed: 'The sugar had come off the pill the moment the states' representatives were to be elected by the states' peoples rather than nominated by the rulers, for under such an arrangement the Muslims would not get from the states in the central legislature the support they required to balance the Congress votes.'[27]

As far as the development of Muslim separatism is concerned, Moore shares the view that the emergence of powerful provincial interests in the Muslim majority provinces was a stepping stone to Pakistan. He believes that 'the very creation of autonomous Muslim provinces under the 1935 Act encouraged and validated the demand for separate nationhood. The Muslim League's achievement was to convert the process of provincialization into the process of separation.' Moore certainly does not see Pakistan as inevitable, but he documents the steady trend towards separation from the late thirties onwards, pinning much of the blame for this on the Congress party. In his view, the Congress converted what he calls 'latent propensity for separate nationhood into strident insistence by its recourse to crude approaches to national integration...'.[28]

Moore's insights into the reactive character of both Indian and Pakistan nationalism reinforce the thesis put forward in *Prelude* that British constitutional strategies helped to shape both the forces of Muslim separatism and of Indian nationalism. It was the British retention of power at the centre under the 1935 Act and the absence of any elected responsibility at that level which evinced an authoritarian response from the Congress and it was this Congress authoritarianism which in turn shaped the response of the Muslim League. As Moore graphically puts it: 'In Jinnah's hands the two nation theory became a psychological weapon to be wielded for political advantage. It was a tyrannical idea formulated to prevail over the Congress totalitarian claim to be the Indian nation in microcosm.'[29]

Given what is known of attitudes in the British parliament, it is questionable whether it would have been possible to establish even a partially responsible central government for British India in 1935, but the debate in the Viceroy's council over this issue shows a wide awareness of what was at stake. By retaining absolute control of the government of India, by pinning their faith on a federal system involving the princes which never took effect, the British created the conditions for a political vacuum at the centre when they eventually ceded power. Ultimately, succession to the Raj meant succession to a system of government which was totalitarian in key areas of imperial control—despite its overt support for democratization elsewhere—and which had no established democratic tradition in dealing with centre-state relations. In 1947, the vacuum was filled by successor governments trying to cope with communal bloodshed and mass migration on an unprecedented scale. It was not surprising in those conditions that they continued to wield many of those powers, despite their own more democratic credentials. However, the problems of over-centralization of power have proved of longer duration than those crises and very difficult to remedy. The successor states inherited the political structures, some of the perceptions and many of the problems of the Raj and they have both found centre-state relations among the most difficult to solve.

Pakistani nationalism and the challenge of regionalism

The view that the attitude of the Congress party was as much responsible for the partition of India as the intransigence of Mr Jinnah has been supported by recent researches on Bengal. Joya Chatterji's *Bengal Divided* may go too far in blaming the *bhadralok* for the communalization of politics, but she shows clearly that the prospect of permanent subordination to a Muslim majority converted many of them to the idea that Bengal must be partitioned and that Nehru and Patel in opting for a truncated Pakistan had the strong support of the provincial Congress.[30] It is also beyond dispute that immediately before partition Jinnah gave his blessings to efforts by Shaheed Suhrawardy and Sarat Bose to float an independent united Bengal. That venture was vetoed by the Congress High Command as well as by the Congress in Bengal, and according to Chatterji was 'never more than a pipe dream' but Jinnah's acceptance of it was a sure sign that even in the last stages of the transfer of power he was not opposed to a future for the Bengalis built around their ethnic rather than their religious identity.[31]

Once the decision to partition India and to create Pakistan had been taken, however, Jinnah and those who worked with him embarked on a policy of centralization of power which was in effect the mirror image of the very trends he had objected to in the political behaviour of the Congress. From the late 1920s onwards, as *Prelude* demonstrates, Mr Jinnah had been arguing for maximum provincial autonomy and a weak central government. But in Pakistan—no doubt partly because of the circumstances of partition itself and the need to build up the new state in the face of hostility from India—he argued for strong central government and he and his successors used the extraordinary powers of the Governor General's office to impose the centre's will on the provinces. Within a matter of months of East Bengal becoming part of Pakistan, the centralizing imperative had taken effect and Jinnah was in Dhaka promoting Urdu as the national language and setting off a long process of disillusionment which was eventually to lead to the emergence of Bangladesh.

Concepts of statehood in the two new dominions had more in common than either side might like to admit not in terms of ruling ideologies but in terms of the structures of power. Just as Nehru and Patel wanted a strong central government to put their stamp on newly independent India, so the official ideology of Pakistan has drawn more on the imperatives of the centralizing Governor General than on those of the liberal politician and the advocate of minority rights. It has emphasized the need for unity and discipline, the binding power of Islam and the primacy of the armed forces in defending the state, and it has been used at various stages of the country's history to justify action by the managers of the state against their critics, particularly those demanding more regional autonomy.

Not surprisingly, therefore, Pakistan governments since 1947 have faced a very similar kind of opposition from their own constituent units as Muslim provinces waged against a strong centre in India before Partition. In Pakistan, however, the issue has not been the rights of Muslims in a Hindu-dominated India but the rights of the country's ethnic minorities in a state dominated by the Punjabis. Over the past fifty years, all the other ethnic groups in Pakistan have revolted against the centre at one time or another over their right to a proper share of power and resources: most notably the Bengalis, who broke away to form their own state in 1971, then later the Baluch and Pashtoons, the Sindhis, and more recently even the Muhajirs who were in the forefront of the demand for Pakistan in the 1940s and left their homes in north India to make it happen.

If *Prelude* showed how all-India Muslim politics during the 1920s and early 30s was the sum of the politics of Muslim provincialism, with the Punjabis playing the dominant role, other works have shown how the forging of Muslim unity, whether under the leadership of Jinnah during the 1940s, or in Pakistan after 1947, continued to involve a problematic suppression of regional and ethnic identities. Yunas Samad in his book *Nation in Turmoil* traces this conflict between Muslim unity and regional identity back to the colonial period and argues that 'there is an element of continuity in the tension between centrifugal and centripetal forces between pre-independence and post-partition Muslim politics.'[32] Samad takes the unusual step of studying the period from 1935 to 1958, a perspective that enables him to pursue the provincial divisions which existed before 1947 into the new state. His chapter on the period from the 1946 elections to the creation of Pakistan is entitled 'A brief moment of political unity', underlining the argument that the unity created around the demand for Pakistan defined the new country in terms of what Indian Muslims did not want, rather than what they did.

Samad points up the contrast between the support for a weak centre by dominant Muslim interests in Punjab and Bengal before 1947 and the League leadership's conviction afterwards that a strong centre was essential for its survival. He also shows how due to authoritarianism in Pakistan, centrifugal forces soon re-emerged, with the rights of Bengal the key issue in the early years. In looking at pre-partition politics, Samad shows that Abul Hashim, the Bengal provincial League secretary who built up a mass movement on an anti-zemindari platform after 1943, was opposed to the two nation theory and favoured a multi-nationality concept for India. Like Suhrawardy, he was a strong supporter of the idea of an independent Bengal in 1947 and warned that the formation of a united Pakistan from the Muslim majority areas would result in the imposition of an alien bureaucracy on the Bengal Muslims. The course of politics in East Bengal after 1947 confirmed many of these presentiments.[33]

Not surprisingly, scholars from Bangladesh have seen the origins of the eventual rupture with Pakistan in these different approaches to Muslim separatism before Partition. In *The Foreshadowing of Bangladesh*, Harun-or-Rashid argues that 'the Pakistan ideal of the larger section of the Bengal Provincial Muslim League was completely different from that of Jinnah, for they developed the ideals of either an independent East Pakistan or some kind of greater Bengal well before 1947'.[34] He says that for Abul Hashim and Suhrawardy, the two nation theory was not an article of faith but 'a strategic framework for the united struggle of Indian Muslims against the common principal enemy' and he contends that what really motivated them was 'the goal of a separate state for North East India'. However, though it can be shown that the two men had developed such a vision by 1944, they appear to have kept it largely to themselves. Harun-or-Rashid describes it as 'incredible' that they did not publicize their ideal, even during the 1946 elections, but he points up the complexity of the choices facing the Bengali Muslims when he says that this was a matter of strategy. As he puts it, they carefully avoided direct confrontation with the League leadership on the form of Pakistan because that would have torpedoed the whole idea. Harun-or-Rashid argues that Suhrawardy's proposal for an independent united Bengal was not just a counter move to prevent Partition but he also has to admit that until early 1947 Suhrawardy gave primacy to the demand for a separate Muslim state and that in any event because of economic differences between the two communities 'a clear and powerful sense of common Bengali nationalism...was not there'.35

Taj ul Islam Hashmi's *Peasant Utopia* concentrates less on high politics and more on the role of the Muslim peasantry, whose politicization was central to the growth of the Pakistan movement in Bengal. Hashmi follows others in highlighting the radical economic agenda of the Bengal Muslim League which went into the 1946 elections promising the abolition of zemindari and major improvements in the lot of the peasantry and he explains the disillusionment with Pakistan after 1947 in terms of the failure of this utopia to materialize. Much of the value of his work lies, however, in the critique it offers of Marxist and Subaltern interpretations of peasant politics.[36] Hashmi argues that before 1947 the Muslim peasantry proved to be less autonomous and less differentiated in its political reactions than many such analysts have suggested; the poorer peasants accepted the leadership of the more prosperous and the peasantry as a whole trusted the ulema, the urban professionals and the Muslim aristocracy to represent their interests at the provincial level. Hashmi does not accept that communalism was instilled in the rural areas from the top downwards; in his view, the re-emergence of the ulema during the Khilafat movement was a major factor. But he argues that from the 1920s the British played an important role in communalizing the peasantry by increasing Muslim representation in local bodies and by taking measures to regulate usury and to increase security of tenure.[37] He follows *Prelude to Partition* in holding that the political power accruing to the Bengali Muslims under the Reforms encouraged the communalization of politics—what he calls' the communalization of the class struggle'—but he argues that the creation of this separate Muslim identity transcending economic divisions turned out to be short-lived. If the 1940s saw the emergence of an alliance between the urban *ashraf* and the richer peasants in support of Pakistan, the coming of the new state brought a new alliance between the *ashraf* and the West Pakistan elite which left the richer peasantry and the Bengali middle class out in the cold. It was their disillusionment which ultimately led to the creation of Bangladesh, though according to Hashmi the 'first victims' on both occasions were the poor Bengali peasants.

While Hashmi concentrates on the economics of communalism, Tazeen Murshid's *The Sacred and the Secular* highlights the complex interplay of religion, culture and language from the late nineteenth century onward. Her work is a useful reminder of the cultural schizophrenia which affected Bengali Muslims, split between the appeal of North Indian role models—the upper class Urdu speaking leaders of the community—and the pull of Bengali culture, which inevitably grew stronger as education and politics spread to the middle class and the rural areas. She acknowledges the role of British constitution-making in consolidating the sense of Muslim community, but she also stresses the impact of Hindu revivalism and chauvinism as seen in the rejection of plans for a united Bengal. Murshid detects a continuing ambivalence about their identity among the Muslim intelligentsia even on the eve of Partition, something which she says persisted after 1947 and deprived them of the initiative in Pakistan. In terms of social and economic change, the emergence of Pakistan temporarily strengthened conservative forces, though it was not long before the Bengali language became a rallying point for the new middle class in their resistance to political and economic domination by the Western wing. The emergence of

Bangladesh in one sense marked the triumph of ethnicity over religion, but Murshid's study makes it clear that old contradictions persist. Religion remains a key marker of identity and has been politically exploited in Bangladesh just as it has in Pakistan.[38]

Indian nationalism: the Nehruvian narrative

While much of the debate in Pakistan since 1947 has been about the extent to which the state defines itself in religious terms and the extent to which other allegiances—of ethnicity, language and class can be accommodated, in India Nehru's commanding influence in the first two decades of independence ensured that his vision held sway. Unlike Jinnah, who committed few of his innermost thoughts to paper, Nehru left an extraordinary corpus of writing, personal and political, which has successfully communicated the thinking of the nationalist and statesman to a very wide readership over several generations. Such works as *An Autobiography* and *The Discovery of India* show how he viewed Indian history and how he re-interpreted it to create a modern secular nationalist discourse for the emerging independent state. It was a process heavily influenced by his own education at Harrow and Cambridge, by his agnosticism and his socialism, by critiques of colonialism coming out of Europe and by what was being done under the Communists to build a modern state in Russia. The result was a new vision of India which downplayed religious and cultural difference and put the emphasis on the elimination of vested interests and economic progress for all under the auspices of a modernizing state. For Nehru, 'the real struggle in India' was 'not between Hindu culture and Muslim culture but between these two and the conquering scientific culture of modern civilisation'. Communal leaders were merely 'a small upper class reactionary group' which exploited religion for their own ends and made every effort 'to suppress and avoid the consideration of economic issues'. As to claims by the Muslim League that the Indian Muslims formed a nation, Nehru wrote: 'Politically, the idea is absurd, economically it is fantastic; it is hardly worth considering...To talk of a Muslim nation... means that no nation in the modern sense must be allowed to grow... that modern civilisation should be discarded and we should go back to the medieval ways...'.[39]

Of course, running alongside the Nehruvian modern, secular nationalist narrative—albeit in a minor key for most of the time—

was a Hindu nationalist narrative which portrayed India as the land of the Hindus and the British as only the last in a long line of conquerors, among whom the Muslims featured most prominently. Sarvarkar's influential work *Hindutva*, scrawled on the walls of a prison in the Andaman islands during the first world war, was an early rallying cry to Hindus to reclaim their birthright after many centuries of foreign domination; it also foreshadowed prophetically the growth of militant Hindu organizations like the RSS and the kind of strategies of organization and proselytization, particularly the demonization of the Muslim, which has been their hallmark since that time. The cohabitation of these two narratives—and others—within the Congress party, which was a feature of the early phase of the nationalist movement, proved more uncomfortable from the 1930s onwards, when Nehru at least was openly intolerant of communalism in all its forms. But even at this stage public posture often disguised tacit tolerance. As all-India politics became communalized, Congress support could not go unaffected, and once the Muslim League was openly demanding a homeland for the Muslims, this trend became more marked. Arguably it was only the assassination of Mahatma Gandhi at the hands of a Hindu extremist that brought India to its senses and gave Nehru the upper hand in suppressing the Hindu right and establishing the ascendancy of his own secular vision of the future.

Much Indian history since 1947 has taken its cue from Nehru's own writings. To read Bipan Chandra's work on communalism, for example, is to be struck by the extraordinary identity of view between the country's first prime minister and one of its most noted Marxist historians. According to Chandra, 'not only did Hindus or Muslims or Sikhs or Christians not form a nation or a nationality, they did not even form a distinct and homogeneous community, except for religious purposes... Hindus and Muslims as such were divided among themselves by economic interest, class, caste, social status, language, culture and social practices and even in religion. In fact an upper class Muslim had far more in common culturally with an upper class Hindu than with a lower class Muslim.'[40] Chandra argues that nationalism emerged in the nineteenth century to express 'the common interests of the Indian people for modern social, economic, political and cultural development ... for liberation from the colonial state and for the formation of an independent state.' He describes this as 'valid or legitimate consciousness' whereas he characterizes communalism, which emerged at the same time, or indeed casteism, as 'false consciousness'.[41] For Chandra, as for Nehru, it is only class consciousness that is valid and communalism is seen as an attempt by vested interests to forestall its growth. Consequently, he agrees with Nehru that a compromise with communal forces was neither feasible nor desirable because 'the terms on which it was available would have destroyed the secular integrity and identity of the nationalist forces themselves, leading to the creation of a Hindu communal, possibly fascist India.'[42] At the same time, he is critical of the Congress for not pursuing the logic of its own analysis. Nehru himself had accepted that 'many a Congressman was a communalist under his national cloak',[43] but Chandra takes the view that it was an 'ideological weakness of the national movement' that 'socially reactionary and obscurantist ideas... were never frontally opposed or rooted out by the Congress leaders.' He supports Nehru's view that national unity should be 'a unity between the masses and not an artifically arranged marriage of convenience between the leaders', but he points out that Nehru's Muslim mass contact campaign in the late 1930s, which was intended to bypass the Muslim middle class and upper class communal leaders, was not only 'ill planned and ill organised' but also opposed by the Congress right wing. As he says, 'it was not possible to heighten the class understanding and social consciousness of the Muslim masses without doing so also in case of the Hindu masses.'[44] For Bipan Chandra's nationalist ideal to have been realized, the Congress party would have had to be less dependent on the middle class, with a stronger social and ideological base among the mass of peasants and workers, and more committed to a policy of socialist transformation. But as he admits himself, this did not happen either before independence or afterwards. He does not find it surprising that the process of modernization should have given rise to all sorts of false consciousness, but he regrets that communalism, regionalism and casteism have remained so powerful.

Historians of the so-called nationalist Muslim school have tended to share these perceptions, though for them Partition has presented more acute dilemmas of identity. As Muhammad Mujeeb wrote in his magnum opus *The Indian Muslims,* Partition did not solve their problems. On the contrary, 'they became a much smaller minority in India, physically not less but more vulnerable by the creation of the separate state of Pakistan, with their loyalties obviously open to suspicion and doubt, and their future nothing but the darkness of uncertainty.'[45] Mushirul Hasan, the leading contemporary historian of the nationalist Muslims, holds virtually identical views. 'For the Muslim communities that remained in India', he writes, 'Partition was a nightmare... the so-called Islamic community in India, which had no place in Jinnah's Pakistan, was "fragmented", "weakened" and left vulnerable to right wing Hindu onslaughts.'[46]

Mushirul Hasan rejects the idea that the Indian Muslims prior to 1947 were 'a monolithic community with common interests and aspirations'. Rather he sees them as 'a disparate, differentiated and stratified segment of society'. So how could so many disparate groups strive for and eventually accomplish their goal of partition? He gives a number of answers, some drawn from an analysis of the Pakistan movement itself and its appeal to the masses in terms of Muslim values and history, some from a political context in which the Muslims were encouraged to develop separately by the British colonial authorities. In his view 'the colonial government created a community in its own image and allowed its war-time ally, the League, to transform a segmented population into a "nation" or "juridical entity".'[47] But he argues that the ground had already been made fertile by Muslim thinkers and clerics themselves. He accepts the point made by Aijaz Ahmad that many so-called Orientalist constructions of the Muslim community had their origins within the community itself and, after an account of the development of separatist Muslim thinking after 1857, he even goes so far as to say that 'by the close of the nineteenth century, the "community", separate and distinct from the "Others", had arrived with its accompanying baggage of concepts *bearing no relation to realities on the ground*' (my italics).[48] Mushirul Hassan's commitment to secularism—as exemplified by Nehru's own thinking and practice—shines through his writings. But his examination of the two most significant episodes in the history of the contemporary Indian Muslim community—Partition itself and the demolition of the Babri Musjid in 1992—reveals a vision under serious threat if not overwhelmed by strong communal currents. He passionately believes that prior to 1947 there was a possibility 'for fervent advocates of Indian nationhood to thwart Hindu majoritarianism and Muslim nationalism'. But his prescription for achieving this—'to evolve an independent/autonomous discourse, discard communal categories, the mainstay of religious mobilisation, and ignore the Muslim elite's self-image and perceptions of its role and destiny and history'[49]—makes clear the enormity of the task.

The Subaltern challenge

The Nehruvian consensus in Indian politics, though still shared by many Indian commentators, particularly those on the left, has suffered, not just from the re-emergence of communalism, but also from a loss of faith in the ability of the state, both in India and more widely in communist or socialist countries, to effect the kind of social transformation on which Marxists previously pinned their hopes. Consequently, with the emergence of all sorts of political challenges to Congress dominance—based on ethnicity, religion and caste—attention has inevitably focussed on the shortcomings and misuses of state power and the viability of the secular, scientific model of nationalism. Various kinds of 'false consciousness' are now the order of the day and while defenders of Nehru's vision attribute this situation to failures of the system, others argue that the vision itself was too limited to do justice to the diversity of India.

In terms of Indian historiography, the steady decline in Congress power has been matched by a questioning of the traditional nationalist discourse—in which the role of the great Congress leaders and the importance of national integration always had pride of place—and a search for alternative explanations which focus less on the unity which was imperative in confronting the Raj and more on the diversity which often underlay it. In this quest, historians of the Subaltern school have been particularly important. Drawing their inspiration from the work of the Italian Marxist Gramsci, they have sought to provide a counterbalance to traditional elite histories of nationalism by looking at the role of subordinate groups, whether as participants in the nationalist movement or rebels against it or indeed as rebels in their own right.

Subaltern history emerged in the late 1970s, criticizing traditional nationalist historiography for concentrating on leaders and institutions and for ignoring a wide range of other responses to colonialism, and finding fault with much European and American scholarship for portraying nationalism too narrowly. What is left out of such history, they argued, is 'the politics of the people... the subaltern classes and groups constituting the mass of the labouring population...' which, at least initially, was their main subject for study. It is important to realize, however, that the Subalterns offered a critique not just of historiography but of Indian nationalism itself. In their view, the leadership of the nationalist movement had failed to speak for the nation; in other words the movement was a social and political revolution that did not happen.[50] As Sumit Sarkar put it in *Modern India* : 'the social and economic contradictions that had provided the deeper roots of popular anti-imperialism had not been resolved, for the privileged groups in town and country had been able to successfully detach attainment of political independence from radical social change.'[51] For the 'subalterns', this failure constituted 'the central problematic of the historiography of colonial India.'

The first phase of Subaltern studies was devoted largely to writing history 'from below' but the second phase has paid more attention to political theory and to the re-examination of key concepts such as nationalism and communalism. In this phase, the influence of Edward Said's *Orientalism*, of Michel Foucault and of post-modern theory has been more marked and the resulting scholarship more contested. However the intellectual critique of Indian nationalism offered by scholars like Partha Chatterjee and Gyanendra Pandey has stimulated a very wide debate about the Nehruvian legacy and about the role of the state in independent India.

In his *Nationalist Thought and the Colonial World*, Partha Chatterjee offers a theoretical perspective on Indian nationalism which focuses on three important personalities—Bankim Chandra Chatterjee, Gandhi and Nehru—who are taken to characterize moments of departure, manoeuvre and arrival in the development of nationalist thought. Chatterjee acknowledges Gandhi's remarkable contribution to the development of mass politics and the originality of his critique of western industrial civilization, but he argues that Gandhi's politics of non-violence was not what he claimed it to be—a means to power for the masses—but a struggle conceived and directed by others which opened up 'the historic possibility by which the ...peasantry could be appropriated within the evolving political forms of the new Indian state'.[52] The role of Nehru, representing the Indian bourgeoisie, was to complete that process, becoming the author of what Chatterjee calls a 'supremely statist' utopia, in which the 'omnipotent and supremely enlightened state' is responsible for planning the progress of the country. In Chatterjee's words, this means that '... the world of differences, of conflict, of the struggle between classes, of history and politics, now finds its unity in the life of the state'. As he puts it 'Nationalism has arrived; it has now constituted itself into a state ideology; it has appropriated the life of the nation into the life of the state.'[53]

Chatterjee argues that nationalism is itself a child of the same post-enlightenment influences as colonialism. In his view, Reason—in which is subsumed science and technology and the power of the European nations to colonize the rest of the world—has always been 'parasitic upon... the universalist urge of capital.' Nationalism may have succeeded to some extent in checking capitalism. But nationalism was 'a derivative discourse'; its arguments were derived from the discourses of the enlightenment; it did not possess the ideological means to challenge the nexus of reason and capital; it merely resolved the contradiction by absorbing the political life of the nation into the body of the state, which then made its peace with global capital.

In Chatterjee's analysis the nation state, as an instrument of capital, is incapable of suppressing the unresolved tensions which are the product of an incomplete revolution. These may take the form of peasant populism or ethnic separatism but whatever the form Chatterjee says they 'bear the marks of the people-nation struggling in an inchoate, undirected and unequal battle against forces which have sought to dominate it.'[54]

This is a theme to which he returns in *The Nation and its Fragments*, where he argues that: 'The modern state, embedded as it is within the universal narrative of capital, cannot recognize within its jurisdiction any form of community except the single, determinate, demographically enumerable form of the nation. It must therefore subjugate, if necessary by the use of state violence, all such aspirations of community identity. These other aspirations, in turn, can give to themselves a historically valid justification only by claiming an alternative nationhood with rights to an alternative state.' For Chatterjee, more explicitly and more controversially in this second work, in the unresolved struggle between capital and community, it is community 'persistent in its invocation of the rhetoric of love and kinship against the homogenising sway of the normalised individual' which has right on its side.[55]

Chatterjee and other 'Subalterns' have been accused by those who support Nehru's secular vision of India of encouraging other, more partial and more dangerous allegiances. Chatterjee's condemnation of the nation-state and his preference for the narrative of community have even been read as an encouragement of the forces of Hindu nationalism. Such criticisms are undoubtedly oversimplified, given the intellectual influences on the Subaltern group, but they do point up the negative character of much Subaltern theorizing, which has for the most part been more proficient in providing critiques of nationalist discourses than in suggesting viable new ones.

Though there is wide agreement on the state of Indian politics which Chatterjee is interpreting—notably the failure of the Congress party to introduce far-reaching economic reforms after independence and its compromises with the capitalist sector—it is by no means clear that the problem of authoritarianism in the 1970s and 80s and the emergence of serious and often violent regional, ethnic and communal challenges to the state at that time arose from the same causes. Nehru certainly embodied the traditions of western 'rationality' in his vision of the post-colonial state, but he also handled the challenges of 'community' during his period of office more democratically than many of his successors. The challenges faced by his successors were arguably more to do with their authoritarianism and the collapse of internal democracy in the Congress party than with the imposition of an ideology which rejected alternative allegiances. There is a danger here of mistaking the discourse for the reality.

There may also be a problem in putting upon Nehru's shoulders the burden of representing nationalism at the point of 'arrival'. My own reading of the pre-independence period is that Nehru emerged as a key nationalist voice in the late 1920s because his theory of economic nationalism and his resistance to appeals in the name of religion and community fitted the needs of Congress political strategy at the time. His scientific socialism and his secularism were not fully shared by his Congress colleagues; indeed, many Congressmen remained very communal in their thinking, as became clear at Partition. By the same token, though Nehru's vision certainly held sway in independent India in the planning of development, the pressures of community and caste continued to bear on the implementation of policy at other levels.

If Nehru carries too heavy a burden in Chatterjee's interpretation of Indian nationalism, the same may also be said of the narrative of 'Capital' and 'Reason' in the post-colonial period. Though European influences have continued to have a major impact on India, not least in the preservation after 1947 of the instruments of colonial government—the civil service, the judiciary and the army—there are obvious dangers, as Sumit Sarkar has pointed out, in ascribing too much influence to ruling forms of power-knowledge; it may mean that power relationships are oversimplified, and subordinate groups are robbed of agency.[56] Chatterjee may be right in pointing up the dichotomy between Nation and Community, but he is unhelpful in locating the problem in the realm of imported ideas rather than in the use made of those ideas by Indians themselves.

If Chatterjee's main thrust has been the deconstruction of Indian nationalism, Gyanendra Pandey in his book *The Construction of Communalism in Colonial North India* looks from similar philosophical perspectives at the growing rift between the two main communities from the late nineteenth century onwards. In a series of essays, he focuses particularly on the role of the British colonial authorities in perpetrating the idea that communalism was inherent in the Indian condition. He argues that this essentialist view—that India was a country of primordial if not primitive allegiances—served imperial purposes and justified colonial rule as the harbinger of enlightenment. However, as Pandey points out, it was not just the Imperialists who rewrote history. Nationalist politicians and historians also rewrote it to serve their purposes, stressing Akbar rather than Aurangzeb, Ashoka and the Buddha rather than Shivaji, the unifying and the syncretistic rather than the plural and the divisive, while on the Hindu right a similar vision of the fundamental unity of India was also emerging, very different in its inspiration but sharing the same perceptions of India's political geography.[57]

Though approaching the subject from a more theoretical perspective, Pandey supports the thesis put forward in *Prelude* that the 1920s are a watershed in terms of changing attitudes to nationalism and communalism. In the late nineteenth century concepts of nation and community had overlapped. India had been seen as an aggregate of its different communities—Hindu, Muslim, Sikh, Christian and Parsi. How else could Gandhi have said with such evident admiration for the Ali brothers: 'The brave brothers are staunch lovers of their country, but they are Mussulmans first and everything else afterwards. It must be so with every religiously minded man.'[58] But the 1920s bring a change—with the growing politicization of both communities and more communal violence and rioting. It is in this period that Hindu and Muslim communal organizations grow in importance and that Congress leaders begin to characterize communalism as the antithesis of nationalism—the result of colonial manipulation which will only disappear with the coming of independence. Pandey explains the growth of communal consciousness in terms of the mass mobilization of Muslims in support of the Khilafat, subsequent evangelical movements in both communities and the growth of rioting in the mid 1920s, whereas *Prelude* places more emphasis on the way in which constitutional change—the introduction of political responsibility in the provinces and the growth of communal politics—underpinned this process. It is common ground that the new Congress approach to nationalism, which was pioneered by Nehru, was a response to this growth of communalism, but Pandey opens up a new field as a result of his analysis of the reconstruction of history which accompanied this process. Pandey argues that much of this rewriting, with its emphasis on unity and synthesis and the role of great leaders, with its discovery of the early roots of secularism in the reign of Akbar, was intrinsically oversimplified. There was no sense of the common people as historical agents, no room for the accommodation of local loyalties, no place for continued attachment to religion or for class or regional perspectives on the Indian national movement. On the contrary, '...nationalism was forced into the kind of statist perspective that colonialism had favoured and prompted for its own reasons. In nationalist historiography, as in the colonial construction of the Indian past, the history of India was reduced in substance to the history of the state.'[59]

Recent explorations of the intellectual origins of nationalism have confirmed that in the late nineteenth and early twentieth century there was an overlap between nation and community. At that stage, many Hindu writers produced work in both Urdu and Hindi—Persianized and Sanscritized—and were champions of the religious and the national. Sudhir Chandra in his work *The Oppressive Present* has shown how Hindu writers on the one hand characterized the Muslim as alien and on the other argued for political cooperation among all the communities in the wider interests of nationalism. He makes it clear, however, that for most Hindus—whatever Nehru's formulation may have been—there was a strong cultural dimension to their perceptions of nationalism which made it an ambiguous inheritance.[60] Moreover, the more politicians attempted to reach out to the masses, as they did from the 1920s, the more important this cultural dimension became.

Attempting to portray nineteenth century Hindu approaches to nationalism during a period of 'ominously rapid Hinduisation of the Indian polity' makes Chandra particularly sensitive to these nuances. We must not forget, he warns us, that in India, as in other nation-states, 'a kind of teleology is at work. Taking its cue from the present, it works backward to confirm the belief that the nation-state, as it is, marks not only an inevitable, but also an inviolable stage in the nation's historical evolution.' Chandra deplores the 'centralising viewpoint' which 'underlies not only the communal Hindu but also certain secular conceptions of Indian nationalism', the tendency to cast the nation-state in a monolithic mould, to project narrow group identities as the only possible Indian identity, to assume that there is an essential opposition between nationalism and all other identities. He laments the disappearance of the earlier harmony between Indian nationalism and regional nationalisms and the fact that 'despite the plurality of Indian society... and the federal spirit of the Indian constitution, the idea of a multi-national Indian state finds no place in these conceptions.' For Chandra, nationalism as an historical phenomenon was a rich mix of the economic, the political, the religious and the cultural, and attempts to reinterpret it more narrowly have been the cause of many of India's subsequent political problems.[61]

New feminist perspectives

In much of this analysis of nationalism and community, Partition, with all its violence, bloodshed and dislocation, has been for many years a spectre at the feast. The lost lives of the partition victims and the traumas of the survivors have reinforced the ideologies of nationalism, justified the centralization of power and the suppression of challenges to it, and helped to perpetuate divisions between the two states and their peoples. But until recently they have not been the subject of extensive historical analysis. Now however, a new generation of scholars has begun to look at Partition from this perspective.

This new work owes its origins partly to the interest of the next generation in answering questions previously too painful to be asked, though perhaps more influential has been the experience of a new wave of communalism in Indian politics, on a scale not seen since Partition, affecting Sikhs and Muslims in particular. It is no accident that a number of those who have begun to re-examine Partition from the perspective of sufferers and survivors were involved in dealing at first hand with the victims of indiscriminate violence against Sikhs in Delhi after the assassination of Indira Gandhi.

It is also significant that this new research has been pioneered mostly by women authors, who have seen Partition as a male narrative, in which women were sacrificed or abducted or recovered in a conflict which gave primacy to community and hierarchy at the expense of individual rights. Their work first attracted attention in 1993 with the publication of two articles in the *Economic and Political Weekly* looking at the role of the Indian state in the recovery of women abducted during Partition.[62] These articles point up the extraordinary sufferings that women went through at that time, in some cases killed by their own families to prevent them from falling into the hands of the other community, in other cases raped and abducted, then recovered and rejected by their original families, in yet others settling for a new life with their abductors only to have their choices overturned by tribunals set up by agreement between the two new states.

Ritu Menon and Kamla Bhasin in their article argue that 'it was a particular construction of the identity of the abducted women that determined the entire recovery operation, one that raises serious questions regarding the Indian state's definition of itself as secular and democratic.' If the tribunals appointed by the two states so decided, the individual woman had no right of appeal; she was in effect deprived of her fundamental rights. Action by the state 'entailed representing the women as ill-treated and humiliated, without volition or choice and most importantly without any rights that might allow her to intervene in this reconstruction of her identity and her life... Only thus could social and moral order be restored and national honour vindicated.'

Urvashi Butalia in her article looks in more detail at the harrowing stories of some of the women caught up in these crises, but her conclusions are very similar. As she puts it: 'This vocabulary of recovery, rehabilitation, homeland was actually a euphemism for returning Hindu and Sikh women to the Hindu and Sikh fold and Muslim women to the Muslim fold. On this point... both countries were agreed. Thus even for a self-defined secular nation (India), the natural place/homeland for women was defined in religious, indeed communal terms, thereby pointing to a disjunction between its professedly secular rhetoric... and its actively communal actions in regard to women. Women who had been taken away by the "other" community, had to be brought back to their "own" homeland: both concepts that were defined for women by the men of the respective countries. They did not have a choice.' Butalia also points up the way in which the crisis caused by Partition, the collapse of civil society and the killing and brutality which ensued, in some sense emasculated the men who would normally protect the women in their own families and forced the leaders of communities to look to the state to intervene on their behalf. In her view, this explains why the issue of gender became so important and why the state 'now provided coercive backing for restoring and reinforcing patriarchy within the family.'[63]

This concentration on the role of women—as sufferers and victims—during the Partition violence has raised important new questions about how community, religion and nationality have been defined, whether at that crucial moment or subsequently, and about the balance between the rights of the state, of communities and of individuals. In her recent book, *Critical Events*, the Indian anthropologist, Veena Das, has examined these questions—and the role of anthropology in addressing them—in relation to this work on Partition and to certain other key episodes in recent Indian history which pitted communities against the state. These include: the Shah Bano Affair, which raised questions about the place of Muslim personal law in a secular state, the revival of *sati* in Rajasthan, which highlighted the tension between the state and the Rajput community in the interpretation of cultural rights, and the growth of militancy among Sikhs in the Punjab in the 1980s, with its discourse of sacrifice and martyrdom and its definition of Sikh identity at odds with both Hinduism and the Indian state. The value of Veena Das's approach—as that of Menon, Bhasin and Butalia—is that by her focus on the victims she puts competing discourses of state and community into a more humane perspective. In fact she puts the case for what she calls a new 'anthropology of pain', 'an anthropology which can be seen as forming one body with the victim',[64] to replace traditional anthropology, which she sees as heavily Eurocentric in its approach and inclined to accentuate the 'otherness' of Indian society.

Das accepts many of the criticisms of the state which have emerged in India over recent years. She delineates very clearly how the state has arrogated or attempted to arrogate to itself rights which have thrown it into conflict with communities and individuals. However she does not see this as a reason to champion the community—as many academics as well as politicians have tended to do—because in her view champions of community rights very often fall into the same trap as the state itself, making absolutist claims which are equally restrictive of individual rights and freedoms. She says the community has traditionally been seen as an area of face to face relationships and therefore a humane counter to the growing power and impersonality of the modern state, but she finds that in India 'community is emerging as a political actor which seeks to reshape not so much the face to face intimate relations of the private sphere but control over law and history in the predominantly public sphere of life.' For this reason she believes that 'unless a very different theory of community emerges, the language of cultural rights cannot help us to remoralise those areas of life which have become denuded of meaning by the dominance of technologies of governance within modern states'.[65] As to the resolution of the conflict between the state and the community, her view is that it will only be possible 'if the state ceases to demand full ideological allegiance from the various collectivities which constitute it; and if communities, instead of demanding complete surrender from individual members on the pretext of preserving their culture recognize the paradoxical links of confirmation and antagonism from their members. An individual's capacity to make sense of the world...presupposes the existence of collective traditions; but indviduals must be able to experiment with these collective traditions by being allowed to live at their limits. The simultaneous development of the rights of groups and individuals will depend on the extent to which these paradoxes can be given voice, both in the realm of the state and the public culture of civil society.'[66]

Intellectually, Veena Das's call for the rejection of 'the seduction of consensus' in the name of either modernity or tradition,[67] and her sceptical treatment of claims to allegiance by both state and community constitute a powerful appeal for more attention to individual rights and more space for individual development. But as she herself makes clear, her main quest has been for a more humane and useful role for the anthropologist, not to provide a blueprint for legal or constitutional reform. By her emphasis on the victim she succeeds remarkably in injecting a new moral urgency into an area where polemics and violence have all too often had the field to themselves. It is a longer term project, however, to reshape state and community to such a prescription and one which will require significant changes in public opinion and much practical thinking in the legislative and judicial field.

Postscript

One of the reasons why Partition remains so absorbing a subject is that it continues to cast its shadow over relations between India and Pakistan. As the recent nuclear escalation in South Asia has proved so dramatically, fifty years of independence have done little to alleviate the rivalry and suspicion between the two countries. Nationalism remains a very powerful force.

But it has not gone unchallenged. In terms of the writing of history, Indians have enjoyed more freedom to call official ideologies into question, but there are obvious comparisons to be made between the kind of reflections emerging from historical research into the independence movement in India and the regular questioning of centralized state power which has taken place in Pakistan, even if in Pakistan the questioning has been done more by politicians than by historians. Nationalism remains powerful, but in both countries it has had to find new clothes, new weapons and new enemies in order to perpetuate itself in the face of serious ethnic, regional and other challenges.

New historical writing has carried research well beyond the areas explored in *Prelude to Partition*. But there are some common assumptions and preoccupations. There is a broad recognition that the 1920s were a crucial period in the shaping of the subcontinent, in preparing the ground for the emergence of Pakistan and in casting the character of Indian nationalism. There is also widespread interest in deconstructing the narrative of nationalism, in arguing the case for a more genuine pluralism and in pointing up the inhumanity of too narrow a definition of citizenship.

What *Prelude* has to say about those years is only part of a complex story. A study of colonial strategy and structures cannot explain how people were mobilized to achieve Pakistan or the continued centrality of those ideas in the future history of the state. But I believe it does help to explain how the building blocks of Pakistan were put in place, how it became possible for Muslim communities from different parts of India to see it as a common goal, and the kind of contradictions involved, not only during the Pakistan movement but in Pakistan itself.

I would also argue, as others have done from different perspectives, that the character given to Indian nationalism—in response to the communalization of politics and the challenges thrown down by imperialism—produced a mirror-image Muslim nationalism. Both these nationalisms have interpreted India and Pakistan in ways which have often proved too narrow to incorporate the diversities which fall under their sway. This is also to some extent an inheritance of the Raj and the way it handled the process of decolonization.

Partition is an event of such momentous significance for states, for families and for individuals, that it needs to be examined in many different ways and re-intepreted by every new generation. Structures do not tell the whole story. But they tell an important part of it. The impact of British imperialism in south Asia continues to be felt long after 1947. *Prelude to Partition* is an attempt to understand that impact at a critical stage in the region's history.

London
June 1998.

Notes

1. Ishtiaq Hussain Qureshi, *The Muslim Community of the Indo-Pakistan Subcontinent (610–1947)* (New Delhi 1985), p. 349.

2. See for example the review by I.A. Rehman in the *Herald*, Karachi, June 1987

3. David Lelyveld's review in the *American Historical Review*, vol. 89, number 2, April 1984.

4. See David Hardiman's review in the *Economic and Political Weekly*, 11 September 1982, and Gyanendra Pandey's review of writings on communalism in *Economic and Political Weekly*, 15 October 1983.

5. See *Journal of Commonwealth and Comparative Politics*, November 1977, pp. 215–34 in which Robinson comments on Brass's views on Muslim separatism and Brass replies.

See also Paul Brass, *Language, Religion and Politics in North India* (Cambridge 1974); Francis Robinson, *Separatism among the Indian Muslims* (Cambridge 1974); and Robinson's new introduction to the paperback version (Delhi 1993).

6. Farzana Shaikh, *Community and Consensus in Islam, Muslim Representation in Colonial India, 1860–1947* (Cambridge 1989), p 233

7. Ibid., pp. 175, 199–200, 207

8. Ibid., pp. 189–93

9. David Gilmartin, *Empire and Islam* (London 1988), chapter 5.

10. Ibid., chapter 6 and conclusion, particularly pp. 205–7 and 221–7.

11. Ian Talbot, *Punjab and the Raj 1849–1947* (New Delhi 1988), chapters 9 and 10.

12. Ian Talbot, *Freedom's Cry: The Popular Dimension in the Pakistan Movement and Partition Experience in North West India* (Karachi 1996), p. 1.

13. Ibid., p. 97.

14. Jawaharlal Nehru, *An Autobiography* (New Delhi 1988), p. 137.

15. See for example Dr Gopal's review of work on the transfer of power, *Hindustan Times*, 11 August 1985.

16. Ayesha Jalal, *The Sole Spokesman: Jinnah, the Muslim League and the Demand for Pakistan* (Cambridge 1985), p. 122.

17. Ibid., p 57

18. Ibid., chapter 5, particularly pp. 191–207 and chapter 6, pp. 211–13.

19. Anita Inder Singh, *The Origins of the Partition of India 1936–1947* (New Delhi 1987), chapter 5, particularly p. 143.

20. Sharif ul Mujahid, *Quaid i Azam Jinnah, Studies in Interpretation* (Karachi 1981), p. 268.

21. Stanley Wolpert, *Jinnah of Pakistan* (New York 1984), p. 340.

22. Saad R. Khairi, *Jinnah reinterpreted, the journey from Indian Nationalism to Muslim statehood* (Karachi 1996), p. 460.

23. I am indebted to Dr. Z.H. Zaidi for this information.

24. Interview with Mahommed Ali Chaiwallah, Bombay, September 1970.

25. R.J. Moore, *The Crisis of Indian Unity* (Oxford 1974), p. 307.

26. Moore shows that prime minister Clement Atlee also subscribed to this diagnosis. As a member of the Simon commission, Atlee had been concerned from its inception that the 1935 Act was 'deliberately framed so as to exclude as far as possible the Congress party from effective powers', though later, as prime minister, trying to maintain the unity of India in the face of the growing rift between the Congress and the Muslim League, he found fault with the Congress for its unwillingness to meet the legitimate fears of the Muslims. At that stage, he took the view that the failure to establish responsible government at the centre had facilitated 'totalitarian dictatorship by the working committee of the Congress party'. See *Escape from Empire: The Atlee Government and the Indian Problem* (Oxford 1983), p. 5.

27. Linlithgow to Zetland, 27 February 1940. This and the following quotation from *The Crisis of Indian Unity*, p. 312.

28. *Escape from Empire*, p. viii.

29. Ibid., p. 53.

30. Joya Chatterji, *Bengal Divided: Hindu Communalism and Partition 1932–1947* (Cambridge 1994), p. 222.

31. Ibid., pp. 259–60. Mountbatten asked Jinnah on 26 April 1947 for his views on Bengal remaining united and outside Pakistan. He is reported to have said without hesitation: 'I should be delighted. What is the use of Bengal without Calcutta; they had much better remain united and independent; I am sure they would be on friendly terms with us.' See Mansergh, *Transfer of Power*, vol. x, pp. 452–3.

32. Yunas Samad, *A Nation in Turmoil: Nationalism and Ethnicity in Pakistan, 1937–1958* (New Delhi 1995), pp. 10–11.

33. Ibid., pp 71—2, 106–7.

34. Harun-or-Rashid, *The Foreshadowing of Bangladesh: The Bengal Muslim League and Muslim Politics 1936–47* (Dhaka 1987), p. vii.

35. Ibid., pp. 344–6.

36. Taj ul-Islam Hashmi, *Peasant Utopia, The Communalisation of Class Politics in East Bengal, 1920–47* (Dhaka 1994), pp. 1–21, 263–70.

37. Ibid., See Chapter 4, pp. 83–123.

38. Tazeen Murshid, *The Sacred and the Secular, Bengal Muslim Discourses 1871–1977* (Calcutta 1995), particularly pp. 204–10, 286–7, 437–41.

39. Jawaharlal Nehru, *An Autobiography* (New Delhi 1988), pp. 467–70.

40. Bipan Chandra, *Communalism in Modern India* (New Delhi 1984), pp. 13–15.

41. Ibid., p. 21.

42. Ibid., p. 290.

43. Jawaharlal Nehru, *An Autobiography*, p. 136.

44. Bipan Chandra, op.cit., pp. 299–304.

45. Muhammad Mujeeb, *The Indian Muslims* (London 1967), p. 440.

46. Mushirul Hasan, *Legacy of a Divided Nation: India's Muslims since Independence* (New Delhi 1997), p. 6.

47. Ibid., p. 98.

48. Ibid., p. 236.

49. Ibid., p. 52.

50. See Ranjit Guha's article 'On some aspects of the Historiography of Colonial India' in *Subaltern Studies I* (New Delhi 1982) pp. 1–8.

51. Sumit Sarkar, *Modern India* (New Delhi 1990), p. 453.

52. Partha Chatterjee, *Nationalist thought and the Colonial World, a Derivative Discourse* (New Delhi 1986), p. 124.

53. Ibid., pp. 160–1.

54. Ibid., pp. 168–70.

55. Partha Chatterjee, *The Nation and its Fragments: Colonial and Post-colonial Histories* (New Delhi 1997), pp. 238–9.

56. See his 'Orientalism revisited: Saidian Frameworks in the writing of Modern Indian history' in the *Oxford Literary Review*, vol. 16, nos 1–2, 1994, pp. 205–24.

57. Gyanendra Pandey, *The Construction of Communalism in Colonial North India* (New Delhi, 1990), chapter 2, pp, 23–65, and chapter 7, pp 247–54.

58. Ibid., pp. 210, 233, 238.

59. Ibid., chapter 7, particularly pp. 235, 253.

60. Sudhir Chandra, *The Oppressive Present* (New Delhi 1992), chapter 3, pp. 116–154.

61. Ibid., pp, 155–9.

62. *Economic and Political Weekly*, 24 April 1993: Ritu Menon and Kamla Bhasin, *Recovery, Rupture and Resistance, the Indian State and the Abduction of Women during Partition;* Urvashi Butalia, *Community, State and Gender, on Women's Agency during Partition.*

63. These authors have since published books elaborating these themes: Ritu Menon and Kamla Bhasin, *Borders and Boundaries: Women in India's Partition* (New Delhi 1998) and Urvashi Butalia, *The Other Side of Silence: Voices from India's Partition* (New Delhi 1998). Gyanendra Pandey is also writing a book on Partition based on interviews with survivors which examines some of the same issues.

64. Veena Das, *Critical Events, An Anthropological Perspective on Contemporary India* (New Delhi 1995), chapter 7.

65. Ibid., p. 17.

66. Ibid., p. 116.

67. Ibid., p. 54.

Acknowledgements to the Paperback Edition

This book was begun more than thirty years ago during a year spent teaching at Edwardes College, Peshawar. It was during that first experience of the subcontinent that I became interested in the origins of Partition and I owe a huge debt to the Principal, the late Dr Phil Edmunds, and to the staff and students with whom I worked.

In writing the original thesis, I received assistance, both financial and academic, from a very large number of people and institutions. The Department of Education and Science supported my first year of studies. The trustees of the Hildebrand Harmsworth Scholarship Fund of Merton College, Oxford, awarded me a three year senior scholarship from 1968–71. The Beit Fund and the Bartle-Frere Fund of Oxford University made possible my research visits to India and Pakistan in 1969 and 70. I was also greatly helped by the staff of the Indian Institute Library, Oxford, the India Office Library in London, the National Archives of India, the Nehru Memorial Museum and Library and the Jamia Millia Islamia, New Delhi, the U.P. Secretariat Archive, Lucknow, the Research Society of Pakistan, Lahore, and Karachi University Library.

In those days, my tutor at Merton college, Dr Roger Highfield, and Dame Lucy Sutherland, historian of the East India Company, with whom I worked on Warren Hastings for my first degree, were important influences. The late Professor Jack Gallagher, the father of the so-called Cambridge school of Indian history, acted as my supervisor during his stay in Oxford and on his return to Cambridge. In his habitually irreverent and thought-provoking way, he encouraged me to keep digging for answers to what sometimes seemed impossibly large questions. I am also indebted to Professor Peter Reeves and Professor Ronald Robinson for helping me to put some of my ideas into a better perspective; to Chris Bayly and Francis Robinson for the opportunity of talking to them about their work; and to Bruce Cleghorn, Peter Kelly, Margaret Macmillan and Gynendra Pandey, for their friendship and for many helpful discussions. Dr Sarvepalli Gopal has been a source of encouragement and advice over many years. I also owe a great deal to my friends Anthony and Ursula King, under whose roof in West Dulwich the thesis was finally completed.

In the preparation of the introduction to the paperback edition, Anthony King and Gynendra Pandey have made valuable comments on several drafts. Urvashi Butalia, Barun De and Sudipta Kaviraj have given me helpful advice on parts of the text. Ruth Kirk-Wilson has demanded greater intelligibility on behalf of the general reader. The section on the historiography of Pakistan was discussed in London at a seminar at the School of Oriental and African studies in December 1995 and at a meeting of the Pakistan society in May 1997.

Finally, my thanks to the Oxford University Press in New Delhi, for seeing the paperback into print.

London
September 1998

Preface

Until the creation of Bangladesh in 1971, most Pakistanis saw the emergence of their country primarily as a religious or ideological phenomenon. This view was shaken by the secession of East Pakistan, which raised important questions about Pakistan's identity as a homeland for the Muslims of the subcontinent. However, it was not rejected. Indeed over the past fifteen years, the rulers of Pakistan have continued to stress the country's Islamic identity, whether in the development of closer ties with the Muslim world, or in an effort to establish an Islamic state in Pakistan itself. Furthermore, the mass media within Pakistan, as well as the educational system and the ulema, have continued to reinforce this perspective.

This book does not seek to question the part played by religion in the formation of the state. For the belief that Islam was in danger was clearly crucial to the growth in support for the Muslim League on the eve of Independence. However, though it is possible to explain in such terms how men were mobilized to achieve Pakistan, such a theory is plainly insufficient to explain how disparate Muslim communities throughout India came to see Pakistan as a common goal.

Many Muslim historians have been aware of this themselves, at least subconsciously, for they have concentrated their attention on two main historical periods: firstly, the period dominated by Sir Syed, from 1857 to the foundation of the Muslim League, and secondly, the period after 1937, when the movement which led to Pakistan began to gather momentum. This book contends, however, that the intervening period was crucial, and it seeks to provide a structural explanation of Muslim politics in that period to complement existing ideological explanations.

It does this by concentrating attention on the formal structure of politics—the Imperial system of control and the manner in which it was modified. In particular, it examines the constraints on political development imposed by the introduction of electoral institutions. This process, which was the chief means by which the government modified its system of control in the last stages of Empire, is seen as crucial both to the quickening pace of politicization and to the steady increase in communal awareness among the Muslims of the different provinces.

The value of this approach is that it illuminates the working of factors previously neglected. In the process, however, important elements in the development of Muslim politics have necessarily been treated less thoroughly. Little is said, in particular, about the cultural context of politics, or about the social and psychological tensions produced by the process of 'modernization'. This is a subject in itself, and one which requires a more detailed study of Muslim society.

Those who open this book in the hope of discovering a detailed examination of Muslim politics in every part of the subcontinent also deserve an apology. The main focus of the work is on political developments in the United Provinces and Punjab, the two provinces with the lion's share of all-India leadership during the period under study. Considerations of time, space and coherence have made necessary this degree of specialization.

The theoretical basis for the analysis is explored in detail in the Introduction. The Introduction also contains an examination of political developments under the Morley – Minto Reforms as an illustration of the working of the theory during that period. It shows how the linkages provided by the Reforms between provincial and district levels of politics drew local issues into the orbit of provincial politics, and how the introduction of a substantial elected element in provincial councils acted as a spur to political confrontation with the Raj. Both the participation of the Muslim League in the politics of confrontation and the rise of communalism in the localities is explained in these terms. The rise of Panislamic politics is treated briefly as a separate theme.

The book itself concentrates on the constitutional Reforms introduced in 1920. These Reforms are considered the most important stage in the process of electoral innovation. For the first time, an element of political responsibility is introduced at the provincial level, and by the time these Reforms give way to the Government of India Act of 1935, provincial autonomy has become a reality and the Congress has emerged as the obvious political successor to the Raj. In the period before 1920, the Muslim League works with the Congress to further the cause of constitutional reform, but by 1937, the dominant Muslim interests in most

Indian provinces have been alienated from the Congress and the scene is set for the emergence of the Pakistan movement.

Chapter 1 examines the effect of the Montagu – Chelmsford constitution on the structure of all-India politics. It suggests that the weight given to the rural interest and the efforts made to balance the representation of different communities within individual councils were deliberate attempts to offset the challenge of the 'nationalist' politicians. It also suggests that these devices were to have an important effect on the nature of respondent political activity, both encouraging the development of communal blocs within councils, and ultimately dictating the logic of the Congress appeal to the countryside. Where all-India Muslim politics are concerned, chapter 1 argues that the Reforms were instrumental in bringing the majority-province Muslims into prominence. By distributing power, at least in some measure, according to population, the Reforms made numerical superiority a political asset. But because the Bengali Muslims were economically and politically weaker than the Punjabis, they were less well-represented within their own council and less capable for that reason of utilizing the Reforms for their own advantage. Chapter 1 concludes with an analysis of the Muslim political interest which emerged in the Punjab under the new dispensation—its leadership, and its tactics for consolidation.

Chapter 2 examines the growth of communal tension which followed the introduction of the Reforms, and assesses its implications for political co-operation between the two communities at the all-India level. Because this tension was most marked in the Punjab and the United Provinces, attention focuses on these two provinces. An attempt is made to explain the worsening communal situation in political terms. In the Punjab, it is suggested that the use of political power by the majority community penalized the urban Hindus and provoked a communal reaction. In the United Provinces, Hindu interests with an eye on office at the local and provincial levels appear to have used communal appeals to undermine the political dominance of an inter-communal alliance. The effect on all-India politics of the resulting polarization of communal relations is then discussed. Where the Khilafat movement is concerned, the growth of communalism in the provinces is shown to have undermined the hold of the Ali brothers on the all-India organization. Where constitutional politics are concerned, Jinnah's career illustrates the same trend. Anxious for a measure of responsibility at the Centre, Jinnah endeavours to produce a new Lucknow Pact to strengthen his hand. But the rise of communalism in the provinces obliges him to demand a higher price than the Congress is prepared to pay. Finally, the same phenomenon is shown to have affected the Congress. The Congress has to compromise with communal parties in order to maintain its coherence and in the process loses much of its Muslim support.

In Chapter 3, a study is made of the process of polarization at the all-India level induced by the appointment of the Statutory Commission. The government's strategy is to encourage provincial ambitions, and particularly Muslim provincial ambitions, to offset challenges to its authority at the Centre. It is at this time that the Punjabi Muslims appear on the all-India stage as the leaders of provincial Muslim opinion.

The exclusion of Indians from the Statutory Commission provokes a re-alliance of all-India interests and gives new momentum to the politics of confrontation. However, support from provincial interests enables the government to stand by its decision, and communal dissension re-emerges. In March 1928, the Muslim League withdraws from the all-parties conference and the Nehru report is drawn up without its assistance.

The formulation of the Nehru report is examined in detail. By this stage, the terms on which the Congress is prepared to frame a constitution are shown to be unacceptable even to important nationalist Muslims. The report's demand for a strong unitary government at the Centre intensifies Muslim demands for safeguards within a Federal framework. It also forces minority-province Muslims to come to terms with the eventual withdrawal of the Imperial power. At the all-parties convention at Calcutta in December 1928, with Jinnah's failure to secure amendments to the Nehru report, the possibility of a genuine all-India agreement between the two communities disappears. The scene is set for the Congress one-year ultimatum to government and the emergence of the All India Muslim Conference, an alliance of provincial Muslim interests, under Punjabi leadership.

The final chapter examines the role of the Muslim Conference during the period of constitutional revision. Attention is drawn to the importance of the Punjabi Muslim leader, Fazli Husain, as the organizer of the Conference and to the value of his membership of the Viceroy's Council. An examination of Fazli Husain's role in shaping the Government of India's proposals for Reform shows he was chiefly concerned to secure Muslim control of the majority provinces and to forestall the introduction of responsible government at the Centre. At the first round-table conference and immediately afterwards, the Muslim Conference faces serious all-India challenges. Liberal efforts to secure Muslim support for a Federal Centre and government overtures to the Congress prompt negotiations on the communal question which threaten the Conference position. But continuing communal tension and astute Conference leadership prevent agreement from being reached on Liberal or Congress terms. The acceptance of the Federal idea also favours the Conference. The princes acquire a virtual veto on constitutional advance, and the establishment of a responsible Centre is made less likely. By the beginning of 1932, with the failure of the second round-table conference and Congress resumption of civil disobedience, Muslim support has become vital to continued Imperial control at the Centre. An increase in Muslim belligerence at this time forces the government to settle the main communal questions according to Conference demands. The Communal Award makes Muslim Raj in Punjab and Bengal a real possibility. It also strengthens those provinces against the emergence of a national government at New Delhi.

The Conclusion examines the implications of the Award for the future of Muslim politics. It suggests that Pakistan only became a reality when the most important provincial interests created by the Reforms had been converted to it. It also points to the continuing importance of the Punjab interest once Pakistan had been achieved. The study ends with an assessment of the role of Imperial policy in the creation of communal consciousness.

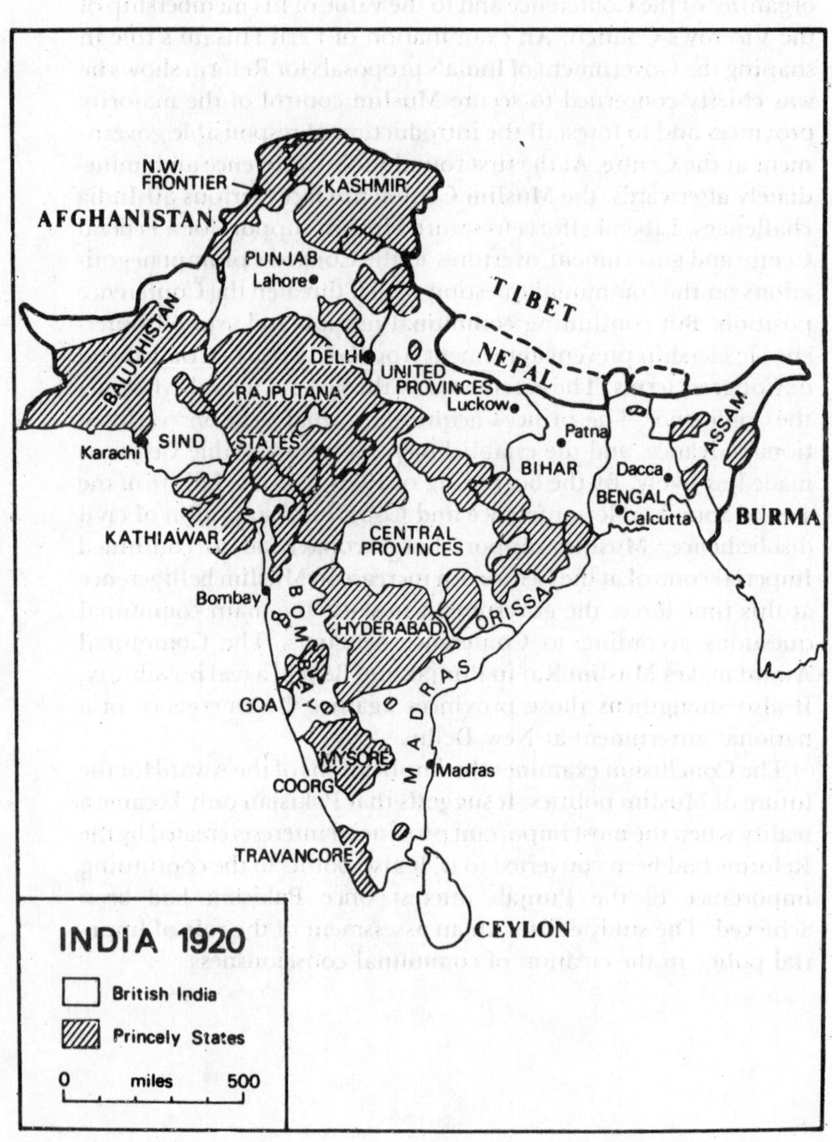

N.W. FRONTIER
KASHMIR
AFGHANISTAN
PUNJAB
Lahore
TIBET
BALUCHISTAN
DELHI
NEPAL
UNITED PROVINCES
RAJPUTANA
STATES
Luckow
ASSAM
SIND
Karachi
Patna
BIHAR
Dacca
BENGAL
Calcutta
BURMA
KATHIAWAR
CENTRAL PROVINCES
Bombay
BOMBAY
ORISSA
HYDERABAD
MADRAS
GOA
MYSORE
Madras
COORG
TRAVANCORE
CEYLON
INDIA 1920
British India
Princely States
0
miles
500

Introduction

Relevance of a study of pre-Partition politics

The Partition of India can lay claim to be one of the most significant events of modern history. Indeed in many respects it has overshadowed the release of the subcontinent from colonial rule, for unlike that event, which is now taken for granted, it continues to be an important factor in the political complexion of South Asia. It took place in 1947 because it seemed the only way of alleviating the rivalry of Hindu and Muslim. But it was accompanied by bloody rioting and the transfer of populations and far from laying discord to rest, it merely institutionalized that discord at an international level. Where party opposed party, state has since opposed state, and on three occassions war has broken out. For this reason, an investigation of the reasons for Partition has a relevance beyond the event itself. It is also important to an understanding of subsequent relations between the two countries.

But the relevance of Partition does not stop there. India was the first major colonial dependency outside the white Dominions to gain its independence, and the communal problems which it faced as it evolved towards that state have since occurred in similar, if not identical forms, in many other countries. In Northern Ireland, communal tension has long been a political problem. In Malaysia, there has been friction between Malays and Chinese. In Nigeria, the Ibos tried to secede from the Federation. In Cyprus, there have been serious divisions between the Turkish and Greek Cypriots. And more recently in Sri Lanka, political differences between Tamils and Sinhalese have erupted into violent confrontation. Consequently, the problem of Hindu-Muslim antagonism in India in the last phase of Empire has a relevance beyond the confines of that particular time and place, and an examination of how it arose may throw light on similar situations elsewhere.

Imperialism and political integration

One of the most important questions for the student of nationalism, whether of Indian or Pakistani nationalism, is: how did politicians succeed in building bridges between district and district and between province and province? In other words, is there a functional explanation for the growth of national consciousness? If one merely looks at the map of India and meditates on the variety of races, castes and customs, the disparities of social and economic development, not to mention the huge physical distances which separated one Indian from another, the question seems impossible to answer. What had the Parsee businessman in common with the Jat farmer? The Allahabad Brahmin with the untouchable of Nagpur? The Moplah with the Pathan? Apparently nothing. But there is an answer. What they all had in common was that they came under the political authority of the Imperial power. Long before the foundation of the Indian National Congress or the All India Muslim League, there existed in India a 'national' organization whose ramifications extended into the remotest village—the Imperial power itself. Rather than asking, therefore, what it was that bound together men of different races, languages and customs, and created Indian or Pakistani nationalism, the historian might more profitably ask in what ways the Imperial power itself contributed to the bridge-building process.

In the years immediately after 1857, the Indian Empire might be described as a three-tiered autocracy. From the 'national' level, where Imperial authority was wielded by the Viceroy in Council, orders travelled down to the next tier in the hierarchy, the provincial level, whence they were relayed by the Governor in Council to the district officers and their assistants, who gave them executive effect. Some decisions were made at the national level, some at the provincial level and some at the district level, and laws regarding what could be decided where were laid down in great detail. But the strength of the system, as of any autocracy, was that the relations between the Raj and its subjects were conducted almost entirely at the district level. India was run by the district officers and each district officer was the 'mother and father' of his district.

From the point of view of the preservation of Imperial rule, the value of this system was that it confined points of irritation within a small compass. Because each district officer was both the embodiment of Imperial power within his own district, and the channel by which men were obliged to approach the provincial and national governments, there was little chance of undermining his authority. And because each district officer ran his district along individual lines, choosing his own allies, dispensing his own justice and utilizing his own methods to keep the peace, the management of provinces was made easy. The greater the number of individual units the provincial government had to deal with, the easier it was to maintain Imperial authority, for with each district run along individual lines, the chances of province-wide agitation were small. Only at times of great economic distress or religious disturbances was this not the case, and in both these instances the causes of province-wide concern were essentially temporary in character.

So what disturbed the placid waters of autocracy? This book suggests that an important part of the answer to this question may be provided by a study of the introduction of electoral institutions. It suggests that this process, which was the main means by which the Imperial power modified its system of control between 1857 and 1947, contributed, in its various stages, to the focusing of district grievances at the provincial level, and to the focusing of provincial grievances at the national level. Moreover, it suggests that the introduction of electoral institutions, by providing permanent political links between the different levels of government, encouraged the settlement of grievances at higher levels than had previously been the case, and so contributed to the building of parties first at the provincial level and subsequently at the national level. Finally, it suggests that the devolution of power to Indian hands, which took place within this electoral framework, by encouraging competition for power, also encouraged an extension of political activity, with the result that new classes, castes, communities and interests were drawn into the political process.

Electoral innovation and political catalysis

Electoral institutions with a substantial elected element were first introduced in local self-government, at the district and municipal level, in the 1880s. But from the point of view of the preservation of Imperial control, this stage of devolution, even when it came to involve real responsibilities, did little to throw the Raj off balance. The same institutions were introduced in most towns and districts but the system did nothing to focus grievances at a higher level of government. Each district board and each municipality continued to be treated as an individual unit. The district officer remained the main vehicle for Imperial control and patronage, and even though many boards were empowered to elect non-official chairmen, they generally made sure that the district officer occupied this important position. In their relations with the provincial government, he was the man most capable of getting things done.

In 1909, with the introduction of the Morley-Minto Reforms, this system began to change. Except in the Punjab, where reasons of military security dictated otherwise, the Reforms introduced a substantial elected element at the provincial level and made election to the provincial councils the prerogative of district and municipal boards. The powers of the new provincial councils were not extensive. Except in Bengal, the elected members were everywhere in a minority. They only had the right to ask questions, to speak in the Budget debate and to introduce private members' bills subject to government approval. Yet their inauguration made a substantial difference to the Imperial system of control. For the first time, the grievances of the districts and municipalities were brought to a permanent provincial focus, with the result that the Raj could no longer deal with such grievances on an individual basis. It became obliged to discuss local grievances in provincial terms and, as a result of the pressure which it faced in the council, to make decisions at the provincial level which it would previously have left to the jurisdiction of its local officers.

Another important feature of the Morley - Minto Reforms was that they gave those with purely provincial grievances their first opportunity to achieve representative status and to confront provincial governments with those grievances. For such politicians, however, there was a price to pay for participation. Because local self-government bodies formed the electorate for the provincial councils, politicians with provincial grievances were obliged to involve themselves in municipal and district board politics. Consequently, competition for power at that level increased; conflicts emerged between provincial and local interests; and, as a by-product of this process, politicization was enormously speeded up.

In the decade after the introduction of the Morley-Minto Reforms, the confrontation with government assumed a new intensity, and at the end of that decade, signs of national consciousness were beginning to appear. But the Reforms did not give anything away at the provincial level. The power to remedy provincial grievances continued to lie in the hands of the Raj, and if the Raj had stood firm at the provincial level, the political spotlight might have shifted back to the district officer. But the Raj did not stand firm. In 1920, the system changed again. In that year, by the terms of the Montagu-Chelmsford Reforms, each provincial council was given a majority of elected members. the franchise was greatly extended, and most important of all, the patronage of such important departments as Education, Agriculture and Local Self-Government was handed over to ministers responsible to the legislatures.

From the point of view of the relations between the districts and the province, this first stage of political devolution at the provincial level was of crucial importance. In those areas of control which had been handed over to Indian ministers, the ground under the district officer's feet began to give away. Patronage ceased to be the prerogative of the district officer. The district officer became the servant of the minister; and the patronage which he had distributed became the reward for political organization. Consequently, in certain important areas of government, those who were not receiving satisfaction at the district level could no longer look to the district officer for redress. Just as their opponents were enjoying the fruits of government patronage because they had allies in the provincial government, so they were obliged themselves, either to find similar allies or, failing that, to join a provincial opposition party. In certain important areas of government, there had ceased to be a local solution to local grievances.

But if the position of the local politician had changed, so had the position of the provincial politician. Under the Morley-Minto Reforms, because no power had been devolved at the provincial level, it had been possible, indeed it had been expedient, for provincial politicians to resolve local conflicts for the sake of provincial advantage. After 1920, however, the council chamber became a battleground between those who had access to the transferred departments and those who did not. This gave local grievances a new importance. Just as those who worked the Reforms were able to consolidate their power province-wide by the distribution of patronage, so those who wished to unseat the ministers were obliged to develop a similar organization themselves. Consequently the exploitation of local divisions, the recruitment of local opponents of ministers and the politicization of new sections of the electorate proceeded apace. The localities were drawn increasingly into the ambit of provincial politics, and the fortune of local and provincial politicians became correspondingly interdependent.

But what of the growth of nationalism? This book suggests that the politicization of the provinces was an essential prerequisite for its emergence. An arena for the expression of 'nationalist' grievances existed at the all-India level at a very early stage, and particularly after 1909, when an Imperial council was instituted along the same lines as those in the provinces, there was never any shortage of eminent men to fill the seats which had been created. Yet though the Morley-Minto Reforms had the same catalysing effect at the national level as they did in the provinces, the demands of 'nationalist' politicians for a share of power at that level fell on deaf ears. In 1920, under the Montagu-Chelmsford Reforms, the Central Legislature was expanded and an elected majority created, but no devolution of power took place. All the departments of the government of India remained firmly in the hands of the Raj and its agents until the very eve of Independence. This had important implications for the nature of nationalist politics. Whereas the devolution of power at the provincial level, both in 1920 and in 1937, had the effect of sharpening conflict at that level between 'in' groups and 'out' groups, causing a polarization of political interests around provincial issues, the failure to devolve power at the all-India level prevented the same yeast from working in nationalist politics. After 1920, confrontation with the Raj continued to be the *leitmotif* of Central Assembly politics, but in the face of Imperial recalcitrance on this issue, the mainspring of nationalist politics remained competition of interest at the provincial level. The assault on the Centre, the last stage in the emergence of nationalism, came not from the nation itself but from the provinces. The Congress party only won its right to succeed the Raj when it had captured a majority of provinces in 1937.

The Imperial system of control: beneficiaries and opponents

The introduction of electoral institutions and the devolution of power to Indian hands *per se* provide a framework for explaining the pace of politicization and the building of bridges between different levels of government. But they do not explain the nature of the bridges which were built and the kind of politicization which was done. They do not explain why certain groups, castes, classes and communities found themselves among the 'nationalists' at any given stage of the process of devolution, nor why certain others did not. More particularly, they do not explain what this book attempts to explain, namely why Muslim separatism became so important a political force. In order to explain these things, one has got to look at the introduction of electoral institutions and the devolution of power not as an autonomous process but in relation to the existing system of Imperial control.

In the system of control which Britain inherited from its predecessors, a man's importance in the eyes of the Imperial power lay in his social and political influence at the local level. No Imperial power could run a country of India's size without the help of local agents, and in the British case, the absence of intensive European settlement and the relative paucity of European personnel made it very necessary for the Imperial power to recruit to its service those who already possessed an established position in society, whether on account of their personal wisdom, their economic influence or their authority as social or religious leaders. In practice, the main criterion for an individual's usefulness was the ownership of land. It was from land that men derived the political and economic leverage necessary to ensure compliance with their wishes, and it was also from land that the government derived the bulk of its income. These were both excellent reasons for the government to develop a firm alliance with the landed class. It confirmed it in its possession of the land, by legal and, if necessary, by military means, and in return the landed class collected the land revenue and delivered a portion of it to the Imperial power. But the ramifications of this system of control did not stop there, for the Imperial power cemented the alliance even more firmly by recruiting the scions of landed houses into the Imperial bureaucracy. It endeavoured, in fact, to create an administrative machine which reflected the established social structure of the country, a machine which operated not only in the collection of land revenue, but in the day-to-day administration of every district, *tehsil* and *pargannah*.

The position of the Muslims within this system of control depended on their social and economic importance in the different provinces. Where they were influential landowners, they formed an important element in the Imperial system. Where they were small farmers and traders, the part they played was less significant. In North India, in the area around Delhi, which had been the centre of Muslim power since the twelfth century, and in the Gangetic plain to the East, where Muslim settlement had been most intense under the Moghul Empire, the Muslim share of land was great and their role within the Imperial system proportionately great. In this area (the United Provinces), and to a lesser extent in Bihar, the decline of the Moghul Empire did not radically disturb the Muslim share of landownership, and even where landed families were coming under pressure as a result of the working of new economic forces, they continued to play a similar role under the British Empire to the one they had played under the Moghuls. In 1913, as Table I shows, though only fourteen per cent of the population, the U.P. Muslims had thirty-five per cent of the most important jobs.

TABLE 1

Hindus and Muslims, by province and population: their share of executive and judicial services, 1913 (Shown in percentages)

Province	Hindus				Muslims			
	Pop.	Exec.	Jud.	Total	Pop.	Exec.	Jud.	Total
Madras	88.90	73.5	91.3	82.9	6.67	11.8	1.3	6.3
Bombay	76.02	81.3	89.1	84.4	20.32	4.9	1.7	3.7
Bengal	44.80	72.9	97.5	84.7	52.74	18.1	2.5	10.6
Bihar anc Orissa	82.40	54.3	76.1	60.2	10.63	22.6	22.7	22.7
United Provinces	85.32	50.7	73.9	60.1	14.11	41.3	24.8	34.7
Punjab*	33.46	38.2	37.5	38.0	54.85	38.2	39.6	38.6
Central Provinces	82.62	53.0	88.2	64.9	4.06	28.0	3.9	19.9
Assam	35.55	62.7	91.7	67.6	50.25	18.6	8.3	16.9

*In the Punjab the Sikhs formed 10.48% of the population and possessed 10.3% of the executive posts and 6.2% of the judicial posts.

Source: Report of the Public Service Commission 1912, vol, i (Calcutta 1917), p. 191.

In Western India, on the other hand, Muslim landowners had suffered at the hands of the Mahrattas, and in the South, where they had been largely confined to the princely state of Hyderabad, they remained so confined at the turn of the twentieth century. Both in Bombay (except in Sind) and in Madras, the most influential Muslims were merchants, and the community did not qualify for special consideration.

In Bengal, though for different reasons, Muslim influence was also negligible. Until the coming of the British, Bengal had possessed a substantial Muslim aristocracy. But as a result of the resumption proceedings of the East India Company, this aristocracy was virtually eliminated. At the turn of the century, despite the emergence of a parvenu aristocracy in the Dacca division, the community consisted primarily of peasant farmers and it was not favoured for government service. In 1913, though over fifty per cent of the population, the Bengali Muslims had only ten per cent of the prestigious jobs.

Outside the United Provinces, the Punjabis were the only community of great importance to the system of control. In the Punjab, Muslim fortunes improved under the British, for after the 'Mutiny', because the Muslims of West Punjab played so notable a part in putting it down, the Punjabi Muslims became a vital element in Imperial military strategy. For this reason, the Raj bolstered Muslim interests in the Punjab, and when irrigation schemes led to the reclamation of large areas of West Punjab in the later nineteenth century, the Muslims of that area were among the chief beneficiaries. This development marked the most important accession of landed wealth to the community during the British period. It gave the Punjabis a landed position to rival that of their co-religionists in the United Provinces, and in the years after 1920, because of their numerical strength, it was to make them politically more powerful.

Opposition to this system of control (and to the Muslim position within it) came from a multitude of sources. It came from the trader facing restrictions; from the landlord refused a revenue remission; from the oppressed tenant who found the administration siding with his oppressor; from the government servant facing a block in promotion; from the unsuccessful job applicant; from the religious zealot with theocratic beliefs; and from all those who felt they suffered discrimination. But particular grievances were not a substantial source of irritation to government. They only became so when they could be generalized—when the same grievance united a large number of opponents, or when a number of different grievances could be brought together under the same umbrella.

In the early stages of the nationalist movement, before the working of electoral institutions began to assist this process, one of the most important sources of generalized opposition to the Raj was the growth of an educated and professional élite, united by a common education, a common language, in many cases by the practice of a common profession, and increasingly, as the volume of graduates grew, by a common search for personal fulfilment in a system loaded against it. For those who were recruited as agents of the Raj were not educationally competitive. They were recruited not on the basis of qualifications obtained in the colleges, but on account of their family background and tried loyalty to Government. In the United Provinces, for example, in 1886, out of 161 Deputy Collectors, only fifteen had passed their intermediate examination and only nine had degrees. Of 225 *tehsildars,* only four had passed the intermediate examination and only one had a degree.[1] Moreover, even after 1886, despite the recommendations of the Public Service Commission that entry into the provincial services should be by competitive recruitment 'wherever the Government of India thinks it not inexpedient', the same system continued. Prior to 1917, the only 'competitive' examination for entry to any provincial service took place in the Punjab, where two jobs were awarded as a result of a competition among nominated candidates.[2] Thus, even though colleges in the Presidency towns were producing hundreds of graduates, the majority of prestigious jobs remained outside their reach unless they fulfilled the broader requirements of Imperial recruitment policy. This inevitably created resentment; and as the number of graduates grew, so did the demand for a change in the system. The foundation of the Indian National Congress was in part the result of these resentments—a recognition that the system would only be changed if a more concerted political approach was adopted, and if pressure was brought to bear not only on the Indian Civil Service but also on the British Parliament and people.

The Muslim part in challenging the system was not initially very

[1] *Report of the Public Services Commission 1886-7* (Calcutta 1888), pp. 34-5.

[2] *Report of the Public Services Commission 1912,* vol. i (Calcutta 1917), p. 29.

large. College education first made headway in the oldest centres of British rule, Calcutta, Bombay and Madras, and the Muslims of those areas were in no position to benefit from it. In Bengal, the community was impoverished and concentrated far from Calcutta in the province's Eastern divisions. In Bombay, and to a lesser extent in Madras, though adequate funds were available, they were invested chiefly in trade, an occupation for which English education was unnecessary. When the Indian National Congress was founded to express the grievances of this class, therefore, the Muslims took virtually no part of it. Those of the Presidencies were not educated enough, and those of North India, though keenly aware of the importance of education, were too far behind to compete with the Presidency elites. By the turn of the century, however, North India had become part of the educational mainstream. In 1911, as Table 2 shows, there were more pupils in colleges in the United Provinces than in either Madras or Bombay; and the Punjab was not far behind. Moreover, because the North Indian Muslims had the funds to invest in education, they also benefited from this process. In the same year, there were more Muslims in colleges in the U.P. than in any other province and the ratio of their share of college places to their share of the population was also considerably higher. By the turn of the century, therefore, insofar as the United Provinces had joined the educational mainstream, the U.P. Muslims had also joined it, and insofar as the educated elite was in the vanguard of the nationalist movement, the U.P. Muslims were also qualified to take part.

The Morley-Minto Reforms: political manipulation and electoral response

It is sometimes assumed in discussions of the introduction of electoral institutions in Britain's dependent territories that Britain's only role was to bestow on her subjects as a free gift a system of government which had been tried and tested by the 'Mother of Parliaments'. Such an assumption belongs more to the realm of myth than of reality. In Britain, parliamentary reform and the extension of the franchise was a positive if reluctant response by the ruling class to a demand for a change in the political system. In 1832, for example, Parliament took note of the social and economic changes wrought by the industrial revolution and gave the vote to

TABLE 2

English education in colleges and secondary schools, showing total numbers of pupils (A), total numbers of Muslim pupils (B), and the percentage of Muslim pupils (C), by province in 1911/12

	A		B		C	
Province	Colleges	Schools	Colleges	Schools	Colleges	Schools
Madras	5,801	110,336	103	5,519	1.8	5.0
Bombay	4,958	74,601	183	5,543	3.7	7.4
Bengal	11,620	205,931	792	20,364	6.6	9.8
East Bengal	3,156	186,641	381	59,439	12.0	31.8
Punjab	3,549	99,418	872	24,774	24.5	24.9
U.P.	5,844	97,056	1,357	10,561	23.2	10.8
C.P.	716	55,295	33	2,054	4.6	3.7
NWFP	38	9,332	23	3,362	60.5	36.0

Source: Progress of Education in India, Sixth Quinquennial Report, Cmd. 7485 (1914), Table 16, p. 203, and Tables 217-18, p. 286.

those whom it had brought into prominence. By the terms of the Reform Bill of that year, the country's ruling class admitted the new industrial and commercial bourgeoisie to a share of the rewards of the political system and so avoided the development of extra-parliamentary confrontations. In India, on the other hand, those who were loudest in demanding reforms were rarely those who benefited from them. In India, as this book will attempt to show, the introduction of parliamentary institutions was not a concession intended to absorb those 'on the outside trying to get in' but an attempt to extend and improve the existing system of control by a new method.

The Morley-Minto Reforms are the first significant electoral monument to this strategy.[3] They endeavoured to put power not into

[3] In the 1880s, when electoral institutions with a substantial elected element were first introduced in local self-government, it was chiefly for financial reasons. It was decided that the localities should bear more of the cost of local administration and it was considered necessary to increase popular participation to make this change more palatable. Lord Ripon, the Liberal Viceroy, did hope that these measures would provide India's emerging élite with a training ground for greater responsibilities. But the élite was still small and the matters in which it was most interested could not be settled at the local level.

the hands of those who demanded reform but into the hands of those on whose co-operation the Raj had long relied. They did this chiefly by making local self-government bodies the electorates for council seats. In the United Provinces, for example, twelve seats were created along these lines. Each of the eight divisions elected one member, the weight of the responsibility lying with the more conservative district boards, and the eight most important municipalities were given the right to elect a member at alternate elections. The aim of this arrangement was to secure the return of the government's allies in the localities. The eight divisional seats were expected to elect 'sound' members of the landed interest, and from the major cities were expected nominees of the substantial indigenous commercial interests whose political influence had hitherto been dominant.[4] The Raj had succeeded for nearly three decades in managing the municipalities and districts with their help, and it hoped to manage the provincial councils in the same style. For those outside the system of control, therefore, and particularly for India's growing educated and professional élite, the Reforms were as much a challenge as a response. If they wished to be returned to the provincial council, either they had to make themselves amenable to dominant local interests or they had to take up arms and oppose them.

Additional constraints were imposed on Muslim political activity by the introduction of separate electorates. Separated by religious conviction and social customs from the bulk of the Hindu community, the Muslims had always received special consideration from government, and particularly in North India, where they formed a vital part of the system of control. But separate electorates had never been generally demanded before, and they had only been introduced in one or two municipalities in the Punjab. Why then were they introduced at this time? Hitherto the debate on this question has been about whether the Muslims really wanted them. Most Pakistani historians have said they did. Many Indian historians have accused the government of pulling strings behind the scenes to arrange for them to be demanded. This scenario is too simple. It does not make sense to suppose that the Simla deputation demanded concessions its members did not want. Nor that the government

[4] To date, the most thorough study of urban politics at this time is C.A. Bayly's *The Local Roots of Indian Nationalism* (Oxford, 1975).

introduced a new system of election without being sure that it would be worked positively by those it was designed to assist. On both sides of the debate, the weakness is the assumption that 'the Muslim community' can be treated as a coherent unit at this time.

From the turn of the century, divisions had begun to emerge between the traditional leaders of the community—those who had a place within the system of control—and the growing body of educated Moslems. This was nowhere more so than at the Aligarh Mahommedan Anglo-Oriental College, the institution founded by Sir Syed Ahmed to bring Muslim India into line with the new educational demands of the Imperial system. There, the increasing interest of Muslim youths in the Congress threatened the credibility of the community's traditional leaders, and if Harcourt Butler, at that time Joint Secretary to the U.P. Government, is to be believed, it was in order to harness these enthusiasms to their own cause that these leaders founded the Muslim League in 1906.

> There never was any splendid loyalty. Moshin ul Mulk and others came to see me at Lucknow to take my advice. They were quite frank. They could not hold their young men and feared their joining the Hindus, which meant ultimate absorption of the Mahommedans. It was purely in their own interests that they formed the Muslim League. I said at that time: What if you can't control the young men in the League? They recognized the possibility of this but regarded the danger as remote.[5]

Seen against this background, the granting of separate electorates appears to have been an attempt by the Raj to shore up a crucial part of its system of control. As in the case of the general electorates, it was an attempt to extend and broaden the base of its rule by extending and broadening the support of its traditional allies. For those Muslims outside the system of control, however, and particularly for the Muslim professional and educated élite, this innovation had serious implications. For it meant that they could only work the Reforms successfully if they came to terms with the grievances of the Muslim localities. In the years after 1912, when the Muslim League began to develop an alliance with the Congress, this was to be a potential source of conflict between the two organizations.

[5] Harcourt Butler papers (IOL MSS F 116) 71: Butler to Allen, 6 April, 1913.

In 1911, the Muslim League moved its headquarters from Aligarh to Lucknow, and shortly afterwards it came to be dominated by a group of politicians, chiefly of the Shia sect, who lived and worked in that city. The group's patron was the Raja of Mahmudabad, one of the largest *taluqdars* of Oudh, and one of the few members of his class with an interest in nationalist politics. In 1914, he became the League's permanent President. Apart from the Raja, most members of the group were lawyers and professional men. Most prominent among them was Wazir Hassan, a man of exceptional intellectual and organizational abilities, who became the League Secretary in 1912. To him belongs the credit for changing the League's creed in 1913, and according to the Raja he was also one of the chief authors of the scheme of Reforms which the Congress and League submitted to the government.[6] Another important member was Samiullah Beg, an advocate of the Lucknow Bar and the group's link-man with the U.P. Congress. The older statesman of the group was Syed Nabiullah, the Chairman of the Lucknow Municipal Board, who had been called to the Bar in England in the 1880s. Within the U.P., the group's political ambitions were focused on the provincial council, and from 1912 to 1914, it was engaged in building up its influence within the province. But after the outbreak of the World War, in co-operation with a number of other politicians, it came to assume all-India importance. Prominent among the politicians with whom the Lucknow group co-operated at that time were Mahommed Ali Jinnah, an ambitious Bombay lawyer with his sights set at the all-India level; Hassan Imam, once a judge of the Calcutta High Court; Ali Imam, his brother, from 1910 Law Member of the Government of India; and Mazhar ul Haq, their protégé, a man of more radical views. The Raja, Jinnah, Ali Imam and Mazhar ul Haq all sat on the Viceroy's Council in the years before the War, and their association with other Indian political leaders in that body provided a basis for subsequent Congress-League co-operation.

But Congress-League co-operation was not achieved easily. Indeed in many parts of the U.P., the policies adopted by the Lucknow group only met with qualified approval. This was because of the different levels of development of the Muslim community in different parts of the province. The province of Oudh, of which

[6] Ali Imam papers (Karachi University Library): Wazir Hassan to Raja of Mahmudabad, 20 July 1917; Raja of Mahmudabad to Ali Imam, 25 July 1917.

Lucknow was the capital, was in two ways an exception: firstly, in that the landed leadership of the community was in a fairly thriving condition; and secondly, in that Lucknow, both as a traditional Muslim centre and as a service centre for the colonial regime, was naturally a focus for the more educated and intelligent Muslims. In the province of Agra, on the other hand, both in the more populous western divisions of Meerut and Rohilkhund, and in the divisions further east, the landed position of the community was under severe attack, and educational advancement, particularly in the highly urbanized Rohilkhund division, was very limited.[7] It is, of course, difficult to claim overwhelming reliability for such generalizations. The evidence for degrees of educational advancement is by no means exhaustive. Nor is it true to say that all Muslims were losing land in the province of Agra. The Sheikhs appear to have been gaining in many districts,[8] demonstrating in all probability that those Muslims who were increasing their holdings were also changing their titles to register their claims to higher social status. But if one examines the sort of questions asked in the U.P. Legislative Council by Muslim members from the different constituencies, it is noticeable that those representing the more economically and educationally backward divisions tend to demand more special treatment for their community. Syed Raza Ali, the member for the backward Rohilkhund division, is the most communal politician in the Council.[9] Samiullah Beg and Wazir Hassan, on the other hand, advocate a better deal for those with higher educational qualifications almost

[7] The evidence for these generalizations has been taken from the U.P. District Gazetteers and the Censuses. See *DG Bahraich* (1903), p. 80; *DG Kheri* (1905), p. 97; *DG Barabanki* (1904), p. 102; *DG Fyzabad* (1905), p. 97; *DG Lucknow* (1904), p. 90; *DG Bareilly* (1911), pp. 98, 100-1; *DG Bijnor* (1909), pp. 107-8; *DG Badaun* (1907), pp. 82 and 84; *DG Moradabad* (1911), pp. 84, 87, 93, 97; *DG Shahjehanpur* (1910), pp.87-8; *DG Bulandshahr* (1903), p. 92; *DG Aligarh* (1909), pp. 91-2; *DG Muzaffarnagar* (1903) p. 120; *DG Meerut* (1904), pp. 83-5; *DG Saharanpur* (1909), pp. 116-17; *DG Allahabad* (1911), pp. 103-4; *DG Fatehpur* (1906), p. 101; *DG Jaunpur* (1908), p. 94; *DG Ghazipur* (1909), p. 95; *DG Azamgarh* (1911), p. 107, *NWP and Oudh Census 1901,* part ii, table viii, pp. 116-120; *U.P. Census 1911,* part ii, table viii, pp. 148-51; *U.P. Census 1921,* part ii, table viii, pp. 130-3.

[8] See *DG Aligarh* (1909), pp. 91-2; *DG Saharanpur* (1909), pp. 116-17; *DG Meerut* (1904), pp. 83-5.

[9] See for example, *UPLC Progs. 1913,* p. 215; *UPLC Progs. 1914,* pp. 515-17; *UPLC Progs. 1915,* p. 449; *UPLC Progs. 1916,* p. 738.

The Punjab (1920), showing districts and divisions

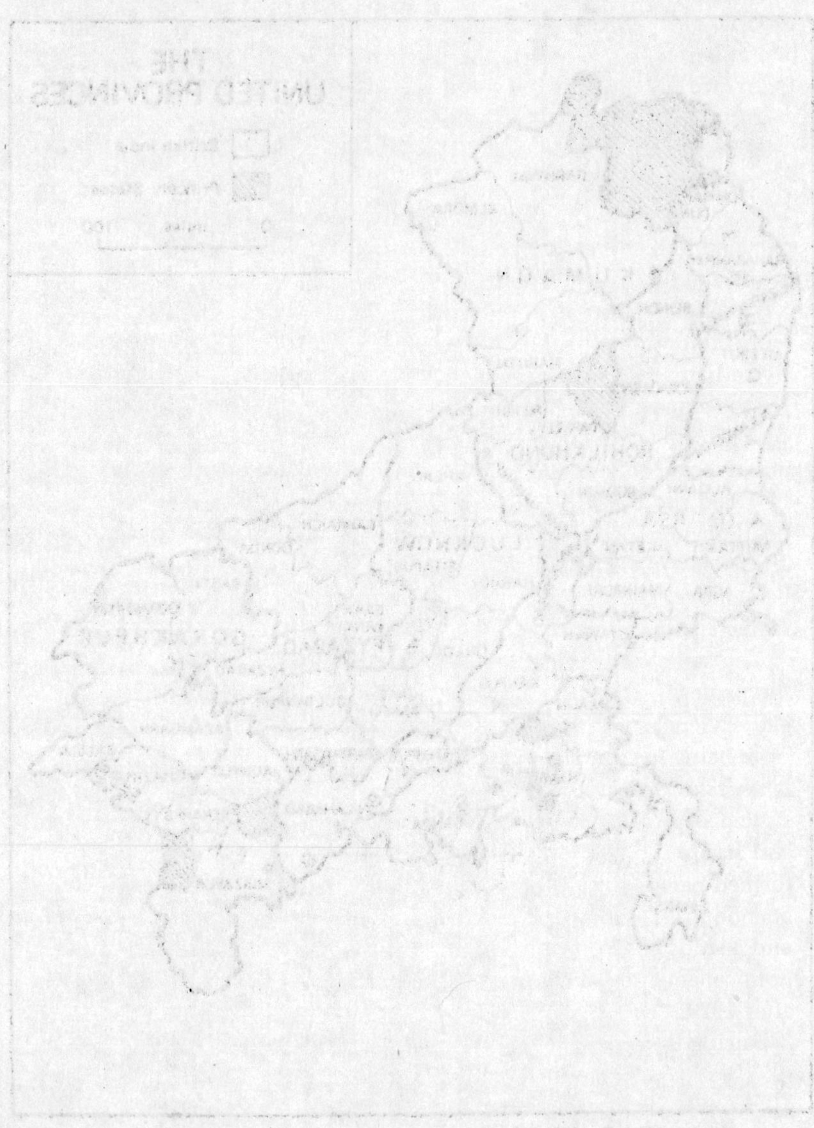

without reservation.[10] Nor is it simply a coincidence that loyalist leadership throughout the British period—from Sir Syed to the Nawab of Chaththari—comes from the province of Agra. It reflects the inherently less competitive character of the community in that province.

But if loss of land to the moneylender and educational backwardness were important sources of communalism, they were not activated significantly at the provincial level at this time. The main reason for this was that in these fields no points of distribution were reached. The emphasis of the politicians was on securing concessions, not on distributing them, and on this basis it was possible for very different interests to combine. In the demand for an Executive Council for the United Provinces, for the replacement of Europeans by Indians, for greater financial devolution to the provincial level, for the expansion of educational opportunities, and for an improvement in the status of the legal profession, Raza Ali was as spirited an advocate as the Lucknow leaders.[11] On these issues, moreover, he stood shoulder to shoulder with the very Hindus who opposed his demands for special treatment for the Muslims of his locality. This was a paradox of the Morley-Minto constitution which was to be removed when Indians were given control of government patronage at the provincial level.

The same kind of paradox is also noticeable in the relations of the professional elite and the landed class. Though accusations of subservience were common enough, the landed class was still far from being the main target of the politicians and it did not consider it necessary to organize itself. Despite the introduction of a new system of representation at the provincial level, the government still had a monopoly of decision-making, and those who already formed part of the system of control had no need to compete for its attention. This is a twilight period between two systems of government and a study of overt political activity only provides one half of the political equation. This paradox was also to be removed in the years after 1920.

During the Morley-Minto Reforms, the most significant challenge

[10] See *UPLC Progs. 1916*, p. 681; *UPLC Progs. 1917*, pp. 146 and 908-18.

[11] The annual Council debates on the Budget give an indication of political feelings on these questions. For Raza Ali's views, see, for example, *UPLC Progs. 1913*, p. 59; *UPLC Progs. 1915*, pp. 203 and 387; *UPLC Progs. 1916* pp. 472-3 and 738.

to the ambitions of the provincial politicians developed as a result of the working of the constitution itself. For by making membership of municipal and district boards a stepping stone to representation at the provincial level, the Reforms awakened a new interest in municipal politics. The result was many more hotly contested elections, much more rivalry for seats on municipal and district boards, and a distinct increase in communalism in the localities. In the U.P. municipalities before 1909, despite the existence of general electorates, there does not appear to have been any persistent communal friction. The municipalities of the Rohilkhund division may have been an exception to this, particularly after the turn of the century, but except in that one division, Muslims did not suffer any severe losses as a result of the working of the general electorate. Indeed in several of the larger towns, just before the 1909 Act was introduced, they made a number of gains.[12] After 1909, however, Muslim losses increased, particularly in the eight most important towns with the right to elect a member to the Council.[13] Quite why this happened is uncertain. Whether it was, as a report from Mirzapur suggests, that the more established members of municipal boards were enrolling members of their own religion to offset the challenge of the *vakils*,[14] or whether it was the *vakils* themselves who were indulging in communal appeals to cut across the electoral alliances of the traditional urban élites, is a question which can pro-

[12] To date, the most detailed examination of Muslim politics in the U.P. municipalities is to be found in F.C.R. Robinson, 'Municipal Government and Muslim Separatism', in Gallagher, Johnson and Seal (eds.), *Locality, Province and Nation* (Cambridge 1973), pp. 69-121. But I have differed from him in his assessment of the effect of the working of general electorates on the Muslim community before 1909. Dr Robinson contends that the Muslims were losing seats in the Meerut, Agra, Rohilkhund and Allahabad divisions from 1883 onwards. But in computing his statistics he does not take the Municipal Reform Act of 1900 into account. This Act reduced the membership of municipal boards in order to provoke keener competition for election. Prior to that time, many municipalities had a record of poor electoral response and infrequent meetings. See annual *Reports on Municipal Taxation and Expenditure in the North Western Provinces and Oudh*, 1891/2-1898/9; *Reports on Municipal Administration and Finances*, 1900/1901-1908/9.

[13] Between 1909 and 1916, the Muslims lost three seats at Meerut, two at Bareilly, four at Benares, three at Lucknow and two at Fyzabad. At Allahabad by 1913, there were no Muslim members on the Board at all. See *Report on Municipal Administration and Finances, 1908/9*, appendix A, pp. ii-v; *U.P. Gazette*, part viii, 2 Sept. 1916.

[14] See *Report on Municipal Administration and Finances 1909/10*, p. 2.

bably be answered in a different way in each locality.[15] What is certain, however, is that except in the very limited number of municipalities where they formed a majority of the electorate, the Muslims, as a minority community, could not help but suffer, and this undoubtedly explains why the demand for an extension of separate electorates increases in volume after 1909.[16]

While the Muslim League leaders pursued their policy of political co-operation with Congress, this rise of communalism in the localities forms a sombre backcloth to their activities. At the All India Muslim League at Agra in 1913, when Jinnah and Mazhar ul Haq attempted to persuade the League not to pass its regular resolution in favour of separate electorates in local self-government as an earnest of its intentions to work with the Congress, they were voted down by the politicians of the U.P. municipalities.[17] At Bombay in 1915, the first year that both Congress and League held their sessions in the same city, local opposition almost wrecked the possibility of a joint approach to the question of Reform, and Jinnah and his colleagues only carried the day against Cassim Mitha and his 'goondas' by locking themselves up in the Taj Mahal hotel and holding their session in private.[18] Finally, in 1915 and 1916, these local conflicts emerged on to the provincial and national stage most threateningly of all as a result of a Government decision to introduce a substantial measure of reform in the U.P. municipalities. The U.P. Municipal Bill, which proposed a large-scale devolution of power to the municipalities, sharpened communal demands in the localities at the very time that provincial and national leaders

[15] C.A. Bayly, in his work on Allahabad, sees 1909 as a definite landmark in the involvement of the professional classes in politics. Before that date, they acted as brokers and publicists, pursuing their ambitions under the umbrellas of dominant *rais* factions. Afterwards the professionals came into their own and electioneering based directly on caste and creed became more frequent. Dr Bayly sees electoral reform as one of the main causes for the change, but he believes it was assisted by modifications in the structure of local taxation. (op.cit., pp. 226-244.)

[16] Syed Raza Ali was the main leader of the communal faction. The campaign to secure separate electorates began in earnest after the provincial council elections of 1912. See *UPLC Progs. 1913*, pp. 20, 60, 214 and 393; *UPLC Progs. 1914*, pp. 410-11, 492 and 517-18.

[17] See S.S Pirzada (ed.), *Foundations of Pakistan, All India Muslim League Documents* 1906-47, vol. i (Karachi 1969), pp. 315-17.

[18] Ibid., vol. i, pp. 324-61.

were anxious to keep them out of sight. It brought the 'separate electorate' issue to a head, it embittered relations between the communities throughout the province, and it came very close to sabotaging the Lucknow Pact itself.[19]

But the scope of the argument goes somewhat beyond the assertion that the working of the Reforms imposed important constraints on the activities of the politicians. It would also suggest that the nature of the Reforms influenced the capacity of such politicians to overcome these constraints, to compose communal divisions, and to produce a united front against the government. Where the controversy surrounding the U.P. Municipal Bill was concerned, it was the fact that there had been no real devolution of power at the provincial level which enabled provincial leaders of both communities to surrender local advantage in the hope of provincial gain. As Tej Bahadur Sapru put it when the final compromise was being debated:

> Were it not that I believed in and hoped for higher things to come, were it not that I hoped that we are not going to rest contented with merely local self-government, I should not be so willing to accept an amendment which I know is not approved of by my friend, the Hon. Babu Brijnandan Prasad[20].

Moreover, when the same controversy re-emerged during the negotiations prior to the Lucknow Pact, it was because of the operation of similar factors at the all-India level—because the Presidency politicians were in no mood to be baulked in their own ambitions—that the recalcitrance of the U.P. communal Hindu party was not allowed to stand in the way of a national agreement[21].

However, even after the Lucknow Pact had been agreed, even after the Congress and the League had met Mr Montagu in joint

[19] For an account of the Municipal Bill controversy, see Robinson, 'Municipal Government and Muslim Separatism', op.cit., pp. 106-15.

[20] *UPLC Progs. 1916,* pp. 217-18. Brijnandan Prasad was the member for Rohilkhund and Kumaon. The Rohilkhund Hindus lost twenty-six seats as a result of the compromise.

[21] For details of the efforts of Mrs Besant, Tilak, Surendra Nath Bannerjee and Bhupendra Nath Basu to produce the Lucknow Pact, and of Jinnah's strategy for ensuring continuing compliance with it, see GUPGAD140/1917. CID report on the Lucknow sessions of the League and Congress.

deputation, the power to modify the constitution still lay with the Raj. How would the Raj respond to their demands? What modifications would it make to the system of control? These were the questions which preoccupied the politicians as first Montagu and then the various constitutional committees toured the provinces. They only met with a definitive response with the passing of the Government of India Act of 1919. But long before that time, as the Raj mobilized its allies to present their case,[22] it had become clear that the politicians did not face a rosy future. For the opponents of the system of control, the Montagu-Chelmsford Reforms, like their predecessors, were to be as much a challenge as a response.

Panislamism: an agitational alternative

Those involved in constitutional politics were hopeful that modifications to the existing system of control would give them a new importance in their own society. But there were other political and quasi-political elements in Muslim society which shared neither their hopes nor their interests. Some considered it inherently unlikely that constitutional methods would secure Reform. Some felt that Reform was not likely to benefit them, whatever methods were employed. Others—notably the religious elements in Muslim society—were not fundamentally interested in the system, except insofar as it imposed limitations on their own areas of activity. In the period before and after the First World War some of these political and religious forces contributed to the rise of Panislamism in India. This development, which owed its impetus to the problems faced by Turkey as a result of European expansionism, reached maximum intensity after the War, when the fate of Turkey was being settled by the victorious allies. At that time in India, the Khilafat movement obtained massive support and presented a serious threat to the stability of government.

The dependence of the Khilafat movement on circumstances outside India necessarily limited its long-term importance. But it was not without significance for political developments inside India. Firstly, it did have a bearing on the constitutional situation. Both before the First World War, in co-operation with the constitutiona-

[22] For details of the U.P. government's efforts in this field, see GUPGAD 553/1917, *passim.*

lists, and afterwards, in co-operation with Gandhi, the Panislamists play an important role as the shock troops of Reformist politics. Secondly, the religio-political alliances formed at this time in some respects foreshadow the Pakistan movement itself. The Khilafat movement was the most significant mass movement among the Muslims before the 1940s, and many of the politicians involved in it were later to figure on the Muslim League platform.

The most convenient place to begin a study of Panislamist politics is the Aligarh Mahommedan Anglo-Oriental College, which was the initial political focus for the two most prominent Panislamists, Mahommed and Shaukat Ali. The structure of power within the college was remarkably similar to the structure of power in Muslim society at large. The management was dominated by the Rajas and Nawabs who figured largely in the Imperial system of control, whilst the students themselves, and particularly the scholarship boys, were in many cases attracted to more radical politics. The Ali brothers, both former scholarship pupils, had their strongest links with the students and the old boys, and their chief aim in college politics was to democratize the court of Trustees in such a way as to gain a position of greater prominence for themselves and their followers. In 1907, Mahommed Ali drew up a scheme of Reforms with this in view; and in 1910, when the Aga Khan launched a campaign to make the college into a university, the two brothers were among his most ardent supporters. They appear to have hoped that the university would be controlled more democratically than the college and that they would benefit from the reorganization.[23]

The coincidence of the Secretary of State's veto on the community's plans for the university and the outbreak of the Balkan wars makes it difficult to assess the precise reasons for Mahommed Ali's involvement in Panislamist politics at this time. Like many Indian Muslims, he took pride in the independence of Turkey as a compensation for the Muslim fall from power in India, and he had great hopes of the Committee of Union and Progress as a vehicle for the revitalization of the decaying Ottoman Empire. As an English-educated Muslim, moreover, he saw in the expansion of European power in the Balkans an exaggerated form of the subjugation which Indians suffered in their own country. It is significant, however,

[23] See G. Minault and D. Lelyveld, 'The Campaign for a Muslim University 1898-1920', *Modern Asian Studies*, 8, 2 (1974), pp. 145-189.

that the Italian invasion of Tripoli in 1911 provoked far less reaction in India than the Balkans wars. It was only after the veto on the university that Mahommed Ali began to campaign politically on Turkey's behalf; only then that the Ali brothers began to develop an alliance with the ulema, and to argue in favour of confrontation with the Raj and co-operation with the Congress. Prior to the veto, Mahommed Ali had argued that the fate of Tripoli and Persia made no difference to the realities of Indian politics.[24] Afterwards, he was to say that the treatment meted out to Tripoli, Persia and Turkey justified the Muslim League's acceptance of self-government as an ideal.[25]

The political alliance which the Ali brothers developed at this time had two poles—Aligarh and Delhi, the first the seat of the college, and the second, the capital of India, where Mahommed Ali edited and published the *Comrade*. At Delhi, Mahommed Ali's chief allies were Ajmal Khan, a hakim with a lucrative practice among the princes, and Dr Ansari, a younger man who had studied and practised medicine in England. These two men shared Mahommed Ali's concern for the position of Turkey, and they co-operated with him in a number of ventures both before and after the War. What gave the Delhi-Aligarh axis a new dimension, however, was the adherence of a number of Punjab and U.P. ulema, chief among whom was Maulana Abdul Bari of Firengi Mahal, Lucknow. An *alim* of a traditional mould, Abdul Bari was apprehensive that secular education would undermine religious allegiances, and he saw the Balkan wars as fertile ground for the extension of ulema influence. In the first decade of the century, he had founded a number of evangelical organizations to recall Muslims to the correct observance of Islamic law, and together with Mushir Hussain Kidwai, a taluqdar of Barabanki, he had made efforts to improve the religious instruction of the English-educated. Abdul Bari was also quicker than most ulema to grasp the political implications of the Balkan wars, for he had visited Mecca and Constantinople only two years before. His association with the Ali brothers, which was to last for over a decade, began in the winter of 1912/13.

Before the First World War, the Delhi-Aligarh axis was involved

[24] See Afzal Iqbal (ed.), *Select Writings and Speeches of Maulana Mahommed Ali*, first edition, (Lahore 1944), p. 70.

[25] *Comrade*, 24 May 1913.

in two main enterprises, the organization of a Medical Mission to Turkey, and the developments of the *Anjuman-i-Khuddam-i-Kaaba*, a society designed to protect the heartland of Islam, and to strengthen the faith by preaching and teaching. Both enterprises enjoyed a measure of success. The Medical Mission, which was led by Dr Ansari, was appreciated by the Turks, and proved a formative experience for a number of Aligarh students who were later to figure prominently in nationalist politics.[26] The *Anjuman* opened an office at Bombay to provide a service for *hajis* en route for Mecca, and under the leadership of Shaukat Ali and Abdul Bari, established branches in Punjab, the United Provinces, Sind and Kashmir. According to one source, it had a membership of 17,000 by 1915.[27]

These activities were brought to an end when Turkey entered the War on the German side. Most Muslims understood that Britain was a reluctant opponent of Turkey, and were reassured by the Allied guarantee that the Holy Places would be immune from attack. Far from campaigning on Turkey's behalf, they concentrated on averting a confrontation, taking it as a foregone conclusion that Turkey would be the loser if one took place. But this was not the attitude of the Ali brothers. At a time when the government was empowered to deal more effectively with challenges to its authority, the Ali brothers campaigned unreservedly on Turkey's behalf and quickly got into trouble. The *Comrade* was obliged to cease publication, and in April 1915, the brothers were interned for the duration of the War.

However, as the War progressed and Turkey came under pressure from the Allies—as the Sharif of Mecca repudiated Turkish rule and Baghdad fell—Muslim anxiety increased and the Ali brothers came to assume a new importance. Their internment in these years becomes symbolic of the plight of Turkey, and the demand for their release a vicarious plea for the restoration of Turkey to her former strength. In September 1917, as preparations were being made for the Congress-League deputation to Montagu, Panislamist pressure on this question was very embarassing to the League leaders, and at Allahabad in October they embarassed the

[26] See Chaudhuri Khaliquzzaman, *Pathway to Pakistan* (Lahore 1961), pp. 20-7.

[27] GI Home Poll., June 1915, B 549-52; Weekly Report of the Director of Criminal Intelligence, 1 June 1915.

Congress by insisting that the issue be given priority.[28] By December, however, with communal organizations marshalling their forces for the revision of the constitution, and feelings embittered by a bout of rioting in Bihar, the situation had changed noticeably. By that stage, the League leaders were under pressure to break with the Congress, and the Ali brothers began to take their place as the symbols of Hindu-Muslim unity. At Calcutta in December, as the League leaders attempted unsuccessfully to renegotiate the Lucknow Pact, the Ali brothers' mother was given royal treatment on the Congress platform.[29] In this lay the embryo of post-War developments.

The prime mover in the development of an agitational alliance between the two communities was Mahatma Gandhi. By February 1918, he had made contact with Abdul Bari; by March he was petitioning the Viceroy for the brothers' release; and by November, he was quite explicit in his strategy. 'My interest in your release', he wrote to Mahommed Ali 'is quite selfish. We have a common goal and I want to utilize your services to the uttermost in order to reach that goal. In the proper solution of the Mahommedan question lies the realization of Swaraj.'[30] But early efforts at co-operation were not successful. Gandhi's hopes that Abdul Bari would be able to mobilize the Muslims to participate in the Rowlatt Satyagraha proved ill-founded. At that time, the plight of Turkey was not serious enough for the Muslims to be allured by offers of a joint front against Government, and it was only after the Delhi riot of 30 March 1919, in which members of both communities were shot dead in police firing, that a joint front developed.[31] The Khilafat movement itself only began to attract serious attention in September 1919, when a decision at the Peace Conference was believed to be imminent. At that stage, meetings of protest were held both in Bombay and in North India, and Gandhi was accepted as a mentor by the Khilafatists of both areas. Under his guidance, a *hartal* was organized on 17 October, and he was also responsible for suggesting a boycott of the

[28] GI Home Poll., Nov. 1917, B 471-74; Weekly Report of the Director of Criminal Intelligence, 3 Nov. 1917.

[29] GI Home Poll., Jan. 1918, B 487-90; Weekly Report of the Director of Criminal Intelligence, 12 Jan. 1918.

[30] *Collected Works of Gandhi*, vol. xv (Ahmedabad 1965), pp. 63-4: Gandhi to Mahommed Ali, 18 Nov. 1918.

[31] See GUPGAD 262/1919.

peace celebrations.[32] By December, when the Ali brothers were released from internment, the Khilafat-Swaraj alliance was already well established.

The Khilafat movement itself was the result of a genuine religious concern for the position of Turkey. To most Muslims, it seemed that the Kaaba really was in danger, and in those circumstances, the call to prayer became a call to action. All over India, there was a spontaneous and widespread groundswell of agitation, and religious leaders mushroomed to give it voice. The problem for the political leaders of the movement was how to harness these religious feelings to a movement directed against the government. For on a question of such moment, the nature of Quranic instruction was one of blunt alternatives. If the government did not interfere with the practice of the Muslim religion, India was to be considered *Dar ul Islam* (Land of peace), but if it did, and no redress was obtained by appeal, India became *Dar ul Harb* (Land of war), and the immediate response of the Muslim people had to be one of *jihad* (war) or *hijrat* (migration). In the nature of things, however, the Raj was too strong to be successfully opposed by *jihad*. Very few people imagined that the Khilafat movement could succeed in an outright war with the administration. And *hijrat* was really a counsel of despair. For the political leaders of the movement, this presented a very real dilemma.

The leadership's answer to this dilemma was the alliance with Gandhi and the adoption of his programme of non-co-operation. This alliance had the obvious strategic advantage that it held out hopes of Hindu support, and it had the practical advantage of providing a stage-by-stage programme for putting pressure on the Government of India. The success of this policy, however, depended on efficient organization and shrewd leadership by the Khilafatists themselves, and the history of the movement suggests that these qualities were lacking. Khilafat committees sprang up all over India. Vast amounts of money were sent to the Central Khilafat Committee at Bombay. The Ali brothers toured India making speeches. Mahommed Ali went to Europe and played the Grand Moghul. The popularity of the brothers was enormous. But the control of the Central Khilafat Committee over the rank and file

[32] See IOR/L/P and J/6/6594/1919: Viceroy to Secretary of State, 16 Oct. 1919; GI Home Poll., Jan. 1920, D 5: Bombay FR I Nov. 1919.

was very circumscribed. Such control as the leadership did exercise was dependent on their ability to convince the ulema and the workers that peaceful pressure according to Gandhi's programme was being successful, and once it became clear that this was not the case, as it did by April 1920, the ulema and workers began to champion a resort to religious solutions. At this point, the deficiencies of the political leadership became most apparent. Because they had failed to organize the movement, they found it difficult restraining the ulema, and because they lacked the necessary political initiative, they failed to take the one step—immediate commencement of all stages of non-co-operation—which might have kept control of the movement in their hands. Instead, they themselves gave voice to the same views which the ulema were propagating, and by doing so encouraged a movement which they hoped to contain. By May 1920, the leadership was in fact following the masses. The Khilafat movement had assumed a momentum of its own. This loss of control by the leadership is shown most graphically in the *hijrat* movement to Afghanistan.[33]

The political dominance of Gandhi in the counsels of the Central Khilafat Committee is the other side of the same coin. This dominance, which was as much personal as political, was not always to the leadership's disadvantage because Gandhi had a shrewder awareness than they of how to organize a political movement. But Gandhi's advice was not principally related to the need to save the Khilafat. His own ambitions were more related to the Indian situation. His reluctance, for example, to give way to Khilafatist demands for full-scale non-co-operation in April and May 1920, when the Khilafat movement began to escalate, was principally motivated by his desire to bring Congress under the same umbrella over the issue of the Hunter report.[34] Delay in the publication of the report thwarted him in this ambition. But even then he only eventually began non-co-operation when it had become clear that the Congress would not come in over the Hunter report, and that the only way of cowing

[33] For the dilemma facing the political leadership and their reactions to it, see Weekly Reports of the Director of Criminal Intelligence, March, April and May, 1920: GI Home Poll., March 1920, D 89; April 1920, D 103; June 1920, D 78. The government's reactions to the *hijrat* movement can be found in IOR/L/P and J/6/5703/1920.

[34] Gandhi's tactics emerge most clearly at the Allahabad meetings of Khilafatists and Congressmen early in June. See Reports of the Commissioner of Police, Bombay, GI Home Poll., July 1920, B 109.

his opponents into submission was by starting the movement unilaterally with Khilafat support. In this plan he was successful. At Calcutta in September, with the Khilafatists strongly behind him, he captured the Congress organization, and he consolidated this victory at Nagpur in December.[35] Yet once he was established in firm control of the Congress organization, Gandhi's political priorities changed. Having obliged the Congress to reject the new constitution, he began reshaping the organization to cope with the new political situation. Party-building became the most important aspect of his political work and it brought him increasingly into conflict with the Khilafatists. In March and April 1921, when the Ali brothers began to throw off Gandhi's leadership and incite their audiences to violence, Gandhi began to dissociate himself from them. In July, when the Khilafat Committee pronounced it *haram* to serve in the Army, Gandhi took no part in the proceedings, and by September, when the Ali brothers were arrested, the most significant phase of Hindu-Muslim co-operation had come to an end.

As a result of his alliance with the Khilafatists, Gandhi increased his political prestige, captured the Congress organization, and reformed and revitalized it so as to give nationalist politics a new sanction. As a result of their alliance with Gandhi, however, the Khilafatists had little effect on British government attitudes towards Turkey. When the government made concessions, it was chiefly due to the resurgence of Turkish military power and not to Pan-islamist support for her position. Within the context of Indian politics, moreover, the Khilafatists made fewer gains. The movement had derived its impetus from events outside India, and it had acquired support for primarily religious reasons. Once the Turks settled the Khilafat question themselves, religious feeling abated and the movement died away For many politicians, however, participation in the Khilafat movement was a formative experience which continued to affect their political outlook long after the Khilafat had been abolished. The belief that Hindu-Muslim unity was the only basis for Swaraj was fostered and strengthened, and the alliance between Gandhi and the Ali brothers, between Congressmen and Khilafatists, which was cemented in these years, continued, though with varying degrees of intensity, well into the 1920s. After the

[35] See J.M. Brown, *Gandhi's Rise to Power: Indian Politics 1915-1922* (Cambridge 1972), pp. 250-304.

Khilafat movement subsided, however, the context of the Khilafat-Swaraj alliance became more exclusively political and pressures on the Khilafat leaders sprang more from the working of purely Indian forces. By the time the Ali brothers were released from gaol in 1923, the new constitution was already beginning to make an impact, and many Congressmen had recognized that they could no longer afford to continue with a policy of boycott. Gandhi himself was never converted to this view, though he did not always oppose those who were; and the Ali brothers, who had built up their careers as Panislamist politicians, continued to work in the same field after their release. In the long run, however, the working of the new constitution prompted political developments which neither Gandhi nor the Ali brothers could afford to ignore, and it was ultimately in relation to those developments that their political future had to be worked out.

CHAPTER 1

The Montagu-Chelmsford Reforms and the Changing Structure of Politics

The changing structure of all-India politics

During the Morley-Minto Reforms, though the introduction of a substantial elected element in most provincial councils did prove a spur to political organization, the councils offered no real power to those elected to them. Except in Bengal, the elected members were nowhere in a majority and even the possession of a majority was not sufficient to move the government to action. The government was not responsible to the Council and it was under no obligation to implement a majority decision. After 1920, however, by the terms of the Montagu-Chelmsford Reforms, provincial councils were enlarged, provision was made for a substantial elected majority, and under a system known as Dyarchy, certain departments of government, notably Local Self-Government, Education, Agriculture, Health, Commerce and Industry, were transferred to the control of ministers responsible to the legislatures. After 1920, therefore, the government no longer possessed a monopoly of power at the provincial level. Very real power had been transferred to Indian hands and the government became dependent on the goodwill and co-operation of others for the administration of important departments.

In many respects, however, the devolution of power which took place in 1920 was less important than the terms under which it took place. Those who had been most active in calling for constitutional reform had been the English-educated professionals of the cities; and what they had demanded was that the urban areas should be given more substantial representation. The power of the government, however, lay in its alliance with the rural élites—the landed families whose offspring filled the ranks of deputy-collectors, *tehsildars* and *naib-tehsildars.* In its formulation of the Morley-Minto Reforms, the government had deliberately used these élites as a counterbalance to the 'advanced' urban politicians, and in framing the Montagu-Chelmsford constitution it continued with the same policy. There were two main techniques. Firstly it kept the number of urban seats at a minimum. Secondly, it extended the franchise beyond the canvassing power of the politicians. An examination of the situation in the United Provinces will illustrate the point.

When the U.P. Congress Committee met Mr Montagu, its main complaint was that under the Morley-Minto Reforms the towns were insufficiently represented:

> It is there that the largest measure of public spirit and capacity can be found and the desire for progress and the comprehension of political questions are keenest. Yet the present system all but ignores them. It allows of the nomination of persons ignorant of English, and ruling chiefs who have no concern with the affairs of British India, but rigorously limits the number of men who can be worthy representatives of their country.[1]

But when the U.P. government's Reform proposals were formulated, this complaint was ignored. In a house of 100 members, the government proposed that there should be seventy elected seats, of which ten were to be for urban interests. The only towns which were to receive such representation were the very largest ones—Lucknow, Benares, Allahabad, Agra, Kanpur, Meerut and Bareilly. All the others—and these included such substantial towns as Moradabad, Shahjehanpur, Aligarh and Jhansi—were to be represented within rural constituencies.[2] As a result of pressure from the politicians, these proposals were subsequently modified. Provision was made for two more urban seats, and the claims of Moradabad, Shahjehanpur and Aligarh were recognized. But this modification did little to alter the substance of the government's proposals. The government kept the urban politician at a disadvantage by ensuring that the balance between urban and rural seats remained the same.

The government's proposals for the franchise also put the urban politician at a disadvantage. The Congress and League scheme had demanded that members of Council be elected 'directly by the people on as broad a franchise as possible'.[3] But at that stage the

[1] Montagu papers (IOL MSS Eur. D 523) 35: Address presented by the U.P. Congress Committee, 26 Nov. 1917.

[2] IOF/L/Parl./409B: The Reforms Committee (Franchise), Proposals of the U.P. Government, pp. 71-3.

[3] S.S. Pirzada, (ed.), *Foundations of Pakistan, All India Moslem League Documents 1906-47*, vol. i (Karachi 1969), p. 492.

politicians were primarily concerned to secure the uniform introduction of direct election[4] and when they spoke of 'as broad a franchise as possible' they appear to have envisaged at the very most giving the vote to zemindars and tenants paying fifty rupees land revenue or rent.[5] The government decided, however, to give the vote to zemindars paying twenty-five rupees land revenue, and not only to secured tenants paying fifty rupees rent but also to non-occupancy tenants paying the same amount.[6] Neither the Congress nor the League protested strongly at these additions, and for very obvious reasons, but the concern both parties showed at the prospect of so large an electorate suggests that the government's proposals went considerably beyond their expectations. The addition of those paying between twenty-five and fifty rupees land revenue added 125,000 to the electorate,[7] the number of non-occupancy tenants paying over fifty rupees rent was 430,937.[8] The government's proposals thus enfranchised over 500,000 more electors than the politicians had anticipated; and this number constituted almost fifty per cent of the new rural electorate. Why had the government gone beyond what the nationalists demanded? There is no explicit evidence on motivation. But if an argument can be made from the effect of the proposals, the government was attempting to extend the electorate beyond the canvassing capacity of the politicians and to secure the return of its old allies in the districts. The existence of a more limited franchise would have made it possible for urban politicians to manage the rural electorate and get elected themselves. By extending the franchise beyond what was demanded, this possibility was considerably reduced.

Another important manipulative device was the distribution of seats between different interests in each council. The Lucknow Pact had stipulated that each council should consist of eighty per cent elected members and twenty per cent nominated members. But the

[4] Under the Morley-Minto Reforms, only the Muslim seats were filled by direct election. Non-Muslim members were elected indirectly by municipal and district boards.

[5] Montagu papers, 35: Address presented by the U.P. Congress Committee, 26 Nov. 1917.

[6] IOR/L/Parl./409B: The Reforms Committee (Franchise), Proposals of the U.P. Government, p. 71.

[7] Ibid., table vii, pp. 90-1: Statement of persons paying land revenue.

[8] Ibid., table vi, pp. 86-7 and table vii, pp. 88-9: Statements of all tenants and of secured tenants.

government laid down that at least thirty per cent of the seats in each council should be allocated to nominated and special interests. The Lucknow Pact had kept the nominated element low for good reason. In granting the Muslim community substantial weightage in Muslim minority provinces, the Hindu community had no intention of depriving itself of its majority position. The government, however, was not concerned to give either Hindu or Muslim majority communities a dominant share in their respective councils. Its main concern was to preserve its own position. Table 3 shows that only in the Central Provinces, where the non-Muslims formed 95.4 per cent of the population, were the elected members of a majority community in a position to command a majority in a legislature. In Bombay, the elected non-Muslims were given 40.4 per cent of the total number of seats; in the United Provinces 48.8 per cent; in Bihar and Orissa 46.6 per cent; and in Madras 49.2 per cent. In the Muslim majority provinces of the Punjab and Bengal, the elected members of the Muslim community were given 34 per cent and 27.9 per cent respectively.[9] Furthermore, even as a proportion of the total number of elected seats, the number of elected seats allocated to majority communities was considerably lower than the percentage laid down at Lucknow—34.2 per cent and 45.1 per cent for the Muslims of Bengal and the Punjab, and 66.3 per cent, 53.5 per cent, 60 per cent and 63.2 per cent for the non-Muslims of Madras, Bombay, the United Provinces and Bihar and Orissa. Only by the addition of nominated Muslims and non-Muslims to the totals for elected Muslims and non-Muslims was it possible to approach the Lucknow proportions.

The significance of this constitutional arrangement is obvious. It meant that in default of a combination of Muslim and non-Muslim elected members the government held the balance of power in all the most important provincial councils. Except in the Central Provinces, the elected members of a majority community could not work the Reforms without government support, whereas the government, provided it could win the support of the minority community and the special interests, was capable of running the

[9] In Bengal, this low figure in some measure reflected the agreement reached at Lucknow whereby the Muslims, though a majority, were awarded only 40 per cent of the elected seats. But the Bengali Hindus, though awarded 60 per cent of the elected seats, did not fare much better. They received only 32.9 per cent of the total number of seats in the council.

TABLE 3A

Provincial representation under the Montagu-Chelmsford Constitution

Province	Elected					Nominated	Total
	M	Non-M	Others	Special	Total		
Madras	13	65	7	13	98	34	132
Bombay	27	46	2	11	86	28	114
Bengal	39	46	7	22	114	26	140
U.P.	29	60	1	10	100	23	123
Punjab	32	20	12	7	71	23	94
B and O	18	48	1	9	76	27	103
CP	7	41	0	7	55	18	73
Assam	12	21	0	6	39	14	53

TABLE 3B

Elected members of provincial councils and their influence

Province	Muslims					Non-Muslims				
	A	B	C	D	E	A	B	C	D	E
Madras	6.7	15	13.2	9.8	10.6	90.0	85	66.3	49.2	73.3
Bombay	19.8	33	31.3	23.7	25.4	78.9	67	53.5	40.4	53.5
Bengal	54.6	40	34.2	27.9	30.8	45.1	60	40.4	32.9	47.9
U.P.	14.3	30	29.0	23.6	26.0	85.4	70	60.0	48.4	58.6
Punjab	55.2	50	45.1	34.0	40.4	32.0	50	28.2	21.3	25.5*
B and O	10.9	30	23.7	17.6	18.5	88.2	70	63.2	46.6	61.2
CP	4.4	15	12.7	9.6	9.6	95.4	85	79.2	56.2	78.0
Assam	32.3	—	30.8	22.6	30.2	65.9	—	53.9	39.6	47.1

* The Sikhs, who formed 11.1% of the population in the Punjab, were awarded 16.9% of the elected seats. This gave them a 12.8% share of the entire council, exclusive of special and nominated members.

A Percentage of population.
B Lucknow Pact proposals.
C Elected members as percentage of elected total.
D Elected members as percentage of total.
E Elected and Nominated members as percentage of total.

Source: Indian Statutory Commission, vol i (*Cmd. 3568*, 1929-30), part ii, ch. 4, appendices iii and iv, pp. 144-7.

administration in the face of a hostile majority community. The distribution of seats ensured, therefore, that the government was in a position to extract the maximum advantage from its enormous powers of patronage. Implicit in the whole structure of the new constitution was the maxim that co-operation with government was a precondition for constitutional success.

But despite the existence of these constraints, the main effect of the introduction of ministerial responsibility was to increase competition for power at the provincial level. Before 1920, though there had been distinct differences of attitude amongst the members of the educated elite, competition for power had been restricted to the municipal and district level where actual power had been devolved to Indian hands. At the provincial level, politicians had stressed the need for unity as a prerequisite for political reform, and they had been prepared, in order to achieve that unity, to adjust their differences and even to sacrifice local advantage to hopes of eventual provincial profit. Once devolution had taken place, however, the objective was no longer to convince the British public that India was ready for reform, but to gain a majority in any given legislature. The desire to obtain office or to prevent others from obtaining office became the mainspring of political activity, and men who had worked together for political reform became competitors in a struggle for power.

This growth of competition at the provincial level provincialized all-India politics. Between 1909 and 1920, all-India politics had been dominated by the educated elites of the most advanced provinces and because they were not competing for power at the provincial level, either amongst themselves or with other interests, they presented a united front at the all-India level. After 1920, however, except during a brief period of successful non-co-operation within the legislatures, the Reforms were worked in all provinces, and political interest groups supported by the Raj established a lien on the resources of government. The Raj needed them to work the Reforms and in most cases they needed the Raj to remain in office. In all provinces, therefore, parties with a vested interest in the continuation of the existing political dispensation came into being. Where a consolidated party worked the Reforms, this vested interest was well-entrenched. Where they were worked by a shifting alliance it was less well-entrenched. Throughout India, however, the exercise of power in the provinces transformed the nature of the all-India confrontation with the Raj. That confrontation no longer derived its strength from those who had no chance of power in the provinces. It drew its support instead from those temporarily excluded from the power which others enjoyed. Consequently it was subject to a greater degree of instability. The magnetic attraction of provincial office drew political energies away from the all-India level, and the all-India confrontation with government lived uneasily under the axe of constitutional collaboration in the provinces.

The changing structure of all-India Muslim politics

The Montagu-Chelmsford Reforms also changed the nature of all-India Muslim politics. Before 1920, Muslim political organization at the all-India level had been in the hands of the Muslims of the United Provinces, Bihar and Bombay. In these provinces, a Muslim educated élite had shared the political aspirations of the Hindu educated élite and had masterminded a political alliance with the Congress in pursuit of constitutional reform. Almost as soon as the government's Reform proposals were formulated, however, the League leaders saw the writing on the wall. There was no need for special representation for the landlords, Raza Ali told the U.P. government, because even without such representation, they would be 'in the ascendant in the first two, maybe three, councils'. 'At present their interests are not imperilled', he said. 'Rather there is a remote danger of their imperilling the interests of others.[10] Raza Ali obviously realized how difficult it would be to canvas such huge constituencies. 'It is important to consider', he wrote, 'whether a huge extension of the vote without a corresponding increase in the size of the councils will not lead to a breakdown of the system.'[11] Wazir Hassan made many of the same points. In his view, the franchise proposed by the government was too low and ought to be raised:

> The danger of a constituency becoming too large to be workable can be very much reduced by enhancing the property qualification to double figures. I think it would be pertinent to observe that in as much as we are not considering the question of franchise in relation

[10] IOR/L/Parl./409B: The Reforms Committee (Franchise), Syed Raza Ali's proposals, p. 143.

[11] Ibid., p. 141.

to complete self-government but only in relation to a step towards it, the broadening of the franchise should be commensurate with the step.[12]

On second thoughts, however, he concentrated his efforts on increasing the number of urban seats. The government had allocated thirty seats for the Muslims, of which three were to be for the towns. In an additional note submitted to the Franchise Committee, Wazir Hassan demanded twelve, including three for Lucknow.[13]

But these protests went unheeded. In the U.P. Council, under the new constitution, twenty-five out of twenty-nine Muslim members were returned by rural electorates, and a majority of these were leading zemindars of their districts.[14] Kunwar Jamshed Ali Khan, the Nawab of Baghpat, was returned from the Meerut constituency for all four councils.[15] The Nawab of Chhatari, a leading Lalkhani Rajput and one of the richest Muslim landowners in the Western divisions, was returned from Bulandshahr;[16] and from the Aligarh, Muttra and Agra constituencies the member for three out of four councils was Mahommed Ubedar Rahman Khan, a close relation of the Nawab of Bhikampur, a man renowned for his loyalty to the Raj.[17] From Muzaffarnagar, the member for the first two councils was Kunwar Inayat Ali Khan, a *Khan Bahadur* with an encumbered estate;[18] and from Bijnor, Chaudhuri Amir Hassan Khan, a leading zemindar paying 18,000 rupees land revenue.[19] From Bareilly, the member for the second and third councils was K.B. Hakim Mahboob Ali Khan, 'a big zemindar of good status';[20] and from Shahjehanpur, the

[12] By 'double figures', Wazir Hassan appears to have meant that the voting qualification should be double what the government was proposing. This would be in line with the suggestions put forward by Sheikh Habibullah, and by Raza Ali. Ibid., pp. 100 and 143.

[13] Ibid., pp. 140-1: additional memorandum submitted by Wazir Hassan.

[14] For the election returns for the United Provinces during the Montagu-Chelmsford Reforms, see *Cmd. 1261* (1921); *Cmd.2154* (1924); *Cmd.2923* (1927); *Cmd.3922* (1931).

[15] GI Home Public 953/1924: Summary of information received about new members of the U.P. Legislative Council, p. 254.

[16] *DG Bulandshahr* (1903), pp. 103-4; *DG Aligarh* (1909), p. 108. Chhatari paid 67,620 rupees land revenue in Bulandshahr and 12,318 rupees in Aligarh.

[17] GI Home Public 953/1924, p. 255; *DG Aligarh* (1909), pp. 110-12. The Pathans of Bhikampur were the wealthiest Muslim landlords in Aligarh.

[18] GI Home Public 953/1924, p. 254.

[19] Ibid., p. 254.

[20] Ibid,. p. 256.

member for all four councils was Fazlur Rahman Khan, 'one of the biggest Mahommedan zemindars in the district'.[21] In the Eastern divisions and in Oudh, a similar pattern was reproduced. Nawab Mahommed Yusuf, the son of Nawab Abdul Majid was regularly returned for Allahabad, Jaunpur and Mirzapur;[22] and Shah Badre Alam for Benares, Ghazipur, Ballia and Azamgarh.[23] From Hardoi, Lucknow and Unao, two taluqdars, Lt. Sheikh Shahid Hussain, a former member of the Morley-Minto council, and the Raja of Salempur were returned for two sessions each. The Fyzabad and Barabanki seat was filled by the Rajas of Pirpur and Jehangirabad and their relations,[24] and the Kheri and Sitapur seat, presumably with the approval of the Raja of Mahmudabad, initially by a Swarajist lawyer,[25] and subsequently by Sheikh Habibullah, the manager of his estate. For the most part, these men were zemindars, not lawyers, but even those who did have legal pracices generally took a conservative stand in politics. Furthermore, because of the nature of the electorate, even in the constituencies where landowners were not returned, the members were conservative intellectuals and educationalists—men like Dr Ziauddin,[26] Sheikh Abdullah,[27] and Professor Shafaat Ahmed Khan[28]—or men like Hafiz Hidyat Hussain of Kanpur, whose earlier dalliance with Panislamism gradually gave

[21] Ibid., p. 256. Fazlur Rahman Khan was also a *vakil* and chairman of the Shahjehanpur Municipal Board. See also *DG Shahjehanpur* (1910), p. 94.

[22] Nawab Mahommed Yusuf was 'the biggest and most influential landholder in the Eastern districts of the United Provinces'. See Nurul Hasan Siddiqui, *Landlords of Agra and Avadh* (Lucknow 1950), p. 273. Siddiqui's work is an invaluable source of information on U.P. landlord politics.

[23] Shah Badre Alam was a member of 'the chief Musulman landowning family of Ghazipur' and one of the leading supporters of the Muslim Defence Association. *DG Ghazipur* (1909), p. 98; GUPGAD 553/1917.

[24] The Raja of Pirpur filled the seat in the first council; the Raja of Jehangirabad's brother-in-law in the second; and the Raja of Jehangirabad himself in the fourth.

[25] Mahommed Habib Ashraf, the famous Aligarh Muslim historian [and brother of Mahommed Mujib], was elected to the seat as a Swarajist in 1923. GI Home Public 953/1924, p. 257.

[26] Ziauddin was returned for Mainpuri, Etah and Farrukhabad in the second council.

[27] Sheikh Abdullah was returned for the same constituency in the third council.

[28] Professor Shafaat Ahmed Khan of Allahabad University, member for Moradabad South in the second and third councils, married into Sir Mahommed Safi's family. He was the leading U.P. Muslim political strategist at the time of the round table conferences.

way to more stolid conservative sentiments.[29]

The League leaders' reactions to this situation varied from person to person. Few were prepared to dance to the rhythms of landlord politics; and even fewer to embrace the logical alternative—agitational politics. The only one to follow this course was Mazhar ul Haq, who participated in the Khilafat movement and subsequently disappeared from national politics altogether.[30] So they were faced with a very limited choice—either to take what jobs they could get from the government, whether political, administrative or judicial, or to opt out of British Indian politics and seek a new future in the States. The Raja of Mahmudabad and Wazir Hassan chose the first course of action; Sir Ali Imam and Samiullah Beg chose the second. The Raja was persuaded by Harcourt Butler to serve for a short while as Home Member in the U.P. government. Wazir Hassan accepted a job as Assistant Judicial Commissioner of Oudh. Ali Imam and Samiullah Beg, on the other hand, deserted British India for Hyderabad, the first to become the Nizam's Prime Minister and the second his Chief Justice. The only League leaders to remain actively involved in the politics of confrontation after 1920 were those whose ambitions were focused at the all-India level. Jinnah was the most notable of such men. He had been working for central responsibility since 1909 and his objective remained the same. It is a measure of the effect of the Reforms in the provinces, however, that many politicians whose interests had previously been strictly provincial should have attempted after 1920 to build themselves a new future at the all-India level. Syed Raza Ali, for example, moved into the Council of State; Mahommed Yakub into the Legislative Assembly. Even at the all-India level, however, politics were not the same, for the non-co-operation movement had taken the initiative, at least temporarily, out of the hands of the constitutionalists, and it was only when non-co-operation was suspended that the constitutional battle could be resumed.

So where did the leadership of the Muslim community lie after

[29] Hafiz Hidayat Hussain joined the U.P. Muslim Defence Association in 1917. In the years after 1920, he was one of the most vociferous protagonists of Muslim rights in the Western U.P. See for example, GUPGAD 429/1925, 246/1926, and 703/1927.

[30] In 1926, after spending the mid-1920s in district politics, Mazhur ul Haq failed to secure election to the Bihar and Orissa Provincial Council. Shortly afterwards, he retired from politics altogether, and spent the rest of his life living in an *ashram* as a virtual recluse.

1920? Certainly not with the landlord politicians of the United Provinces. Of course, these men did share in the responsibility of government. Men like the Nawab of Chhatari and Nawab Mahommed Yusuf, because of the support they commanded among the Muslim landlords in the U.P. Council, were given charge of the transferred departments and even appointed to the highest offices of state.[31] They held these honours, however, not as leaders of the Muslim party *per se,* but as leaders of the Muslim arm of the U.P. landed interest. It was only in combination with the Hindu landed interest that they secured their ministerships, and whilst their participation in the responsibilities of office undoubtedly preserved the position of their community within the collaborative system, it was not possible for them to make radical changes in the distribution of political patronage without the consent of the Raj.

This is not to imply that the Muslim landlord in the Muslim minority province was not concerned with communal advantage. Even if he was not involved in communal politics himself, he was certainly subject to pressures from below and at times when communal tensions exercised a polarizing infuence on politics, he followed his religion like everyone else. But while a Hindu landlord in a Muslim minority province could choose to join a communally oriented party in the hope of securing majority support for a solely Hindu ministry, a Muslim landlord, even taking into account the distribution of seats within the legislature, had only the slenderest hope of achieving office as the leader of communally oriented block. In the Muslim minority province, the exercise of power by the Muslim landlord was dependent on the solution of communal difficulties in a spirit of compromise under the auspices of the Raj.

The real power of the Muslim community after 1920 lay with the Muslim majority provinces of Punjab and Bengal; and the main reason for this was that under the Montagu-Chelmsford Reforms, for the first time, power began to be distributed, at least in some measure, according to population. The criterion for distributing power was no longer solely the social standing of the community's leaders in the districts, though the government did its best to ensure that they continued to thrive. Numbers began to matter. Consequently, the Punjabis and Bengalis, simply because they possessed

[31] Chhatari was appointed a Minister in 1923; he became Home Member in 1926; he acted as Governor in 1928. Nawab Yusuf served as a Minister from 1926 to 1937.

a greater share of the seats in their respective councils, were put in a better position to work the Reforms for their own advantage than their co-religionists in the minority provinces. After 1920, therefore, the political spotlight moves away from the United Provinces and Bihar, and focuses instead on the North-West and the North-East.

The Reforms in Bengal

Of the two Muslim majority communities, the Bengali Muslims were in the weaker position. They had been given a minority share of the elected seats under the terms of the Lucknow Pact and despite both the protests of their leaders and the recommendations of the government of India their position did not improve when the constitution was finally framed. They received only 34.2 per cent of the elected seats and even if they could secure the support of the government bloc this low figure put them in a less commanding position than their Punjabi co-religionists.

The main stumbling block to their enjoyment of power, however, was not the poor deal they had received at Lucknow but the existence of internal divisions within the community itself. These were threefold. Firstly, in the Dacca, Mymensingh and Murshidabad districts there was a small but influential aristocracy which collaborated closely with the Raj and provided the community with its loyalist leadership. Secondly, in the other rural areas of Northern and Eastern Bengal, in default of an aristocratic leadership, political power was in the hands of small proprietors who were closely in touch with the mass of Muslim and Namasudra tenant farmers. Thirdly, in Calcutta itself, and in Barrackpore, Howrah and the municipalities of the twenty-four *pargannahs,* there was a Muslim educated class akin to that of North India. Between these groups there were three main lines of division. Firstly, there was a division of economic interest between the aristocracy of the Dacca division and the mass of Muslims elsewhere. The aristocrat was favoured by the Raj; the *raiyat* was not. The aristocrat collaborated closely with the Raj; the *raiyat* was more likely to join the forces of opposition. Secondly, there was a cultural difference between both the urban educated Muslim and the aristocrat on the one hand and the *raiyat* on the other. The first spoke Urdu and looked nostalgically towards North India; the second spoke Bengali and shared a common culture with his Hindu counterpart. Lastly, between the urban élite of West Bengal and the rural society, whether landlord or peasant, of the North and East, there was a gulf created by hunger for employment and the innumerable waterways of Southern Bengal. The urban élite had co-operated with the Congress in the years before 1920 and given the right terms it might do so again.

These divisions within the community were not politically significant during the first council because the elections of 1920 had been boycotted both by the Congress and by the Khilafat committee, and the floor had been left to co-operating interests. By 1923, however, the All India Congress Swaraj party had been formed, and in Bengal, under the leadership of C.R. Das, it was advocating a policy of non-co-operation within the council. Because of the manner in which the seats in the council were distributed, however, the success of this policy depended on a combination of Muslim and non-Muslim members, and Das was therefore obliged to make a bid for the support of those Muslim interest groups which were least closely allied with the government. These fell into two categories—firstly the Muslim *raiyats*, and secondly the urban educated Muslims—and of the two the first were the more important. Long before the elections, Das directed his attention to the Muslim majority areas of the province and utilizing the connections which he had built up during the Khilafat movement, he succeeded in securing the return of an appreciable number of Swarajist Muslims. It was significant, however, that where the aristocracy was strong, Das was not successful. Of the fifteen Swarajists returned from the rural areas, five were returned from the Rajshahi division, four from the Chittagong division and four from the Presidency division. From the Dacca division only one was returned, and the Dacca, Mymensingh and Murshidabad districts returned seven loyalists and a Minister.[32] After the election had been fought, Das also secured the support of a number of urban Muslims. These men had supported the campaign for Reforms but once the Reforms had been granted they found themselves with an unattractive range of choices. For those like Sir Abdur Rahim who were taken into government, personal advancement was not impeded, but for others like Dr Abdullah Suhrawardy and Hussain Shahid Suhrawardy,

[32] See R.A. Gordon, 'Aspects in the history of the Indian National Congress with special references to the Swarajya party 1919-1927', unpublished D.Phil. thesis (Oxford 1970), pp. 152 and 336-9.

hopes for political success were small in a council so largely dominated by the rural interest. When Das produced the right terms, therefore, they were not slow to join him.

Though the Pact by which Das secured the support of these Muslim interests was only ratified by the Bengal Provincial Congress Committee on 16 December 1923, its terms were known to Das's Muslim supporters during the campaign, and they were so enormously to the Muslim advantage that they almost certainly exercised an important influence on the polling. The Pact laid down that the Muslims should be represented in the Council according to population and by separate electorates; it divided the spoils of local self-government on a sixty: forty basis according to which community was in the majority in each district; it gave the Muslims fifty-five per cent of the services, and an eighty-per-cent share of recruitment until this quota was complete; and it ordained that music should not be played before mosques, and that the Muslim right to slaughter cattle should be respected.[33]

The Muslim support which Das won as a result of this Pact enabled him to make Dyarchy unworkable. In March 1924, supported by twenty-one Muslims, he defeated the government over many important heads of the Budget. The demands for ministerial salaries and for the salaries of civil servants in the Medical and Education department were rejected and the government was obliged to have recourse to extraordinary powers to keep the administration running.[34] Yet though Muslim support for Das made the difference between success and failure, the alliance which he had created was a very unstable one. The educated Hindu middle class adhered to the Pact with reluctance because it struck at their preponderant share of the services. The Hindus from the Muslim majority areas did not relish the prospect of permanent minority status; and the Hindu landlord dwelt uneasily in a camp overflowing with Muslim *raiyats*. Das's alliance, therefore, was essentially an alliance for opposition. Promises could produce a temporary unity, but any attempt to implement those promises was bound to create divisions.

As far as opposition was concerned, Das proved his point. He

[33] For an account of the making of the Pact from the Muslim point of view, see Maulvi Abdul Karim, *Letters on Hindu-Muslim Pact* (Calcutta 1924).

[34] J.H. Broomfield, *Elite Conflict in a Plural Society* (Berkeley and Los Angles 1968), p. 249.

made Dyarchy unworkable and despite the instability of the alliance he managed to maintain his majority and to prevent any ministry from functioning for more than a matter of weeks. He did not succeed, however, in bending the government to his will. Indeed, far from offering to negotiate with Das, the government sought to undermine his hold over the Council by driving a wedge between the Hindu and Muslim Swarajists. No better example exists, in fact, of the power of patronage enjoyed by the government under the Reforms than that provided by the creation in Bengal between 1924 and 1927 of a homogeneous community working closely with the government out of the disparate material of pre-1920 Muslim politics.

In March 1924, when the demand for ministerial salaries was rejected, the government made much of the fact that the two ministers were both Muslims, and it retained them in office and encouraged them to make communal profit out of this issue.[35] A Muslim supporter of government was given the task of moving a resolution calling for the implementation of that clause of the Bengal Pact which referred to the Muslim position in the services; and though Das prevented a split over this issue by moving for an adjournment, the communal atmosphere became fouler as a result.[36] By April 1924, a communal party which included the two Suhrawardys had come into existence, and Das's majority began to look shaky. The government's efforts to secure majority support for a ministry, however, did not meet with success. Both in August 1924 and in March 1925 Das succeeded in defeating the government over this issue by exploiting factional differences within the Muslim community. In August 1924 he won back the support of the urban Muslims,[37] and in March 1925, when the inscrutable Fazlul Haq and his eight followers put their votes up for auction, Das appears to have been the highest bidder.[38] Even so, these successes brought no tangible rewards. The net result was merely the suspension of the constitution and an increased determination on the government's part to win the support of the Muslims by unilateral concessions.

The man most responsible for separating Das from his Muslim

[35] Ibid., pp. 252-3.

[36] Ibid., pp. 254-5.

[37] Ibid, p. 256.

[38] IOR/L/P and J/6/1193/1925: Chief Secretary, Government of Bengal, to Home Secretary, Government of India, 28 March 1925.

followers was Sir Abdur Rahim, a former judge of the Madras High Court and an executive councillor in the Bengal government. He saw where Das was strongest and persuaded government to offer the Muslims of those areas more tangible concessions. Firstly, in order to win back the support of the urban educated, he persuaded government in July 1925 to review the Muslim position in the services. In October, it was agreed that the Muslims should receive more favourable treatment, and in December, the terms of this new deal were made public. Secondly, he encouraged government to make concessions to the agriculturalists; to extend primary school education to the rural areas, and to amend tenancy legislation in favour of the *raiyats.* Both these measures were opposed tooth and nail by Das's Hindu supporters and served to alienate his Muslim supporters from Northern and Eastern Bengal. Thirdly, he supported government's efforts to organise communal organizations in the districts; and in late 1925, following his resignation from the Executive Council, took up the task of political organization himself, making communal appeals through the press and building up a communal party to contest the 1926 elections. In all these activities Rahim had remarkable success. But the event which did most to polarize the two communities was the Calcutta riot of April 1926, which raged for a fortnight virtually unchecked, and which saw whole bazaars razed to the ground and the death of over fifty citizens, both in open combat and in isolated revenge killings. The part played by Hussain Shahid Suhrawardy both in the April riots and in the July riots[39] casts grave suspicions on Rahim's own role, because Suhrawardy was Rahim's son-in-law and the two men worked closely together. Nor can the government itself be entirely cleared of responsibility because the ineffectiveness of the administration, both in preventing the riot and in bringing it under control, suggests at best a culpable degree of negligence and at worst an element of political vindictiveness.[40] Whilst the responsibility for the riot must remain a matter for conjecture, however, its effect need not. By the time of the 1926 elections, the Muslims had been thoroughly alienated from the Congress party, and the Congress itself was so aware of its poor standing with the

[39] For a discussion of Suhrawardy's activities at the time of the July riot, see GI Home Poll. 209/1926.

[40] See GI Home Poll. 11/vii/1926: Note by Haig, 11 July 1926; also Hailey papers (IOL MSS Eur. E 220) 9A: Craik to Hailey, 28 April 1926.

community that it made no effort to secure the return of Muslims on the party ticket.[41] Of the thirty-nine Muslim members elected, only one was a Swarajist, and the other thirty-eight pledged themselves to work the constitution in the interests of the community. In the Bengal Legislative Council, the days of sympathy with the Congress were over.[42]

The Reforms in Punjab: the government's role

Though the Muslim community in Bengal was made more homogeneous by the government's subtle use of political patronage, it remained a tool in the government's hands. The government of Bengal was not enamoured of the Bengali Muslim; he merely served as a useful counterweight to the power of the Swarajists. Abdur Rahim was the architect of Muslim unity; but the plans he drew up were only adopted by the government because it was in its own interest. Even after 1927, therefore, the same political necessity which had forced Das to bid for the support of the Muslims forced the Muslims to adjust their political programme to the wishes of the government bloc. Such was not the case in the Punjab. The Punjab Muslims were a vital element in the government's administrative and military strategy; they started off with a better share of the seats in the council; and they succeeded from the beginning in making more use of the Reforms.

In the Punjab before 1920 the political activity that did take place was confined to the large towns and particularly those of the Lahore and Jullundur divisions.[43] The most important centre was Lahore, the capital of the province, a town of over 280,000 inhabitants. Second in importance was Amritsar, one of the most important commercial centres of North India; and in the third rank stood Sialkot, Jullundur, Ferozepur, Ludhiana and Hoshiarpur. When the most advanced

[41] Gordon, op.cit., pp. 297-8.

[42] For an account of Abdur Rahim's activities in 1925 and 1926, see Broomfield, op.cit., pp. 269-81.

[43] Before 1920 the Punjab had a reputation for political inactivity. A letter to the *Tribune* at the height of the Home Rule movement complained that 'the Punjab and the Punjabis, despite their boasted matter of factness, are indolently dozing over their affairs as if it were no business or concern of theirs to keep pace with the rest of their countrymen in the race for the political goal of Self-Government for India. The valorous and practical Punjabis are, alas, showing themselves to be Tennyson's veritable lotus-eaters.' (*Tribune,* 25 May 1917).

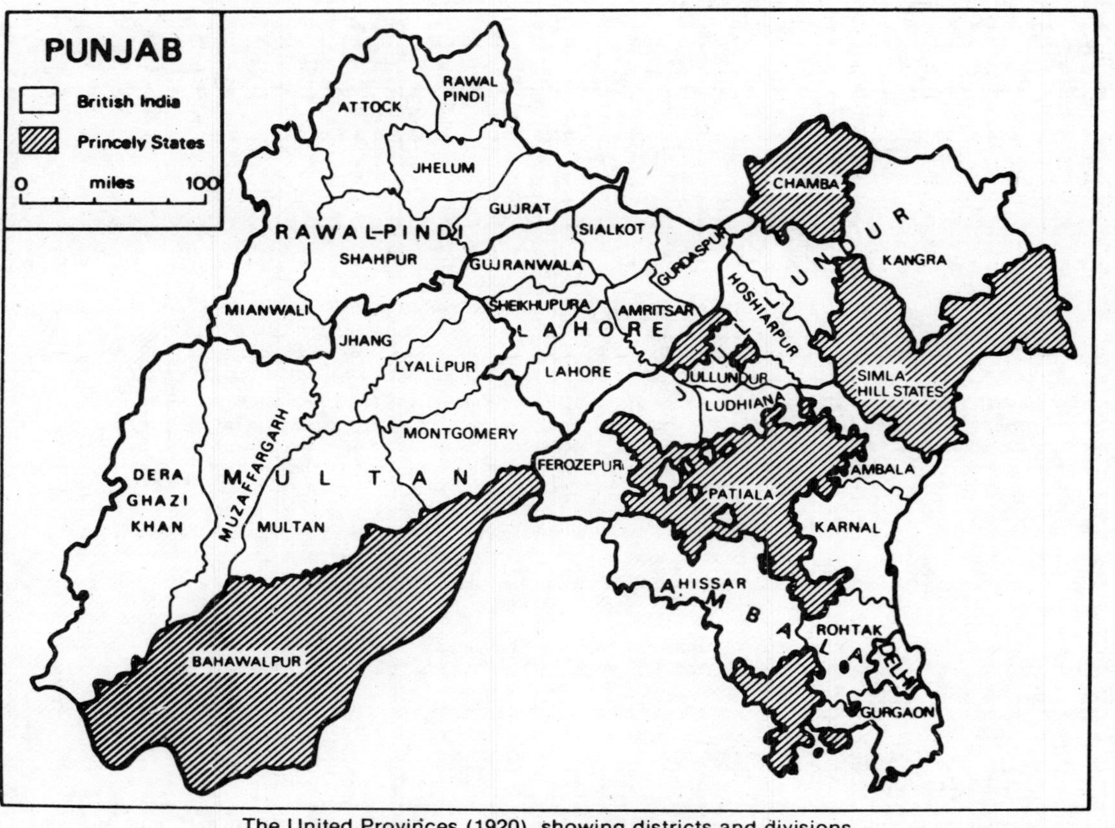

The United Provinces (1920), showing districts and divisions

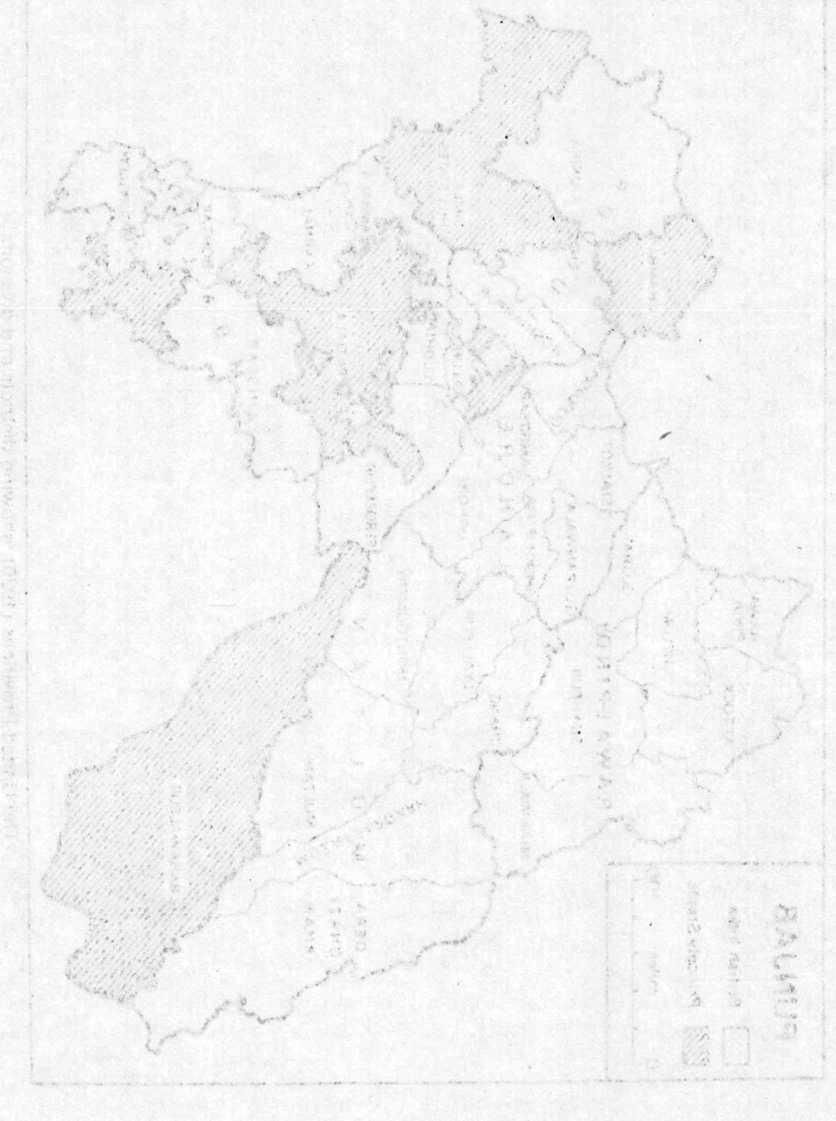

political organization in the Punjab, the Punjab Provincial Conference,[44] met Montagu in 1917, it consisted chiefly of Hindu and Muslim lawyers, merchants and industrialists of these cities; and what was true of this deputation was also true of the active communal organizations, the two branches of the Muslim League and the Hindu Sabha.[45] After 1920, however, as a result of the Montagu-Chelmsford Reforms, the Old World was called into play to redress the balance of the New: power was transferred to the rural areas and the urban centres of the Central Punjab ceased to be the focus for provincial politics. Where the Muslim community was concerned, this shift in the balance of power was particularly significant. The majority of urban Muslims, as is shown by Tables 4a and 4b, was concentrated in the districts east of Lahore, whereas the majority of rural Muslims was concentrated in the districts to the west. After 1920, therefore, the focus of Muslim politics shifted from Central to Western Punjab. Of the thirty-four seats allocated to Muslim representation under the Montagu-Chelmsford Reforms, only four went to the urban areas of the Lahore, Jullundur and Ambala divisions, whereas twenty-nine were allocated to the rural areas, and twenty-three to rural areas of the Muslim majority districts west of Lahore.

TABLE 4A

Distribution of Muslim population in the Punjab

Division	Total	Muslims	Urban	Muslims
Ambala	3,826,615	1,006,159	452,975	183,863
Jullundur	4,181,898	1,369,648	350,788	171,504
Lahore	4,977,441	2,848,800	773,214	425,310
Rawalpindi	3,460,710	2,973,371	335,008	196,188
Multan	4,218,360	3,246,343	300,207	166,241
Total	20,685,024	11,444,321	2,212,191	1,142,108

[44] The Punjab Provincial Conference contained representatives of the Punjab Provincial Congress, the Hindu Sabha and the more advanced branch of the Muslim League. It withered away when these organizations came to frame their detailed Reform proposals.

[45] Montagu papers, 35: Deputations from the Punjab to the Secretary of State.

TABLE 4b

Towns over 50,000 in the Punjab

Division	Number	Towns	Total	Muslims
Ambala	1	Ambala	76,326	31,448
Jullundur	3	Jullundur	71,008	42,261
		Ludhiana	51,880	30,921
		Ferozepur	54,351	
Lahore	3	Lahore	281,781	149,044
		Amritsar	160,218	71,180
		Sialkot	70,619	44,846
Rawalpindi	1	Rawalpindi	101,142	47,653
Multan	1	Multan	84,806	55,864

Sources: Punjab Census 1921, part 2, Tables I, V, VI, pp. 2-3, 22-6, 30.

The Muslim community of West Punjab was a far more homogeneous community than the Muslim community of Eastern and Northern Bengal. Table 5 shows the number of Muslims, Hindus and Sikhs paying over twenty rupees land revenue and over 500 rupees land revenue in the Rawalpindi, Multan and Lahore divisions in 1918. It demonstrates firstly that west of Lahore the Muslims were the main landholding community and secondly that they also possessed a majority of the largest estates in all districts except the Sialkot district. In districts opened up by irrigation projects, notably Gujranwala, Lyallpur and Montgomery, they shared this pre-eminence with the Sikhs,[46] but further west, in the districts where the Muslims formed more than eighty per cent of the population, their pre-eminence was unqualified. In those districts, as is demonstrated by reference to Griffin's *Chiefs and Families of Note in the Punjab,* the Muslims provided not only the bulk of the agriculturalists but also the most firmly established social leadership. Except in the Rawalpindi, Jhelum and Gujrat districts, where Muslim tribes possessed an influence which is not made apparent by a mere counting of heads, every family of note in these districts was a Muslim family.[47]

[46] Table 5 also makes clear, however, that the Muslims were recruited in overwhelmingly superior numbers as crown tenants in Montgomery, Lyallpur, Jhang and Shahpur.

[47] Sir Lepel Griffin, *Chiefs and Families of Note in the Punjab* (rev. edn. Lahore 1940), vol. ii, pp. 165-466.

By comparision with Bengal, therefore, the Muslim majority community of Punjab possessed a well-entrenched landed leadership; and for this reason, if for no other, it had a favoured position in the political thinking of the Raj.

The relations between the Muslim landed leadership and the Raj fell under two related heads, the first administrative and the second military. Recruitment to the services in the Punjab was, if anything, more geared to the preservation of the old landed aristocracy than elsewhere in India. In the United Provinces tried loyalty to the Raj was a very important criterion in the recruitment process but with the spread of education, educational qualifications were required even of the scions of landed houses. In the Punjab, however, the administration showed a much more pronounced bias towards the landed classes and a determination to maintain their position at all costs. This was shown by the regulations for recruitment to the services laid down in the late nineteenth century[48] but it became most apparent in 1900 when the Punjab Government passed the Land Alienation Act to prevent indebted landlords from losing their property to the urban moneylender. From that time forward a distinction was drawn between agricultural and non-agricultural tribes and those unfortunate enough to fall into the second category suffered severe discrimination. They could not purchase land in their own right and those of them who practised moneylending were restricted in their ability to foreclose on their debts.

One of the main reasons why the Punjab government alone amongst the various provincial governments took such strong measures was because it relied very heavily on the landed interest in the recruitment of soldiers for the Army. The Muslims of West Punjab had played an important role in the annexation of the province, and both the Muslims and the Sikhs provided the forces which enabled the government to put down the Mutiny of 1857. In the aftermath of the Mutiny, therefore, the Punjab became the main recruiting area for the Indian Army, and acquired a reputation as the 'Sword Arm of India'. The extent to which the government relied on Punjabi soldiers could be demonstrated in the later nineteenth century by reference to the part they played in the Afghan Wars. At that time fear of Russian expansion was the guiding prin-

[48] *Proceedings of the Public Services Commission* (Calcutta 1887), vol. i, *Proceedings relating to the Punjab*, pp. 49-59.

TABLE 5

Landholding in the Lahore, Rawalpindi and Multan division
Showing land revenue payments of tenants by Community

District	Over 500 rupees			Over 20 rupees					
	Muslim (CT)	Hindu (CT)	Sikh (CT)	Muslim	CT	Hindu	CT	Sikh	CT
Lahore	19 (2)	11	24	3,001	419	614	44	7,261	605
Amritsar	4	10	26	2,475	0	517	0	13,158	0
Gurdaspur	6	50	16	6,074	0	4,639	0	8,054	0
Sialkot	7	8	10	9,124	0	5,815	0	4,166	0
Gujranwala	119 (4)	51 (1)	90 (7)	11,864	867	2,810	80	6,692	1,057
Gujrat	8	3	2 (1)	8,471	511	508	13	208	62
Shahpur	128 (34)	23 (8)	11 (7)	8,531	4,212	658	190	183	887
Jhelum	19	2	1	4,395	33	267	2	105	1
Rawalpindi	3	0	3	3,222	1	139	0	176	0
Attock	45	0	1	4,557	6	165	2	87	2
Mianwali	33	3	0	2,427	4	293	1	8	1

District	Over 500 rupees			Over 20 rupees					
	Muslim	Hindu	Sikh	Muslim	CT	Hindu	CT	Sikh	CT
Montgomery	21 (12)	11 (3)	19(10)	2,492	3,979	840	383	898	761
Lyallpur	195 (32)	68 (3)	175 (3)	19,982	7,881	1,167	119	13,839	478
Jhang	85 (38)	6 (1)	1	6,603	4,280	859	159	87	25
Multan	95 (20)	46	4	6,583	1,499	2,577	134	263	375
Muzzafargarh	39 (1)	11	0	4,205	6	1,725	1	7	0
Dera Ghazi Khan	16 (2)	3	0	1,773	97	922	8	0	0
Total for 3 divisions	842(155)	306(16)	383(28)	106,139	23,795	24,675	1,036	55,192	4,254
Total for Punjab	939(155)	511(16)	439(28)	134,549	23,824	90,601	1,144	92,088	4,255

(CT) = Crown Tenant:

Source: IOR/L/Parl./409B: Proceedings of the Reforms Committee (Franchise), Proposals of the Punjab Government, pp. 156-67.

ciple of Indian military strategy, and the location of the Punjab astride the route from Central Asia made a strong Punjab essential for India's defence. The most eloquent proof of government reliance on the Punjabi soldier, however, is provided by the statistics for recruitment to the Army during the First World War. Out of a total of 683,149 combatant troops recruited in India between August 1914 and November 1918, 349,688 came from the Punjab.[49]

The government's reliance on the Punjab in its recruitment to the Army was essentially a reliance on the rural Punjab. The urban classes made a very poor response to the government's exhortations to enlist and they became increasingly a subject for government derision as the War progressed.[50] Even amongst the rural classes, however, there was a significant difference in the degree of commitment from one area to another. Of the 250,000 soldiers recruited up till April 1918, the lion's share had been provided by three main communities, the Muslims of West Punjab, the Jat Sikhs of Central Punjab and the Hindu Jats of the Ambala division. The first community provided 98,000 combatant troops, the second 65,000 and the third 22,000. The finest record, however, belonged to the Muslim majority districts of the Rawalpindi division. From Rawalpindi and Jhelum over thirty per cent of the manhood of the district went to the War; in Attock the figure was sixteen per cent, in Gujrat thirteen per cent and in Shahpur ten per cent. These five districts were amongst the eight most heavily recruited districts in the entire Punjab, the other three being Ludhiana and Amritsar, the two main Sikh recruitment areas, which sent fourteen and eleven per cent respectively, and Rohtak, the main Hindu Jat recruitment area which sent fifteen per cent.[51]

The degree of favour shown by the Punjab government to the

[49] *India's contribution to the Great War,* published by authority of the Government of India (Calcutta 1923), appendix C, p. 276.

[50] In the Spring of 1918 O'Dwyer informed the Viceroy that the urban areas had only produced 250 recruits for the Indian Defence Force. He described the strained feelings which existed between the urban and martial classes as a result of the failure of the first group to make sufficient sacrifices during the War, and he argued that any increase in taxation should be borne by those who had not sent their manpower to the front line. Chelmsford papers (IOL MSS Eur. E 264) 20: O'Dwyer to Chelmsford, 12 April and 6 May 1918.

[51] J.P. Thompson papers (IOL MSS Eur. F 137) Box File 4: Speech by O'Dwyer in the Punjab Legislative Council, 26 April 1918.

landed interest was made clear by the Lieutenant Governor, Sir Michael O'Dwyer, in a characteristically blunt speech delivered to the Imperial Council in September 1917. At a time when the government of India was endeavouring to convince the urban politicians of the Presidencies and the United Provinces of its good faith where the prospects of Reform were concerned, O'Dwyer threw out a derisive challenge to the urban classes and spelt out the special relationship between the Raj and the landed interest which the Punjab government had been at pains to develop. Speaking against a resolution introduced by Sardar Sundar Singh Majithia in favour of the assimilation of the legislative and administrative system in the Punjab to that of the province of Bihar and Orissa, O'Dwyer explained that the Punjab government relied on two main classes, the landed aristocracy and the mass of peasant proprietors, and gave his opinion that these classes were not interested in political reform:

> The political and administrative reforms already discussed and others that may follow in due course [he said] will appeal primarily to the educated urban class which is in the best position to appreciate and profit by them: but they will leave the vast majority of the two classes in question cold.

O'Dwyer then went on to answer the question posed by Sundar Singh as to what the Government proposed to do to reward these classes:

> I am glad to think [he said] that we have already a good record on the credit side. The great improvement in the pay, pensions and allowances of the Indian army has already given a powerful stimulus to the fighting classes, the earmarking of 180,000 acres of colony land for allotment to men who have rendered distinguished services in the field is a further encouragement, while the recent announcement in regard to the grant of Commissions will specially appeal to the landed gentry.

Next, after casting aspersions on the courage of the urban classes and hinting at future legislation to regulate usury, he laid stress on the importance of the Land Alienation Act.

> It is to it [he said] that we owe the fact that we are appealing today not to be a sullen, discontented and half-expropriated peasantry, eager perhaps for a change which might restore them to their own, but to a loyal and contented body of men who realise that the

Government has stood and still stands between them and ruin and who consequently rally in their tens of thousands to its support.

But [he continued] we have not only done what legislative and administrative measures could do to maintain the zemindars in possession of their paternal acres, we have also relieved congestion and increased their prosperity by opening up to them several millions of acres in the great canal colonies. In allotting those lands we have invariably given them priority seeking not so much the profit of the Government as the advantage of the rural population.

In the older colonies we have allowed the colonists who came in as Government tenants to purchase for Rs 12-8-0 per acre, or even less, land which they could sell next day for Rs 200 to Rs 300 per acre; and even in the more recent colonies they are allowed to purchase the proprietory right, which has a present average value of Rs 250 per acre, for a sum which must not exceed Rs 100 per acre—the payment being spread over 30 years.

Again, take the question of land revenue settlements. The Punjab government has long accepted it as a principle of revenue administration that the peasant proprietors, especially in those districts from which the Indian army is largely drawn, shall receive special favour in assessment. The re-assessment of all the rich districts of the Central Punjab has been completed within the last 5 or 6 years and I am in a position to say that Government has rarely imposed a demand above half of the half net rental which is supposed to be the standard of assessment in the Province. At the same time, where agricultural conditions are fairly stable and fully developed it has raised the terms of settlement from 20 to 30 years. The result of this leniency is to appreciate enormously the value of proprietory rights which 50 years ago sold at from 5 to 10 times but now sell at an average of 170 times the land revenue demand, a figure which excites the envy and admiration of other provinces, even those under permanent settlement.

All these things are done in the interests of our zemindars and especially of those tribes and classes which enlist so freely in the Indian Army.[52]

In O'Dwyer's view these tangible rewards were a substitute for political reform. Like most Punjab civilians he was extremely conservative in his political inclinations[53] and this was made abundantly clear when his Government put forward its franchise proposals. The Montagu-Chelmsford Report had laid down that each

[52] *ILC Debates*, 1917-18, 13 Sept. 1917, pp. 233-4.

[53] For the views of leading Punjab civilians on the Montagu-Chelmsford Report, see IOR/L/Parl./409A: Enclosure to the Punjab government's letter no. 19351 of 5 Nov. 1918.

council should contain a minimum of fifty members and that thirty per cent should be nominated; the Punjab government proposed a council of fifty-one members with a thirty-three per cent nominated element. The most striking evidence of the government's conservatism, however, lay in its proposals for the distribution of urban and rural seats and in its recommendations concerning the franchise. Where the distribution of rural and urban seats was concerned, the government showed a strong bias towards the rural areas. Of the thirty-four elected members, twenty-five were to be allocated to the rural areas, ten to the Muslims, six to the Hindus, five to the large landowners and four to the Sikhs, and only six to the urban areas, three to the Muslims and three to the Hindus. And where the franchise was concerned, the desire to obtain a conservative electorate in both the rural areas and the towns was very apparent. In the rural areas the government proposed that the payment of fifty rupees land revenue should be the main voting qualification. This qualification was twice as high as that proposed by other governments and would have made the Punjab electorate by far the smallest in India. It also proposed quite unashamedly that in each village the officially appointed *lambardar* should be given the vote, a proposal which made the 65,327 *lambardars* a substantial element in the total rural electorate of 161,610.[54] Finally, it prevented the urban politicians from standing in rural constituencies, even if they possessed land in those constituencies, by laying down that candidates for rural seats must fulfil a three-year residence requirement; and it restricted the influence of the small-town politician in rural politics by excluding all towns with a population of over 5,000 from the rural constituencies.[55] In the urban areas the government restricted the number of urban seats to a bare minimum and proposed extremely high voting qualifications. To vote in urban elections it was necessary either to pay income tax, or to possess immovable property to the value of 10,000 rupees, or to occupy premises valued at

[54] The most amazing proposal of all was put forward by one 'Jullundur Smith'. He had an ingenious scheme for running English candidates for all the rural constituencies and believed they would get in everywhere. J.P. Thompson papers, Diary, 20 August 1918.

[55] This proposal contrasted markedly with the practice in the United Provinces where even Jhansi, a town of over 60,000 inhabitants, was included within a rural area.

20,000 rupees. These stipulations restricted the vote to three per cent of the urban population.[56]

In making these proposals the Punjab government made clear its suspicions of the urban politician and its reliance on the rural areas. It justified the allocation of five special seats to the landed gentry in terms of their importance for the administrative services and for the Army and, while stressing their lack of English education and their aristocratic reluctance to tout for votes amongst their social inferiors, it clearly saw them as a useful counterweight to more radical politicians. 'Their representatives', ran its proposals, 'will form a valuable steadying influence in the council chamber where their practical experience and conservative tendencies should prove a healthy check on the impatient idealism of middle class politicians.'[57] A similar calculation was also evident in the government's acceptance of separate representation for the Sikhs, a measure it justified in terms of their share of the land and their military importance;[58] and in its desire to secure adequate representation for the Army interest, not only by nomination but also through the rural electorates: 'Retired military men', it believed, 'would form an element in the electorate whose intelligence has been sharpened by contact with the outside world and has moreover been subjected to the wholesome influence of regular discipline.'[59] Finally, in acceding to the Muslim demand for separate representation, it was clearly endeavouring to restrict the influence of the educated and moneyed Hindu middle class. Not only did it fear that within a joint electorate this class would dominate the urban seats; it also feared that it would have an influence in rural elections because of its economic power. In a joint electorate, moreover, the Hindus would form a larger proportion of the electorate than they did of the population. For all these reasons, separate electorates were held to be essential.

> . . . the Lieutenant Governor calculates [ran the proposals] that assuming the Sikhs to be given special electorates of their own and the other two communities to compete in general rural and urban electorates coterminous with Revenue divisions, the Mahommedans

[56] IOR/L/Parl./409B; Franchise proposals of the Punjab government, pp. 147-205.
[57] IOR/L/Parl./409B: Franchise proposals of the Punjab government, pp. 149-50.
[58] Ibid., p. 148.
[59] Ibid., pp. 150-1.

could not count on obtaining more than 9 out of 16 rural seats and 2 out of 6 urban seats, or 11 in all against 11 Hindus though they outnumber the Hindus by 70%.... This calculation is based on a view favourable to the Mahommedans but the result would certainly not satisfy their expectations.[60]

As a result of the Franchise Committee report, the recommendations of the government of India and the decision of the Joint Select Committee, these proposals were subsequently modified. The Punjab government was obliged to accept a larger council and a larger electorate than the one it had originally proposed. The council was increased to ninety-four members and the rural and urban franchises were lowered, the first to include those who paid twenty-five rupees land revenue and the second to include those possessing immovable property to the value of 4,000 rupees. Where the main features of the earlier proposals were concerned, however, no substantial changes took place and as a result of the terms of the final constitution, urban educated politicians were deprived of any real share of political power.

In the demands of the main urban political associations, the Punjab Provincial Congress Committee, the Hindu Sabha and the two branches of the Muslim League, the main emphasis had been on the enfranchisement of the urban areas. The Congress Committee in a memorandum drawn up in March 1920 had demanded that thirty per cent of the elected seats should be given to the urban areas, sixteen seats in a council of eighty-seven or twenty in a council of 100.[61] The Hindu Sabha had demanded eighteen seats for the urban areas and three seats for the University in a council of 100.[62] The more advanced branch of the Muslim League had demanded a council of 125 members, eighty per cent being elected and six urban seats being created for every ten rural seats.[63] All these demands were disregarded. Only ten seats were allocated to the urban areas; the urban franchise was not lowered to the level demanded by the urban politicians;[64] and the three-year residence

[60] Ibid., p. 148.

[61] GI Reforms Office, Franchise B, May 1920, nos. 129-34.

[62] IOR/L/Parl./409B: The Reforms Committee (Franchise), p. 226.

[63] Ibid., pp. 218-9.

[64] The Punjab Provincial Congress Committee wanted the urban vote to be given to those possessing property valued at 3,000 rupees. The government was not prepared

requirement, against which the urban educated protested, was increased by one year to keep urban influences out of rural politics for the second council as well as the first.[65] The most important feature of the final constitution, however, was its provisions with regard to the military vote. In its first constitution the Punjab government proposed to enfranchise only retired and pensioned Indian military officers above the rank of *jemadar,* estimating their number at 2,000 and opposing the enfranchisement of lower ranks 'for fear of enfranchising too large an electorate'.[66] By July 1920, however, as a result of a pressure group in the House of Commons under the leadership of Sir Charles Yate,[67] Montagu had agreed, contrary to the wishes of the government of India that the vote should be given to the ex-sepoy,[68] admitting in a speech to the House in the same month that this concession would add 200,000 soldiers to the Punjab electorate.[69] In the final constitution, therefore, despite the opinion of the Joint Select Committee that 'this might mean that soldiers in the Punjab would have a preponderating voice in elections.'[70] the Punjab soldier was enfranchised and the military vote became a very substantial element in the electorate. It cannot be claimed that this particular concession was desired by the Punjab government itself but its effect certainly was to strengthen the government's hand under the new constitution. Calculations based on the government's own figures suggest that nearly forty per cent of the rural electorate had served in the Army and over fifty per cent had derived direct benefit from Government

to accept that such a person compared well with the rural voter who paid 25 rupees land revenue.

[65] GI Reforms Office, Franchise A, Sept. 1920, nos. 133-80: C.J. Hallifax, Punjab Reforms Commissioner, to S.P. O'Donnell, 23 March 1920.

[66] IOR/L/Parl./409B: The Reforms Committee (Franchise), p. 208, H.D. Craik, called and examined.

[67] Sir Charles Yate served in the Indian political service from 1868 to 1904. He spent most of his time in North-West India and Afghanistan. His last post was as Agent to the Governor-General in Baluchistan. Between 1910 and 1924, he was MP for the Melton division of Leics.

[68] IOR/L/P and J (R)/6/881/1920: Mr Montagu to Sir Charles Yate, 22 July 1920.

[69] *House of Commons Debates (Hansard),* vol. 132, Friday 23 July 1920, cols. 869-74.

[70] This was Sir James Meston's verdict on the Joint Select Committee decision. See GI Reforms Office, Deposit, April 1920, no. 5: Proceedings of the Governors' Conference on the Reforms, 23 Jan. 1920, p. 1.

patronage.[71] Those returned to the council after 1920, therefore, were men heavily committed to the maintenance of the Punjab military machine. It was these men who formed the government, and it was the classes recruited to the Army that derived most benefit from the power which had been devolved.

The Reforms in Punjab: beneficiaries and policies

The men who benefited most from the Reforms were the Muslim interests represented by the Punjab Muslim Association, and the Sikh and Hindu Jat interests represented by the Punjab Zemindar Central Association. The similarity between the arguments used by Umar Hayat Khan Tiwana,[72] the leader of the agriculturalist Muslim lobby, and those put forward by the government itself, is a remarkable feature of the Punjab debate on the Reforms and it must be taken as a measure of the dependence of the government on men of Umar Hayat's class in the maintenance of the Punjab military machine. His demands for special representation for landholders,[73] if not his demand for a second chamber,[74] were accepted and enforced. His wariness of the trading class and his desire to see its influence over the rural voter curtailed by constitutional provisions was met by the government's insistence on a residence requirement for rural candidates.[75] His demand that the discharged

[71] The total rural electorate at the 1920 elections was 379,409. Of these 168,714 paid land revenue over 25 rupees, 38,000 were *lambardars* not included in this category, 5,500 were payers of income tax and 9,610 were *zaildars*, jaghirdars, non-official members of district boards, presidents of co-operative societies, registered graduates and civil pensioners. The total electorate excluding soldiers amounted to 216,324. On these calculations 163,085 had the right to vote on account of their military services to Government. The figures on which these calculations are based can be found in the Franchise proposals of the Punjab government (IOR/L/Parl./409B, pp. 151-3, 156-67) and in the Electoral Returns for the 1920 election (GI Reforms Office, Franchise B, March 1921, nos. 34-99).

[72] Umar Hayat was recognized by the administration as 'probably the most influential individual in the Punjab' (see GI Reforms Office, General, Deposit, Dec. 1919, no. 12: Note by H.D. Craik, 8 July 1919). For a history of the Mitha Tiwana family and of Umar Hayat's own career, see Griffin, op.cit., vol. ii, pp. 191-208.

[73] IOR/L/Parl./409B: The Reforms Committee (Franchise), p. 236: Proposals of the Punjab Muslim Association.

[74] GI Reforms Office, Franchise A, Sept. 1920, nos. 133-80, appendix iii.

[75] GI Reforms Office, General, Deposit, Dec. 1919, no. 12: Memorandum by Umar Hayat, July 1919.

soldier should be given the vote was ultimately accepted by the Secretary of State; and though his request that the military classes should be given their own representatives[76] was not accepted, men representing those interests were returned in very large numbers from the rural electorates. Finally, the political programme which he put forward, the main item of which was the stoppage of recruitment to government service of non-zemindars 'till equilibrium is restored and the aggrieved class of zemindars has got its rightful share',[77] was later to be implemented by the Muslim agriculturalist party.

A similar emphasis on the rights of the zemindars and the military classes was evident in the Reform proposals of the Punjab Zemindar Central Association,[78] and the comprehensive programme put forward by the Association was also to be significant for the future. The Association demanded government action, firstly to improve the lot of the agriculturalists and secondly to give them greater control of their own affairs. The detailed programme included, under the first head, demands for free and compulsory primary-school education, agricultural and technical education, a sixty-year land revenue settlement, subsidized irrigation, the expansion of cooperative credit, improved pay for the Indian Army, adequate representation of peasant proprietors in the legislatures, and recruitment of personnel for the Agricultural, Revenue, Canal, Police and Registration departments 'mainly from the agricultural classes'. Under the second head, demands were made that the village should be made the main unit for local self-government; that every village should have a panchayat elected by the people with powers to raise local taxes; that sanitary, educational and policing arrangements should be placed in the hands of the panchayat; and that District and Municipal Boards should be made wholly elective and freed from official control. The government noted that these demands were 'more radical in some respects than even the Congress scheme' and concluded that the programme was the product of befuddled agriculturalist thinking.[79] Under the Reformed constitution, how-

[76] GI Reforms Office, General, Deposit, Dec. 1919, No. 12: Memorandum by Umar Hayat Khan Tiwana, July 1919.

[77] Ibid.

[78] For the personnel of the deputation and the text of the programme, see Montagu papers, 35.

[79] See Montagu papers, 35: Note by the Punjab government.

ever, a large number of these demands were implemented as part of the agriculturalist party programme.

The Muslims who dominated the Punjab council under the Montagu-Chelmsford Reforms were those represented by the Punjab Muslim Association; and a large number of them were from 'families of note' who had been involved in recruitment during the War. Umar Hayat Khan Tiwana served first in the Council of State from 1920 to 1929 and then on the Secretary of State's Council during the crucial period when the 1935 Act was being framed.[80] Syed Mehdi Shah of Gojra was elected for Lyallpur South in 1920.[81] Makhdum Syed Rajan Shah of Multan sat in the Central Assembly from 1920 to 1936, and his nephew, Syed Mahommed Raza Shah, sat in the Punjab council for West Multan during the same period.[82] Raja Mahommed Akbar of Jhelum was elected to the provincial council in 1920 for West Punjab towns.[83] Captain Ajab Khan, one of the leading members of the military lobby, was nominated to the Central Assembly in 1923.[84] Captain Mumtaz Mahommed Khan Tiwana, the younger brother of Nawab Malik Mubariz Khan Tiwana,[85] was returned from Shahpur West in 1923, and Mahommed Hayat Qureshi was elected from the same seat in 1926 and 1930. Malik Khan Mahommed Khan was the member for Sheikhupura from 1923 to 1930. Karam Ilahi, a leading member of the Chatha family, was returned from Gujranwala in 1920 and his second cousin, Riasat Ali, was elected from the same constituency in 1930.[86] All these men appeared before Montagu in the Punjab Muslim Association deputation.

Other leading Muslims in the legislative council after 1920 were also of a similar origin. Ahmed Yar Khan Daultana, who was elected

[80] Griffin, op.cit., vol. ii, pp. 207-8. His son, Khizr Hayat, became the second Premier of the autonomous Punjab in 1942.

[81] Mehdi Shah was recommended for the OBE in 1918 for his services to recruiting. He was largely responsible for an offer of 20 lakhs made to the government by the Lyallpur zemindars. Chelmsford papers, 21: O'Dwyer to Chelmsford, 2 Sept. 1918.

[82] For the history of the Jilani family of Multan, see Griffin, *op.cit.*, pp. 395-7.

[83] Mahommed Akbar was the chief of the Chib Rajputs of Jhelum (*ibid.*, vol. ii, pp. 243-5).

[84] For an instance of Ajab Khan's lobbying, see Chelmsford papers, 20: Ajab Khan to Chelmsford, 11 Jan. 1918.

[85] Mubariz Khan was the head of the Mundial Tiwana family of Shahpur (Griffin, op.cit., vol. ii, pp. 218-20). He was awarded the CBE for his services during the War.

[86] Griffin, op.cit., vol. ii, pp.120-3.

from East Multan in 1920 and 1926 and from the Moslim landholders constituency in 1930, had an estate of 45,000 acres in that district.[87] Alan Khan, the member for Dera Ghazi Khan from 1920 to 1923, came from the well-known Drishak family.[88] Sardar Jamal Khan who represented the Baluch tumandars throughout the period of the Montagu-Chelmsford Reforms was President of the Chiefs' Jirga in that district after the death of Sir Behram Khan in 1923.[89] Chaudhuri Fazl Ali, who represented Gujrat West from 1920 to 1923 and Gujrat East from 1923 to 1936, was one of the leading landowners of the district.[90] Firoz Khan Noon, who represented Shahpur West from 1920 to 1923 and Shahpur East from 1926 to 1936 and who became Minister for Local Self-Government in 1927 and Minister for Education in 1931, came from the Noon family of Mitha Tiwana, a related branch of Umar Hayat's clan.[91] Karimullah Khan and his brother Nawab Major Talib Mehdi Khan, who were elected from Jhelum in 1920 and 1926 respectively, were both senior members of the Darapur branch of the Janjuah tribe.[92] Mahommed Abdullah Khan, elected from Muzaffagarh in 1920 and 1923, was one of the main zemindars of that district.[93] Mahommed Saifullah, the member for Mianwali from 1920 to 1930, came from the wellknown Isakhel family,[94] and Khan Sahib Malik Muzaffar Khan, who succeeded him, was the eldest son of the chieftain of the Bhachar tribe.[95] K.B.

[87] Purushotamdas Thakurdas papers (Nehru Memorial Museum, New Delhi) 362: Thakurdas to NR and Company Limited, Bombay, 25 July 1946. Daultana met Thakurdas at Murree in the summer of 1946 and asked for his help in setting up a cotton-ginning factory on his estate.

[88] Griffin, op.cit., vol. ii.

[89] Ibid., vol. ii, pp. 417-21. For an account of Dera Ghazi Khan in the early years of the twentieth century, see Sir Malcolm Darling, *Apprentice to Power* (London 1966), pp. 45-132.

[90] Griffin, op. cit., vol. ii, pp. 188-90. Fazl Ali provided 1,500 recruits during the War and was awarded the MBE.

[91] Firoz Khan Non was educated at Wadham College, Oxford. He was subsequently Indian High Commissioner in London (1936) and Chief Minister in the post-Partition Punjab Government (1953), Ibid., vol. ii, pp. 232-5; see also Firoz Khan Noon, *From Memory* (Lahore 1966).

[92] Griffin, op.cit., vol. ii pp. 262-5. Almost all the men in this family had served in the Army.

[93] Ibid., vol. ii, pp. 401-2.

[94] Ibid., vol. ii, p. 346.

[95] Ibid., vol. ii, p. 357.

Malik Mahommed Amin of Shamsabad, the member for Attock from 1926 to 1936, was the head of the Awan tribe and was awarded the OBE for his services to recruiting.[96] Finally, Sikunder Hayat Khan, who was elected from Attock in 1920 and 1923 and from the Punjab landholders constituency in 1926, and who became Revenue member in 1929, Acting Governor in 1932 and the first Premier of the autonomous Punjab in 1937, came from a zemindar family of Wah with great military and administrative traditions. His grandfather had marched with Nicholson to Delhi in 1857 and he himself had been commissioned during the War. His brother, Liaquat Hayat, began life in the police service and was responsible for detecting the leaders of the Ghadr Conspiracy. He later became Prime Minister of Patiala. His cousin, Muzaffar Khan, after a distinguished service in the Political Department, became Director of Information in the Punjab Government in 1924, Reforms Commissioner in 1929 and Revenue member in 1935.[97] This was the only family to rival the influence of the Tiwanas in the period between 1920 and 1947.

In the period after 1920, these Muslim zemindars formed the backbone of the agriculturalist party. But they worked very closely with the agriculturalists of other communities and particularly with the Hindu Jats of the Ambala division. The two main leaders of the Hindu Jats were Chaudhuri Lal Chand and Chaudhuri Chothu Ram, both of Rohtak. In 1919, Lal Chand had been associated with Umar Hayat, and with Gujjan Singh of Ludhiana[98] in an effort to produce a united front of rural and military Muslims, Sikhs and Hindus at the time of the Joint Select Comittee,[99] and in 1920, together with Syed Mehdi Shah, Mirza Ikramullah, Captain Bhagowal

[96] Ibid., vol. ii, pp. 322-6. In recommending Mahommed Amin for the OBE, O'Dwyer informed Chelmsford that Attock had provided 14,000 men for the Army and that a 'very large proportion' had come from 'his Awan tribe'. (Chelmsford papers, 21: O'Dwyer to Chelmsford, 2 Sept. 1918).

[97] Griffin, op.cit., vol. ii, pp. 332-6. Sikunder Hayat himself was educated at Aligarh and University College, London. In the Aligarh junior school, he, the Nawab of Chhatari and Khwaja Nazimuddin shared the same dormitory. Much later they were to work together in all-India Muslim politics.

[98] Gujjan Singh was a Jat pleader of Ludhiana. He contributed 64,000 rupees to the War effort and produced 104 recruits in his own name. He was awarded the CBE in 1918. See Chelmsford papers, 21: O'Dwyer to Chelmsford, 2 Sept. 1918.

[99] GI Reforms Office, General, Deposit, Dec. 1919, 12: Telegram, Umar Hayat Khan Tiwana to the Secretary, Home Department, Government of India, 10 July 1919.

Singh and Sonah Lal, he had served on the Punjab Reforms Advisory Committee, which had produced a report criticizing the government's revised proposals for including towns under 10,000 in the rural electorates.[100] Both he and Chothu Ram had been members of the Punjab Zemindar Central Association, and both had performed huge services during the War as recruiting agents for the government. Lal Chand's 'tactful working and personal influence' were held to have been 'a great factor' in the recruitment of 20,000 Jats from Rohtak district, and he was recommended for the OBE in 1918.[101] Chothu Ram was awarded the title of *Rai Sahib* for his recruiting work.

Of the two, Chothu Ram was the earthier character. Like all those involved in the war effort, he was at pains to stress the contribution of his community and to demand that it should be given politicial rewards. Yet he was more concerned than most with practical questions. A man with a following amongst both Jat Sikhs and Hindus, and something of a guru for the small numbers of those communities who were slowly receiving education, he was a perennial wearer of khaddar and one of the earliest advocates of rural uplift. He possessed the Jat's fulsome loathing of the bania, and when the Provincial Congress Committee showed a bias in favour of the urban areas in its Reform proposals, he made plain his annoyance, though he himself was at that time President of the Rohtak District Congress.

> The Punjab Provincial Congress Committee [he wrote] has adopted a distinctly sectarian attitude in its memorandum, has wholly identified itself with the urban and commercial classes and deals with the rights and the claims of the rural population as if the latter formed no part of the Indian nation and should be content with such crumbs of political rights and privileges as their urban—shall I say—masters might be pleased to throw over to them.[102]

In the same memorandum, moreover, he showed clearly that if he had to choose between the Muslim agriculturalist and the urban Hindu his sympathies lay with the first:

> While the general urban population of Jullundur town has received a suspiciously generous treatment, the poor rural Mahommedan

[100] GI Reforms Office, Franchise B. May 1920, nos. 129-34, pp. 29-31.

[101] Chelmsford papers, 21: O'Dwyer to Chelmsford, 2 Sept. 1918.

[102] GI Reforms Office, Franchise B, May 1920, nos. 129-34, pp. 36-9: Memorandum by Chothu Ram, 10 May 1920.

population of that district seems to have been entirely lost sight of....Am I to suppose that 3,16,148 Mahommedans living in the rural tracts of the Jullundur district will go without any representation in the new council?

In this lay the seeds of the future agriculturalist combination in the council. Lal Chand, who had been associated with Umar Hayat in in 1919, was appointed Minister of Agriculture in 1924, and when he was unseated as a result of an election petition in the same year,[103] it was Chothu Ram who took his place.[104] From that year onwards, Chothu Ram became a key member of the government, and throughout the 1920s and 1930s he worked closely with the Muslim agriculturalists to implement a political programme favouring the rural areas.

If the agriculturalists benefited most from the Reforms, however, the architect of agriculturalist policy was Mian Fazli Husain, a man of strictly urban origins whose political record before 1920 made him a thoroughly unlikely candidate for the job. Though he claimed Rajput descent, and possessed a small estate in Gurdaspur district, his was essentially a 'service' family. His grandfather had served in the Sikh armies, his father had risen to the rank of District Judge, and he himself was a Cambridge graduate with a lucrative practice at the Lahore Bar.[105] In the years before 1920, like many leading lawyers, he had been a member of the Congress, and had been elected to the Morley-Minto Council from the Punjab University. This in itself was a measure of his acceptability to Hindu opinion because Hindu graduates far outnumbered Muslim graduates and he could not have been elected without their support. His political attitudes at that time were considered 'advanced' and he

[103] Hailey papers, 6A: Sir Malcolm Hailey to Sir Malcolm Seton, 17 July 1924. 'I deeply regret', wrote Hailey, 'the result of the election petition in regard to my minister Lal Chand. He was a very good fellow and though a Hindu had the support of the agriculturalist party; he was therefore able to work with the agricultural Mahommedans who form a practical majority in the council. I shall be at very great difficulty in replacing him.'

[104] Chothu Ram stood for the South-East Rohtak seat in 1920 and was defeated. Returned in 1923 from the same seat, he was appointed Minister of Agriculture in Sept. 1924. Hailey was sorry that he could not appoint a more distinguished man but Chothu Ram was ultimately to disappoint his critics.

[105] For an account of Fazli Husain's family background, his early life at Cambridge, Sialkot and Lahore, and his political activities before 1920, see Azim Husain, ***Fazli Husain, a political biography*** (Bombay 1946), pp. 1-129.

was one of the government's most prominent critics. He supported the Lucknow Pact and heartily concurred in the censure of Mahommed Shafi, the Punjab Muslim League President, who opposed it.[106] He dissociated himself from the Shafi League, formed a separate League of his own, and while the Reforms were being framed, he and his colleagues worked closely with the Congress. He appeared before Montagu as a member of the Punjab Provincial Conference deputation, and in the franchise proposals which his League laid before the Southborough Committee his desire for substantial urban representation and his opposition to residence requirements for rural seats are clearly stated.[107] He was not, it is true, unaware of the importance of representing Muslim opinion. He had played a leading role in the foundation of Islamia College, Lahore,[108] and the constitutional demands of his League were heavily laced with demands for communal concessions.[109] Yet considering his Congress sympathies, his urban bias and, more particularly, the fate of other urban Muslim politicians after 1920, his survival requires explanation.

For most urban Muslim politicians, whether of Shafi's League or Fazli Husain's League, the terms of the Montagu-Chelmsford constitution spelt political eclipse. Even before the Franchise Committee visited the Punjab, Shafi and his associates had given up hope of playing an important provincial role and had come to see their future in all-India politics. By September 1918, Shafi was working assiduously to secure a place on the Viceroy's council,[110] and in the franchise proposals of his League, significantly reborn as the All India Muslim Association, there is a strong emphasis on the distribution of seats at the Centre.[111] Nor were these calculations misconceived. None of those who appeared with Shafi before Montagu was to be elected to the provincial council between 1920

[106] Mahommed Shafi was an Arain lawyer with one of the largest practices in Lahore. His grandfather had been an artillery commander in the Sikh armies. He himself was the leading urban Muslim collaborator of the Raj in the years before 1920. An interesting insight into Shafi's social and political circle is provided by his daughter, Jehanara Begum Shahnawaz, in her autobiography, *Father and Daughter* (Lahore 1971).

[107] IOR/L/Parl./409B, p. 218.

[108] Azim Husain, op. cit., p. 78.

[109] Montagu papers, 35.

[110] J.P. Thomson papers: Diary, 14 Sept. 1918.

[111] IOR/L/Parl./409B, pp. 216-17.

and 1936, and it was at the all-India level that they were to exercise what little political influence remained to them. Shafi himself was appointed to the Viceroy's council in 1919 on the resignation of Sir Sankaran Nair,[112] and two of his colleagues were elected to the Central Legislative Assembly, Mian Abdul Hai from the East Punjab Muslim constituency in 1923 and 1926 and Mian Ghulam Bari from the West Central Punjab Muslim constituency in 1923.[113]

Fazli Husain's colleagues shared the same fate as Shafi and his colleagues. Except for Fazli Husain himself, the leading members of his group, Mirza Yakub Beg, Pir Tajuddin, Malik Barkat Ali and Khalifa Shujauddin, played no role either in the Central Assembly or in the provincial council during the Montagu-Chelmsford Reforms.[114] Like their Congress counterparts they were deprived of a constitutional role by the terms of the Reforms and though some of those with whom they were more loosely associated, men like Dr Kitchlew, Aga Mohammed Safdar and Ataullah Shah, became involved in the Khilafat movement, even this proved only a temporary panacea. Once the movement was over, they too were condemned to the wilderness. There were, of course, a number of exceptions. Sheikh Abdul Quadir and Chaudhuri Shahabuddin, both politicians of similar origins, played an important role in the Muslim agriculturalist party. Both acted as President of the Punjab council and Sheikh Abdul Quadir was Minister for Education and Revenue Member during Fazli Husain's absence from the province. Yet for these and a handful like them, a constitutional role was only possible insofar as they were prepared to work with the agriculturalist Muslims, and to that extent it involved a change of political direction.

Considering the fate of his colleagues, Fazli Husain's emergence as the architect of agriculturalist policy must be considered largely fortuitous. Though there are suggestions that he had some zemindar

[112] Chelmsford considered that Shafi had 'no moral backbone' and only appointed him when Ibrahim Rahimtoolah refused to serve. He proved, however, to be of very material help to Government. See Chelmsford papers, 5: Chelmsford to Montagu, 28 May, 18 July and 20 Sept. 1918.

[113] Another colleague, K.B. Mian Mahommed Khan, stood against Nawab Ibrahim Ali Khan of Kunjpura for the East Punjab Muslim constituency in 1920.

[114] Malik Barkat ali, the most important of these men, was to become the main supporter of the Muslim League in the Punjab in the period immediately after the introduction of provincial autonomy. See Rafiq Afzal, *Malik Barkat Ali, His Life and Writings* (Lahore 1969).

support even before the first council met,[115] his main springboard to fame and fortune was his appointment as a minister in 1921. Like most politicians of the moderate school, he had broken with the Congress in 1920 when Gandhi's policies were approved. But though at this point his political future looked very bleak, he benefited from the government's desire to appoint liberal ministers as a means of disarming the forces of non-co-operation.[116] As a result of this policy, he and Lala Harkishen Lal were appointed ministers in the Punjab, and C.Y. Chintamani and Jagat Narayan Mullah in the United Provinces. Unlike most politicians appointed at that time, however, Fazli Husain consolidated his position. Chintamani and Jagat Narayan proved too independent to work well with government, and Harkishen Lal could not command a sufficiently large following. All three failed to be reappointed after the second election in 1923. Fazli Husain, on the other hand, became the leader of the Muslim bloc in the Punjab council and was reappointed Minister for Education and Local Self-Government in 1924.[117] By contrast with the fate of his colleagues, therefore, as a minister no less than as an urban politician, Fazli Husain's success was remarkable.

Fazli Husain always maintained that his success was due to the implementation of Congress policy. 'What did I do as a Minister?' he asked a Unionist gathering in 1930. 'Nothing more than carrying out the Congress programme that had been initiated before the Reforms. I venture to assure the members of the party that they have done more in the Punjab in carrying out the Congress programme than has been done in any other part of India'.[118] In one respect he was right. The Congress had talked a good deal of the

[115] Fazli Husain was elected to the first two councils from the Muslim landholders' constituency.

[116] Fazli said later of his appointment as a minister that 'although from one point of view that time may be considered as unfavourable to the starting of responsible government, at the same time, from another point of view, it was not altogether unsuitable. We were really received by the Government with open arms.' See Mihr collection (Research Society of Pakistan, Lahore): Fazli Husain, 'Our Political Programme', a speech delivered in 1930 before leaving the Punjab to join the Viceroy's Executive Council.

[117] For Governors' comments on the strengths and weakness of these Ministers, see Reading papers (IOL/Mss/Eur. E 238) 25: Marris to Reading, 2 May and 15 July 1923, and Maclagan to Reading, 30 Aug. 1923.

[118] Mihr collection, 87:Fazli Husain, 'Our Political Programme.'

need to improve the condition of the people, and Fazli Husain's policy had been to aid the backward sections of society. 'The principle that I stand by', he told the Punjab council in March 1923, 'is the principle of helping the backward community, irrespective of their religion, be they Muslim, Hindu or Sikh.'[119] Nor was this mere propaganda. The legislation which he introduced in his first period of office to decrease official control of District and Municipal Boards and to establish largely autonomous panchayats and small-town administrations was strictly in accordance with the demands put forward by the Jat Zemindar Association in the pre-Reform period. The introduction of compulsory primary-school education and the building of dispensaries, high schools and intermediate colleges in the rural areas did not only benefit the Muslims.[120] Other communities also benefited, and on occasion their needs were supported even in the face of urban Muslim opposition.[121] Moreover, between 1926 and 1930, when Fazli Husain was Revenue Member, whilst resisting strident appeals by zemindars for large-scale reductions in land-revenue assessments and water rates, he did his best to persuade both Hailey and de Montmorency to keep the zemindars of all communities contented.[122] Like government itself, he relied on the support of those rural classes which were recruited to the Army, and in order to maintain the position of his party these men had to be appeased.

Many of his policies, however, were more exclusively to the advantage of the Muslims. In November 1921, he laid it down that places at the Lahore Medical College and at Government College, Lahore, should be distributed amongst Hindus, Muslims and Sikhs

[119] *PLC Debates,* vol. iv, 15 March 1923, p. 1318.

[120] No definitive analysis of the distribution of political patronage in the Punjab under the Montagu-Chelmsford Reforms has yet been published. But statistics on the introduction of compulsory primary education suggest that the Hindu Jats secured very favourable treatment. Another pointer to this conclusion is the increase in the number of Fazli's Hindu Jat supporters in the Punjab council after the 1923 elections. See *Indian Statuory Commission,* vol. x, *Memorandum Submitted by the Government of the Punjab* (London 1930), pp. 122 and 132; also GI Home Public 953/1924, p. 225.

[121] A motion for the establishment of a committee to report on the educational needs of zemindars was supported by all the rural Muslims, all the Sikh members and the Hindu Jats of the Ambala division but it was opposed by all the urban Hindus and by Mohorram Ali Chishti, the Muslim member for Lahore city. See *PLC Debates,* vol. ii, 25 Oct. 1921, pp. 374-5.

[122] Mihr collection, 87: Fazli Husain, 'Our Political Programme'.

TABLE 6

Muslims in the Punjab Educational and Medical Services, 1921

	Total	Muslims	Muslims %
Punjab Educational Service	74	19	25.7
Subordinate Educational Service	32	7	21.9
District Inspectors	30	11	36.7
Headmasters	40	11	27.5
Civil Surgeons	9	2	22.2
Assistant Surgeons	227	34	15.0
Sub-Assistant Surgeons	603	132	21.8
Clerks	87	18	20.7

Source: PLC Debates, vol. ii, 4 Nov. 1921, p. 509: Answers to Questions 1077 and 1078.

in the ratio 40:40:20. This was of undoubted benefit to the Muslims. They had formed only 15.2 per cent of Government College admissions in 1917-18[123] and their share of Medical College places was probably much lower.[124] Similar orders were also issued with regard to recruitment to the medical and educational services; and with similar effects, as Table 6 shows.[125] It is significant, however, that Fazli made no attempt to persuade government to apply the same quota system to the Muslim-dominated police force. In 1922, the Muslims formed forty-eight per cent of the permanent police force, fifty per cent of the temporary force, and seventy-five per

[123] *PLC Debates*, vol. iii, 10 Jan. 1922, p. 66. Answer to question 1176.

[124] Of 65 pupils who passed the first examination in Medicine in 1917, six were Muslims, and of 45 who passed the second, four were Muslims. (*Tribune*, 31 May and 3 June 1917). The B.A. results for Punjab and Delhi also told the same story. Muslims numbered five out of 34 successful candidates at St Stephen's College, Delhi; five out of 33 at Khalsa College, Amritsar; four out of 94 at Dayal Singh College, Lahore; six out of 63 at Government College, Lahore; 13 out of 71 at Foreman Christian College, Lahore; and 26 out of 26 at Islamia College Lahore. Out of a total of 411 successful candidates, 59 or 14.3 per cent were Muslims. (*Tribune*, 7 June 1917).

[125] Those who lost most heavily as a result of these orders were the urban Hindus. In 1921, in the Medical service, 66 per cent of the assistant surgeons, sub-assistant surgeons and clerks were Hindus, and in the Educational services, Hindus held 56.3 per cent of the posts in the provincial service and 51.8 per cent in the subordinate service. See *PLC Debates*, vol. ii, 4 Nov. 1921, p. 509; *Punjab Civil List 1922* (Lahore 1922), pp. 188-210.

cent of the officiating force, and the implementation of such a quota would have undermined his position with his Muslim followers.[126]

The same concern for communal advantage also lay behind the terms of the Municipal Amendment Act of 1923. Between 1917 and 1920 the Punjab Government itself had greatly increased the number of municipalities which possessed communal electorates and the percentage of Muslim seats rose from forty to forty-four per cent during those years. As a result of Fazli's Bill, however, the Muslims improved their position still further. The Bill itself redistributed seats where communal electorates already existed and redrew electoral boundaries where joint electorates were still in operation. The criterion for this redistribution of power was the mean difference between voting strength and population strength and as such it was calculated to benefit the numerically preponderant Muslim community at the expense of the educationally and economically superior Hindu community. The statistics for the changes which took place, however, do not give an entirely clear picture of the impact of the legislation. In the forty-one municipalities where joint electorates had previously existed, the balance of power remained unchanged in thirty-three cases, and the redrawing of electoral boundries benefited the non-Muslims in two cases and the Muslims in one case. Where election was introduced for the first time, six municipalities were given non-Muslim majorities and only two Muslim majorities. In the most important municipalities, however, where communal electorates already existed, the Muslims did derive the greatest benefit. In eighteen out of thirty-eight of these municipalities the Muslims gained seats, whereas the non-Muslims gained seats in only five; and in seven municipalities, including Lahore and Ambala, the Muslims gained majorities or equalities, whereas the non-Muslims gained majorities in only two. Where municipal power was most substantial, therefore, the Muslims benefited most, and by 1930 their share of the total number of municipal seats had risen from forty-four to forty-nine per cent.[127]

The reality of power in the Punjab council was made very clear

[126] It is also significant that British officials, while supporting Fazli's efforts in other departments, rejected an urban Hindu demand to this effect in 1922. See *PLC Debates*, vol. iii, 10 Jan. 1922, pp. 61-2.

[127] *Indian Statutory Commisssion (ISC)*, vol. x (London 1930), p. 141.

in March 1923 when Raja Narendra Nath,[128] the leader of the urban Hindu bloc, moved for a cut in Fazli Husain's salary as a protest against his policies. He complained that insufficient weightage had been given to minorities in the Panchayat Act, the Municipal Act and the District Board Act. And he alleged that the effect of the policy of communal representation in the services was to replace competent Hindus by incompetent Muslims.[129] Against both these charges Fazli Husain defended himself most eloquently. He showed that he had supported many of his policies even before he became a minister, and he defended the policy of reservation both by reference to individual cases and in terms of his general desire to aid the backward. With regard to his local-government legislation, moreover, he held that he had implemented one principle throughout the province and that whilst Muslims had gained in the west, Hindus had gained in the east.[130] The voting on Raja Narendra Nath's motion, however, was very instructive. Apart from Lala Harkishen Lal and Sundar Singh Majithia, both of whom held official posts, the only non-Muslim to support Fazli Husain was L.K. Rallia Ram, a nominated Christian. Twenty-three Sikhs and Hindus supported Narendra Nath's motion and forty-seven Muslims and British officials opposed it. It was defeated by twenty-three votes to fifty. In the last resort, therefore, even Fazli's Hindu Jat supporters were reluctant to side with him in a confrontation with the Hindu and Sikh blocs.[131] It was the Muslim bloc on which he ultimately relied and, because this bloc was the most substantial bloc working the Reforms, it was the Muslims who obtained the maximum amount of official support. After 1920, therefore, the Muslim interest in the Punjab grew and prospered, and Fazli's party was soon the most powerful Muslim constitutional party in the sub-continent.

[128] For the history of Narendra Nath's family and his own career, see Griffin, op.cit., vol. i, pp. 271-80. Though he came from one of Lahore's most respected families and possessed 'an inherited sympathy with the big landlords', Narendra Nath was recognized as the leader of the urban Hindus throughout the 1920s and 30s. This was a measure of their dependence on the protection of the Raj after 1920.

[129] *PLC Debates,* vol. iv, 13 March 1923, pp. 1274-7.

[130] *PLC Debates,* vol. iv, 15 March, 1923, pp. 1313-20.

[131] Chaudhuri Bans Gopal, Chaudhuri Lajpat Rai and Chaudhuri Ghasi Ram voted against Fazli Husain. Chaudhuri Lal Chand and Chaudhuri Daya Ram abstained (ibid., vol iv, p. 1320).

CHAPTER 2

The Growth of Communalism and the Polarization of Politics

From the point of view of Hindu-Muslim relations, the period after the introduction of the Reforms stands out in stark contrast with the period which preceded it. During the War years, the Muslim League and the Congress worked together for constitutional reform, and after the War, Gandhi and the Ali brothers joined forces to preserve the Khilafat and to gain Swaraj. After the introduction of the Reforms, however, and particularly after the subsidence of the Khilafat and non-co-operation movements, communal unity gave way to communal antagonism, the fraternization of 1919 seemed an aberration, and many parts of North India were plunged into scenes of bloodshed and strife which were to have no parallel until Partition itself. Nor was this development merely of temporary significance. On the contrary, because it polarized relations between the two communities in the crucial period before the Montagu-Chelmsford constitution was reviewed, it had far-reaching implications for the future of the subcontinent. This chapter will attempt to explain, therefore, why communalism became so rampant and how it affected the chances of political agreement between the two communities at the all-India level.

It is not possible within the scope of this study to investigate the causes of communal tension on an all-India scale. Yet, as Table 7 shows, except in 1926, when the statistics were adversely affected by three bouts of intensive rioting at Calcutta, over fifty per cent of those dead or injured between 1923 and 1927, and a considerably higher proportion in the first two years, were victims of riots in the Punjab, the United Provinces and the two administrations most closely connected with them, the Frontier and Delhi. This survey will deal, therefore, with the communal situation in those two provinces, the one a Muslim majority province and the other a Muslim minority province. The experience of Muslims in these provinces was not identical with that of Muslims elsewhere, but insofar as the growth of communalism related to the constitutional status of the community the evidence from these two provinces is of more general significance.

TABLE 7

Deaths and injuries in communal disturbances by province 1923-1927

Province	1923 D.	1923 I.	1924 D.	1924 I.	1925 D.	1925 I.	1926 D.	1926 I.	1927 D.	1927 I.
Frontier	0	0	36	145	0	0	0	0	0	0
Punjab	1	83	0	0	0	35	17	90	39	289
U.P.	14	335	19	312	6	182	1	21	39	384
Delhi	0	0	16	150	1	56	4	114	3	79
Bombay and Sind	0	0	0	20	2	115	1	49	10	320
B and O	0	0	1	34	0	0	2	34	14	84
Bengal	0	0	0	6	1	9	151	1,490	22	50
CP	2	18	14	91	3	40	0	7	20	173
Madras	0	0	0	0	0	0	0	0	1	7
Grand Total	17	436	86	758	13	337	176	2,207	148	1,386
Punjab/Delhi Frontier/U.P.	15	418	70	607	7	273	22	233	81	752

Source: ISC, vol. iv (London 1930), memoranda submitted by the government of India and the India Office, pp. 108-20.

Communalism in the United Provinces

The growth of communal antagonism in the United Provinces may be dated from the inception of the *shuddhi* campaign directed by the Arya Samaj against the Malkana Rajputs of Agra in 1923. This is a verdict explicitly supported by a U.P. government survey of 1925[1] and it is borne out by the fortnightly reports of 1923 itself. Concern was expressed in March that the communal situation in Agra might get out of hand; by early April, the controversy had spread to the Muttra and Aligarh districts; by the end of May, incidents had been reported in Etawah, Fatehgarh, Saharanpur and Mainpuri; and by the end of August, the western divisions of the province were thoroughly inflamed. At the Moharram festival of

[1] GI Home Poll. 206/1926: Chief Secretary, U.P. Government, to Secretary, Government of India, Home Department, 2 Jan. 1925.

that month, communal antagonism was reported to have spread to the villages of Rohilkhund; and the District Magistrate of Bareilly informed the government that the utmost vigilance had been required to avert disorder.[2] Explicit evidence of the connection between this Arya Samaj campaign and the growth of communal rioting is not available. Yet the fact that those areas which were most inflamed by the campaign were the very ones where communal riots took place suggests that such a connection did exist. In 1923, the most serious outbreaks took place at Saharanpur, Shahjehanpur and Agra, and in 1924, apart from two riots at Allahabad and Lucknow, the main outbreaks took place at Muzaffarnagar, Hapur, Sambhal and Shahjehanpur.[3]

It is not the purpose of this survey to stigmatize the Arya Samaj. That was done by countless mob orators at the time. If any comment is necessary it is that the *shuddhi* movement was not unprovoked. In all probability, it was a Hindu reaction to the superior powers of mobilization demonstrated by the Muslims during the Khilafat movement. What is equally important, however, is that it appears to have been religious in origin. Swami Shraddhanand, one of its main instigators, had certainly played a prominent role in the scenes of fraternization in Delhi in 1919. But though many Hindu politicians had become disenchanted with Gandhi's policy of Hindu-Muslim unity after the Malabar disturbances of 1921, there is little evidence to suggest that any of them lent their wholehearted support to Shraddhanand in 1923. Malaviya, who was elected president of the revived Mahasabha which met at Benares in August, was outspoken in his support of *shuddhi* and offended many orthodox pandits by making them listen to the exhortations of a *chamar* from Nagpur.[4] But like Chintamani, who resigned his ministership in April 1923 and paid court to the Arya Samaj in the columns of the *Leader*,[5] he found it inexpedient to do more than flirt with the movement before the 1923 elections.

The reluctance of orthodox Hindu politicians to make political profit out of the *shuddhi* campaign was dictated by the national political situation. When Gandhi suspended non-co-operation after

[2] GI Home Poll 25/1923: United Provinces FR II March, I April, I May, II May, II June, II Aug.

[3] *ISC*, vol. iv, pp. 108-10.

[4] ***Indian Annual Register (IAR) 1923***, vol. ii (Calcutta 1924), pp. 130-3 and 139.

[5] GI Home Poll. 25/1923: U.P. FR I June 1923.

the Chauri Chaura incident, Congress ranks became divided with regard to future policy. One faction led by Gandhi's lieutenants, Vallabhbhai Patel, Rajendra Prasad and Rajagopalacharya, advocated the continuation of non-co-operation outside the councils. Another, led by C.R. Das and Motilal Nehru, who formed the Congress-Khilafat Swaraj Party, advocated entering the councils with a view to bringing them to a standstill. This was the main debate in the Congress between April 1922 and September 1923, and Malaviya and Chintamani found themselves firmly on the side of Nehru and Das. They undoubtedly wished, as Chintamani's acceptance of a ministership demonstrates, to work the councils rather than to bring them to a standstill, but they were aware of the pressure of nationalist opinion and they worked on the principle that half a loaf was better than no bread at all.

This preference for the policy of Nehru and Das involved a compromise over communal questions. Both Nehru and Das, as the title of their party showed, were basing their council-entry programme on the same political alliance with the Khilafatists which Gandhi had fostered during the non-co-operation movement, and for Malaviya and Chintamani to have lent their wholehearted support to the Arya Samaj would have been to create communal divisions within the council-entry party at a time when it needed to be strengthened. A more important factor, however, was that Nehru and Das were in the ascendant. At the municipal elections of 1923 their Congress-Swaraj party had been voted into power at Lucknow. Allahabad, Benares, Kanpur, Aligarh and Bareilly; and in Allahabad, Malaviya and Chintamani's home town, Motilal's son, Jawaharlal, had been elected chairman of the Municipal Board.[6] Whilst Malaviya and Chintamani flirted with the Arya Samaj in the period before the 1923 elections, therefore, they showed themselves most anxious of all to come to terms with Nehru.[7] They knew how well-positioned he was and they feared for their survival if they did not keep on good terms with him.

Their anxiety to win their way into Nehru's favour, however, was not reciprocated. Nehru was anxious to keep them in hope but he had no intention of coming to terms with them. Indeed, before the

[6] GI Home Poll. 25/1923: U.P. FR II March and I April 1923.

[7] Ibid., U.P. FR I July, I Aug. and I Sept. 1923.

provincial election took place, he was confident of superseding Chintamani's Liberal Party completely.[8] As soon as the elections were over, however, it became clear that his party would not be able to bring the council to a standstill. Out of 100 elected seats, the Mahommedans and landholders won fifty-one, the Swarajists thirty-one, the Independents seven, and the Liberals, Progressives and Europeans four each.[9] Even with the support of all the other parties, therefore, the Swarajists were not strong enough to defeat the landlord-Muslim combination. In January 1924, a motion of no-confidence in the government was defeated without official support,[10] and in March 1924, the only Budget demand to be rejected, the Land Revenue demand, was only rejected because the Swarajists obtained an accession of landlord support.[11] By the spring of 1924, therefore, it had become clear that the policy of non-co-operation within the U.P. Council would only be of limited success, and for those like Malaviya and Chintamani, who were anxious to use the Reforms for the advantage of the Hindu party, the time had come for a reappraisal of their political strategy.

To plot the connection between political ambitions at the provincial level and the growth of communal antagonism in the localities is too ambitious a project to receive detailed attention here. Not only is evidence of local disputes in poor supply but what is known of provincial political networks suggests that they were limited in influence, and poorly co-ordinated.[12] Whilst co-ordination was poor, however, local and provincial politicians did share common interests. The same Swarajist party which had been returned to the provincial council had secured control of the largest municipalities in the previous municipal elections, and local control and provincial success were clearly interrelated. Any party endeavouring to undermine the position of the Swarajists at the provincial level, therefore, would obviously encourage their opponents in the locality. More-

[8] Ibid., U.P. FR II Nov. 1923.

[9] GI Home Public 953/1924: Tgm Chief Secretary, U.P. Government, to Secretary, Government of India, Home Department, 22 Dec. 1923.

[10] GI Home Poll. 25/1924: U.P. FR II Jan. 1924.

[11] *Ibid.*, U.P. FR I March, 1924.

[12] See, for example, All India Congress Committee (AICC) papers (Nehru Memorial Museum and Library, New Delhi) 9/1925: Motilal Nehru to G.B. Pant, 15 Aug. 1925. In this letter, Nehru discloses that he had reliable agents in only thirteen districts outside Allahabad.

over, because the same political alliance of Hindus and Muslims had been successful in both spheres, both local and provincial networks could be undermined by the same methods. A wedge driven between Hindu and Muslim Swarajists in the locality was also a wedge driven between the two communities at the provincial level. Evidence for this sort of manipulation is not plentiful but the communal situation at Allahabad and Lucknow was watched with particular care by the authorities and the reports on the riots which took place in these two centres provide an interesting insight into the methods which were later to be used by the same politicians at the provincial level.

The evidence for the connection between political ambition and the stimulation of communal antagonism at Lucknow comes from very detailed reports on the situation in that city during and after the communal riot of September 1924. That riot, which broke out on 12 September over a dispute regarding the regulation of prayers in Aminabad park, led to two deaths and 163 injuries. It did not compare in magnitude with the Saharanpur or Allahabad riots of the same year but its political implications were nonetheless far-reaching. The political battle which raged round the *arti-namaz* controversy was to dominate local politics in Lucknow throughout the 1920s and 30s.[13]

The extent to which the politicians were responsible for provoking the riot is uncertain. Both Hindus and Muslims had said their prayers in the Aminabad park for many years, and the development which intensified religious feeling was the increasing Muslim attendance at evening prayers. Attempts to produce an amicable settlement failed and an order under section 144 had to be passed by the District Magistrate. This was followed shortly afterwards by an attack on a Muslim shop and from that point the riot spread.[14] The situation never got out of control but it was necessary to station two squadrons of cavalry in the troubled areas and it was some days before the situation returned to normal.

Though there is no direct evidence of political provocation, the

[13] For information on the working of the same political factors in 1927-28, see GUPGAD 503/1927.

[14] GUPGAD 479/1924: Cassels, Commissioner of Lucknow, to Lambert, Chief Secretary, U.P. Government, 13 Sept. 1924.

Commissioner laid the responsibility for the riot at the Hindu door.

As I read the events [he wrote] the Hindus have really been the aggressors. In January 1924, there was the incident of the Alambagh temples. The Hindus seized a very good opportunity presented to them by the mistake of the Railway and the Hindu Sabha asserted itself successfully in the eyes of the world. All no doubt part of the aggressive *shuddhi* and *sangathan* movements—both of them in their objects anathema to the orthodox Hindus but still used by these same orthodox Hindus for political purposes. Then came the Amethi incidents. In the building of one of the two temples in dispute a few months ago the Hindus were really the provocative party: though the Muslims gave themselves away by their desecration of the other temple. Blowing of *sankhs* by Hindus during the *tazia* procession may also have occurred. Then came the *Ram Dol* incidents at Amethi. Ruttledge made a concession to the Hindus. Thereupon the Muslims got up and threatened and were only held back by the troops being warned. Then the *Ram Dol* incidents in Lucknow cantonment carried through in the end by the Hindus with much blare and noise. Then at last the dispute about Muslim prayers and Hindu *puja* and the time for each. Hindu leaders would not agree. Hence an order under section 144. Then the Hindus held their meeting in a *dharamsala*. Inflammatory speeches no doubt: and then disorder got going, the Hindus starting it. The Muslims retaliated and won all along the line, the Hindus getting panic-stricken and sending continuous calls for assistance. Now panic is slowly disappearing and 'leaders' are re-emerging.[15]

This Hindu provocation was undoubtedly related to the political situation in the municipality. Even during the riot itself it was noted that Narayan Swami, a leading Hindu agitator, was living in the house of Raja Sir Rampal Singh, and this suggested to the officials that Rampal Singh's political ambitions were being furthered by the Swami's activities.[16] In the aftermath of the riot, however, more substantial evidence was forthcoming. The Hindu party unearthed a bye-law which forbade the use of the Aminabad park for any purposes except recreation, and Dr Laksmi Sahai, one of the Hindu party leaders, called for its enforcement at a meeting of the Municipal Board.[17] This was an attempt to divide the Hindu Swarajists from their Muslim colleagues, and the majority party, unwilling to

[15] GUPGAD 479/1924: Cassels to Lambert, 16 Sept. 1924.

[16] Ibid., Cassels to Lambert, 18 Sept. 1924.

[17] Ibid., Cassels to Lambert, 10 Nov. 1924.

see such a development, refused to accept the doctor's suggestion. This refusal, however, merely served to intensify the Hindu campaign against the Swarajists,[18] and communal relations deteriorated still further.

This intensification of communal feeling tended to obscure the political manipulation which lay behind it but it was clear to the Commissioner, as it was to Swarajists themselves, that 'party jealousy between Liberals and Swarajists amongst the Hindus has much to do with it.'[19] The most perspicacious comment on the affair, however, came from 'a Hindu', undoubtedly a Congressman, who wrote to the *Indian Daily Telegraph* on 8 November. The basic point, as far as he was concerned, was that 'the defeated members of the last Board are leading the present movement in almost every ward'.

> In plain words there is little doubt that an electioneering campaign is surging behind the veil of *Arti* and *Namaz.* But nay, this is not yet the worst phase. Sermons are openly being preached against Swaraj and non-cooperation. The movement is being knowingly confused with personalities. Strange logic is being used in heaping all sorts of abuses upon Congressmen because Congressmen are thought to have failed in their duty at the last meeting of the Board. The *Amanists* of Lucknow are striving heart and soul to turn the Municipal Board into an arena for communal strife meaning thereby to kill two birds with one stone, i.e., exalting their position and aiming a death blow at the future hopes of Hindu-Muslim unity in this unfortunate city.[20]

Nor was this campaign unsuccessful. Mr Gwynne, the new District Magistrate, succeeded in December in persuading the two parties to agree to a settlement but feelings continued to be embittered and in the municipal elections of late 1925 every Swarajist lost his seat.[21]

Much the same sort of political analysis can be made of the communal situation at Allahabad. There Nehru and Malaviya confronted each other on their own home ground. Nehru's party had been victorious in the municipal elections of 1923, and Malaviya's party exploited religious passion as a means of displacing their oppo-

[18] Ibid. 'This has given offence to the militant Hindus, especially Dr. Kaiker, the Secretary of the Hindu Sabha, who is asking what the Hindu members are doing. The inevitable cry is sack the lot.'

[19] Ibid.

[20] *Indian Daily Telegraph,* 8 Nov. 1924 (enclosed GUPGAD 479/1924).

[21] GI Home Poll. 112/1925: U.P. FR I Dec. 1925.

nents. The first serious communal incident was the *Ram Lila* riot of 1924, which had its origins in the blowing of a *sankh* in front of the Colonelgunj mosque when the *azan* was being sounded. The bad feeling which this occasioned was further exacerbated by a provocative Hindu demonstration in front of the Jumma Musjid on the first day of *Dusehra* and, before that festival was over, Allahabad was rocked by a riot in which twelve were killed and over one hundred injured.[22] It cannot be claimed authoritatively that the Malaviyas were responsible for this riot but the circumstantial evidence against them is strong. They were the most virulent of all the Hindu groups in the city and it seems likely that the exclusion of Muslim musicians from the *Ram Lila* celebration was their work. This was a crucial predisposing cause of the riot. The part played by Muslim musicians in earlier celebrations had ensured that music was not played before mosques, and to the District Magistrate their exclusion seemed a clear indication that the Hindus intended to be provocative.[23] Nor was his judgement wrong, for the incidents which provoked the riot were of precisely this character. Further evidence against the Malaviyas is also provided by their behaviour once the riot was over. When Zahur Ahmed and Purushotamdas Tandon made a tour of the bazaars in an attempt to secure a return to normality they received assurances from the *mukhyas* of almost all the *mohallas* that the people were calm and that prospects were good. When they reached the Malaviya stronghold, however, they met with a very different reception:'...they were received with a volley of foul abuse by the Malaviyas and told that if he [Zahur Ahmed] and the other Mahommedans had not been in the company of Srijut Purushotamdas they would have killed them and been glad to get it done.'[24] The Malaviya family, indeed, did their best to prevent the restoration of normal relations. 'There are no signs of reconciliation', wrote the District Magistrate. 'Conversations between even respect-

[22] GUPGAD 613/1926: Crosthwaite, the District Magistrate, provided this information in a survey of *Ram Lila* troubles at Allahabad written for the Chief Secretary's benefit on 10 Oct. 1926.

[23] Ibid. Crosthwaite informed the Chief Secretary that Knox, the District Magistrate in 1924, had written in the DM's Confidential notebook: 'Muslims were not employed to play music in the procession this year for fear that they should stop playing of their own accord in front of mosques.'

[24] GUPGAD 520/1924: Knox, District Magistrate, to Alexander, Commissioner, Allahabad division, 9 Oct. 1924.

able members of the two communities generally end in recriminations and the Malaviya tribe is especially virulent.[25] Moreover when the Unity Conference called at Delhi after the Kohat riot offered prospects of peace at the national level, the local Hindu Sabha, of which the Malaviyas were the leading lights, lessened the chances of any benefit accruing to Allahabad by passing a resolution to the effect that it would not be bound by the conference's decisions.[26]

In all these reports from 1924 little mention is made of political ambitions but by the time of the *Ram Lila* in 1925 these ambitions had become a good deal more evident. The municipal elections were only a matter of weeks away and communal antagonism was clearly being aroused in order to secure the defeat of the Swarajists at the polls. The controversy of 1925 centred on the *Ram Lila* procession and the increasingly hoary question of music before mosques. The Hindus refused to guarantee that the procession would be over before the sunset prayers and they would not agree to stop the music if the procession was still in progress. The District Magistrate persuaded the Muslims to close fifteen out of the seventeen mosques on the route if the Hindus would guarantee to allow no music before the two remaining mosques, but the Hindus were not even prepared to accept this stipulation.[27] The District Magistrate was thus obliged to issue an order under section 144 and the Hindus responded to this order by calling off the *Ram Lila* altogether. No riot ensued, as it almost certainly would have done without the order, but the communal temperature rose and the relations between the two communities became increasingly polarized.

All the officials agreed that the Malaviyas were at the bottom of this incident. 'The Malaviya family have deliberately stirred up the Hindus and this has reacted on the Muslims', wrote Crosthwaite, the District Magistrate.[28]

Mr Crosthwaite [wrote the Commissioner] has been more than reasonable in his attitude to the Malaviya family and he had done

[25] Ibid., Knox to Alexander, 12 Oct. 1924.

[26] GUPGAD 520/1924: Alexander to Lambert, 19 Oct. 1924.

[27] GUPGAD 680/1925: Report by Crosthwaite on the proceedings of a joint Hindu-Mussulman committee held at the Collector's house on Saturday, 5 Sept. 1925.

[28] Ibid., Crosthwaite, District Magistrate, to Smith, Commissioner, 14 Sept. 1925.

all that any one could possibly do to avert strife but they are bent on extremes. I had a visit from them and they were clearly against any *modus vivendi.*[29]

Why were they against any *modus vivendi*?

To a very large extent [wrote the Commissioner] the whole movement has been political, with a view to its result on the coming elections. In addition to a display of their stalwart Hinduism, the Malaviya party evidently wanted a passage of arms with Government, and when they found that Crosthwaite refused to be bounced they decided to shirk the ultimate issue and have cancelled the processions. In my opinion they have come very badly out of the affair.[30]

Yet though the Commissioner saw the Malaviyas in a bad light he was the first to admit that their tactics had succeeded admirably in cowing their opponents.

A lamentable feature [he wrote in the same letter] is that out of all the well-known public men and prominent politicians among the Hindu community of Allahabad, not one has had the courage to stand up and point out the danger or folly of the attitude taken up by the Malaviya party.

Nor indeed were they likely to take up such a position when their electoral position was at stake. What was the value in being conciliatory to either the government or the Muslims when the community itself was up in arms againt them? Yet though other Hindu leaders were cowed into silence, the Malaviyas were the main beneficiaries. Even at the time of the *Ram Lila* dispute the District Magistrate had been convinced that their motive was 'to show the Nehru family that they do not rule the Allahabad Hindus'[31] and in this ambition they amply succeeded. In the municipal elections of 1925, the Swarajists were almost totally eliminated and the Malaviya family resumed control of the Municipal Board.[32]

Malaviya's decision to turn to the exploitation of communal differences in 1924 and 1925 appears to have been as related to the provincial and national political situation as his reluctance to accept

[29] GUPGAD 680/1925: Smith, Commissioner, to Alexander, Chief Secretary, 14 Sept. 1925.

[30] Ibid., Smith to Alexander, 19 Sept. 1925.

[31] GI Home Poll. 112/1925: U.P. FR I Sept. 1925.

[32] Ibid., U.P. FR I Dec. 1925.

such a policy in the period before the 1923 elections. He was unable to act in support of his interests as long as his opponents were likely to acquire kudos in the localities by their efforts at the provincial and national level. Once it became clear that the Swarajists were unable to make any provincial gains, however, the time was ripe to move against them, first at the municipal level, because the municipal elections were to take place before the provincial elections, and next at the provincial level. It was always possible, of course, that they might redeem themselves at both these levels by a spectacular success at the national level. The possibility was not great—because the Raj was unlikely to give way to national pressure when the provincial situation was turning in its favour. But it was a sufficient argument for caution and it was only when the Swarajist initiative had failed demonstrably at the national level that Malaviya openly advocated a communalist platform outside his own municipality.

In the growth of communalism in the U.P. the part played by the Muslims was a secondary one. Their powers of mobilization may have sparked off the Arya Samaj campaign and that campaign in its turn did undoubtedly galvanize the maulvis into action. But what created a permanent state of communal tension in the province was not the evangelical zeal of Hindu and Muslim religious leaders but the political rivalries of the Swarajists and Liberals. The lurid pictures of an all-devouring Muslim leviathan conjured up by such intelligent men as Malaviya and Chintamani bore almost no relation to the Muslim position as a minority community with only thirty per cent of the elected representation in the council. They bore a great deal of relation, however, to the reality of power within the Hindu community itself. Such propaganda exercises must be seen, therefore, as a means of outmanoeuvring the Swarajists rather than as a response to a Muslim challenge. The implications for Muslim politics, however, were no less serious. It was one thing to set the communal bandwagon rolling downhill: it was quite another to arrest its progress in full motion.

Communalism in the Punjab

Communal rioting in the Punjab was never as extensive as in the United Provinces. Until 1926 fewer people were killed or injured, and even after 1926 those riots that did take place were largely confined to the urban centres. There was a serious riot at Multan during Moharram in 1922, a further riot in the same city in April 1923 and another at the same festival in 1927. Amritsar witnessed two riots in April and May 1923, Panipat two riots in July 1923 and August 1925, Rawalpindi a major communal outbreak in June 1926, and Lahore a mammoth conflagration in May 1927. Outside these centres, however, no serious riot took place and only two other riots, in Ludhiana and Gurgaon, receive any official mention.[33]

The number of towns affected by riots, however, provides little indication of the depths of communal tension. The Punjab, indeed, had the worst reputation for communalism of any province in India, and in the urban areas the relations between Hindus and Muslims became implacably hostile at a very early stage. When C.R. Das, Motilal Nehru, Sarojini Naidu, Kalam Azad and Ajmal Khan visited the province in March 1923 in an effort to compose communal differences before the elections of that year, they found the communal situation virtually beyond hope: 'On our arrival here', ran their report, 'we found that the relations between the Hindus and Mussulmans, both educated and uneducated, were so greatly strained that each community had practically arrayed itself in an armed camp against the other.'[34] 'In fact', commented the government at the same time, 'it is generally conceded by Congress and Khilafat leaders alike that political life in the Punjab is stagnant and that for the present, at all events, Hindu-Muslim unity is out of the question.'[35] In assessing the reasons for this state of affairs, both the Congress and the government agreed that the *shuddhi* movement had been an important contributory factor, but they placed the main burden of responsibility on political manipulators.

The conclusion to which we have arrived [continued the Congress report] is that while it is true that almost the whole Hindu and Mussulman population of the Punjab is more or less affected, the reasons which apply to the so-called educated classes are entirely different from those which apply to the masses and we feel constrained to say that the latter have to no small extent been exploited by interested persons among the former for their own selfish purposes.

[33] *ISC*, vol. iv, pp. 108-10.
[34] AICC papers, 3/1923.
[35] GI Home Poll. 25/1923: Punjab FR I April 1923.

This was also the view of the Deputy Commissioner of Amritsar, who was faced with two communal riots shortly after the Congress report was completed. In his view there was no uncontrollable religious fanaticism or communal ill-will amongst the masses. Ill-will was confined to the upper middle class and to public men, and it was these elements who were responsible for introducing communal tension into the general population from above.[36] 'It is notorious', he wrote to the Commissioner of Lahore after the first riot in April, 'that excitement has deliberately been fanned by interested men of position, principally by prospective candidates at the next elections.'[37]

It is not possible within the scope of this study to investigate the individual rivalries which stimulated this sort of manipulation. It seems clear, however, that a political explanation such as has been given for the growth of communalism in the United Provinces will not fit the facts in the Punjab. There the conflict was not between two parties excluded from power by the structure of the constitution but between a Muslim majority working the Reforms and an urban Hindu minority suffering from the legislation introduced by the Muslim Minister for Education and Local Self-Government. It is, of course, difficult to lay the blame for the riots on Fazli Husain's ministerial activities but an examination of the effect on the life of the province of his most controversial piece of legislation, the Municipal Amendment Act of 1923, makes it clear that these activities did have a polarizing effect on communal relations.

The reconstitution of municipal committees which took place under the terms of the Municipal Amendment Act was chiefly to the benefit of the Muslims. No Hindu seats were lost but the provision of extra Muslim seats changed the balance of power in several municipalities and the resulting Hindu resentment was very great. As early as January 1923, the Hindus were reported to be suspicious of Fazli Husain's motives and opposed to the changes which he proposed.[38] By April, Hindu resignations were reported to be imminent and by August the whole province was affected. At Lahore, where the municipal boundary was extended to give the

[36] GI Home Poll. 25/1923: Punjab FR II May, 1923.

[37] GI Home Poll. 125/1923: Dunnett, Deputy Commissioner, Amritsar, to the Commissioner of Lahore, 18 April 1923.

[38] GI Home Poll. 25/1923: Punjab FR II Jan. 1923.

Muslims a majority, the Hindus resigned *en masse* early in June. Then followed a bitter press campaign against both Fazli Husain and Chaudhuri Shahabuddin and as the communal temperature rose the educated of each community maligned all that the other held sacred. The editor of the *Kesri* was prosecuted for alleging that the Prophet had been immoral; two Muslims were arrested for disparaging Hindu customs; and Zafar Ali, ever ready to boost his circulation by fanning the flames of dissension, urged the Muslims to take the law into their own hands.[39] Had it not been common knowledge that the Army was being held at the ready a riot would almost certainly have broken out. Even without a riot, however, Lahore had been divided into two hostile camps and communal relations elsewhere were soon similarly affected. In July, mass resignations followed at Ambala, where the Hindus had also been reduced to a minority, and at Ferozepur, where the motive was to demonstrate communal solidarity with the Lahore Hindus.[40] By August, these resignations had provoked others at Gujrat and Jhelum[41] and by October, as a result of the communal antagonism which had been aroused, there had also appeared two para-military organizations, the *Mahabir Dal* and the *Ali Gol.*[42] As a result of this one piece of legislation, therefore, the relations between the two communities were seriously affected. The use of executive powers provided by the Reforms provoked a backlash from urban Hindu interests, and from that point forward the process of deterioration assumed a momentum of its own.

That the origins of this communal tension were political is also shown by the fact that the urban Hindus sought a political solution to their difficulties. In March 1923, even before the Municipal Amendment Act had been passed, Narendra Nath had moved unsuccessfully for a reduction in Fazli Husain's salary as a protest against his communal policies.[43] When the Act was passed and took effect this opposition increased considerably. Loud demands were made that Fazli Husain should not be reappointed after the 1923 elections and when he was not only reappointed but given a

[39] Ibid., Punjab FR I June 1923.

[40] Ibid., Punjab FR I July 1923.

[41] GI Home Poll. 25/1923: Punjab FR I Aug. and I Sept. 1923.

[42] Ibid.. Punjab FR I Oct. 1923.

[43] *PLC Progs.*, vol. iv, 13 March 1923, pp. 1274-7.

colleague from amongst the agriculturalist Hindus, the majority of Hindus and Sikhs boycotted the Governor's speech at the opening of the second council.[44] They did not confine themselves, however, merely to a policy of boycott. They also brought an electoral petition against the new Minister of Agriculture, Chaudhuri Lal Chand, and succeeded by this means not only in unseating him but also in reopening the whole question of how ministerial appointments were to be made. The urban Hindus argued that ministers should be appointed to represent communities and not parties and they requested the new Governor, Sir Malcolm Hailey, to appoint Narendra Nath, who had the support of a majority of Hindu members. When discussions between Fazli Husain and Narendra Nath proved disappointing, however, Hailey decided to reject Narendra Nath in favour of Chaudhuri Chothu Ram of Rohtak, another agriculturalist Hindu.[45] This decision further alienated the urban Hindus and communal tension continued to run high.

But the urban Hindus were in a political cul-de-sac. They could find no solace in the policies of the all-India Congress leadership, whom they suspected of a desire to win over the Punjabi Muslims, if necessary at their expense; they resented Gandhi's attacks on the Arya Samaj;[46] and particularly after the Kohat riot of September 1924, as a result of which large numbers of Hindus were obliged to flee the Frontier and to take refuge in Rawalpindi, they slowly began to reorder their political priorities. The first significant evidence of this trend came in December 1924, when Gandhi visited Lahore in an endeavour to improve communal relations. On that occasion, the urban Hindus stood sternly aloof from his efforts, and Hailey, who was watching the situation carefully from Government House, saw this as an indication of a change of heart:

> It is generally felt by Punjab Hindus [he wrote to the Home Member] that Gandhi has been much too favourable to the Mahommedans, but local feeling goes somewhat further than this. It is clear that our Hindus are beginning to regret the fact that they have practically thrown the Mahommedans into the arms of Government and have begun to see that if they are to get protection as a minority it must be from Government and that they can hope for

[44] GI Home Poll. 25/1923: Punjab FR II Dec. 1923. This same policy of boycott was also extended to the municipal elections at Lahore and Ambala in March 1924.

[45] Hailey papers, 6B: Note by Hailey, 15 Sept. 1924.

[46] GI Home Poll. 25/1924: Punjab FR II June 1924.

little from the Mahommedans.[47]

This shift of political emphasis was formally approved by the Punjab Hindu Sabha in January 1925, and Malaviya, who was already opposing the Swarajists in the United Provinces, gave the new policy his blessing.[48] Though they had changed their policy towards government, however, they had done so only to improve their chances of arriving at the same end. They still wished to secure a ministership for their own party and to reduce the influence of Fazli Husain. In a memorandum written in February 1925 on behalf of the Hindu Sabha, Narendra Nath complained that Fazli Husain had been given 'mere dummies' as colleagues; he lamented the fact that the Hindu minority had been given no opportunity 'to modify, if not to eradicate the evils caused by the administration of the Mahommedan minister'; he called for the establishment of a convention whereby minorities would have some control over the appointment of ministers; and he held that the first priority for the following ten years was the eradication of the communal contagion which dominated Punjabi life. This, in his view, was far more important than the achievement of yet more political concessions. Indeed the Hindu minority would not be prepared to agree to such concessions until this work had been done: 'To introduce provincial autonomy hedged around by communalism of all sorts', he wrote, 'is to sow the seed of the plant of self-government with the seed of a pernicious creeper which will eventually destroy the plant.'[49] By 1925, therefore, the urban Hindus had not only identified the working of the political system as the cause of their communal difficulties; they had also taken a firm stand against any further political concessions until those difficulties had been removed.

The government also saw the growth of communalism in political terms, but it chose to cast itself, officially at least, in the role of spectator. In a review of the working of the Reforms prepared for the Reforms Enquiry Committee in August 1924, the Chief Secretary wrote:

It is doubtful if the Mahommedans at large or the agricultural

[47] GI Home Poll. 37/1925: Sir Malcolm Hailey to Sir Alexander Muddiman, 11 Dec. 1924.

[48] GI Home Poll. 112/1925: Punjab FR I Jan. 1925.

[49] Hailey papers, 7B: Memorandum by Narendra Nath, 18 Feb. 1925.

community were yet entirely aware of the opportunities which the ballot box would give them for developing their own interests. Certainly the authors of the scheme cannot have foreseen the speed with which its working would drive the two main communities into open dissension and would develop a declared antagonism between the urban and rural interests.[50]

Yet having disclaimed any premeditated desire to produce such a state of affairs, the Chief Secretary held that the use of executive power by the majority for its own advantage was only to be expected.

That the Minister should attempt to secure definite opportunities to the community which constitutes his chief support in the council is not in itself unreasonable; it may indeed be admitted as one of the inevitable results of the Reforms scheme. His action again could be justified on its merits, for the community was backward in education and had not so far gained in the administration a representation at all commensurate with its numbers.[51]

This statement was a defence, not only of the Mahommedan minister but also of the British administration. The authors of the constitution had given the Muslim agriculturalists the largest share of seats in the council but they had not laid down that ministers should only be selected from the agriculturalist party. Indeed in 1920, Sir Edward Maclagan had in mind a policy of communal representation.[52] There are grounds for believing, therefore, that the appointment of an agriculturalist Hindu in 1924 was prompted by more than just a concern for constitutional niceties. Hailey justified Maclagan's appointment of Chaudhuri Lal Chand because it had been made on grounds 'more constitutionally correct' than the appointment of Lala Harkishen Lal in 1921, but when he himself appointed Chaudhuri Chothu Ram in September 1924 he was clearly motivated by his opposition to the Swarajist element amongst the supporters of Narendra Nath.[53] In part this was sound tactics. There was a possibility that Lajpat Rai, who was in Europe, would withdraw his support from Narendra Nath on his return, and in that case Narendra Nath, with only seven supporters of his own,

[50] *Reforms Enquiry Committee, Views of Local Governments on the Working of the Reforms*, (London 1925), *Cmd. 2362*, p. 197.

[51] *Reforms Enquiry Committee, Views of Local Governments..., Cmd. 2362*, pp. 200-1.

[52] Chelmsford papers, 25: Sir Edward Maclagan to Lord Chelmsford, 16 July 1920.

[53] Hailey papers, 6B: Note by Sir Malcolm Hailey, 15 Sept. 1924.

would scarcely be a better choice than Chothu Ram. When Hailey informed Sir Michael O'Dwyer of his choice however, he did not justify it on these tactical grounds but more bluntly in terms of his opposition to Swarajist ideology. 'To begin with', he wrote, 'I do not care to have in the Ministry a man who owes his support to the Swarajists.'[54] Seen in this light, the government's support for Fazli Husain appears more sinister. The Punjab administration could not make the Reforms work without Muslim support but it was obviously prepared to allow Hindu noses to be rubbed in the dirt in order to teach that community a lesson. Communalism, provided that it did not lead to a community's permanent alienation from government or to political chaos from which the opponents of the Raj might benefit, was an acceptable corrective to excessive nationalist zeal.

This is shown most clearly by the government's reaction to the change of policy of the Hindu Sabha in 1925. When it had become clear that the Swarajists were losing ground and that the body politic was being divided along communal lines, Hailey began to woo the urban Hindus with political concessions. When Fazli Husain returned from Delhi where he had officiated as a member of the Viceroy's council between August and November 1925, Hailey did not reappoint him to the Ministry of Education and Local Self-Government. He gave that Ministry instead to Chothu Ram; he gave Chothu Ram's ministry to Jogendra Singh, a Jat Sikh landholder; and he promoted Fazli Husain to his own Executive Council as the Member for Land Revenue. This reshuffle was the first step towards a reconciliation with the urban Hindus and the reasons for Fazli Husain's promotion made a mockery of the constitutional arguments which had been advanced only a year before.

> His appointment [Hailey wrote to Reading] would have some advantage in removing him from the sphere of transferred subjects, in which his position as a supporter of Muslim claims has brought him under general criticism from the Hindus. One is obliged to give to a Minister a certain latitude in regard to appointment and promotion of officials, control of grants to schools and local bodies and the like which one need not give to a Member.[55]

Hailey's reshuffle was calculated to limit Fazli Husain's activities

[54] Hailey papers, 6B: Sir Malcolm Hailey to Sir Michael O'Dwyer, 19 Sept. 1924.

[55] Hailey papers, 8B: Sir Malcolm Hailey to Lord Reading, 1 Dec. 1925.

and to encourage the urban Hindus to turn more wholeheartedly to government. And this they soon began to do. In February 1926, the Hindus of Ambala and Lahore were persuaded by Chothu Ram to return to their respective Municipal Committees[56] and as the 1926 council election approached, though they campaigned along unashamedly communal lines, they satisfied the government where their attitude towards council-entry was concerned. Indeed the government's reaction to the election results was indicative of its general political outlook. Twenty-five Swarajist candidates had been set up but only two had been returned and the government quickly commented that this constituted 'an unmistakably adverse verdict on the policy of non-co-operation'.[57] The stage was therefore set for the appointment of an urban Hindu minister. Chothu Ram was dropped as Minister for Education and Manohar Lal was appointed in his place.

The arguments put forward by the government when Manohar Lal was appointed, however, illustrate the complexity of the situation in which it found itself. On the one hand, it disapproved of Swarajist ideology and was prepared to take action which was likely to encourage communalism as a means of outmanoeuvring the Swarajist party. On the other hand, the development of a communal ideology amongst the Hindu minority was no permanent guarantee that it would continue to look to government. Some form of political concession to the Hindus was essential if they were not to feel themselves permanently excluded from the political process. At the same time, to make concessions to the Hindu minority involved in some degree alienating the Muslim agriculturalist and, because they were the strongest party in the council, the government could not afford to let that happen. Hailey, therefore, decided to appoint a third minister, in charge of Local Self-Government, from amongst their ranks.

> . . . even as it is [he wrote to Muddiman] there will be a good deal of strain on their feelings and some charge that I am dropping them after depending for three years on their support; the best that I could do was to give them a Minister of a distinctly rural type. Feroz Khan, who is a barrister, is also a representative of the 'county families'.[58]

[56] Hailey papers, 9A: Chaudhuri Chothu Ram to Sir Malcolm Hailey, 7 Feb. 1926.

[57] GI Home Poll. 112/xii/1926: Punjab FR I Dec. 1926.

[58] Hailey papers, 10A: Sir Malcolm Hailey to Sir Alexander Muddiman, Jan. 1927.

Though there can be no doubt, therefore, that the government had supported what was in effect Muslim control of the transferred departments for political reasons during the second council, its capacity for manoeuvre was not what it had been before 1920. It could use its powers of appointment to ministerships as a corrective either to the nationalist zeal of the Hindus or to the communal zeal of the Muslims but it was obliged in the last resort to throw its weight behind the Muslim bloc. Though it could indulge, therefore, in any amount of sophisticated political jugglery in order to preserve its own position, it would not ultimately be capable of saving the Hindu minority from the subjection and discrimination which it feared.

Communalism and all-India Muslim politics

The effect of the communalization of provincial politics on the nature of all-India politics was not to be seen clearly until the Montagu-Chelmsford constitution was revised. Until that time, though many politicians pressed for immediate reform, the Raj's recalcitrance made it unnecessary for all parties to declare themselves. In particular, those who were enjoying the power provided by the Reforms had no reason to involve themselves prematurely in lobbying at the all-India level because they already had a share of their respective administrations and were preoccupied with the daily tasks of political consolidation. Whilst these vested interests did not participate openly in all-India politics, however, the pattern of politics produced by their activities soon influenced all-India politicians. From 1920 onwards they were the guy-ropes and pegs anchoring the Imperial balloon and no amount of hot air produced by all-India politicians at the Centre could raise the balloon whilst its was thus firmly anchored in the provinces. For an all-India confrontation with the Raj to be successful after 1920, therefore, it was not only necessary to outmanoeuvre the Raj; it was also necessary to outmanoeuvre the vested interests created in the provinces by the Montagu-Chelmsford Reforms.

In the early 1920s, the two Muslim political groups most involved in all-India politics were the Khilafatists and the Constitutionalists. Both these groups had been successful politically when they had advocated a policy of Hindu-Muslim unity and of co-operation with the Congress, and both were slowly obliged, as a result of the growth of communalism in the provinces, to veer away from this policy and to turn instead to the representation of provincial communal interests. In the second part of this chapter, the political activities of these groups in the period before the 1926 elections will be discussed. The relations of the Khilafatists with the Congress organization, however, will not receive detailed treatment. When the Khilafat movement collapsed, many Khilafatists turned to the pursuit of more local objectives and a study of their activities would pay few dividends. Even where Khilafatists remained involved in all-India politics, however, their relations with the Congress *per se* are less illuminating than their relations with their own colleagues. Even important figures like the Ali brothers had always been Khilafatists first and Congressmen second, and their control over their own organization was more important to them than their standing with the Congress. From the point of view of the measurement of the effect of the growth of communalism on the Khilafatist, therefore, it is more rewarding to study the activities of the Khilafat organization than to study the activities of individual Khilafatists within the Congress. By so doing, the trap of treating individual activities as significant in themselves is avoided and a clearer idea of the increasing isolation of the all-India politicians is obtained. Where the activities of the Constitutionalists are concerned, however, their relations with the Congress are of paramount importance. They were working, as they had done during the War years, for a devolution of power at the Centre, and co-operation with the Congress was essential to achieve that end. In a study of their activities, therefore, the effects of the growth of communalism not only on their own position but also on the Congress organization can be more accurately measured.

The fate of the Khilafatists

For the Khilafatists, the publication of the government's dispatch on the Turkish question in March 1922 was a watershed. The movement had derived much of its impetus from the fact that the British government was opposing the Turks at the Peace Conference and once it became clear that the government of India was representing the Indian Muslim position, non-co-operation seemed less justifiable. At that time, therefore, two of the main groups involved in the movement, the Bombay moderates and the ulema of North India, showed signs of a change of policy.

The moderates had been eclipsed politically as early as May 1920, and from that time forward, though they continued to render the movement invaluable financial assistance, political control had rested in the hands of the North Indian politicians and ulema. After March 1922, however, the dissociation of the moderates became complete. At a meeting of the Congress Working Committee at Ahmedabad on 17 and 18 March 1922, Mahommed Chothani, the President of the Central Khilafat Committee and the leader of the Bombay group, broke with the politicians over the attitude to be adopted to Montagu's resignation and drew upon himself the enmity of the North Indian faction.[59] Chothani, however, was not alone. Many of the most influential ulema were similarly affected by the same development. After the government's dispatch was published, Abdul Bari and Hasrat Mohani and many leading U.P. Khilafatists issued a manifesto urging Muslims to cease hostilities against the government,[60] and Abdul Bari, in a letter intended for the Viceroy's eye, declared that his opposition to the government had been solely with a view to preserving the Khilafat and that the government's changed attitude warranted a similar change on the part of the Muslims.[61] Most spectacular of all, however, was Hasrat Mohani's reaction. He had been the most virulent protagonist of independence for India and his activities had been curbed with difficulty by Gandhi at Ahmedabad in December 1921,[62] but by March 1922 he showed himself prepared to drop non-co-operation altogether[63]. By March 1922, therefore, those ulema who did remain politically active were not those who had led the movement from the beginning but the secondary leaders, men like Abdul Majid

[59] GI Home Poll. 501/1922.

[60] GI Home Poll. 501/1922: Mahommed Abdullah to Sir Mahommed Shafi, 15 March 1922.

[61] Ibid., Abdul Bari to Mahommed Abdullah, 15 March 1922.

[62] GI Home Poll. 461/1921.

[63] GI Home Poll. 501/1922: Mahommed Abdullah to Sir Mahommed Shafi, 15 March 1922.

Badauni, whose antipathy towards the Raj went deeper than their aversion to particular policies.

After March 1922, the movement began a rapid decline. Most of the leading politicians were in gaol, subscriptions began to fall off,[64] and though the government continued to be wary of any developments in Europe which might spark off a resumption of civil disobedience, it was gratified by the enhanced esteem in which it was held.[65] The only major revival of Muslim feeling took place in September and October when the British opposed the retaking of Smyrna and Eastern Thrace. At that time, a clash between British and Turkish forces seemed imminent and the Khilafatists organized a body of semi-military volunteers called the Angora legion.[66] Government fears were allayed, however, by British concessions to the Turks and the signing of an Armistice[67] and after that time the Angora legion ceased to be treated seriously. Finally, in November, the Turks themselves delivered the death-blow to the movement in India by abolishing the temporal powers of the Khalifa. This action went clean contrary to the demands of the Khilafat organization and though they rationalized the position as best they could it was a blow from which they never recovered.[68]

By the beginning of 1923, Khilafat activity had virtually come to an end.[69] The masses had lost interest; with few exceptions the ulema had dissociated themselves from the work of the Khilafat Committee; and the politicians, finding themselves to be leaders without a following, sharpened their knives for internecine war. The North Indian faction made public Chothani's embezzlement of 18 lakhs of Khilafat funds and preoccupied themselves with retrieving the money by the liquidation of his assets,[70] while Chothani's colleague, Khatri, the Treasurer of the Khilafat Committee, gave plentiful

[64] GI Home Poll. 741/1922: from March (and even earlier in some provinces) subscriptions were getting smaller and by July they were scarcely coming in at all.

[65] Reading papers (IOL MSS Eur. E 238) 5: Reading to Peel, 8 June and 5 Oct. 1922.

[66] GI Home Poll. 868/ii/1922.

[67] Bernard Lewis, *The Emergence of Modern Turkey* (London 1961), p. 249.

[68] IOR/L/P and J/6/6151/1922: a survey of Indian Muslim opinion on this question.

[69] GI Home Poll. 25/1923: Punjab FR I Jan. 1923; Bihar and Orissa FR II Jan. 1923; U.P. FR II Feb. 1923.

[70] The meetings of the Khilafat Committee at Muzafferabad on 25 April, at Bombay on 26 and 27 May, and at Bombay on 8 July were largely concerned with this issue. See GI Home Poll. 15/II, 15/III and 15/V/1923.

evidence to the Khilafat Accounts Enquiry Committee of the parasitical activities of the Ali brothers and Dr Mahmud.[71] Neither of these disclosures improved the public image of the leadership, and future efforts to raise funds were treated with justifiable cynicism. Yet though the Khilafatists were leaders without a following, they found themselves in an identical dilemma to that faced by their Congress counterparts. Were they to follow Gandhi and his lieutenants in the continued pursuit of non-co-operation outside the legislatures or were they to join the Congress-Swaraj-Khilafat party, under the leadership of C.R. Das and Motilal Nehru, in order to contest the elections and make the Reforms unworkable? Like the Congress, the Khilafat Committe was deeply divided over this issue and this added to its ineffectiveness.

The main protagonists of the 'no-change' party were the Ali brothers, Dr Kitchlew of Amritsar and Dr Mahmud of Patna. For the Ali brothers, the obstacles to a policy of council entry were the same as the obstacles to their participation in constitutional politics in the years before 1920. As individuals, they might have secured election to either the U.P. Council or the Central Assembly, yet they were too committed to non-constitutional activity to change their policy overnight, and too accustomed to straddling the subcontinent to confine themselves to being small cogs in a constitutional machine. For Dr Kitchlew, the existence of a zemindar party in the Punjab which despised his Kashmiri origins as much as he despised its consistent loyalism left him no alternative but to continue as a political activist, and for Dr Mahmud, habitual vacillation and an emotional attachment to Jawaharlal Nehru, himself a fervent no-changer, provided on this occasion, as on many others, a stumbling block to rational action. Lastly, in early 1923, when the Swaraj party was formed, all these men were in gaol and incapable for that

[71] GI Home Poll. 15/1923: The Khilafat Accounts Enquiry Committee Report. The Committee found that 50,000 rupees could not be accounted for. For a further lakh no satisfactory accounts were available. It discovered that Dr Mahmud had received 21,000 rupees for the publication of a book on *The Khilafat and England* and that only 1,600 rupees had been spent on the printing. It also discovered that most Khilafat officials travelled first class on the railways and that huge sums had been spent on taxis and entertainment. 'When the Secretary travels', ran the report, 'the cloud of bounty showers rupees on all sides, Muhajirs, deserving persons, newspapers, servants, are all fully satisfied from the fountain of generosity...'

reason of participating in the new political initiatives which were being taken.

The main protagonists of the Swarajist policy were the young men who had followed Mahommed Ali since their Aligarh days, Tassaduq Ahmed Khan Sherwani, Abdur Rahman Siddiqui, Chaudhuri Khaliquzzaman, Abdul Aziz Ansari, Khwaja Abdul Majid and Shuaib Qureshi. These men were secondary leaders; they were mostly from the United Provinces; and whether through disenchantment with the Turks produced by their activities as emissaries of the Khilafat Committee in Europe[72] or through a closer relationship with Motilal Nehru developed after the imprisonment of the Ali brothers, they supported a policy of council entry. Sherwani and Khaliquzzaman both served as secretaries of the Swaraj party from its inception in January 1923, and as they freed themselves from their Panislamic entanglements the others threw their weight behind these two men.

Somewhere between these two groups but progressively inclining to the second were Hakim Ajmal Khan, Dr Ansari and Kalam Azad. The role of Ajmal Khan and Ansari in the Khilafat movement had been strictly limited. They were men of caution, opposed to violence, reluctant to participate in mass politics and wary of the extremism of the Ali brothers and the *ulema.* At the height of the Khilafat movement they remained in the background and when they did emerge again after the imprisonment of the Ali brothers it was largely as a moderating influence, working hand-in-hand with Gandhi in an endeavour to co-ordinate the two movements under his leadership.[73] After the government's dispatch of February 1922, they continued to follow the same policy, urging both the *ulema*

[72] Shuaib Qureshi and Abdur Rahman Siddiqui were sent to university in England in 1919 but they gave up their studies to be Mahommed Ali's right-hand men in Switzerland. Shuaib returned to India and became the editor of *Young India* in Nov. 1921 and was imprisoned for his writings in June 1922. Siddiqui returned to Lausanne as an emissary of the Khilafat Committee in Oct. 1922 but his efforts to persuade the Kemalists to restore the temporal power of the Khalifa met with no success. See GI Home Poll. 60/1923 and 253/1924.

[73] See, for example, GI Home Poll. 137/1921: CID Report on the meetings of the Central Khilafat Committee and the *Jumiat ul Ulema i Hind* at Delhi on 21 and 22 Sept. 1921.

and the moderates, in the name of Hindu-Muslim unity, not to make any gesture of conciliation to the government.[74] Over the question of council entry, however, they differed. Both considered a return to civil disobedience the resort of desperate men,[75] but Ansari was more anxious than Ajmal Khan to keep both wings of the movement together. Ajmal Khan came out in favour of council entry in October 1922[76] but Ansari continued to favour the no-change party and worked to prevent party divisions from becoming deeper.[77]

After the defeat of council entry at Gaya, these differences increased. Ansari continued to support the no-changers; Ajmal Khan joined the Swarajist party and endeavoured to persuade the ulema, though with little success, to amend the *fatwa* passed in 1920 on this question.[78] In this he was aided by Kalam Azad, who had resigned from the Khilafat Committee in January 1923 when he saw that the Swarajist star was in the ascendant.[79] He had been obliged to admit by this stage that his hopes to become *Sheikh ul Hind* would not be fulfilled and he chose a broker's role instead.[80] These differences persisted until September 1923, when the Special Congress gave the green light to the Swarajists. After that time, Ansari ceased to support the no-changers and applied himself instead to the task of healing Hindu-Muslim divisions.

These differences over council entry did not entirely dominate the proceedings of the Khilafat Committee. Indeed, even after November 1922, it pursued Panislamist policies which were unani-

[74] GI Home Poll. 501/1922: Report on the Congress Working Committee meeting at Ahmedabad on 17 and 18 March 1922.

[75] After the revolutionary oratory of the Congress Committee meeting at Lucknow on 10 and 11 June 1922, Ansari and Ajmal Khan made plans to retire from political life. See GI Home Poll. 941/1922.

[76] Mahommed Ali papers (Jamia Millia Islamic Library, New Delhi): Statement by Ajmal Khan, 27 Oct. 1922.

[77] In Nov. 1922, for example, at the AICC meeting at Calcutta, Ansari opposed Nehru's motion in favour of council entry and took the lead in securing an adjournment of the discussion until the Gaya Congress in Dec. See AICC papers 8/1922, pp. 57 and 91.

[78] GI Home Poll. 25/1923: Delhi FR I Feb. 1923.

[79] Ibid., Bombay FR II Jan. 1923.

[80] For evidence of Azad's ambitions to become *Sheikh ul Hind,* see GI Home Poll. 180/1921: CID Report on the conference of Bihar ulema held at Patna on 25 and 26 June 1921.

mously supported by all factions. Reactions to the abolition of the temporal and spiritual powers of the Khalifa and to Sharif Hussain's bid for election to that office, all fall into this category. Not all Panislamist issues, however, can be disentangled from Indian issues, because particularly for the Ali brothers, the pursuit of Panislamist policies was largely dictated by their need to maintain themselves as credible Muslim leaders after the decline of non-co-operation. Their advocacy of Panislamist activities, therefore, did not always meet with widespread support. Indeed, it often brought them into conflict with those Khilafatists who wished to use the Khilafat organization for purely Indian purposes.

In 1923, the main opposition within the Khilafat Committee to its continuing preoccupation with Panislamic ventures came from the Muslim Swarajists who had joined Nehru and Das in January. These men had involved themselves in the U.P. municipal elections in March, and Khaliquzzaman and Khwaja Abdul Majid had emerged as the Chairmen of the Lucknow and Aligarh Municipal Boards.[81] This involvement in Swarajist politics made them less sympathetic to Panislamic activities. Their feeling was that the Khilafat organization should be used to strengthen the pro-change party, and this feeling grew stronger as the battle between the no-changers and pro-changers became more acute. One small indication of the emergence of this feeling was provided at the Khilafat Committee meeting at Muzafferabad in April 1923, when Khaliquzzaman and Sherwani fought with Ansari over the allocation of 12,000 rupees to Kalam Azad for propaganda in Persian and Arabic in the Khilafat cause.[82] Matters got worse, however, after the Ali brothers were released from gaol, for they proceeded to nail their colours firmly to the Khilafat mast and to plan three deputations to the Middle East. This escapist political thinking won them few friends among the Swarajists, and at Coconada in December the differences between the two groups came to a head. Khaliquzzaman led the Swarajists in an attack on the Ali brothers' proposals for three deputations, holding that one would be quite sufficient, and when this attack failed, he, Shuaib Qureshi and Abdul Aziz Ansari refused to stand

[81] GI Home Poll, 25/1923: U.P. FR II March 1923.

[82] GI Home Poll. 15/ii/1923: CID Report on AIKC meeting at Muzafferabad, 25 April 1923.

for election as secretaries of the organization.[83] By this stage, the political rift between the Ali brothers and their former *chelas* was virtually complete.

But the Ali brothers were not only faced with opposition from their former followers. They also had to face a Muslim community throughout North India which was becoming less interested in the problems of Turkey and more preoccupied with the growth of communal tension in its own back yard. By June 1923, communal feeling in the U.P. was already intense, and on the eve of Mahommed Ali's release from prison, rumours were rife that he would respond to this situation by breaking with the Congress and by leading an anti-*shuddhi* campaign.[84] Consequently, when he turned a blind eye to these developments and plunged himself into Middle East affairs, there was much disappointment and opinion hardened against him. The Moradabad Municipal Board decided in July by the casting vote of the Chairman not to present him with an address,[85] and though the Aligarh and Lucknow Boards did so in September and October he met with a very poor reception in both places. At Lucknow, where he campaigned for the freedom of the *Jazirat ul Arab,* he only collected fifty rupees for his projected deputations, and at Jhansi, whither he proceeded the following day, he was 'so chagrined' by his reception at the railway station 'that friends had some difficulty in persuading him to proceed to the city to receive the address.'[86] By the end of 1923, therefore, it had become clear that the fortunes of the Ali brothers were in decline. The Panislamic questions with which they were concerning themselves were only of peripheral appeal to the masses, and it was not to be long before the rise of communal antagonism in the provinces began to erode their control of the Khilafat organization.

In 1924, after their successes in the elections, the Swarajists took less interest in the affairs of the Khilafat Committee, and the main opposition to the Ali brothers came from the Punjabi Khilafatists under the leadership of Dr Kitchlew. His Amritsar Khilafat party

[83] GI Home Poll. 253/1924: CID Report on the Khilafat conference at Coconada, 26 Dec. 1923. Dr Mahmud, who had become depressed at the poor response to his Khilafat tours, also refused to stand.

[84] GI Home Poll. 25/1923: U.P. FR II June 1923.

[85] Ibid., U.P. FR II July 1923.

[86] Ibid., U.P. FR II Oct. 1923.

had sided with the no-changers in the debate over council entry, but as communal tension increased, Kitchlew was obliged to become more communal himself. Even in 1923 there had been a split in the Punjab Khilafat Committee over the *shuddhi* movement,[87] but at that stage Kitchlew had worked hard to reduce communal tension[88] and to revive non-co-operation by forming a united front with the Akalis.[89] What he lost by these endeavours, however, was considerably greater than what he gained. The Muslims of Amritsar were offended by the introduction of Akalis into their mosques[90] and in the early months of 1924, in the face of waning support for his policies,[91] Kitchlew was obliged to give up his hopes of an alliance with the Akalis and to concentrate on constructive work amongst his own community.

The plans which he initially put forward were not of a communal character but his ambitions were clearly political and he met with opposition from both the Swarajists and the Panislamists on this score. The Swarajists did not relish the idea of mass mobilization: they were involved in constitutional opposition to the Raj and given the nature of the franchise, they were obliged to take into account the prejudices of the more established sections of the community. When Kitchlew's programme was debated by the Central Khilafat Committee at Delhi in June 1924, Khaliquzzaman emphasized the fact that 'most of the rich men, the landholders and the Shia community will not like to work on any organization founded under the Khilafat committee, and he suggested that the best plan would be 'the capturing of the Muslim League by the Khilafatists'. The Muslim League had a history behind it and any work done through it would carry more weight.[92] He pointed out, furthermore, that the Muslim League had appointed a committee to confer with other nationalist organizations and he said that it would be inadvisable to pre-empt the work of the League before it had been given a chance to prove itself. This advice was in line with Swarajist policy, and Kitchlew did not take exception to it. His differences with the Ali brothers,

[87] GI Home Poll. 25/1923: Punjab FR I May 1923.

[88] Ibid., Punjab FR I Sept. 1923.

[89] Ibid., Punjab FR II Sept. 1923.

[90] Ibid., Punjab FR II Nov. 1923.

[91] GI Home Poll. 25/1924: Punjab FR II Feb., II March and II April 1924.

[92] GI Home Poll. 167/1924: CID Report on the meeting of the CKC at Delhi on 24 and 25 June 1924.

however, were more fundamental. They were less opposed than the Swarajists to his plans for political mobilization[93] but they reacted strongly against two of his proposals which struck at their chances of political survival. Of the two, the proposal to convert the Jamia Millia into a school for propagandists was the less serious because the Delhi and U.P. Swarajists were as opposed to this as the Ali brothers. But his proposal for the transference of the Khilafat office from Bombay to Delhi met with the support of both these groups and placed the Ali brothers in a very threatened position. It amounted to a vote of censure on Panislamist politics and a demand for a Khilafat organization geared to the North Indian situation. The Ali brothers resisted it to the hilt, tempers rose on both sides, and they only escaped defeat by much blistering rhetoric and a thinly veiled attack on Ajmal Khan and Ansari which produced a characteristic plea for compromise from these two men.[94]

After this, Kitchlew became progressively more communal. By September 1924 he had offended not only Malaviya but also Das and Nehru by his advocacy of Muslim economic independence,[95] and though he still remained a member of the Congress he concentrated more on attacking Hindu communalists than on settling Hindu-Muslim differences. When Gandhi visited Lahore to improve communal relations in early December, neither Kitchlew nor Zafar Ali took any part in the proceedings[96] and when Kitchlew composed his presidential address for the Belgaum Khilafat conference he included virulent attacks on Malaviya and Lajpat Rai which provoked an uproar even after modification.[97] His disenchantment with the Congress was also shown by his refusal to attend the Belgaum session and the difficulty with which he was persuaded to meet Gandhi. By February 1925 he had begun a *tanzim* tour of Northern Punjab and was reported to be 'on the point of breaking

[93] Mahommed Ali accused Kitchlew of stealing his ideas, but though he had been reported in April to be 'contemplating the spending of his time in the propagation of Islam and the combating of the shuddhi movement...', he had produced no coherent plan of his own. See GI Home Poll 25/1924: Delhi FR I April 1924.

[94] GI Home Poll. 167/1924: CID Report on the meeting of the CKC at Delhi, 24 and 25 June 1924.

[95] GI Home Poll. 25/1924: Punajb FR I Sept. 1924.

[96] Ibid., Punjab FR I Dec. 1924.

[97] GI Home Poll. 167/III/1924: CID Report on the All India Khilafat Conference at Belgaum on 23 Dec. 1924.

with the Congress and joining the ordinary Muslim progressive party in the Punjab.'[98]

Kitchlew's new strategy strengthened his position amongst the Amritsar Muslims, and in March 1925, amid much excitement, all his candidates were returned to the Municipal Board.[99] This success made it less essential for him to capture the Khilafat organization and he concentrated instead on setting up a new central organization for the *tanzim* movement. Even in this, however, he met with the opposition of the Ali brothers, and the all-India Muslim parties conference at Amritsar in July witnessed still more accusations and counter-accusations between the two parties. Once again a compromise was reached. But this time it was to no avail. Kitchlew had reached the end of his tether and he resigned the Presidency of the Khilafat organization at the same meeting.[100] He had come to the conclusion that the pursuit of non-co-operation was no longer a viable policy. He was thoroughly disenchanted with the Congress and he concentrated increasingly on *tanzim* and left the Ali brothers to stew in their own juice.

The plight of the Ali brothers was scarcely enviable. As early as August 1924, in the hope of a financial return from journalism, Mahommed Ali had considered reviving the *Comrade*. But though he received an initial offer of help from Shuaib Qureshi, he was ultimately disappointed[101] and it was not until November, following a donation of 10,000 rupees from Haji Abdullah Haroon, that the project got off the ground.[102] By October 1924, such was the financial plight of the Ali brothers that they were obliged to espouse sectional interests in order to survive: they began supporting Ibn Saud, the Wahabi king of Saudi Arabia, in his ambitions to take over the Hedjaz.[103] This provoked a Sunni backlash and ultimately alienated their old colleagues, Hasrat Mohani, Abdul Bari and Mushir Hussain Kidwai,[104] but so long as Ibn Saud and his Indian followers provided

[98] GI Home Poll. 112/1925: Punjab FR II Feb. 1925.

[99] Ibid., Punjab FR 1 March 1925.

[100] GI Home Poll. 112/1925: Punjab FR II July 1925.

[101] Mahommed Ali papers: Mahommed Ali to Shuaib Qureshi, 27 Aug. 1924.

[102] Ibid., Mahommed Ali to Haji Abdullah Haroon, 24 Oct. 1924; GI Home Poll. 25/1924: Bombay FR II Oct. and Delhi FR I Nov. 1924

[103] GI Home Poll. 1924: Bombay FR II Sept. 1924.

[104] C. Khaliquzzaman, *Pathway to Pakistan* (Lahore 1961), pp. 80-2; GI Home Poll. 112/1925: U.P. FR I May 1925 and I Nov. 1925; Punjab FR II Nov. 1925.

them with cash the Ali brothers refused to throw him over.[105] Like Zafar Ali, however, who was also in Ibn Saud's pay, the Ali brothers were placed in a difficult position when his troops desecrated the Prophet's tomb at Medina in August 1925.[106] Shaukat did his best to play down Wahabi excesses but he met with considerable opposition, not least in Bombay, where Chothani took the opportunity to wreak his revenge. On 28 September, on leaving the Juma Musjid, Shaukat was met by Chothani at the head of a hostile mob and was only saved from serious injury by the intervention of the Afghan consul.[107]

This particular reversal of fortune was perhaps the most dramatic from which the Ali brothers suffered, but it was not untypical, and if they remained Panislamist politicians it was largely because they had nowhere else to go. By May 1925, the *Comrade* had proved a failure and Mahommed Ali had taken to the printing of seditious articles in the hope of a cheap martyrdom. The Chief Commissioner of Delhi informed the government of India that Mahommed Ali was 'thoroughly discredited and almost penniless' and refused to prosecute him in order to watch him flounder still further.[108] And flounder he did. He went cap in hand to his former associates and colleagues,[109] and having failed in almost all quarters he finally secured a grant of 6,000 rupees from the deposed Maharaja of Nabha to do propaganda for his restoration.[110] This acceptance of employment from a Sikh is perhaps the best illustration of his loss of credibility with his own community. By the end of 1925, the growth of

105 By the summer of 1925 collections for Panislamic activities from traditional sources had reached their nadir: Mahommed Ali collected 153 rupees on the Id day at Delhi in April and two rupees from 400 people at the Juma Masjid, Aligarh, in June. In May, however, he collected 12,000 rupees from the Delhi Wahabis, and by Sept., the Ali brothers were considered Ibn Saud's chief paymasters in India. See GI Home Poll. 112/1925: Delhi FR II April and II May 1925; U.P. FR I June 1925; GI Home Poll. 99/xiv/1925: Deputy Commissioner, Lahore, to Chief Secretary, Punjab Government, 4 Sept. 1925.

106 For an account of Zafar Ali's activities at this time, see GI Home Poll. 99/xiv/1925.

107 GI Home Poll. 112/1925: Bombay FR II Sept. 1925.

108 GI Home Poll. 226/1925: Chief Commissioner, Delhi, to the Home Member, Government of India, 14 May 1925.

109 Mahommed Ali papers: Mahommed Ali to Ahmed Moola Dawood Madani, 11 July 1925; Mahommed Ali to the Editor of the *Daily Herald*, 30 July 1925.

110 GI Home Poll. 112/1925: U.P. FR II Oct. 1925.

communalism in the provinces had made the Ali brothers look like prehistoric animals unable to adapt to a new environment.

The fate of the Constitutionalists

In the field of constitutional politics, the most notable politician to share the predicament of the Ali brothers was Mahommed Ali Jinnah. Jinnah had been a leading member of the nationalist movement before 1920 but he had been disappointed by the Reforms. Unlike his U.P. colleagues in the Muslim League, he had been ambitious for power at the Centre, and when Dyarchy was only introduced in the provinces he was obliged to reconcile himself to fighting the same old battles all over again in the new Legislative Assembly.[111] Nonetheless he showed no inclination to adopt non-constitutional methods of agitation. On the contrary, he sided with Gandhi at Amritsar in securing a qualified acceptance for the Reforms and he had every intention of working them with a view to securing their early revision.[112] In September 1920, however, when Gandhi stampeded the Congress into non-co-operation at Calcutta, this intention became politically irrelevant and Jinnah was obliged to rethink his policy. Where non-co-operation was concerned, he had no second thoughts. He condemned it unequivocally and he resigned from both the Home Rule League and the Congress on this issue.[113] It is noteworthy, however, that he did not stand for election to the Assembly in 1920. He was anxious for Reform at the Centre and the support of the Congress was essential for that purpose. He could not afford, therefore, to alienate Congress sympathy by working the Reforms when Congressmen were rejecting them. All he could do was to take a back seat until political conditions returned to normality.

While the non-co-operation movement was in progress, Jinnah performed a broker's role. In the summer of 1921, he visited England and lobbied there for a constitutional response to Gandhi's activities. He warned the British public of the dangers of driving

[111] For evidence of Jinnah's desire for power at the Centre, see *ILC Debates 1917-18*, 17 Sept. 1918, p. 135; *Joint Select Committee on the Government of India Bill*, vol. ii, Minutes of Evidence (London 1919), p. 212.

[112] IOR/L/P and J/6/1337/1920: CID Report for Upper India, 2 Jan. 1920.

[113] *The Times*, 3 Jan. 1921; GI Home Poll. Dec. 1920, D59: Bombay FR I Oct. 1920.

the Indian intelligentsia to rebellion and he suggested that if the Punjab wrong were righted and the constitution amended to allow for provincial autonomy and Dyarchy in the central government, India might be restored to an even keel.[114] It was an appeal which fell on deaf ears. The Secretary of State was anxious to reassure Indian opinion over the Jallianwalabagh tragedy but he would not revise the constitution and Jinnah returned to India empty-handed.[115]

He then tried to break non-co-operation, not by securing political concessions from the Raj but by driving a wedge between Hindu and Muslim non-co-operators. He set about discovering the terms on which the Khilafatists would cry halt, and like Shafi, who was also about the same business, he urged upon Reading 'a settlement of Turkish affairs which would restore Smyrna and Thrace to her, leaving the Hedjaz and Mesopotamia under the two present rulers, Hassan and Feisul'.[116] These terms were virtually identical to the ones subsequently enshrined in the famous government dispatch of February 1922. But before they could be acted upon, the All India Congress Committee declared in favour of civil disobedience, Gandhi and his Muslim supporters drew closer together, and the whole scheme was foiled.

Before the year was out, however, Jinnah was given one more chance of achieving the same end. The Prince of Wales landed at Bombay on 17 November 1921 to the accompaniment of a very serious riot. Gandhi, proclaiming that Swaraj stank in his nostrils, suspended the civil disobedience movement, and the government, which had long been urged to act against the extremists, saw its opportunity and struck. As was so often the case, however, the use of extraordinary powers to ban public meetings and imprison leading Congressmen provoked a backlash in Gandhi's favour. The very men who had called for action criticized the government for going too far[117] and the brokers seized their chance to profit from a buyers' market. Malaviya led a deputation to Lord Reading on 22 December;[118] Purushotamdas Thakurdas, through Ambalal Sara-

[114] *The Times*, 29 June 1921.
[115] Reading papers, 10: Tgm Reading to Montagu, 2 Nov. 1921.
[116] Ibid.
[117] Ibid., 3: Reading to Montagu, 15 Dec. 1921.
[118] IOR/L/P and J/6/7961/1921.

bhai, the Ahmedabad mill-owner, persuaded Gandhi to discuss terms for a truce with government;[119] and Jinnah, Malaviya and other moderates planned a meeting with Gandhi which took place in mid-January.[120] As it turned out, however, Gandhi was not interested in parleying with government. He did not wish to alienate moderate opinion by appearing to be uncompromising but he declined to discuss peace on the terms suggested by Jinnah and Malaviya. He persuaded them to raise their terms to a point at which they were unacceptable to government, and having brought them down on his side of the fence, he resumed civil disobedience with his position re-established.[121] Jinnah could only throw up his arms in exasperation and let Gandhi and the government fight it out.

Jinnah re-entered the political arena once Nehru and Das had committed themselves to council entry. In March 1923, in an effort to woo the Muslims away from the Khilafat Committee, he called a meeting of the Muslim League at Lucknow and invited his old friend, G.M. Bhurgri,[122] to deliver the presidential address. Bhurgri proceeded cautiously. He had no desire to offend the Khilafatists and he paid tribute to their activities. He condemned the British government for siding with the Greeks, he praised the achievements of Mustafa Kemal and he looked forward to the formation of a Federation of Oriental States. The burden of his song, however, was that non-co-operation had proved a failure, that the British Raj had come to stay and that the only feasible course of action was to work the Reforms and to press for the early appointment of the Statutory Commission. This was very much Jinnah's own view, but it was opposed tooth and nail by Ansari and his Khilafatist followers, and the two sides were so evenly balanced that no decision was forthcoming. A five-hour session of the Subjects Committee on 31 March resolved nothing and though Jinnah's motion for council entry was rejected by twelve votes to nine the following day this was only because Ansari contrived to have the vote taken during the lunch interval. Jinnah was confident that he would win in the

[119] Purushotamdas Thakurdas papers, 24: Ambalal Sarabhai to Thakurdas, 9 Jan. 1922.

[120] *The Indian Social Reformer*, 8 Jan. 1922.

[121] For an account of the meeting at Bombay at which Gandhi outmanoeuvred the moderates, see GI Home Poll. 461/1921.

[122] For a detailed account of Bhurgri's political history, see GI Home Poll. 66/1924, KW4.

open session but his confidence was not put to the test. After only two resolutions had been passed, Zahur Ahmed, a non-co-operating barrister from Allahabad, objected to the continuation of the proceedings on the grounds that there was not a quorum of *bona fide* members. This objection was sustained and the session was adjourned *sine die.* Jinnah had failed in his endeavours and it was to be over a year before the League met again.[123]

Jinnah only re-emerged as a significant political force after the 1923 elections. He was returned to the Assembly by the Muslims of Bombay city and he became the leader of the Independent party. In that capacity he co-operated with Nehru's Swarajist party, and together the two parties were known as the Nationalist party. Nonetheless Jinnah held the upper hand. There were 101 seats in the Assembly and the Swarajists had won only forty-one of them. Jinnah with a party of some seventeen members, held the balance between the Swarajists and the government.

From the beginning the two parties were separated by political ideology. Nehru's party was recruited chiefly outside the Presidencies, from those areas which had either co-operated wholeheartedly with Gandhi or seen the wisdom of compromising with him. Of its forty-one members, ten came from the United Provinces and Delhi, seven from Bihar and Orissa, five each from the Punjab and the Central Provinces, and two from Assam. Only twelve came from the Presidencies, five from Bengal, where Das had bowed to Gandhi, four from Bombay, and three from Madras.[124] Jinnah's party, on the other hand, was recruited almost entirely from the Presidencies, six of its seventeen members coming from Bombay, six from Madras, three from Bengal and only two from the United Provinces.[125] Unlike the Swarajists, the Independents had mostly

125 Pirzada, op.cit., vol. i, pp. 566-74.

124 Gordon, op.cit., Table 7, p. 182.

125 The seventeen Independents were: Jinnah (Bombay city Mahommedan urban), G.M. Bhurgri (Sind Mahommedan rural), Purushotamdas Thakurdas (Indian Merchants' Chamber and Bureau, Bombay), Kasturbhai Lalji (Ahmedabad millowners), Sardar Mutalik (Sardars of the Deccan), Harchandrai Vishindas (Sind non-Mahommedan), K.K. Nambiyar (Madras landholders), Venkatapatiraju (Ganjam cum Vizagapatam), Ramchandra Rao (Godavari cum Kistna), Venkatarama Reddi (Guntur cum Nellore), Shanmukhan Chetty (Salem and Coimbatore cum North Arcot), Rama Iyengar (Ramnad and Madura cum Tinnevelly), B.C. Pal (Calcutta non-Mahommedan urban), K.C. Neogy (Dacca division), Ranglal Jajodia (Marwari Association), Madan Mohan Malaviya (Allahabad and Jhansi divisions) and Mahommed Yakub (Rohilkhund and Kumaon, Mahommedan rural).

opposed non-co-operation and several had contested the elections of 1920. If they could be identified with any political group at all, it was with the school of 'moderate' nationalism which had broken with the Congress over the acceptability of the Reforms. Though Jinnah was the President of the Muslim League, therefore, the differences between the two parties were political, not communal. Motilal Nehru, indeed, had more Muslim supporters than Jinnah. Of the forty-one Swarajists, eight were Muslims,[126] whereas of the seventeen Independents, only three were Muslims, and after the death of G.M. Bhurgri the number was reduced to two. The outcome of their co-operation, however, was of great importance for communal relations in North India. If Jinnah enabled Nehru to carry the day against the government and to obtain political concessions with which to pay off his supporters, the Swarajist-Khilafat alliance would be strengthened, but if Nehru, through Jinnah's recalcitrance, failed to carry the day, his opponents were poised and ready to exploit communal differences to destroy him. It was an awesome responsibility but Jinnah was not entirely aware of the burden which he carried. He had his eyes firmly fixed on the central government and he had his own notions of the best methods to achieve the political revision which he sought.

The initial period of co-operation was cordial enough. The ground was prepared by Das, Jayakar and Jinnah at Bombay after the Coconada Congress.[127] A National Demand, calling for provincial autonomy and responsibility in the central government, was subsequently approved by the Swarajist Executive at Lucknow,[128] and the two parties agreed to make this the basis of a joint political programme at Delhi on 3 February. On 18 February, Motilal Nehru moved this demand as an amendment to Diwan Bahadur Rangachariar's resolution calling for the early appointment of the Statutory Commission. It was supported by virtually all the elected

[126] Nehru's Muslim supporters were Sarfaraz Hussain Khan (Patna and Chota Nagpur cum Orissa), Shafi Daudi (Tirhut division), Nawab Ismail Khan (Meerut division), Yusuf Imam (U.P. Southern divisions), Khwaja Abdul Karim (Dacca division), Mahommed Kasim Ali (Chittagong division), Ahmed Ali Khan (Assam) and Samiullah Khan (Central Provinces). Syed Murtuza (South Madras) was elected as a Khilafatist, but subsequently joined the Swarajists. Biographies of these men ae to be found in GI Home Poll. 66/1924, GI Home Public 953/1924, and Gordon, op.cit., pp. 364-73.

[127] M.R. Jayakar, *The Story of My Life*, vol. ii (Bombay 1959), p. 182.

[128] AICC papers, 8/1924 and 31/1924.

Indian members of the Assembly and it was passed by a handsome majority. Even before Nehru moved his amendment, however, the Home Member's reply to Rangachariar's resolution had made it clear that the government of India was in no mood to make concessions. All manner of obstacles to advance were erected, not least the problem presented by the position of minorities and all that was offered ultimately was a departmental enquiry to remedy justifiable complaints within the terms of the Act itself.[129] The main hopes of the Swarajists, however, rested not with the government of India, but with the new Labour government in England. They had friends in the Labour party and they continued throughout the summer to expect a summons to a conference.[130]

The first response to the National Demand by the new Secretary of State, Lord Olivier, however, was distinctly disappointing. In a speech to the House of Lords on 26 February, he made it plain that he was not prepared to go any further than the government of India, and as Nehru was later to remark, this response was 'not only insufficient, but highly unsatisfactory and disappointing.'[131] When it came to pressing home this disappointment, however, the Swarajists and Independents were at loggerheads. Many Swarajists wished to reject the Budget in its entirety, but the Independents were not prepared to resort to such tactics and because their agreement was necessary for any policy to be successful they ultimately won the day. It was agreed that the first four heads should be rejected and that the rest of the Budget should be treated on its merits. This was the first instance of Jinnah using his advantage to modify Swarajist policy, but it was very clear from the statement which he made to the Assembly on 11 March that it was not to be the last. The whole tone of the speech suggests not only a desire to reassure the government as to the reasonableness of the Nationalist position but also an ambition to bring the Swarajists under his own more constitutional umbrella.

...the Nationalist party [he said] is a party which is formed to work in this Assembly and nothing more; and in this Assembly we stand

[129] *ILA Debates,* vol. iv, part i, 18 Feb. 1924, pp. 355-66.

[130] See speech by Nehru, *ILA Debates,* vol. iv, part ii, 19 Feb. 1924, p. 783; report of speech by Jinnah at Hindu College, Delhi, GI Home Poll. 25/124: Delhi FR II March 1924; B.R. Nanda, *The Nehrus* (London 1965), pp. 230-3.

[131] *ILA Debates,* vol. iv, part ii, 10 March 1924, p. 1382.

to pursue a policy and a programme of a constitutional character. We shall pursue that policy and that programme until the last stages of the constitutional struggle are exhausted. There is no idea in the mind of the Nationalist party to resort to civil disobedience. There is no idea in the mind of the Nationalist party that we want revolution. There is no idea in the mind of the Nationalist party that we are going to carry on the campaign of non-payment of taxes.[132]

In Reading's view, Jinnah was making a bid for leadership[133] and his activities over the next three months do not belie that impression.

He first attempted to achieve this ambition by direct methods. After the Assembly session ended, he returned to Bombay and held almost daily conferences with Nehru, Jayakar, Purushotamdas Thakurdas and V.J. Patel with a view to producing a new, inclusive, constitutional party. Gandhi also participated in a number of these discussions, as did Das on his arrival from Bengal.[134] Ultimately, however, Jinnah's efforts foundered on the rock of internal Congress differences. Nehru and Das were under pressure from Gandhi and, though they did not bow before him, they were too wary of his antics to ally openly with men who repudiated his creed. It was only after the promulgation of the Bengal ordinance in October 1924, when Gandhi agreed to suspend non-co-operation and to place the Swarajists in charge of the Congress organization, that Jinnah's ambitions stood any chance of being fulfilled and by then new obstacles had been thrown into his path.

Jinnah's other *ballon d'essai,* the revival of the Muslim League, had more ominous consequences. When Jinnah called the Council of the League at Delhi on 16 March and persuaded his colleagues to agree to a session at Lahore,[135] he was undoubtedly motivated by a desire to strengthen the chances of a government response to the National Demand. The choice of Lahore was not fortuitous. The Punjab was the only province where the Muslims were working the Reforms for their own advantage, and the Punjabi Muslims were the most likely to support a policy of constitutional advance. Such a demand, coming from the premier Muslim political organization, would be a complete answer to the argument that communal differences were an obstacle to advance, and Jinnah, as the man who

[132] Ibid., 11 March 1924, pp. 1443-4.

[133] Reading papers, 7: Reading to Olivier, 13 March 1924.

[134] Jayakar, op.cit., vol. ii, p. 264.

[135] Shafi Daudi papers, Diary, 16 March 1924.

had secured Muslim support for this purpose, would also add to his own political stature. So it must have seemed. But the reality was different. Fazli Husain was keen on provincial autonomy, but he was wary of selling his support too cheaply and he made sure that he was in a position of overwhelming strength at the League meeting.[136] This preparation paid dividends; and when the main resolution defining the Muslim position emerged from the Subjects Committee it was an almost entirely Punjabi affair. It looked forward to a Federal Government at the Centre, 'the functions of the Central Government being confined to such matters as are of general or common concern'; it demanded that no measure of territorial redistribution should affect Muslim majorities in Punjab, Bengal and the Frontier; and it made scant provision for the position of minorities. Representation was to be by population,

> except that very small minorities may be given representation in excess of their numerical proportion in those cases in which they would remain entirely unrepresented in the absence of such exceptional treatment, subject, however, to the essential proviso that no majority should be reduced to a minority or even to an equality.

This last clause was a direct product of the Punjabi situation, the stress on 'very small minorities' being calculated to exclude the Hindus and the Sikhs, and the proviso itself to improve the position of the Muslims at their expense. As such it was resented by the minority-province Muslims, and particularly by those working the Reforms, and an amendment eliminating the reference to 'very small minorities' and replacing it with a demand for 'adequate and effective representation for minorities in every province' was moved by Dr Ziauddin Ahmed and carried by one hundred and twenty-six votes to eighty-three. This amendment was supported by the Punjabi agriculturalists, suggesting that their original resolution had reflected parochialism but not prejudice, but it was vociferously opposed by the Khilafatists and notably by Ghazi Abdur Rahman of Lyallpur, Chaudhuri Khaliquzzaman and Mahommed Ali. These were the men who had worked closest with the Congress and they saw that these terms would not be accepted by that body. It had become clear when Dr Ansari and Lala Laipat Rai tried to formulate their National Pact that even separate electorates had ceased to be

[136] Fazli Husain papers; Fazli Husain to Amir Din, 24 Nov. 1932.

universally accepted,[137] and a communal majority by separate electorates had already been rejected by the Congress at Coconada.[138] If the League were to demand this concession again without giving any compensation in the minority provinces, the result would be a foregone conclusion.[139] Nonetheless, by the passage of the amendment, the League did demand just that, and Jinnah emerged from the Lahore session, not only armed with a declaration in favour of a complete overhaul of the Government of India Act, but committed to securing an improvement on the Lucknow Pact as a precondition for united action. He did not shirk this responsibility but even his powers of persuasion ultimately proved insufficient.[140]

Within a week of the Lahore session, Nehru and Jinnah were invited to sit as non-official members on the Reforms Enquiry Committee, an extended version of the departmental enquiry promised by Hailey in February.[141] Nehru would have liked to accept this invitation but opposition from the Swarajist Executive obliged him to turn it down.[142] Jinnah, being less subject to external pressure, accepted with alacrity. It gave him an ideal opportunity to pursue his ambitions for Reform, to explore the views of others, and where necessary to convert them to his point of view. His questions to witnesses suggest three main preoccupations. He seeks firstly to show that Dyarchy has failed and that the constitution needs overhauling; secondly to counter the argument that communal tension is an obstacle to advance; and thirdly, to discover terms on which a new Lucknow Pact might be devised. His path was not smooth, however, for he met with considerable opposition from the Chairman, Sir Alexander Muddiman, who was also the Home Member,

[137] Ansari and Lajpat Rai had failed to agree about separate electorates. Dr Ansari wanted them extended to municipalities and local boards. Lajpat Rai not only disagreed with this but desired their abolition throughout the system after a fixed time. When the Pact was circulated for opinion, most Hindus agreed with Lajpat Rai and most Muslims with Ansari. See AICC papers, 25/1924.

[138] Mahommed Ali, as President of the Coconada Congress, had done his best to get the Bengal Pact passed, but he had been defeated by the efforts of Lajpat Rai and Malaviya. See GI Home Poll. 152/1924.

[139] Khaliquzzaman, op.cit. p. 77.

[140] For an account of the League session at Lahore, see Pirzada, *op.cit.*, vol. i, pp. 575-82.

[141] The other non-officials invited were Sir Tej Bahadur Sapru, Sir Sivaswamy Iyer, Dr Paranjpye, Sir Arthur Froom and the Maharaja of Burdwan.

[142] IOR/L/PO/278: Tgm. Viceroy (Home) to Secretary of State, 3 June 1924.

and from Sir Mahommed Shafi, the Law Member, who had been put on the committee to represent the communal point of view.[143]

As at Lahore, Jinnah obtained the greatest co-operation from the Punjabi Muslims. They were anxious for Reforms and willing to minimize the significance of communal tension in order to achieve it. Furthermore they had already come to an understanding with Jinnah and based their position on the resolution passed by the League.[144] Malik Barkat Ali, who represented the Punjab Muslim League before the committee, was the best witness Jinnah could have hoped for. He condemned Dyarchy unequivocally; he gave his opinion that communalism was restricted to the large towns and inspired by disputes over loaves and fishes; he held that these disputes would be easier to handle with provincial autonomy; he supported the view that separate electorates did not necessarily imply communal politics; and he expressed his willingness to accept a Muslim majority in the Punjab of only one per cent.[145] This evidence was of very material assistance to the Nationalist cause and it figured prominently in the committee's Minority Report.[146]

Jinnah also received support from three U.P. Muslims, Maulvi Mahommed Yakub, a member of his own party, Syed Raza Ali, a member of the Council of State, and Professor Shafaat Ahmed, a member of the U.P. Legislative Council. Mahommed Yakub was the most outspoken. He held it 'a malicious subversion of facts to say that the Mussulmans are not in favour of responsible government' and he opposed the argument that communal discord was an obstacle to political advance. He admitted, however, that he was 'more keen for an extension of democratic powers in the Central Government than in the provinces'.[147] As an all-India politician he wished for responsibility at the Centre, but as a Muslim from a minority

[143] Ibid., Tgm. Viceroy (Home) to Secretary of State, 26 May 1924.

[144] See memoranda by Pir Tajuddin and Malik Barkat Ali, *Reforms Enquiry Committee,* Appendix 5, *Written Evidence* (London 1925), pp. 374-80; also memorandum by Fazli Husain and Chaudhuri Lal Chand, 21 May 1924, *Reforms Enquiry Committee, Views of Local Governments on the Working of the Reforms* (London 1925), *Cmd.2362,* pp. 211-13.

[145] *Reforms Enquiry Committee,* Appendix 6, *Oral Evidence,* part i (London 1925): Barkat Ali called and examined, 20 Aug. 1924, pp. 411-20 and 426-9.

[146] *Reforms Enquiry Committee, Report* (London 1925), *Cmd.2360,* pp. 150-1 and 177.

[147] *Reforms Enquiry Committee,* Appendix 5, *Written Evidence* (London 1925), pp. 270-3.

province he had his scruples about provincial autonomy. The same dichotomy was also noticeable in the evidence of Raza Ali. He was less bold than Mahommed Yakub with regard to the central government, holding that Dyarchy, though unpopular, would be a more sensible beginning than complete responsibility, but more sceptical about provincial autonomy, declaring quite openly that communal tension was an obstacle to further devolution.[148] Shafaat Ahmed's views were less precise. On the one hand, he held that full advantage had not been taken of the opportunities afforded by the Act; on the other, that it would be possible even within the terms of the Act to abolish dyarchy and to introduce responsibility at the Centre. Did he wish for the overhaul of the Act? It is not clear. He did demand, however, that Muslim representation should be increased both in the provinces and at the Centre, and as this appeared to be an escalation of the League demand made at Lahore, Jinnah was anxious to clarify the position.[149] Shafaat agreed almost immediately, however, that the minority-province Muslims were satisfied with the Lucknow Pact, and Jinnah proceeded no further.[150]

The main opposition to a renegotiated settlement with the Congress came from the Bengali Muslims. Fazlul Haq and A.K. Ghuznavi, both ministers whose salaries had been refused by the Swarajists, and Nawab Ali Chaudhuri, who was to suffer the same fate in 1925, were all of the opinion that Dyarchy was a necessary training ground for full responsible government and that it should run for the entire statutory period.[151] They undoubtedly had hopes of a Muslim majority in the Bengal Council but with half of their co-religionists voting for Das their first priority was to disrupt Das's alliance and to regain control of their own community. They were prepared, therefore, to play up communal differences as an argument against concessions, and Jinnah, in his examination of Bengali Muslim witnesses was on a much more difficult wicket. He and Shafi were at cross-purposes and their clashes over Sir Abdur Rahim's evidence

[148] Ibid., pp. 264-9.

[149] This demand was also supported by a public meeting at Agra under the Presidency of Dr Ziauddin Ahmed. See *ibid.*, pp. 324-9.

[150] *Reforms Enquiry Committee,* Appendix 6, *Oral Evidence,* part ii (London 1925): Shafaat Ahmed called and examined, 30 Aug. 1924, pp. 122-5.

[151] *Reforms Enquiry Committee,* Appendix 5, *Written Evidence:* memoranda by Fazlul Haq, A.K. Ghuznavi and Nawab Ali Chaudhuri, pp. 207-9, 210-11, 217-21.

provided one of the most heated sessions of the entire committee. Abdur Rahim ultimately agreed that the Lucknow Pact, though unsatisfactory, did provide a basis for renegotiation, but he would not adopt a flexible attitude towards the size of the Bengali Muslim majority, and he was aided and abetted by both Shafi and Muddiman. Jinnah was prepared to accept a majority by separate electorates but he wanted leeway for negotiation and he sought Rahim's approval for a scheme to give weightage to the Hindus on the basis of their voting strength. This, however, was not forthcoming. While Jinnah was questioning Rahim, Shafi interrupted him to elicit the view that population was the principle criterion, Muddiman hurried him along, and ultimately Rahim himself refused to budge from fifty-six per cent.[152] If any revision of the Lucknow Pact were to be attempted, it was plain by this stage that among the Muslims, the Bengalis were the biggest obstacle to success.

When the work of the Reforms Enquiry Committee was completed, Jinnah, Sapru, Sivaswamy Iyer and Paranjpye refused to sign the Majority Report and produced a Minority Report instead. In that report, they condemned Dyarchy unequivocally and they demanded the introduction of provincial autonomy and responsibility in the central government. They used the evidence of Barkat Ali to show that communal tension was a phenomenon of restricted importance; they quoted the Muslim League resolution to prove that the Muslims were not opposed to advance; and, whilst admitting that the Bengali Muslims were of a different view, they held that even they would be satisfied if their majority was recognized. '...the correct interpretation of their attitude', they said, 'is that if the conditions mentioned above are fulfilled and no majority is reduced to a minority in any province, they will agree to political advance.'[153] Their chief concern, however, was for advance at the Centre, and they showed some anxiety lest the Government should cheat them of their prize, as in 1920, by conceding the demands of the provinces whilst leaving the Central Government untouched. They therefore invoked the spectre of centrifugalism as an argument for simultaneous advance:

...with provincial governments fully responsible to their legislatures

[152] *Reforms Enquiry Committee,* Appendix 6, *Oral Evidence,* part ii: Abdur Rahim called and examined, 23 Oct. 1924, pp. 415-16 and 419-22.

[153] *Reforms Enquiry Committee, Report* (London 1925), *Cmd. 2360,* p. 179.

and the Central Government irresponsible in the last resort, the control of various kinds which it is desired to be continued in the Central Government will be more difficult to enforce and the centrifugal tendency observed in many Federal states and especially marked in the history of India will manifest itself more and more making stable Government unworkable.[154]

This was perhaps the first time that Partition had been foreshadowed in constitutional terms and it provides a very significant marker on the road to that destination. In the short term the argument was specious, for while British control was retained at the Centre, there was no such danger. But it was based on an anxiety which proved well-founded. In 1935, only provincial autonomy was conceded, and in the absence of an Indian government to replace the Raj, the transfer of power eventually took place in conditions which maximized the leverage of the provinces. All this was only seen hazily in 1924, but that it was seen at all shows how strong provincial interests had become. Between the millstone of provincialism and that of the Raj, the *pukka* all-India politician was being ground to a fine powder.

On 3 December 1924, when the Reforms Enquiry Committee Report was signed, Jinnah's ambitions looked capable of fulfilment. The government, by its promulgation of the Bengal Ordinance, had provided a real spur to unity; Gandhi, by his suspension of non-co-operation, had paved the way for a new accession of strength to the Congress; and already, on 21 November, an all-parties conference had met at Bombay and set up a representative committee to devise a united front against the government.

Nonetheless, Jinnah was wary of taking part in unity discussions on other people's terms. Strictly speaking, the suspension of non-co-operation enabled him to rejoin the Congress. But when he considered attending the Belgaum session he found himself in two minds. 'He is apparently of the view', Venkatapatiraju wrote to Purushotamdas Thakurdas, 'that we need not bother ourselves outside the Assembly. My point is that to carry any influence in the Assembly we should have public support.'[155] This was a crucial

[154] Ibid., p. 172.

[155] Purushotamdas Thakurdas papers, 40: Venkatapatiraju to Thakurdas, 12 Nov. 1924.

difference not only between Venkatapatiraju and Jinnah, but more importantly, between Jinnah and the Swarajists. Jinnah wanted the Swarajists to adopt purely constitutional methods but he had no desire to fight their battles for them. His own position, both as leader of the Independents and as President of the Muslim League, was already secure, and he did not wish to compromise his chances of negotiating with the Congress as an equal by becoming a party to its decisions. The same considerations also affected his participation in the all-parties conference. He only agreed to sit on Gandhi's Unity Committee providing its decisions were not taken by vote. Decisions by majority implied differences of opinion and he was only prepared to subscribe to an agreement which was voluntarily adopted by all parties.[156]

Jinnah was saving himself for negotiations with the Congress. But Mahommed Ali, as Congress President, had already put a number of spokes in his wheel. Jinnah's self-importance, his fine clothes and his precise manner of speech had long been a subject for Mahommed Ali's satire, but by the middle of 1924, with Panislamist enthusiasm at low ebb, Jinnah was no longer just good material for the gossip column of the *Comrade.* If Mahommed Ali had any chance of re-establishing himself as a political leader it was as a purveyor of Hindu-Muslim unity, and Jinnah's efforts to revive the League and to renegotiate the Lucknow Pact provoked a jealous response for that reason. Mahommed Ali opposed the revival of the League;[157] he attended it only to object to the resolution on communal safeguards; and when the session was over, he turned with a new zeal to the promotion of communal harmony.[158] Jinnah was not unduly perturbed so long as Mahommed Ali confined himself to pouring oil on troubled waters: within the League his opposition was manageable and the reduction of communal tension was a desirable end in itself. But he was considerably inconvenienced when Mahommed Ali stopped playing peace-maker and

[156] *Indian Quarterly Register,* 1924, vol. ii, p. 190.

[157] GI Home Poll. 25/1924: Bombay FR II May 1924.

[158] Both Mahommed Ali and Gandhi saw the pursuit of Hindu-Muslim unity as a means of retrieving their political pre-eminence and they worked closely together. In August, they attempted to mediate between the two communities at Delhi after a riot at *Bakr-Id,* and in September, Mahommed Ali was chairman of the reception committee at the Unity conference called during Gandhi's penitential fast after the Kohat riot.

started playing politician.

During the Lahore League, a committee had been appointed to formulate a consitution in consultation with other organizations. This was Jinnah's brainchild and he had great hopes of it.[159] When it made overtures to the Congress, however, it was unceremoniously snubbed. This was the first instance of Mahommed Ali's activities influencing the relations between the two organizations and it prevented the holding of a joint session at Belgaum.

> Some of the members of the council [Mushir Hussain Kidwai wrote to Motilal Nehru] were so ruffled by the contemptuous treatment with which the Secretary of the Congress treated the request of the Muslim League constitution committee. . . that it rejected the suggestion of holding the session at the same place where the Congress is going to be held.[160]

More significant still, however, was the attempt made by Gandhi and the Ali brothers to solve the communal tangle in the Punjab by political means. Early in December they visited Lahore and offered the Muslims proportionate representation in the legislatures and services in exchange for the abolition of separate electorates.[161] This offer was both an affront to the League's claim to represent the Muslims and a clear indication of Congress unwillingness to accept the terms laid down at Lahore. It was not ultimately accepted but it showed the way the wind was blowing.[162]

Though relations between the League and the Congress had become testy, both Jinnah and the Swarajists remained anxious for a settlement. When Motilal learned that the League had decided to hold its session at Bombay, he urged Jinnah to change the venue to Belgaum, and Jinnah, though he claimed it was too late to do so, did postpone the meeting for several days to allow for Congress attendance.[163] At the League itself, the President, Syed Raza Ali,

[159] See *Reforms Enquiry Committee*, Appendix 6, *Oral Evidence*, part i: Barkat Ali examined by Jinnah, pp. 426-7.

[160] AICC papers, 37/1925: Kidwai to Nehru, 5 Dec. 1924. The Congress Secretary during Mahommed Ali's presidency was Motilal's son, Jawaharlal.

[161] GI Home Poll. 37/1925: Sir Malcolm Hailey to Sir Alexander Muddiman, 11 Dec. 1924.

[162] Fazli Husain did enter into correspondence with Gandhi but duscussions broke down over separate electorates. See *Collected Works of Gandhi* (*CWG*), vol. xxvi, p. 215: Gandhi to Fazli Husain, 2 March 1925.

[163] AICC papers, 37/1925: Motilal Nehru to Mushir Hussain Kidwai, 8 Dec. 1924.

warned his audience against a merger with the Congress.[164] But Jinnah, whilst acknowledging the differences which had emerged over separate electorates, renewed his plea for an attempt at a settlement.[165] Nor was he unsuccessful. The constitution committee appointed at Lahore was refashioned to accommodate a significantly larger Congress Muslim element, and presumably as a result of Gandhi's intervention, this new committee was subsequently co-opted bodily on to the Unity Committee of the all-parties conference.[166] All this shows that hope was not yet dead.

The main obstacle to a settlement came from the communalist Hindus of the Punjab and the United Provinces. Lajpat Rai, the Punjabi Swarajist leader, was slowly being alienated from the national leadership, and like Malaviya and Chintamani, who had already begun to break Nehru's alliance with the U.P. Muslims in the municipalities, he found the communal war-cry a useful means of consolidating his political position. For both these parties a policy of concession to the Muslims was incompatible with the exploitation of communal fears for political ends, and for the Punjabi party in particular there was the added danger that such concessions would involve their permanent subordination to a Muslim majority by separate electorates.

The most vociferous of these communalists was Lajpat Rai. Between 26 November and 17 December 1924, he published thirteen articles in the *Tribune* criticizing Muslim insistence on absolute rights, stigmatizing Jinnah as a recruit to the communalist Muslim party and condemning communal electorates in the most provocative terms. He told his readers that communal electorates, once accepted, would not be abolished without civil war; that to accept them was to divide the country into Hindu India and Muslim India; and that as the Punjabi Muslims were unwilling to grant weightage to minorities it would be better to partition the Punjab, and if necessary Bengal, and to establish a federation of autonomous Hindu and Muslim states.[167] At the same time, in a circular to prominent Hindus of all provinces, he condemned the Congress for its

[164] Pirzada, op.cit., vol. ii (Karachi 1970), p. 17.

[165] *Indian Quarterly Register,* 1924, vol. ii, p. 481.

[166] Mahommed Ali papers: Syed Zahur Ahmed to Mahommed Ali, 12 Jan. 1925.

[167] *Lala Lajpat Rai, His Writings and Speeches,* ed. V.C. Joshi, vol. ii (Delhi 1966), pp. 175-8 and 210-14.

part in the Lucknow Pact and urged them to make the Hindu Mahasabha their political mouthpiece.[168] This call to arms met with a ready response at Belgaum where the Mahasabha's activities took a distinctly political turn for the first time. A committee was appointed to formulate Hindu opinion on the communal question, and its composition was ominous for the future. Amongst others, it consisted of Lajpat Rai, Raja Narendra Nath, Chintamani, Raja Sir Rampal Singh, Jairamdas Daulatram of Sind and, most ominously of all, Nehru's Swarajist allies from the Central Provinces, B.S. Moonji and N.C. Kelkar.[169]

It was these Mahasabhites who frustrated the chances of a new Lucknow Pact when the all-parties conference reconvened at Delhi on 23 January 1925. During the preliminary consultations, when Jinnah urged the committee to attend first to Hindu-Muslim differences, the Mahasabhites did not actually oppose a new settlement. They feigned ignorance of Muslim demands and having first preempted Jinnah's position by condemning both communal representation and the Lucknow Pact they claimed that there was no point in discussing the question until the Muslims laid their cards on the table. It became obvious the following day, however, that this position was mere camouflage. Jinnah's speech demanding recognition for Muslim majorities in Bengal and the Punjab was followed by an uncompromising harangue from Lajpat Rai and there was some danger of the committee being disrupted. This danger was averted by the acceptance of Mrs Besant's proposal for the establishment of two committees, one to formulate a scheme for Swaraj and the other to solve the communal question, but no sooner had the second committee started work than Chintamani announced that its decisions would not be acceptable to the Hindus until they had been endorsed by the Mahasabha. Both Jinnah and Nehru objected to this condition and it was eventually withdrawn at Gandhi's insistence, but the relations between Hindus and Muslims within the committee became steadily worse and on 26 January Hakim Ajmal Khan had to propose an adjournment to allow for the removal of misunderstandings. These misunderstandings, however, were too substantial to be removed and after a further five-minute session on 28 January the committee was adjourned for a month. That in effect

[168] Purushotamdas Thakurdas papers, 40: Circular letter, dated 13 Dec. 1924.

[169] *Indian Quarterly Register*, 1924, vol. ii, pp. 485-8.

marked the end of it. It met briefly on 28 February and 1 March but on both occasions the attendance was too poor for any profitable discussions. After the January session, even Jinnah had ceased to take any real interest in it, and apart from Swami Shradhanand, the attendance was confined to Gandhi, Motilal Nehru, the Ali brothers and a few Assembly politicians.[170]

The Mahasabhites, having achieved their purpose, stayed well away. But it was significant for the future that they were able to hold the Congress to ransom. Nehru and Gandhi, though keen for a settlement, were not prepared to make concessions in the face of Mahasabha opposition. They chose instead to leave well alone. In a communiqué issued at Delhi on 2 March, they informed the public that there was no likelihood of a settlement; and three days later in Bombay, Gandhi told reporters that he intended to put the Hindu-Muslim problem on one side. It was an insoluble riddle and he had no alternative but to wait on God for its solution.[171]

After the failure of the all-parties conference, the division between Nehru and Jinnah definitely widened. Nehru, faced with the political machinations of the Mahasabha, became more obstructionist in the Assembly, whereas Jinnah, despite his sense of disappointment, refused to lend support to what he considered wrecking tactics. In the spring of 1925 the two men began to disagree publicly, and the united front against government collapsed. Jinnah thwarted the Swarajists in their attempt to throw out both the Railway Budget and the Finance Bill, and they in their turn made him the butt of prolonged attacks during both these debates. The speeches of Vithalbhai Patel were largely devoted to criticism of Jinnah,[172] and Jamnadas Mehta, in the debate on the Finance Bill, even accused him of being 'the leader of communal strife in this country'.[173] This was a stray allegation from a personal enemy and Jinnah repudiated it with some heat.[174] Moreover, the fact that it was not made in this form by either Patel or Nehru suggests that it did not ring true. Nonetheless, though Jinnah could not legitimately be accused of

[170] AICC papers, G72/1925; *Indian Quarterly Register,* 1925, vol. i, pp. 66-7.

[171] *CWG,* vol. xxvi, pp. 232-4.

[172] *ILA Debates,* vol. 5, part ii, 25 Feb. 1925, pp. 1504-10; *ILA Debates,* vol. 5, part ii, 16 March 1925, pp. 2422-41.

[173] Ibid., 16 March 1925, p. 2462.

[174] Ibid., p. 2478.

stirring up communal strife, he had undertaken to secure better terms for the majority-province Muslims and having failed in that endeavour he could not both be true to his Muslim clients and support the Swarajists unreservedly. There is no explicit evidence that he modified his position as a result of the all-parties conference but the likelihood remains very strong.

However, this was only one side of the story. Jinnah had been anxious for a settlement to strengthen his hand in the debate on the Muddiman report,[175] and though no settlement was forthcoming he continued to press the government to allow the report to be debated.[176] As Lord Reading was about to visit England to confer with the new Secretary of State, however, the government decided to postpone the debate until his return. Both Jinnah and Nehru condemned this decision, and a vote was carried against the government on this issue.[177] Jinnah, however, continued to coax the government with offers of co-operation, whereas Nehru adopted a derisive attitude towards government promises. The response of the new Secretary of State, Nehru told the Assembly, could easily be predicted. Butler, Sly, Wheeler, Vincent and Blackett would all be in London at the same time as the Viceroy and they would effectively quash any proposals for advance. The House had been gagged over the Reforms Enquiry Committee Report, and its effect on Government policy was about as great as the squeaking of a rat in an Honourable Member's bedroom.[178] Though the two men disagreed publicly, however, privately they appear to have seen each other as complementary elements in the same endeavour. Nehru was the stick; Jinnah the carrot. 'Please do not allow yourself to be disturbed', Nehru wrote to Purushotamdas Thakurdas, 'until you come to the end of the chapter. Do not for a moment think that we are creating an impassable gulf between ourselves. We can afford to fight like Kilkenny cats and still be friends.'[179]

[175] Indian Quarterly Register, 1925, vol. i, p. 73.

[176] Birkenhead papers (IOL MSS Eur. D 703) 1: Reading to Birkenhead, 19 Feb. 1925.

[177] The political situation was debated when the demand for the expenses of the Viceroy's Executive Council was put to the Assembly. See *ILA Debates*, vol. 5, part iii, 14 March 1925, pp. 2344-404.

[178] Ibid., pp. 2346-7.

[179] Purushotamdas Thakurdas papers, 40: Motilal Nehru to Thakurdas, 27 April 1925. See also Broomfield, *op.cit.*, pp. 263-6. These sources suggest that both Nehru and Das hoped that Reading's visit to England would result in an honourable peace.

As it turned out, Nehru's derisive utterances were more apt than his private hopes. Reading visited England not to discuss political reform but to devise a formula for pouring cold water on nationalist aspirations. He had viewed the Muddiman Committee merely as an expedient for holding the situation in check,[180] and contrary to Jinnah's expectations he had been thoroughly unimpressed with the policy of rational protest.[181] In 1924, with a Labour government in office and the Nationalists in control of the Assembly, he had shown distinct signs of strain; in 1925, with a Conservative government in office and Jinnah and Nehru at loggerheads, he was strengthened in his determination to stand firm.[182]

On 7 July, in the House of Lords, Lord Birkenhead put paid to hopes of immediate reform. He did not entirely rule out the possibility of an early statutory commission but he made it plain that no concession could be expected until Indian leaders had co-operated in the working of the Reforms.[183] This speech was a turning-point for the politics of confrontation. Until that time, Nehru's leadership and Swarajist tactics had been unchallenged and a victory at the all-India level seemed possible. Afterwards, both were rejected, and many provincial battalions withdrew from the battle and made overtures to the enemy. Consequently, Nehru was obliged to cease front-line operations and to take up the task of quelling rebellion amongst his own forces. To do that successfully, however, he eventually had to quit the legislature and to resume non-co-operation.

But the most crestfallen politician was Jinnah. It was his policy which had suffered a reverse and when the Muddiman Report was eventually debated his patience for once gave way to a mood of unrestrained exasperation :

I again here ask the Government, I ask Lord Birkenhead, I ask Lord Reading, what is your answer to those men who have cooperated with you? None. Your answer to me as one who has not non-

[180] Birkenhead papers, 1: Reading to Birkenhead, 26 March 1925.

[181] Reading had considered the Muddiman Committee valuable precisely because it was likely to split the Swarajists and the Independents. See Reading papers, 7: Reading to Olivier, 17 April and 22 May 1924.

[182] See Reading papers, 7: Reading to Olivier, 13 March, 17 April, 13 Aug., 18 Sept. and 28 Oct. 1924; also Birkenhead papers, 1: Reading to Birkenhead, 12 Feb. 26 Feb. and 19 March 1925.

[183] *Indian Quarterly Register,* 1925, vol. i, pp. 337-47.

cooperated with you is this: 'Will you bring a section of the politically minded people, who happen to be the largest political party, will you bring them down to their knees? Will you bring Pandit Motilal Nehru to bow before the throne at Viceregal Lodge and say: 'Sir, I am humble, I crawl before you, and will you now graciously be pleased to give me a Royal Commission?" Is that what you want? What has Pandit Motilal Nehru been doing in this Assembly? Has he not been cooperating with you? I want to know what more you want, and may I know what evidence, what proof, documentary or oral, do you want me to produce or adduce that the responsible leaders are willing to cooperate with you? Have you no eyes, have you no ears, have you no brains?[184]

This was the speech of a man who had fought and lost an important battle. Unlike Nehru, Jinnah could find no solace in non-co-operation. All he could do was to take up Birkenhead's challenge and work the Reforms for what they were worth. He had already pursued this policy on a small scale in Bombay[185] and he proceeded to advocate it on a national scale. In July, he made overtures to Jayakar, the Bombay Swarajist, and in November he also tried to form a party with discontented Congressmen from the Central Provinces.[186] Yet the further he moved towards Congress dissidents, the further he moved away from the most powerful elements in the League. This was a paradox which could not be resolved. To support Nehru was to support a policy of non-co-operation and Hindu-Muslim Unity: to support his opponents was to support a policy of co-operation and Hindu-Muslim antagonism. Jinnah could not have his cake and eat it. He escaped to Europe in 1926 as a member of the Skeen Committee and he did not become prominent again until after the 1926 elections.

Communalism and the Congress: the 1926 elections

After Birkenhead's announcement, the confrontation with the Raj ceased to hold the centre of the stage and its place was taken by a conflict between Nehru and his opponents. Opposition to Nehru came from two main sources; firstly from his own allies in the Central

[184] *ILA Debates*, vol. 6, part ii, 8 Sept. 1925, pp. 940-1.

[185] Purushotamdas Thakurdas papers, 40: Jinnah to Thakurdas, circular letter, 22 May 1925; M.R. Jayakar, op.cit., vol. ii, pp. 558-60.

[186] Jayakar, op.cit., vol. ii, pp. 590-1 and 705-6.

Provinces and Bombay, and in particular from the Tilakite Congress organizations in Maharashtra, C.P. (Marathi) and Berar; and secondly from the communal Hindus of the Punjab and the U.P. and their allies in Sind, C.P. (Hindi), Bihar and Orissa, and Bengal. The main point at issue was office-acceptance. Nehru had built his all-India organization on the rejection of the Reforms and a demand that the constitution be completely overhauled. Yet having failed to budge the British, he had to face a demand that the Reforms be worked for what they were worth. This had been Tilak's advice to his followers in the Deccan in 1920 and though they had bowed first to Gandhi and then to Nehru they now sought to implement that advice. In early October, Tambe, a Swarajist leader in Berar, flouted party discipline and accepted office. Nehru condemned his action only to find it being compared to his own in accepting a seat on the Skeen Committee; and before the year was out, despite efforts to patch up differences, a full-scale revolt had taken place.[187] At the same time, in North India, Malaviya's activities had become more overtly political. In August, the working committee of the Mahasabha decided to set up candidates for the forthcoming elections if other candidates were inimical to Hindu interests,[188] and in September, Malaviya began to give all-India importance to the issue of music before mosques. On 5 September, his relative, Pandit Rama Kant Malaviya, told a joint Hindu-Muslim meeting at the Collector's house at Allahabad that local Hindus could not agree to stop music before mosques until there was an all-India settlement[189] and on 21 September, Malaviya himself saw the Home Member in this connection.[190] Malaviya was slower than the Maharashtrians to come out in favour of responsive co-operation but this escalation of communal issues from the local level to the all-India level was an indication of his rising political ambition.

Both these groups clashed jointly with Nehru at the Kanpur Congress. Nehru proposed a resolution reaffirming the faith of the Congress in civil disobedience, insisting on non-acceptance of office as the party programme for the 1926 elections, and calling for a

[187] See Nanda, op.cit., pp. 263-5.

[188] AICC papers, G 47/1926: Pandit Dev Ratan Sharma to Motilal Nehru, 29 April 1926.

[189] GUPGAD 680/1925: Note by Crosthwaite, Collector of Allahabad, enclosed with Smith to Alexander, 7 Sept. 1925.

[190] GI Home Poll. 368/1925: Note by Sir Alexander Muddiman, 21 Sept. 1925.

withdrawal of Swarajists from the legislatures if the National Demand had not been met by February 1926. Malaviya proposed an amendment urging the Congress to work the Reforms to the best possible advantage, replacing the National demand of February 1924 with the less extreme demand of September 1925, and deleting all reference to civil disobedience and resignation.[191] Malaviya was supported by Jayakar, the leader of the Bombay Swarajists, Kelkar, Tilak's lieutenant at Poona, Aney, the party leader in Berar, and Moonji, the key man at Nagpur, but Nehru ultimately carried the day.[192] Nonetheless, the scene was set for a substantial political battle in the crucial months before the 1926 elections.

The Mahasabhites and the Maharashtrians were fighting a political battle but they were using communal weapons. Malaviya had already found communal war-cries useful for dividing Nehru from his Muslim supporters in the U.P. municipalities; and in the Central Provinces and Bombay, though the Muslims were less of an obstacle to office-acceptance, the same cries of Hindu unity served to rally support for the Brahmin party and to divert attention from the growing non-Brahmin challenge both in local self-government and in the services. The battle between Nehru and his opponents, therefore, was not only significant for the political future of the Congress but also for the chances of Hindu-Muslim unity at the all-India level. The crucial factor was Nehru's ability to cope with the opposition which now faced him. Would he be able to defeat the forces of communalism or would he be obliged to compromise with them in order to survive?

The central plank in Nehru's platform—non-acceptance of office—was dictated by his concern to preserve a strong national opposition to the Raj. Unlike in 1937, when the Congress possessed majorities in eight provinces and could take office without compromising its national position, in 1926 the Congress possessed only one strong majority, in the Central Provinces, and one shaky one, in Bengal. Elsewhere, with the communal temperature running high and alliances with Muslim members virtually out of the question, office-acceptance involved not only compromising the Congress creed in order to ally with other parties but also co-operating with the Raj itself. It

[191] For the demand of Sept. 1925, see *ILA Debates,* vol. 6, part ii, 7 Sept. 1925, pp. 854-5.

[192] *Indian Quarterly Register,* 1925, vol. ii, pp. 331-40.

involved, in short, the end of the Congress as a disciplined national opposition party and the transformation of the national confrontation into a number of fragmentary provincial confrontations. Moreover, in the U.P., Nehru's own political base, it was tantamount to capitulation to Malaviya. Thus both for personal and national reasons, office-acceptance had to be resisted.

Nonetheless, the trend towards office-acceptance had to be balanced against the need to preserve the Congress as a comprehensive political organization: Nehru did not proceed recklessly when the allegiance of entire Congress provinces was at stake. If the Swarajists of Maharashtra, C.P. (Marathi) and Berar were totally alienated, the Congress would be virtually unrepresented in those provinces and Nehru thus strove manfully to discover common ground between his own position and that of his former allies. Between October 1925, when Tambe accepted office, and May 1926, when the Sabarmati Pact became a dead letter, he held innumerable meetings and wrote endless letters cajoling and encouraging the Maharashtrians to stand by the Swarajist creed until after the 1926 elections. Indeed he was prepared to hold out hopes of office-acceptance after the elections as an incentive for continued allegiance.[193] It was only when these negotiations broke down irretrievably that he disaffiliated the committees in question and appointed fresh ones to take their place.[194]

Nehru's efforts to retain the allegiance of the Bombay and C.P. Swarajists illustrate the working of a principle which had important repercussions for Hindu-Muslim unity when applied to the Punjab and Bengal. The Punjab Congress was divided into two main factions, the first led by Lajpat Rai and closely associated with the Hindu Sabha, and the second led by Dr Satyapal and Girdharilal and based on a cross-communal alliance of Hindus, Muslims and Sikhs. Lajpat Rai was the leading Punjabi Swarajist,[195] but after his return from Europe in 1924 his activities had become increasingly communal. He had campaigned against the Congress leadership on the Mahasabha platform; he had repudiated the Lucknow Pact and he had demanded the abolition of separate electorates. Had Nehru put the

[193] AICC papers, 21/1926: Motilal Nehru to M.S. Aney, 7 Jan. 1926.

[194] See Gordon, op.cit., pp. 261 and 264-6.

[195] Lajpat Rai was returned to the Assembly as a Swarajist at a by-election in Dec. 1925. See V.C. Joshi, op.cit., vol. i, pp. xlix-1.

secular image of the Congress first, he would have withdrawn his support from Lajpat Rai and backed Satyapal and Girdharilal instead. This he did not do. Indeed so long as Lajpat Rai toed the party line on office-acceptance, Nehru did nothing to offend him. He realized that relations between the communities in the Punjab were thoroughly polarized and that the Congress stood little chance of success without an electoral adjustment with the Hindu Sabha.[196] Consequently even when Satyapal and Girdharilal succeeded in reaching an agreement with the Khilafatists whereby joint electorates would be accepted after six years, he ignored their appeals and showed signs of sacrificing them to Lajpat Rai.[197] When both factions put forward nominations for the 1926 elections, the working committee approved only those names which appeared on both lists, and left all others to be discussed with Lajpat Rai himself.[198] It was only in September when Lajpat Rai ceased opposing office-acceptance and joined Malaviya in opposing the Congress that Nehru threw his weight behind Satyapal.[199] In order to secure better Congress representation, he was obviously willing to back a communally oriented party, providing it did not err on office-acceptance, in preference to a more secular party with less chance of success.

A similar situation also obtained in Bengal where the death of Das exacerbated internal divisions within the Congress organization. As a result of Gandhi's intervention, Das's mantle fell first on J.M. Sen Gupta, a native of Chittagong with a following in the Northern and Eastern divisions. Sen Gupta continued Das's policy, particularly with regard to the Bengal Pact, but he met with intense opposition, notably from the *Karmi Sangh*, a Congress workers party with revolutionary sympathies. The *Karmi Sangh* derived much of its ideological impetus from Hindu mythology and, encouraged by Malaviya and G.D. Birla, it sought by hook or by crook to secure the Pact's abrogation. The Pact was first rescinded on 22 May 1926, after Sen Gupta had adjourned a stormy meeting for fear of defeat; it was then reinstated on 13 June, in the presence of Sarojini Naidu and Kalam Azad; and finally, it was quietly dropped by Sen Gupta

196 AICC papers, G 47/1926: K. Santanam to Nehru, 6 April 1926.

197 AICC papers, G 57(ii)/1926: Girdharilal to Motilal Nehru, 11 June 1926; Girdharilal to Sarojini Naidu, 30 June 1926.

198 AICC papers, G 57 (iii)/1926: Rangaswami Iyengar to Nehru, 14 July 1926.

199 AICC papers, G 57(v)/1926: Rangaswami Iyengar to Nehru, 20 Oct. 1926.

himself as the price of an electoral alliance with the *Karmi*. Where Das's Muslim alliance was concerned, the working committee was not impassive. Yet a note written by Nehru at the height of the Bengal dispute shows that beyond sending Sarojini Naidu to Calcutta it was a virtually powerless spectator:

I do hope that all parties will join to save the Congress. If they do not, we can only do our duty and leave it to the party in power to carry out the Congress resolutions as best they can. If this party turns hostile to the Congress nothing can save it and we must submit to the inevitable.[200]

Faced with a choice between no representation in Bengal and a party of communal inclinations, the Congress inevitably chose the communal party; and it did not cease to support Sen Gupta even after he had dropped the Pact and alienated his Muslim supporters.[201]

Nehru also wooed the Mahasabha. In a statement read in his absence to the Hindu Mahasabha at Delhi on 15 March 1926, Nehru urged the Sabha to join the Congress rather than start a separate political organization of its own.[202] Moreover, even when this advice was disregarded, and the Mahasabha both confirmed its decision to set up candidates where necessary and demanded that all political parties should allow free voting on communal questions, Nehru continued to be conciliatory. He took his stand not on the need to protect minorities but on the demands of party discipline, and as in his dealings with the Maharashtrians, he encouraged the Mahasabhites to remain in the Congress in the hope of securing a victory for their policy when the elections results were out.[203] Nehru also showed distinct signs of flexibility where separate electorates were concerned. The working committee laid down that no Congressman could move a resolution for the abolition of separate electorates until there was general agreement between the Hindu and Muslim members of the legislatures in question, but it conceded a free vote for Congressmen on motions introduced by non-Con-

[200] AICC papers, G 57(iii)/1926: Note by Nehru on the situation in Bengal, 27 June 1926.

[201] For a fuller discussion of the Bengal dispute, see Gordon, op.cit., pp. 270-6; also *Indian Quarterly Register*, 1926, vol. i, pp. 65-100.

[202] *Indian Quarterly Register*, 1926, vol. i, pp. 407-8.

[203] AICC papers, 24/1926: Nehru to Dev Ratan Sharma, 22 May 1926.

gressman and this was a clear loophole for the Mahasabha.[204] It also attempted to secure from Lord Irwin, the new Viceroy, through the offices of Vithalbhai Patel, a guarantee that there would be no further extension of communal electorates to local self-government.[205] This was a cardinal plank in Lajpat Rai's platform and it shows how anxious Nehru was to keep him happy.

But it was Nehru's attitude towards Reforms for the Frontier which caused most suspicion amongst his Muslim followers. The Muslim League had supported Reforms for the Frontier from May 1924,[206] but the Mahasabha had never been sympathetic towards the idea, and after the Kohat riot of September 1924, its opposition intensified. Lajpat Rai played on Hindu fears of an Afghan invasion both at the all-parties conference in January 1925[207] and as President of the Mahasabha in April,[208] and faced with these divided counsels, the Congress remained silent. Matters came to a head in February 1926, however, when Syed Murtuza, a Swarajist from Madras, drew first place in a ballot to move a resolution on this question in the Assembly. The ballot took place on 1 February, and on 9 February, allegedly at Lajpat Rai's instigation, Nehru called a Swarajist meeting and opposed the moving of the resolution, firstly on the technical ground that the Executive had not been given twelve hours notice, and secondly on the political ground that the Swarajist party could not support the introduction of Dyarchy on the Frontier whilst condemning it elsewhere. All four of the Swarajist Muslims at the meeting wished the resolution to be moved, if necessary by a non-Swarajist, but Nehru remained adamant and the meeting was adjourned. The following day, owing to a secession of Muslim support, the Swarajists failed to prevent the consideration of a Government Bill to amend the Criminal Procedure Code,[209] and

[204] AICC papers, 57(ii)/1926: Nehru to Rangaswami Iyengar, 25 June 1926. Mahommed Ali objected to this decision but he was overruled.

[205] Halifax papers (IOL MSS Eur. C 152) 2: Irwin to Birkenhead, 8 July 1926.

[206] See Pirzada, op.cit., vol. i, p. 580, and vol. ii, pp. 26 and 70.

[207] AICC papers, G 72/1925.

[208] *Indian Quarterly Register,* 1925, vol. i, pp. 379-80.

[209] The resolution to consider the Bill was carried by 52 votes to 45. Five Swarajists (Syed Murtuza, Shafi Daudi, Yusuf Imam, Nawab Ismail and Khwaja Abdul Karim) and three other likely Muslim supporters (Mahommed Yakub, Sadiq Hassan and Mahmood Schamnad) did not vote. See *ILA Debates,* vol. 7, part ii, 10 Feb. 1926, p. 1081.

efforts were then made to produce a compromise. Nehru produced a formula to the effect that the Reforms demanded by the Assembly in February 1924 and September 1925 were intended for the people of India as a whole, including the inhabitants of the Frontier, but though this was acceptable as a bare minimum to the Frontier Muslims, it was made unacceptable at a party meeting on 15 February by the addition, on Lajpat Rai's insistence, of the clause, 'subject to such redistribution of provinces as may be found necessary'. This addition gave rise to the suspicion that Congress was only prepared to support Reforms for the Frontier at the cost of the Frontier's independence, and this suspicion was strengthened when Nehru made amalgamation with the Punjab a party question. At that point Syed Murtuza and Shafi Daudi resigned from the party, Syed Murtuza proceeded to move his original resolution, and the scene was set for a party split along communal lines in the Assembly. Nehru ultimately avoided that contingency by revising his original order and instructing the party to remain neutral,[210] but he did nothing further to reassure his Muslim supporters and the whole matter was eventually debated in the press.

Syed Murtuza's charge against Nehru was that he had sacrificed the Frontier Muslims in order to gain Lajpat Rai's support in the 1926 elections:

I was driven to the conclusion [he wrote] that a considerable part of the Hindu opposition to the extension of the Reforms to the Frontier province was based on considerations that are not provincial but are imported into these discussions from other provinces of India, and in particular from the Punjab. In no other province are the Hindus in such a small minority as in the Frontier and being in most provinces in large majorities...the most communally minded Hindu can pose as a Nationalist and pretend that he asks for the abolition of communal representation and of separate electorates only because their existence is incompatible with nationalism...If the Frontier province remains a separate province and also secures the Reforms this pose of Nationalism cannot possibly be maintained any longer. One need not be a prophet to predict that the moment the Reforms are granted...the Hindu minority, which is as insignificant as our own in my own province, will begin to clamour as vociferously as the most nervous or the most greedy Mussulman seeking adequate and effective separate communal representation....

[210] On 16 Feb., the debate was adjourned on a government motion, and when it resumed on 18 March, the Swarajist walk-out had already taken place.

This is the reason why the Punjab Hindus and their Hindu supporters of other provinces brought pressure to bear on the leader of the Swaraj party, who is openly and obviously in need of their support against Pandit Madan Mohan Malaviya and the Hindus Sabhas at his back....[211]

Nehru did not attempt to refute this charge in detail: he merely reaffirmed his personal opposition to all forms of communalism.[212] Yet, as Shafi Daudi pointed out in reply to Nehru's statement, there was a difference between personal ideology and political practice:

I have not charged him, nor has any other Mussulman, so far as I know, with 'positive hostility to Musulman interest' as he has stated. But what I, and all Mussulmans with whom I had occasion to talk over the matter, do charge him with is his weak surrender to those who are universally credited with 'positive hostility to Musulman interest.' He is not himself communally biassed and he will never find me hesitating to admit his lifelong freedom from that kind of communalism, but it is not true that he has been fighting against that vice. It is his failure to fight that vice when that fight was most necessary in the interests of the country and of the Swaraj party itself that is our charge against him. Freedom from a vice in one's person is one thing and fighting against that vice in others is quite another thing.[213]

In the United Provinces, Nehru faced not the secession of an entire Congress organization but a challenge to his own control of the party machine. Malaviya was supporting office-acceptance, maximizing his contacts with Hindu landlords and using a communal platform as a means of rallying support. He had already defeated Nehru's Swarajist alliance in the 1925 municipal elections,[214] and from the Spring of 1926 he began to use the same methods for provincial ends.[215] Nehru did not want an outright battle with

[211] *The Frontier Question in the Assembly, being the statements of Pandit Motilal Nehru, MLA, Maulvi Shafi Daudi, MLA, and Syed Murtuza, MLA* (Comrade Press, Delhi 1926), pp. 26-7.

[212] Ibid., p. 36.

[213] Ibid., p. 40.

[214] GI Home Poll. 25/1924: U.P. FR I Dec. 1925.

[215] See GUPGAD 246 and 613/1926, and GI Home Poll. 112/iv/1926: U.P. FR I June, I July, II Aug. and I Sept. 1926. The chief issue was music before mosques. Malaviya attempted to secure a general ruling from the government: the government stuck rigidly to precedent and custom. Riots took place both at the *Id* and the *Ram Lila*.

Malaviya: he realized the implications of Malaviya's activities for communal relations and he knew that with the aid of Birla's lakhs Malaviya would be in a strong position. Nonetheless, though he wanted a compromise, he was not prepared to compromise on Malaviya's terms, and after September, when negotiations broke down, an outright battle took place.[216] In that battle, Malaviya used every communal device available. Nehru was accused of being a beef-eater; the Congress was stigmatized as a prostitute of Muslim India; and such was the communal hatred aroused that Nehru afterwards considered retiring from public life in disgust.[217] Yet though his every personal sentiment revolted against Malaviya's tactics, Nehru could not ignore the atmosphere which those tactics created.

An indication of the depth of communal tension and its political implications is provided by a letter from the Secretary of the Delhi PCC to the Congress President, Sarojini Naidu:

> You know [he wrote] that Delhi is the one place in the whole of India where we have got joint electorates; and during the coming elections the question of having joint electorates all round in future will be put to the test here. The Muslim and Hindu votes are in ratio of 1 to 2 and the PCC Delhi has put up Mr Asaf Ali, bar at law, as their candidate for the Assembly. It has to be admitted that Mr Asaf Ali's work and his sacrifice during the noncooperation have been of a very high order. And if judged impartially the choice of the PCC Delhi in this respect cannot be questioned.
>
> It is a matter of very great regret, if not of positive shame, that the Hindus of Delhi do not realise the importance and significance of the Delhi elections, and swayed by communal currents are determined upon putting up Hindu candidates on communal tickets. . . . The result is a foregone conclusion; the Muslim candidate fails simply because he is a Muslim. *And quite naturally this incident would furnish a very strong illustration, to be quoted in and out of season by all those who swear by separate electorates all round.*[218] [original italics].

Elsewhere, Nehru had to campaign within a solely Hindu electorate, and with communal feeling running high he was obliged to recruit

[216] See AICC papers, G 57(iv)/1926: Tgm, Nehru to Rangaswami Iyengar, 5 Sept. 1926 and draft reply. The negotiations broke down because Nehru and Iyengar, primarily for reasons of party discipline, were not prepared to concede free voting on communal questions.

[217] *A Bunch of Old Letters, written mostly to Jawaharlal Nehru and some written by him* (Bombay 1960), pp. 51-3: Motilal to Jawaharlal, Dec. 1926.

[218] AICC papers, G 52(i)/1926: Shankar Lal to Sarojini Naidu, 22 Aug. 1926.

candidates who would fare well in that political atmosphere. At Jhansi, the Swarajist candidate would gladly have stood as Malaviya's nominee and did in fact receive his blessing. 'Men like Pandit Bhagwat Narayan Bhargava and Jhanni Lal Pande are not Swarajists in the old sense,' commented the government, 'and in voting for them the majority of people have no idea of a vote subversive of Government. All parties are in the end opposition parties. The only difference is that the Swarajist party will be a better organised opposition.'[219] Another comment on Nehru's campaign is provided by his attempt, even before negotiations with Malaviya broke down, to capture the U.P. Hindu Sabha,[220] and by his willingness, once the campaign was under way, to exploit orthodox Hindu opposition to Malaviya as a means of disarming his communal appeal.[221] Recourse to such tactics did not imply that Nehru had become more communal in his personal outlook, yet in recognizing the necessity of combating Malaviya with his own weapons, he inevitably increased his reliance on communal forces. Indeed, in Rohilkhund, such was the impression created by Swarajist tactics that it was commonly thought the two men would join hands after the election.[222]

Though Nehru made considerable concessions to communal feeling, the election results were disastrous for his party. In both the U.P. and the Punjab, the Swarajists lost seats to the communalists. In the U.P., from thirty-one members in 1923, they were reduced to sixteen members in 1926. Nehru was thoroughly routed by Malaviya in Oudh, and without Pant's activities in the west the result would have been even more disappointing. In the Punjab, the party lost six seats, only two of Nehru's nominees being elected compared with nine of Lajpat Rai's. In the Central Provinces, the Congress lost its hold over the council. From a strength of thirty-five in 1923, the party was reduced to seventeen members in 1926. The Res-

[219] GI Home Poll. 112/X/1926: U.P. FRII Oct. 1926.

[220] AICC papers, 13/1926: Sitla Sahai to Motilal Nehru, 13 July, 20 July, 23 July, 27 July and 4 Aug. 1926.

[221] See, for example, AICC papers, 10/1926: Tgm Motilal Nehru to the manager, *Aj*, Benares, 26 Nov. 1926: 'Print immediately 5000 copies manifesto of sanyasis Benares published in recent issue of *Aj* against Malaviya's party and send by special messenger to Nandkumar Sahai Vakil Sivan.'

[222] GI Home Poll. 112/X/1926: U.P. FR I Nov. 1926.

ponsivists won nine seats and Malaviya's Independent Congress party ten. Both these parties accepted office, and salaries were voted by 55 votes to 16 on 11 January 1927.[223] In Bombay, the party lost thirteen seats and was reduced to a strength of twelve, and in Bengal, though it retained its original size, largely by an amalgamation of Hindu Swarajists and Independents, it lost all its Muslim support and failed to prevent the formation of a ministry.[224] The only bright spots were Madras and Bihar. In Madras, from a strength of ten in 1923, largely by absorbing liberal defectors and followers of Mrs Besant, the party secured the return of forty-seven members in 1926. As in Bengal, however, it achieved success at the cost of its connections with non-co-operation. In Bihar, one of the strongholds of non-co-operation, only eight Swarajists had been returned in 1923, but in 1926, following the conversion of Rajendra Prasad, the number increased to thirty-five. In the Assembly, the size of the party was not greatly altered but it ceased to be dominated by the United Provinces. Of thirty-eight members, eleven came from Madras and nine from Bihar and Orissa. Only five came from the U.P., four from Bengal, three each from Bombay and the Punjab, two from Assam and one from the Central Provinces.

The loss of support amongst Muslims was even greater. In the Central Provinces, where the Swarajists had possessed one Muslim follower in the local council and sent one to the Assembly, no Muslim was returned to either legislature in 1926. In Bengal, relations between the Congress and the Muslims were so bad that no Muslim stood on the Congress ticket. There had been fifteen Muslim Swarajists in 1923: there was none in 1926. In the Punjab, no Muslim stood on the Congress ticket in 1923 and none stood in 1926. Even those Khilafatists who sympathized with the Congress realized that to do so would be self-defeating whilst separate electorates persisted.[225] In the United Provinces, where eleven Muslims had been nominated and four returned in 1923, only six were nominated and only one returned in 1926. Of the original eleven only one was renominated, Maulvi Zahuruddin, the member

[223] IOR/L/P & J/6/267/1927: Secretary, GI Home (Public) to Secretary, Public and Judicial Department, India Oiffice, 20 Jan. 1927.

[224] In Bengal, ministerial salaries were voted by 94 votes to 38 on 17 Jan. 1927. See *Bengal Legislative Council Progs.*, vol. 24, pp. 51-2.

[225] AICC papers, 47/1926: K. Santanam to Nehru, 6 April 1926.

for Bareilly and Shahjehanpur cum Moradabad, and he was the only one returned. Not only had Muslim support decreased: there had been a virtually complete change of personnel. Indeed the indications are that Nehru concentrated on supporting Independent candidates in the hope that they would join the party once elected.[226] Only in Bihar was this dreary picture relieved, chiefly as a result of Shafi Daudi's activities. Despite his differences with Nehru over the Frontier question, Shafi Daudi campaigned vigorously for the Swarajists and prevented Muslim Congressmen from being alienated by Malaviya's activities. On 6 October, he wrote to Nehru from Monghyr:

As to running about in 3rd class and in bullock carts and wading through kneedeep waters to approach the influential voters in the interior, you will hardly find another example except in Bihar. We had to struggle hard for want of funds when came Malaviyaji to Patna and opened up the strings of his purse and carried away some of our zealous but avaricious Hindu workers. Mussulmans were seen to be anxious to follow the example of their Hindu brethren but could not succeed in creating disruption in Muslim workers' ranks and the proposed party fell through. Now the Mussulman candidates are being opposed by Government men or men of pro-Government tendencies but in their individual capacity.[227]

Ultimately fourteen Swarajist Muslims stood for eighteen seats and six were returned. These were almost the only Muslims returned to provincial councils on the Congress ticket throughout North India.[228]

In the Central Assembly, of the eight Swarajist Muslims returned in 1923, only three were returned in 1926. The two Bengalis and the Assamese did not stand, nor did the C.P. Muslim, Samiullah Khan of Nagpur. Of the other four, Shafi Daudi, Sarfaraz Hussain Khan and Yusuf Imam were returned again on the Swarajist ticket,

[226] Halfiz Mahommed Ibrahim, who was returned from Bijnor, got the best of both worlds. He was not only supported by Nehru, unofficially, but also by the pro-government elements. He undertook to support the Swarajists after his election. He utilized the same tactic, though with more dramatic consequences, in 1937. See AICC papers 21/1926: Nehru to the Rani Sahiba of Dhampur, 24 Oct. 1926; Abdul Latif to Nehru, 30 Nov. 1926.

[227] AICC papers, 21/1926: Shafi Daudi to Nehru, 6 Oct. 1926.

[228] Apart from four Muslims returned on the Swarajist ticket in Madras, the only others elected to local councils were two Khojas in Bombay and Maulvi Zahuruddin in the U.P.

while Nawab Ismail Khan got back as an Independent.[229] Syed Murtuza, a Khilafatist in 1923, was returned as a Swarajist in 1926. The only new blood came from Bihar and the U.P. From Bihar, Maulvi Badiuzzaman was returned by the Bhagalpur Muslims, and from the U.P., Tassaduq Sherwani from the Cities and Rafi Ahmed Kidwai from Oudh. Both Sherwani and Kidwai, however, were close friends of the Nehru family,[230] and their election was not an indication of a mass following in the U.P. Indeed, the narrower Assembly franchise may well have worked in their favour: their colleague, Khaliquzzaman, who stood for the U.P. Council from the Lucknow, Unao, and Hardoi constituency, was soundly defeated by the Raja of Salempur.[231]

When Nehru contemplated these results[232] with the Gauhati Congress in prospect he was profoundly discouraged:

> The Malaviya-Lala gang [he wrote to his son] aided by Birla's money are making frantic efforts to capture the Congress. They will probably succeed as no counter effort is possible from our side. I shall probably make a public declaration after the Congress and with it resign my seat in the Assembly though I am still acclaimed as the leader of the strongest party in the country. We can do no possible good in the Assembly or the Councils with our present numbers and the kind of men we have.[233]

As it turned out, such despondency was unwarranted. The Malaviya-Lala gang did not make a bid for power at Gauhati: Nehru's leadership was confirmed and all Swarajist motions were carried by large majorities. Nonetheless, where Congress relations with the Muslims were concerned, the Gauhati Congress produced an incident which augured ill for the future. If the Congress had retained any Muslim support at all, it was because it had not repudiated separate electorates, yet at Gauhati fifty-four members, including not only communalists like Gauri Shanker Misra and M.S. Aney,

[229] Nawab Ismail had disagreed with Nehru's 'walk-out' policy as early as Oct. 1925. AICC papers, 9/1925: Motilal Nehru to Nawab Ismail Khan, 2 Oct. 1925.

[230] Kidwai was Motilal's Secretary and Sherwani was a close friend of Jawaharlal's from their Cambridge days.

[231] See Khaliquzzaman, op. cit., pp. 87-8.

[232] Except where otherwise acknowledged, the foregoing anylysis of election results is based on information contained in Gordon, op. cit., pp. 181-2, 291-312 and appendices i to ix, pp. 321-79.

[233] *A Bunch of Old Letters, p. 52: Motilal to Jawaharlal, 2 Dec. 1926.*

but also progressive Congressmen close to Nehru like Sitla Sahai and Narendra Dev, proposed a resolution for the abolition of separate electorates.[234] This resolution was overruled as a result of pressure from Nehru and Gandhi but the time was not far off when Nehru would have to take a stand on this issue in order to retain the support of even his closest followers.

[234] AICC papers, 20/1926: I am indebted to Mrs Jolly of the Nehru Memorial Museum for the translation of a number of Hindi signatures.

CHAPTER 3

The Emergence of Punjabi Dominance

In the treatment of all-India politics, whether from the point of view of the Congress party or the Muslim League, it is customary, whilst dealing with the period of operation of the Montagu-Chelmsford Reforms, to pay considerably less attention to the period between 1920 and 1927 than to that between 1927 and 1935. Such a concentration of attention appears to be governed less by explicit choice than by the nature of the material available. In the first period not only is material a good deal less plentiful; it is also more intractable. The non-co-operation movement very often obscures the importance of the new constitution, and concentration on the Swaraj party at the all-India level gives only a limited insight into the all-India politician's dilemma. In the second period, on the other hand, the constitution itself is being revised and the various procedural stages make for a wealth of evidence and documentation. Political loyalties become explicit; provincial interests emerge on to the all-India stage; and conflict both between the government and the Congress and between the Congress and the Muslims becomes intensified. For all these reasons, the second period provides a more obvious subject for study than the first. It is the contention of this book, however, that the seeds of this dramatic conflict were sown during the first period; that the constitution itself fostered the political developments of the later years; and that the result of the battle between centrifugalism and centripetalism might have been predicted in 1926. If the second period receives less detailed treatment than the first, therefore, it is not because its importance is underestimated but because attention is being paid less to the events themselves than to their place within the context of politics already delineated.

The Montagu-Chelmsford Constitution produced two main trends in all-India politics, a centrifugal trend and a communal trend. Between 1923 and 1927, every all-India confrontation with the Raj was beset by provincial pressures, and the lesson which the all-india politician learnt during these years was that he either had to bow before these pressures or to bow out of politics altogether. Particularly after 1925, the Congress Swaraj party resembled a Colossus doing the splits, one leg planted at the Centre, the other pulled ever nearer to the provincial periphery; and the Muslim League and the Khilafat Committee, though possessed of fewer organizational resources, displayed similar tendencies, as may be demonstrated by reference to the careers of the Ali brothers and of Jinnah. Of a piece with this centrifugal trend was a trend towards communal polarization. Because separate electorates were continued, the introduction of ministerial responsibility set the two communities at each other's throats. Either one community effectively dominated the transferred departments to the detriment of the other, as in the Punjab, or politically depressed sections of a majority community exploited communal feeling for their own regeneration, as in the United Provinces. In either case, the result was the same : Hindu was divided from Muslim at the provincial level, and all-India politics soon came to be affected.

In the battle between the forces of centrifugalism and centripetalism, the government was not a disinterested party. In 1920 it had not only resisted devolution of power at the Centre: it had also endeavoured to devolve power to the provinces in such a way as to reproduce within the conciliar sphere the collaborative system which already worked well in the sphere of administration. In effect it sought the cooperation of provincial interest groups in maintaining the *status quo*. In exchange for an extension of their provincial privileges, these interests were to acquiesce in continued British control at the Centre: 'The Raj hath given and the Raj may give more: Blessed be the name of the Raj.' In 1918, these decisions were based more on instinct than on sinister calculation. Even the demand for provincial responsibility had only just been voiced and the government of India was in a position of overwhelming strength. By 1928, however, the non-co-operation movement had produced a considerable change in the political atmosphere. Dominion status was a widely recognized ambition and the government of India was much more sensitive to challenges to its authority. Furthermore, the working of the Reforms had reinforced the wisdom of the decisions taken ten years previously. In the provinces, devolution of power had produced staunch allies in the Punjab and Madras;

workable combinations of Hindu and Muslim landlords in the United Provinces, Bihar and Orissa, and Bombay; and even in Bengal and the Central Provinces, the Swaraj party had only succeeded in bringing the Reforms to a standstill for the duration of one council session. In the Central Assembly, on the other hand, the government had constantly been in difficulties, and even though the Legislature had no power over the Executive, without the Council of State even the pretence of democracy could not have been maintained. By 1928, therefore, what had begun as an instinctive reaction to all-India pressure had hardened into a deliberate policy: in response to challenges to its authority at the Centre, the Raj was to rely increasingly on the provinces.

This reliance on the provinces involved maximum reliance on the Muslims. There were, it is true, other important interests—the non-Brahmins of Madras and the various landlord parties of U.P., Bihar and Orissa and Bombay—yet from the all-India point of view, the Muslims formed the most coherent group. Not only did they form majorities in the Punjab and Bengal: they also formed important minorities in U.P., Bihar and Orissa, C.P. and Bombay. Moreover, where the reform of the constitution was concerned, all Muslim groups had good reason to combine. Given the prevailing atmosphere of communal antagonism, the inauguration of provincial autonomy threatened to subject the minority-province Muslim to a communal Hindu majority; and in the majority provinces, because of the backwardness of the community educationally and economically, the concession of provincial autonomy was less important than the terms under which it was introduced. For these reasons, in both Muslim minority and majority provinces, separate electorates were held to be essential for the maintenance of the Muslim position. And because only the government was prepared to make such a political concession, almost all provincial Muslim groups found themselves in the government camp. Finally, where the majority-province Muslims were concerned, there was the additional fear of Hindu control at the Centre. This added to the community of interest between these Muslims and the Raj: the continuation of British control at the Centre was a small price to pay for a free hand in one's own province.

Pride of place amongst the Muslims belonged to the Muslims of the Punjab. Fazli Husain's Unionist party was the most substantial provincial party in India and no other party was better placed to benefit from provincial autonomy. Provincial ambitions were thus strongest in the Punjab, and during the crucial years of constitutional revision, owing to their superior political leverage, it was the Punjabi Muslims who played the leading role in Muslim politics. Even the U.P. Muslims, who habitually prided themselves on their sophistication and despised the Punjabi for his lack of it, were obliged to recognize the facts of the situation:

> The eyes of your brethren in other parts of India [a leading U.P. politician told a Lahore audience in 1929] are directed towards the Punjab at this critical juncture. . . . They ask their Punjabi brethren: 'Are you willing and able to undertake the task of keeping Muslim India effectively organised and united in order that it may play a part in the rearrangement of the Indian constitution which is in consonance with its historical past and glorious culture?[1]'

And of course they were. Yet whilst the Government's reliance on the Muslims increased with the intensity of the challenge it faced from the Congress, the same officials who sought to use the Muslims as a counterweight to Congress were unwilling to allow them to encroach beyond a certain point on what they considered their own preserves. Much depended, therefore, on how the Muslims played their cards. And in the period between 1927 and 1935, that is tantamount to saying, how Fazli Husain played his cards, for during those years the bulk of the responsibility fell on his shoulders. Between 1927 and 1930, as Revenue Member of the Punjab government, he exercised his influence for the most part privately, through such lieutenants as Firoz Khan Noon, Sikunder Hayat, Chaudhuri Zafrullah and Ahmed Yar Khan Daultana, but after 1930, when he became a member of the Viceroy's Council, his became a key voice in the counsels of the government of India. Between 1930 and 1936, his political vision was a crucial factor in the process of constitutional reform, and his success or failure in achieving his objectives was to influence the future of the subcontinent as a whole.

The four proposals of March 1927

The first significant development in all-India politics after the 1926

[1] Mihr collection, 223: Shafaat Ahmed Khan's presidential address to the 8th Punjab Educational Conference, Lahore, 11 Oct. 1929.

elections was an offer by a conference of Muslims which met at Delhi on 20 March 1927 to give up separate electorates if four proposals were accepted. These proposals were as follows: the separation of Sind from Bombay; Reforms for the Frontier and Baluchistan; representation by population in the Punjab and Bengal; and thirty-three per cent for the Muslims in the Central Legislature. No such offer had previously been made by so representative a gathering, and the evidence suggests that Jinnah was the moving spirit behind it. Even for Jinnah, however, it marked something of a *volte-face*. In 1916, he had accepted that separate electorates were indispensable so long as the Muslims demanded them; and his career in the mid-1920s suggests that he saw the wisdom of sticking by the demands of the League. Why then did he put forward a proposal which he must have known would be rejected by provincial opinion?

The reason lies in the changed balance of power within the Central Assembly after the 1926 elections. The elections took place in an atmosphere of communal antagonism and Jinnah's Independent party suffered most. In the previous Assembly, Jinnah had held the balance between the Congress and the Government: in the new one, he was a leader without a following. 'There is a touch of humour', reported one unsympathetic correspondent, 'about the position of Mr M.A. Jinnah, who in the last Assembly led the Independents. It seem unlikely that there will be any such party this session..'..[2] If Jinnah was to continue to play an important role in the Assembly, therefore, it was essential for him to discover a new following, and even before the Assembly met, the same correspondent reported that he was fishing for the leadership of the Muslim group. The father-figure of the group, Sir Abdul Quaiyum, however, was not an easy fish to land, and Jinnah's subsequent behaviour suggests that no agreement was reached. He continued to judge all legislation on its merits, supporting the government over the Steel Protection Bill but opposing it over the Currency Bill, whereas the Muslim bloc, under Quaiyum's leadership, voted solidly for the government and so thwarted the ambitions of the Swaraj party and the Nationalist party.[3] The obvious lesson to be

[2] *The Times*, 20 Jan. 1927.

[3] The government had worked hard to secure this accession of Muslim support, notably by their part in the election of Mahommed Yakub as Deputy President. See

learnt from this situation was not lost on the Congress. It was already divided, and without Muslim support it was likely to become ineffective. As the session closed, therefore, the Congress President, Srinivasa Iyengar, made an appeal to Muslim members to join his party in pressing for political reform.[4] It was in response to this appeal that the conference of 20 March was called.

What makes it doubly clear that the four proposals were a response to Central Assembly conditions is the fact that of twenty-nine Muslims who attended the conference sixteen were members of the Central Assembly and two were members of the Council of State.[5] No member of a provincial legislature attended; and the remaining Muslims were either Congressmen, Panislamists or all-India constitutional politicians. It is also noteworthy that the terms themselves make no provision for the continuation of weightage in the minority provinces despite the fact that almost all those present were either from minority provinces or from minority divisions of majority provinces.[6] This suggests that the four proposals were a new political initiative by politicians who had little chance of power in their own provinces. The first group might be termed 'Independents' pure and simple: Jinnah, Mahommed Yakub (though he had become more pro-government since his election as Deputy President of the Assembly), and the Raja of Mahmudabad. The second was a group of Swarajists who had come to adopt a more independent stance: Shafi Daudi and Shah Mahommed Zubair from Bihar, Syed Murtuza and Nawab Ismail. The third was a group of urban politicians from the Muslim majority provinces: Sir Mahommed Shafi and his son-in-law, Shah Nawaz, whose political base was in east and central Punjab, and Abdullah Suhrawardy, Calcutta's original Young Turk. Shafi and Shah Nawaz had no chance of political power in their own province while the Maliks of Shahpur were

Halifax papers, 3: Irwin to Birkenhead, 3 Feb. 1927; also *ILA Debates*, 3rd Assembly 1st session, vol. i. 31 Jan. 1927. pp. 301-3. For the voting list on the Steel Industry Protection Bill, see ibid., vol. i. 21 Feb. 1927, p. 1114; for the vote on the ratio during the Currency Bill debate, see ibid., vol. ii. pp. 1894-5.

[4] *Indian Quarterly Register*, 1927, vol. i, pp. 32-3.

[5] IOR/L/P and J/6/1197/1927: Indian News Agency tgm. 20 March. 1927.

[6] Apart from the Frontiersmen, there were only three Muslims present from Muslim majority areas: Raja Ghazanfar Ali of Jhelum. Sardar Mahommed Nawaz Khan, who represented the Punjab landholders, and Anwar ul Azim of Dacca. All were members of the Assembly.

running the show, and Suhrawardy, after jumping from Das's pocket into Rahim's pocket and back again, had decided in 1926 that Central Assembly politics might be more to his liking. A fourth group consisted of Mahommed Ali, Dr Ansari and Abdur Rahman Siddiqui. Mahommed Ali was uncomfortable in the Congres; and Ansari and Siddiqui, though less uncomfortable, saw the urgency of the communal situation. Lastly, there were the Frontiersmen, Sir Abdul Quaiyum and Abdul Aziz. Like the Sindhis, they were possessed of a grievance which gave them a ready reason to join a new confrontation and the promise of Reforms for the Frontier was enough to sweep them into the net.

Even more significant than the terms themselves, however, was the response to them, for, as the Viceroy anticipated, whatever Jinnah's original intentions (and these were by no means clear at the time), the result of his initiative was to 'widen rather than diminish the breach between the two communities.'[7] The response, indeed, did no more than illustrate two recurring features of the all-India political scene, the importance of provincial Muslim opinion and the reluctance of the Mahasabha to accept any terms which did not amount to total submission.

On 23 March, certain Hindu legislators, under Malaviya's presidency, gave the first indication of the communal Hindu response to the terms. They snatched at the concession over separate electorates. They turned the demand regarding representation by population in the Punjab and Bengal into a demand for the abolition of weightage in Muslim minority provinces. And they declared, regarding the Frontier and Sind, that the time was not ripe for the discussion of such questions.[8] It did not augur well for the future. On 29 March, seeing the way things were going, Jinnah issued a statement to the press making it clear that the four proposals had to be accepted or rejected *in toto*.[9] But this did not improve the situation. Indeed, when the Mahasabha met at Patna on 16 April, Jinnah's own statement was used as an excuse for not discussing the offer at all. The same meeting did not fail to express its opinion, however, that consideration of the proposals by the Congress would be premature and harmful, and it made its position doubly clear by de-

[7] Halifax papers, 3: Irwin to Birkenhead, 24 March 1927.

[8] *Indian Statutory Comission*, vol. iv (London 1930),p. 169.

[9] *Indian Quarterly Register*, 1927, vol. i, pp. 36-7.

manding new discussions on the basis of joint electorates and a uniform franchise. Reservation of seats was only to be for a prescribed period and reservation by population was only one of several alternatives. Voting strength and taxation, criteria which particularly favoured the Hindus of the Punjab and Bengal, were also to be considered.[10] This response suggests that the Mahasabha was not interested in coming to terms at all.

The provincial Muslim response was not much better. By the end of April, the Muslims of the U.P. and Madras councils had condemned the offer, and by the middle of May, similar sentiments had been expressed by representative gatherings in the Punjab, Bengal and Bihar. At a meeting at Lahore on 1 May, the Punjab Muslim League, under the presidency of Sir Mahommed Shafi, whilst acknowledging the good faith of the Muslims who had made the original offer, condemned the Hindu press and political organizations for showing it such scant courtesy. The four proposals, it was said, were virtually the same as those put forward by Mr Kelkar at the Kanpur Mahasabha in 1925, and the fact that they had been rejected by the same organization at Patna was taken as an indication of the grasping mentality of the communal Hindu politician.[11] Seven days later, at Barisal, Sir Abdur Rahim presided over a meeting of the Bengal Provincial Muslim Conference which came to the same conclusions. Had conditions been more peaceful, he said, the Muslims might have been more inclined to accept joint electorates, but given the state of communal tension, negotiations were unlikely to be productive.[12]

The provinces were vetoing Jinnah's all-India initiative, and several supporters of the original offer began to change their minds. In the aftermath of the Delhi conference, for example, Sir Mahommed Shafi received a flood of abusive and threatening letters, not only from the Punjab but from all parts of India, and it was these letters, quite as much as the Mahasabha response, which produced his *volte-face* at Lahore.[13] Another man who had second

[10]*Indian Quarterly Register*, 1927, vol. i, pp. 422-3: Proceedings of the All Indian Hindu Mahasabha at Patna, 16-18 April 1927, Resn no. xvi.

[11] IOR/L/P and J/6/1442/1927: Resolutions of the Punjab Muslim League meeting at Lahore on 1 May, enclosed in GI. Home Public dispatch 74/1927, 26 May 1927.

[12] *Indian Quarterly Register*, 1927, vol. i, pp. 432-3.

[13] Halifax papers, 3: Irwin to Birkenhead, 26 May 1927.

thoughts was Sir Abdul Quaiyum. In his case, however, it seems likely that official pressure was partly responsible. He may well have been told that the Frontier would get Reforms more quickly if it backed the official horse.[14] Two men who did stand by the proposals were Shafi Daudi and Sir Ali Imam. They convened a special meeting at Patna on 8 May, and put forward their case with some passion. The opposition of Sir Mahommed Fakhuruddin and the Bihari Muslim rural interest, however, was too substantial to be overcome.[15] By the middle of May, the proposals had been rejected by every important provincial group.

Unlike in 1925, the Congress did not hide behind the Mahasabha. The day after the proposals were announced, the working committee welcomed the Muslim initiative and set up a subcommittee to examine its implications. This subcommittee, consisting of Srinivasa Iyengar, Motilal Nehru, Sarojini Naidu nad Mahommed Ali, was clearly sympathetic towards the Muslims, and it recommended that the Congress accept the proposals. Indeed two additional concessions were also recommended, the first guaranteeing liberty of conscience, and the second giving minorities the right to veto legislation affecting their community by a seventy-five per cent vote.[16] The AICC which met at Bombay on 15 May, however, was less easily convinced than the members of the subcommittee. Jayakar, Moonje and Kelkar were not initially prepared to accept the proposals regarding Sind and the Frontier, and what came to be known as the Delhi-Bombay compromise was only adopted when two of Jayakar's amendments had been carried. Reforms for the Frontier became conditional on the provision of a suitable judiciary, and the separation of Sind conditional on the separation of Andhra. Neither of these conditions militated against the spirit of the four proposals, however, and both Dr Ansari and Mahommed Ali were happy to accept them[17]

But though the Congress accepted the proposals, they never became a landmark to rival the Lucknow Pact, largely because the political will necessary for a new confrontation was singularly lack-

[14] Ibid., Irwin to Birkenhead, 11 and 19 May 1927. In the second letter, Irwin confesses to Birkenhead that some members of his council are keen for an extension of Reforms to the Frontier before the Statutory Commission is appointed, 'partly ...to build a dyke against the Statutory Commission . . . and partly in order to please Muslim opinion for general purposes'.

[15] *Indian Quarterly Register,* 1927, vol. i, pp. 39-40.

[16] Ibid., 1927, vol. i, pp. 14-21.

[17] Ibid.

ing. The Congress put itself in a favourable light by accepting the Muslim offer but it did very little more. Jinnah was the only politician to use the Congress resolution in an attempt to consolidate his position and even he realized that paper agreements would not alter provincial opinion. When he visited Lahore in June, he not only advocated the acceptance of the Delhi-Bombay compromise: he also claimed that as a result of his influence with the Government of India, Reforms would be granted to the Frontier.[18] This was an appeal based not on reason but on power, and though the claim was false, as Muddiman hastened to inform Hailey,[19] it touched on the essential factor in the situation. To make an agreement was one thing: to implement it quite another. And where implementation was concerned, the government had the satisfaction of knowing that its position was supreme. As Muddiman put it, while commenting on a draft dispatch relating to these events: 'It is a case of manoeuvring for a political position and as usual the Muslims will be out manoeuvred but neither side can deliver the goods even if they wished to do so.'[20]

The appointment of the Statutory Commission

The divisions of Indian political life demonstrated by the various reactions to Jinnah's initiative were undoubtedly a source of confidence to the government. It was in a stronger position than it had been for many years, and its strength was on the increase. At the provincial level, Hindu was divided from Muslim, and at the all-India level, not only was cooperation both between Gandhi and the Ali brothers and between Nehru and Jinnah virtually a thing of the past: Swarajist was also set against Mahasabhite and the confrontation with the Raj had all but broken down. Indeed all the evidence suggests that the government's main opponents, the Swarajist leaders, recognized the weakness of their position and were searching for a good excuse to give up non-co-operation.[21]

18 Hailey papers, 10B: Sir Malcolm Hailey to Sir Alexander Muddiman, 13 June 1927.

19 Ibid., Muddiman to Hailey, 15 June 1927.

20 GI Home Poll. 6/1927: Note by Muddiman, 24 May 1927.

21 Halifax papers, 3: Irwin to Birkenhead, 6 Jan., 3 Feb., 24 Aug., 31 Aug. and 29 Sept. 1927. On 2 Feb., discussions actually took place between Muddiman, Nehru, Rangaswami Iyengar and Srinivasa Iyengar about how the government could help to extricate the Swarajists from this situation.

In such circumstances, the government made a serious miscalculation in appointing an entirely Parliamentary Statutory Commission. This was the one development calculated to lift the entire conflict between government and its all-India opponents from the political to the racial plane and to reunite those who were slowly being divided from each other. And this is precisely what happened. A large body of Indian opinion was alienated, opposition was intensified, demands sharpened and, as Irwin himself anticipated in a rare moment of insight, the game on each side was thrown 'very much into the hands of the extremists both in India and out of it.'[22] What is surprising is that the government did not realize the wisdom of making some concession to Indian *amour-propre.* The entire course of politics after the collapse of non-cooperation serves to show that the working of the Reforms in the provinces was making a successful confrontation with the Raj more and more difficult. The appointment of Indians to the Statutory Commission, particularly as selection would have been the government's prerogative, was only likely to reinforce the divisions which had already become apparent. At best, it would have produced a salutary change in the relations between the Congress and the Raj; at worst, merely a minority report. Why, then, did the government make such a Himalayan blunder? The answer lies in the origin of the advice on which the Viceroy based his decision.

When Lord Irwin arrived in New Delhi in April 1926, raw and untutored in Indian problems, he fell under the influence of Sir Malcolm Hailey, the Governor of the Punjab. By his own admission, Hailey was one of his chief advisers,[23] and his private secretary, whom he inherited from Lord Reading, was Geoffrey de Montmorency, one of Hailey's greatest friends and closest colleagues.[24] There are grounds for believing, therefore, that Irwin was introduced to India in his first months as Viceroy with the help of a Punjabi guidebook. It was Hailey and de Montmorency who ad-

[22] Ibid., Irwin to Birkenhead, 26 May 1927.

[23] Irwin subsequently admitted that he had 'relied greatly' on Hailey's advice 'from the time I first landed in India'. See Frederick, 2nd Earl of Birkenhead, *F.E.* (London 1965), pp. 323-4.

[24] De Montmorency had served as Hailey's assistant when Hailey was Chief Commissioner of Delhi. He was appointed private secretary to Lord Reading when Hailey was Finance Member of the Viceroy's Council. In 1928, he was to succeed him as Governor of the Punjab.

vised him in the appointment of the Statutory Commission and it was this first step which set the scene for what followed. Moreover, though Irwin later differed with Hailey over broad outlines of government policy, he continued to rely on his advice where recruitment to the government of India secretariat was concerned. Apart from de Montmorency, a number of other Punjab civilians held key posts at this time. James Dunnett, who served in the Home Department from 1926 to 1930, first as Joint Secretary and then as Additional Secretary, was appointed Reforms Commissioner in 1930 and held the post throughout the period of constitutional revision. A man of very outstanding intelligence, his part in reshaping the constitution has yet to receive proper attention. In 1929, when a Muslim was required for the Secretary of State's Council, it was Malik Sir Umar Hayat Khan Tiwana, the most influential agriculturalist Muslim in the Punjab, who was appointed. In 1930, when a new Muslim member was needed on the Viceroy's Council, it was Fazli Husain who received the summons. And in 1931, when the government of India wanted a competent man to manage the administrative difficulties produced by the Gandhi-Irwin Pact, it was Herbert Emerson, the man whom Hailey had used to win Sikh support for government legislation on the Gurdwaras, who was appointed Home Secretary. The Punjab had long been considered the sword-arm of India, but from the early 1920s, as a result of Hailey's influence, it also became the soul in the machine.

This reliance on Punjabi personnel was not mere favouritism: between 1909 and 1937, with the possible exception of Sir Reginald Craddock, there was no government of India official to compare with Hailey, de Montmorency, Emerson or Dunnett: their clarity of mind and political shrewdness were in a class of their own. Yet such reliance did have important implications: it involved accepting Punjabi ideas and managing all-India politics from the Punjabi point of view. What did this imply in detail? At the simplest level, the Punjab civilian had three main characteristics: firstly, contempt for the political classes; secondly, a political vision that was essentially communal in outlook—the belief that the government could maintain its prestige by holding the balance between the two communities; and thirdly, a distinctive *esprit de corps* which separated him from other civilians elsewhere. Because of the importance of the Punjab as a recruiting ground for the Army, genuine loyalty to the

Crown still existed amongst large sections of the community, and the growth of Indian political ambitions had yet to sap civilian morale. If Indian politics were to go the way of Bengal, therefore, the Punjab civilian wished to have nothing to do with it. What he wanted—and here his ambitions coincided with those of the Punjabi Muslims—was continued British control at the Centre and the freest possible hand in his own province. These three characteristics, through the influence of Hailey and his men in the secretariat, were to have a very extensive influence on the government of India's attitude to Reform.

The Statutory Commission took the form it did almost exclusively as a result of Hailey's advice. On 19 August 1926, in reply to a suggestion by Birkenhead that Indians should be appointed to the Commission, Irwin confessed to grave doubts as to the wisdom of such a step. The danger, he said, was that the Commission would become unwieldy and that two reports would be produced, one of which could well have been written beforehand.[25] These grave doubts may well have been sown by Hailey. In a letter written to Lord Irwin on 20 August, in which he referred to an earlier discussion, Hailey reaffirmed his preference for a Parliamentary Commission: 'If the Commission is to include Indian politicians, then it must be representative of all communities, and it will be impossible to expect from it a clear view on such questions as communal representation'. This stress on the importance of communal divisions was a reflection of Hailey's experience of Punjabi politics. There, communal polarization had reached such a point that all communities understood the dangers of boycott:

I have some feeling [Hailey wrote in the same letter] that Indians themselves, divided as they are at present on communal lines, would prefer a Commission composed as I suggest. At the moment, the communal question is even more important than the form which political advance may take.[26]

Undeterred by this advice, in March 1927, Birkenhead again pressed for the appointment of Indians. Irwin forwarded his letter to Hailey for comment, and Hailey replied along much the same lines as before. If Indians were to be appointed, the Commission

[25] Halifax papers, 2: Irwin to Birkenhead, 19 Aug. 1926.

[26] Hailey papers, 9 C: Hailey to George Cunningham (Private Secretary to the Viceroy), 20 Aug. 1926.

would have to be representative. But if it were representative, it would not be unanimous, and if it were not unanimous, Parliament would not be satisfied. Openmindedness was essential: hence the need to exclude all experienced civilians and politicians.[27] This letter was submitted by Irwin to Birkenhead on 19 May.[28]

By May, however, Irwin was beginning to have second thoughts. On 7 May, in a letter to Hailey, whilst adhering to the principle of a Parliamentary Commission, he suggested either that Indians should be associated with the Commission as adjutors or that the Commission report should be submitted to a joint committee of the Central Assembly and the Council of State.[29] On 21 May, Hailey and de Montmorency discussed this question, and the following day, de Montmorency replied on Hailey's behalf. The letter gives away more than Hailey's earlier epistles: it is clear that the main fear of the Punjab civilians was that all-India politicians would secure the lion's share of Indian representation.

> The men chosen will be too deeply imbued with the All India politician point of view. The provinces already feel that the All India politician does not represent the real interests of the people of a province, and is too apt to attach himself to parties in and outside the Central Legislature with labels which have no true meaning and no reality as far as the living issues are concerned. The provinces, on the other hand, have had more practical experience of representative institutions. They are anchored to facts. They know or think they know what they want. They are more likely to know what will work.[30]

And the corollary of this view was that there should not be one body of adjutors but several, indeed one for each province as well as one for the Central Legislature.[31]

For Irwin, the value of Indian adjutors was that they would lessen the chances of boycott. And to that extent, Hailey's acceptance of the principle involved, was clearly welcome. Yet fears of boycott still persisted,[32] and by the end of May Irwin was again considering putting Indians on the Commission. He wrote to both Hailey and

[27] Hailey papers, 10A: Hailey to Irwin, 23 April 1927.
[28] Halifax papers, 3: Irwin to Birkenhead, 19 May 1927.
[29] Hailey papers,10A; Irwin to Hailey, 7 May 1927.
[30] Ibid., de Montmorency to Irwin, 22 May 1927.
[31] This suggestion was ultimately adopted by the government of India.
[32] Halifax papers, 3: Irwin to Birkenhead, 26 May 1927.

Birkenhead on this score and even suggested personnel on the Indian side.[33] Once again, however, he was steered away from this suggestion by Hailey and de Montmorency. At the same time that he was voicing his fears of boycott to the Secretary of State, Hailey, de Montmorency and Muddiman were putting forward 'their very definite view...that as things are today a general boycott is in the highest degree improbable.'[34] A certain number of Irwin's advisers, notably Sir Mahommed Habibullah, the Muslim member of his council, took another view. They pointed out the unwisdom of giving the Swarajists a racial grievance at the very moment when they found themselves in an unprofitable cul-de-sac.[35] But this advice was ignored. Throughout that summer at Simla, whilst Irwin paced Viceregal Lodge making his decision, it was Hailey, only a stone's throw away at Barnes Court, whose advice carried most weight.

Hailey's position was one of reliance first on the provinces and second on the Muslims. In his advice to the Viceroy, whether with regard to the composition of the Statutory Commission or the various other expedients put forward as means of satisfying Indian opinion, he continually stressed the unreasonableness, the unpracticality and the unrepresentative status of the all-India leaders, and he made sure that the coincidence between his own views and those of the Punjabi Muslims was well-known to the Viceroy. He appears to have established a close working relationship with Firoz Khan Noon, his Minister for Local self-Government, and both in the corridors of the government of India and in the councils of the Muslim League, Firoz worked assiduously to secure the triumph of the Punjabi point of view. At the end of August, Irwin informed Birkenhead that 'Hailey's Muslims' had definitely come out for a Parliamentary Commission,[36] and a month later, in an interview with Firoz Khan Noon, he heard the same news himself at first hand:

[33] Hailey papers, 10A: Note by Lord Irwin, forwarded by George Cunningham to Hailey, 24 May 1927: Halifax papers, 3: Irwin to Birkenhead, 2 June 1927. No names were suggested to Birkenhead, but to Hailey, Irwin suggested Motilal Nehru, Fazli Husain, C.P.,Ramaswami Iyer and Sir Chunilal Mehta. In addition, there were to be 'three good Englishmen', one official and one non-official. The Indians would have been in a minority of one.

[34] Halifax papers, 3. Irwin to Birkenhead, 26 May 1927.

[35] Ibid., Irwin to Birkenhead, 2 June 1927.

[36] Ibid. Irwin in Birkenhead, 24 Aug. 1927.

The upshot of his conversation [he reportea to Birkenhead] was that communal electorates were as vital to Mussulmans as they had ever been, and that on this point there was, as I have already said, substantial unanimity of opinion in Moslem circles. They were anxious as to the influence that might be exerted against their views by what they considered to be mugwump politicians like Jinnah, Mahmudabad, Ali Imam etc., and had been considering very anxiously how best to forestall this danger in connection with the Statutory Commission. He insisted that in this matter all Hindus were unanimous in their desire to get rid of communal electorates, and therefore any Hindus who might be placed on a Mixed Commission would be advocates in this sense.For this reason, it was of the utmost importance to them that,if there were to be any Moslems at all on the Commission,the Moslems to be placed on it should be men about whose staunchness on this vital question from the Moslem point of view there could be no doubt. The only two names he mentioned as names in whom the whole Moslem community would have confidence on this issue were Fazli Husain and Abdur Rahim. Unless these two men could be appointed on the Commission, he was charged by all his Moslem friends to tell me that they would definitely prefer a Parliamentary Commission with no Indians at all.[37]

By degrees, therefore, Irwin's doubts and worries were calmed down and Birkenhead's own suggestions rejected by the Viceroy on the basis of civilian knowledge and experience. By July 1927, the question was no longer in doubt. Simon had accepted the chairmanship of the Commission,[38] and attention was being paid more to the preparations for its announcement than to the form it should take. Such features as the interview with Firoz were used, not as arguments for one sort of Commission or another, but as evidence that the decision to appoint a Parliamentary Commission was meeting with Indian approval. By July, despite a good deal of dillydallying, Irwin had swallowed the Punjabi bait, and by October, in letting the Secretary of State know about his plans for the Commission, he was putting forward the very strategy which Hailey himself had advocated. He told Birkenhead that the government would be able to rely on three main sources of support, firstly the Muslims, secondly the provinces and thirdly the liberals.[39] Except with regard to the liberals, whose position the government never fully appreciated,

[37] Ibid., Irwin to Birkenhead, 29 Sept. 1927.

[38] Irwin approved Simon's appointment in a letter to Birkenhead on 14 July.

[39] Halifax papers, 3: Irwin to Birkenhead, 5 Oct. 1927.

this was an accurate prediction of future developments. But whereas this strategy was appropriate to the conditions in the Punjab, where the majority community was cooperating with the government and where the minorities could not afford for that reason to boycott the Commission, it was less defensible elsewhere. In other provinces, where divisions between communities did not work so effectively to the government's advantage, it was to provoke a confrontation with Indian opinion which put a very severe strain on the government's credibility and resources.

The Punjabi breakaway

The announcement of the all-white Commission led to a considerable strengthening of national feeling. Lord Irwin had seen Congress leaders before the announcement was made and had reported to Birkenhead that they were not very happy at the prospect.[40] But it was only when the news became public that the real depth of Indian feeling could be gauged. 'The shouting at present', he wrote to Birkenhead on 16 November, 'is rather louder and more uncompromising than I had perhaps anticipated.'[41] It was a typical case of understatement. On 10 November, Dr Ansari, who had just been elected Congress President, issued a statement enjoining all Congressmen to boycott the Commission completely.[43] On 16 November, to the surprise of both government and Congress, Sir Abdur Rahim presided over a boycott meeting at Calcutta.[43] And on 18 November, Fazli Husain, just returned from representing India at the League of Nations, told reporters that he opposed the Parliamentary commission and would support a Muslim League boycott providing the Hindu Mahasabha came out for the same policy.[44] In all probability this was simply political manoeuvring; the threat to withdraw Muslim support from Government was to be used to good effect on a number of occasions in the future. Yet these manoeuvrings added to government's anxiety. Only a fortnight after the announcement had been made, the calculations behind Irwin's decision looked unsound.

Where all-India Muslim politics was concerned, the effect of the

[40] Ibid., Irwin to Birkenhead, 3 Nov. 1927.

[41] Ibid., Irwin to Birkenhead, 16 Nov. 1927.

[42] *Indian Quarterly Register, 1927*, vol, ii, p. 14.

[43] Ibid., p. 15.

[44] *Indian Daily Mail*, 1927; *The Herald*, 19 Nov. 1927 (enclosed, Hailey papers, 11 B).

announcement was to force politicians like Jinnah and the Ali brothers back into the mainstream of nationalist protest. The exclusion of Indians boded ill for the chances of any substantial devolution at the Centre, and all those interested in such a development consequently closed their ranks. Jinnah was particularly active at this time. He did not actually come out for a policy of complete boycott because he hoped that Indian appeals would produce a change of personnel on the Commission.[45] But he worked hard to produce a united national front. Before the parliamentary debate on the Viceroy's announcement, he organized a telegram of protest and circulated all important leaders for permission to add their signatures[46]. And when the Parliamentary debate produced no change, he organised a joint meeting of all political organizations at Bombay on 12 December.[47] Mahommed Ali was less active but inclined to the same view. He favoured holding a joint session of the Congress and the League at Madras and he wired his brother, Shaukat, to get Jinnah to make the necessary arrangements.[48]

These tendencies to unity were encouraged by the Congress. Dr Ansari, the President, wrote to all prominent Indian politicians, Hindu and Muslim, co-operator and non-co-operator, urging them to use the opportunity provided to reunite nationalist forces. Reactions to the Commission had convinced him that divisions in the body politic were merely over matters of detail: on matters of principle they were all virtually unanimous.[49] He received a number of encouraging replies, some from unexpected sources. Hassan Imam and the Raja of Mahmudabad supported boycott, Mahommed Yakub agreed that 'a large number of Muslims should attend the Congress,' and Abdur Rahim, though unprepared to meet other leaders on the Congress platform, wished to make plans for concerted action. Only Hafiz Hidayat Hussain of Kanpur indulged in

[45] See Halifax papers, 3: Irwin to Birkenhead, 9 Nov., 1927.

[46] Mahommed Ali papers: Jinnah to Mahommed Ali, 11 Nov. 1927; Purushotamdas Thakurdas papers: Thakurdas to Birla, 16 Nov. 1927.

[47] Mahommed Ali papers: Jinnah to Mahommed Ali, 20 Nov,; Purushotamdas Thakurdas papers; Malaviya to Thakurdas, 7 Dec. 1927. Jinnah was also instrumental in organizing a protest meeting of Bombay politicians on 3 Dec. at the Sir Cowasji Jehangir Hall.

[48] AICC papers, G64/1926-8: Mahommed Ali to Srinivasa Iyengar, 21 Nov. 1927.

[49] Ansari papers (Jamia Millia Islamia, New Delhi): circular letter, 1 Dec. 1927.

outspoken criticism.[50] Moreover, if the composition of Ansari's personal entourage for the Madras Congress is any indication of his success, his efforts certainly bore fruit. It included Mahommed Ali, Shaukat Ali, Shuaib Qureshi, Abdur Rahman Siddiqui, Chaudhuri Khaliquzzaman, Abdul Aziz Ansari, Farid ul Haq Ansari and Dr Zakir Hussain.[51] The politicians of the old Delhi–Aligarh axis had been brought together again.

But if Panislamists, Congressmen and Constitutionalists were drawing closer together, the seeds of division within the Muslim League had already been sown. Whatever Fazli Husain may have told reporters at Bombay, there had never been any question of the Punjabi Muslims boycotting the Commission. Indeed, even before it was announced, preparations had been made at Lahore to ensure it a prompt and favourable reception. A preliminary meeting of Muslim leaders was held on 6 November. The editors of important newspapers were canvassed and a consensus in favour of co-operation was obtained. Firoz Khan Noon had a long session with Sir Mahommed Shafi, Sir Abdul Quadir and Abdullah Yusuf Ali, and reported to the Governor that matters were 'likely to take a correct course'[52] This prediction proved accurate. On 13 November, only five days after the Commission was announced, the Punjab Muslim League met officially and voted for co-operation by twenty-two votes to four. The only opponents of the resolution were Dr Kitchlew, Zafar Ali, Malik Barkat Ali and Ghulam Mohiuddin.[53] Thus even before Jinnah sent off his protest telegram to the Secretary of State, the Punjabi Muslims had fulfilled the government's expectations. They had placed themselves in the forefront of the battle against boycott, and made a confrontation with Jinnah and his followers inevitable.

Ever since Jinnah's March initiative, the Punjabis had been suspicious of his intentions. At the beginning of October, when the Muslim League Council met at Simla, they had prevented him from holding the annual session at Madras for fear that he might secure a

[50] Ibid., Mahommed Yakub to Dr Ansari, 7 Dec. 1927; Hassan Imam to Dr Ansari, 7 Dec. 1927; Raja of Mahmudabad to Dr Ansari, undated; Abdur Rahim to Dr Ansari, 7 Dec. 1927; Hafiz Hidayat Hussain to Dr Ansari, 12 Dec. 1927.

[51] Ibid. Dr Ansari to Secretary, Reception Commitee, Madras Congress, 9 Dec. 1927.

[52] Hailey papers, 11B: Firoz Khan Noon to Hailey, 6 Nov. 1927.

[53] Ibid., Firoz Khan Noon to Hailey, 13 Nov. 1927. See also Mahommed Rafiq Afzal, *Malik Barkat Ali, his Life and Writings* (Lahore 1969), part i, pp. 19-20.

verdict in favour of the Delhi-Bombay compromise. They made it plain, as did the U.P. contingent, that the League must be held in North India. Fazli Husain, then in London, received the news direct from the Governor: 'It was clear', he wrote, 'that the advocates of the joint electorate were outnumbered. I fancy as a result that we shall certainly have a meeting at Lahore instead of Madras.'[54] But though Jinnah had been warned, he was disinclined to submit. He gave up the idea of a joint session with the Congress but he did not settle for Lahore. Instead, he began to lobby in favour of Calcutta. This choice did not initially meet with Punjabi objections. 'The political views of the Muslims of the two provinces coincide', Firoz Khan Noon wrote to Hailey, 'and a collection of all-India Muslims may unite the scattered forces of Muslim politicians in Bengal.[55]' After Abdur Rahim had joined the boycott camp, however, Calcutta seemed a good deal less suitable. Because the Punjabis had voted for co-operation, it was of vital importance to them that the All India Muslim League should be held in a province where their policy would be approved. They therefore viewed the League Council meeting at Delhi on 20 November with some concern. If they were not to become isolated, it was essential that they emerge from that meeting with agreement that the League should be held at Lahore.

Thanks to the preparations made by Firoz Khan Noon, the Muslim League Council at Delhi was a triumph for the Punjabis. In the face of opposition from Jinnah and the Ali brothers, a verdict was recorded in favour of Lahore, with Sir Mahommed Shafi as President. It seemed as if a major tragedy had been averted.[56] For Jinnah, however, a Lahore meeting was as unsatisfactory as a Calcutta meeting was for the Punjabis, and if he was not to lose his representative status, it was essential that the decision be reversed. Mahommed Yakub, his Assembly colleague, agreed wholeheartedly. He encouraged Dr Kitchlew, the Secretary, to call another meeting of the council, and he urged Dr Ansari to use his influence to secure a majority for Calcutta, with the Aga Khan as President.[57] As a result, on 11 December, the council met again. Twentythree

[54] Hailey papers, 11B: Hailey to Fazli Husain, 6 Oct. 1927.

[55] Ibid., Firoz Khan Noon to Hailey, 2 Nov. 1927.

[56] Ibid., Hailey to Irwin 23 Nov. 1927.

[57] Ansari papers: Mahommed Yakub to Dr Ansari, 7 Dec. 1927.

people attended, and Firoz Khan Noon and his followers were in fact in a majority. On this occasion, however, absentee votes swung the decision in Jinnah's favour. By eightyfour votes (seventyfour absentees) to fiftyfour (fortyone absentees), the previous decision was reversed. It was decided that the session should be held at Calcutta.[58] But though Jinnah had won, it was a Pyrrhic victory. Firoz Khan Noon, Sir Mahommed Iqbal, Hasrat Mohani and a number of Firoz Khan's Punjabi followers left the meeting in disgust: the time had come for the Punjabis to strike out on their own.

As a result of the clash at Delhi, there were two Muslim Leagues in 1927, one at Lahore and one at Calcutta. Sir Mahommed Shafi, who had been elected President at both council meetings, presided over the Lahore session, and Maulvi Mahommed Yakub presided at Calcutta. Predictably, the Lahore resolutions followed those passed by the Punjab Muslim League on 13 November. The main resolution advocated a settlement between Muslim and non-Muslim communities 'with a view to the joint preparation of a draft constitution for India ... for presenting the same before the Statutory Commission or the British parliament or both'. Several others reiterated demands for the separation of Sind, the introduction of Reforms in the Frontier and Baluchistan and the concession of majority rights to the Punjabi and Bengali Muslims. More significant than the resolutions, however, was the consolidation of U.P. and Punjab Muslims which the session produced. The more vocal Punjabi leaders, Sir Mahommed Shafi, Sir Mahommed Iqbal, Sir Zulfiquar Ali Khan, Mian Shah Nawaz and Chaudhuri Zafrullah were supported by a number of important U.P. Muslim politicians, notably Shafaat Ahmed Khan, Mahommed Yamin Khan, Masudul Hassan, Shaikh Abdullah and Hasrat Mohani, and this co-operation, which was also evident in the selection of new office-bearers, foreshadowed the alliance between these two provinces in the All India Muslim Conference.[59]

The likelihood of a Punjabi breakaway had been inherent in the pattern of power introduced by the Montagu-Chelmsford Reforms. As early as 1924, when the League met at Lahore, it was clear that the Punjabis were the strongest provincial faction. Though supported vocally by many U.P. politicians, the demands put forward on that occasion had displayed a very distinct Punjabi bias and their rejection

[58] *Indian Quarterly Register*, 1927, vol. ii, p. 438.
[59] See Pirzada, op. cit., vol. ii. 128-38.

by the all-parties conference of 1925 showed clearly enough how forces were likely to be divided when the time for constitutional revision arrived. All that happened after the Delhi Muslim League Council meeting of 11 December was that the implicit became explicit. As a result of the clash between provincial and all-India interests, the Punjabis decided to cut themselves adrift from their co-religionists elsewhere and to stake out a claim for themselves less in relation to the subcontinent as a whole and more in relation to the Muslim North-West. Sir Malcolm Hailey narrated this change of mood to Sir Arthur Hirtzel, Permanent Secretary at the India Office, in a letter which shows how far this separatist trend had progressed:

> They see that they can never have quite the same interests as Muslims in the provinces with large Hindu majorities and they seriously think of breaking away from the All India Muslim League and starting a Federation of their own. This will seek to embrace the Punjab, parts of the U.P., the North West Frontier, Baluchistan and Sind; it is part of the programme to secure Sind for the Punjab and to give up to Delhi some of our Hindu districts in the South East of the province. they openly say that this in itself is only a preparation for a larger Federation which shall embrace Afghanistan and perhaps Persia.

This was far-reaching enough. But, to complete the picture, Hailey made plain also the very significant attitude of the Punjabis to their brethren inBengal: 'You will notice that the dream of the future to which I had alluded does not include Bengal. For the moment, the Northern India Moslem has given up his coreligionist in Bengal as hopeless and seems to expect no assistance from Bengal in the cause of Islam'[60] Twenty years before the creation of Pakistan and forty-five years before the creation of Bangladesh, these were prophetic insights.

The Nehru report: end of the road for Hindu-Muslim unity

For those Muslims interested in agreement at the all-India level, the Punjabi breakaway did not mark the end of the road. Indeed for a further year they tried to produce an agreement to which all parties could happily subscribe. Their endeavours, however, only serve to illustrate the working of the factors already outlined—the obstructionism of the Mahasabha, the inhibiting effect of communal pressure

[60] Hailey papers, 11B: Sir Malcolm Hailey to Sir Arthur Hirtzel, 15 Dec. 1927.

on the Congress leadership and the unwillingness of provincial Muslim opinion to come to the conference table because co-operation with government seemed likely to pay higher dividends.

Those who attended Jinnah's League at Calcutta in December 1927 were essentially the same people who had attended his meeting at Delhi in March. Apart from Jinnah himself, the Independents were represented by Sir Ali Imam and Maulvi Mahommed Yakub, and the Congress-Swaraj-Khilafatist group by Shafi Daudi, Syed Murtuza, Kalam Azad, the Ali brothers, Chaudhuri Khaliquzzaman and other members of the consolidated Delhi-Aligarh axis. Two groups had by then defected, the Frontiersmen (Sir Abdul Quaiyum and Syed Abdul Aziz) and the urban constitutionalists from the majority provinces (Sir Mahommed Shafi, Mian Shah Nawaz and Dr Suhrawardy). But the place of the second group had been taken by a number of other urban politicians from the same provinces, chiefly Khilafatists. The Punjab was represented by the four men who had dissented from the Punjab Muslim League resolution of 13 November—Dr Kitchlew, Zafar Ali, Barkat Ali and Ghulam Mohiuddin—and Bengal by a less homogeneous group, including Congressmen like Maulana Akram Khan and former Swarajists like Tamizuddin Ahmed.[61]

The Congressmen and Khilafatists met first at Madras, where the annual sessions of their two organizations produced two developments reminiscent of the palmier days of non-co-operation. The first was the Independence resolution passed by the Congress at the instigation of Jawaharlal Nehru. This did not have any immediate impact on politics. Indeed, many Congress politicians quickly repudiated it.[62] But it did provide a powerful indication of the racial animus provoked by the Statutory Commission, and in the long run it was to be important.[63] The second was a concession, albeit temporary, by Malaviya, to the Congress school which favoured Hindu-Muslim unity. Malaviya had not been present at Bombay in May, and his absence, together with that of Lajpat Rai who was in Europe, was taken, at least in government circles, as an indication of the unaccept-

[61] For an account of the Calcutta League, see Pirzada, *op.cit.*, vol. ii, pp. 107-27.

[62] See *A Bunch of Old Letters...*, pp. 57-8: Gandhi to Jawaharlal Nehru, 4 Jan, 1928; also Nanda, *op. cit.*, pp. 295-8.

[63] Subhas Bose believed the resolution to be the 'logical fulfilment' of continuing demands by the youthful element in the Congress for a more extremist ideology. See *The Indian Struggle 1920-42* (London 1964), pp. 145-6.

ability of the Delhi-Bombay compromise to the communal Hindus of North India.[64] At Madras, however, Malaviya was subjected to immense pressure, both private and public, to make him agree to the Bombay proposals, and this pressure succeeded.[65] He endorsed the Bombay proposals and the AICC resolutions passed at Calcutta in October concerning cowslaughter and music before mosques; and he also subscribed to a resolution empowering the Congress working committee to convene an all-parties conference for the purpose of formulating a Swaraj constitution. These developments generated some hope that the communal question might be nearer solution. Mahommed Ali, for example, looked forward at the Congress session to the day when Muslims would turn not to government but to Malaviya for protection. Srinivasa Iyengar, for his part, announced that the day of perfect nationalism was not far off.[66] However this optimism turned out to be unwarranted. For even before the Madras session began, the Bombay and Calcutta resolutions had provoked a Hindu backlash. In December, letters and telegrams had poured into the Congress office, from Punjab, Bihar and Bengal, criticizing the Calcutta resolution permitting cowslaughter, and from Sind, opposing the Bombay terms for separation.[67] Malaviya had chosen to step down, but others were waiting in the wings to take his place.

At the Muslim League at Calcutta, the question of a declaration in favour of Independence was never officially raised, and this was a comment both on the schizophrenia of the Khilafatists and the ascendancy of the Independents—Jinnah, Ali Imam and Mahommed Yakub. These last three men dominated the session, Jinnah as the permanent President, Yakub as the session President and Ali Imam as the mover of the boycott resolution. Their position was a pragmatic one. They were not outside the mainstream of constitutional politics and they were consequently disinclined to declare for Independence, or even for unconditional boycott. This indeed had been their policy from the beginning. When the Commission was first announced, Jinnah had made a point of not committing himself to boycott irretrievably. He had added his voice to the general chorus of

[64] GI Home Poll. 6/1927: GI Home Department Dispatch 74/1927, to Secretary of State, 26 May 1927.

[65] See speech by Sarojini Naidu, moving the Madras resolution on communal unity, Indian Quarterly Register, 1927, vol. ii, pp. 408-9; also Khaliquzzaman, *op. cit.,* p. 90.

[66] *Indian Quarterly Register* 1927, vol. ii, pp. 409-11.

[67] See AICC papers, G 64 (1926–28).

condemnation but he had kept in close touch with the Viceroy, pressing him continually to alter the arrangements which had been made. He told him in mid-December, for example, that if he, Chimanlal Setalvad and Sapru were allowed to sit with the Commission and to cross-examine witnesses, he would in fact declare for co-operation. He was only supporting boycott, he said, for fear of being supplanted by men of a less compromising disposition.[68] Similar sentiments were also voiced by Ali Imam. He told the League gathering that he was only supporting boycott because he had no alternative: 'We were called partners. We were told of a change in the angle of vision. Our blood and mixed in the battlefields of Flanders. I frankly tell you I fully believed in a change in the angle of vision but I have been disillusioned'.[69] Like Jinnah, however, Ali Imam belonged to a category of Muslims who would be satisfied with the Commission if Indians were appointed, and such being the leadership of the Calcutta League, it was not surprising that the boycott resolution was of a general umbrella type. It accommodated all shades of opinion and left plenty of room for manoeuvre.

The Calcutta League organizers also laid great stress on communal unity. But it became clear during the proceedings that Jinnah's four proposals would not be swallowed hook, line and sinker, even in Bengal. Maulvi Mujib ur Rahman, the Chairman of the Reception Committee and a leading Congressman, told his audience that separate electorates were 'the corner-stone of Muslim politics' and should not be given up.[70] Moreover, when Wahid Hussain of Chittagong supported joint electorates because of his experience in that municipality, he was quickly told that there were only two such cases in the whole of Bengal. Elsewhere, said his critics, joint electorates were not to the Muslim advantage.[71] Consequently, where the four proposals were concerned, though the League leaders remained anxious to cement their alliance with the Congress, they were obliged to tighten their negotiating position. The League resolution on this question made it plain that only *when* the Frontier had received the Reforms and Sind had actually been constituted a separate province would separate electrorates be given up.[72] It was

[68]Halifax papers, 3: Irwin to Birkenhead, 16 and 22 Dec. 1927.

[69] Pirzada, op. cit., vol, ii, p. 115.

[70] Ibid., p. 109.

[71] Ibid., p. 122.

[72] Ibid., p. 118-21.

the first of series of retreats which were to culminate in Jinnah's fourteen proposals of March 1929; and what Jinnah himself said about it suggests that he was beginning to lose hope :

We have got a majority in this house, but shall we be able to carry the majority in the country? Nothing will please me more, but at the same time, it will be fair to say that I am not sure that I am satisfied that the majority of Mussulmans throughout the country are in favour of it. That remains to be decided ....[73]

Despite this cautiousness, the League leaders did pass a resolution accepting the Congress invitation to an all-parties conference at Delhi, and they set up a sub-committee for that purpose, urging it to safeguard Muslim interests in its transactions.[74] When the conference convened on 12 February, however, it became apparent that agreement would not be easy. Malaviya, who was increasingly under suspicion for being too much in the Congress pocket,[75] was deprived of the limelight by Moonji, who effectively tore up the Delhi-Bombay compromise by refusing to agree either to the separation of Sind or the reservation of seats for majorities.[76] Jinnah met this intransigence with a reiteration of the terms of the League's Calcutta session and a deadlock ensued. On 5 March, when the Muslim League Council met to discuss these developments, it determined to stand firm, and when the conference reconvened three days later the position soon became critical. No appeals seemed capable of shifting the Mahasabha, and the Congress leaders refused to commit themselves to one side or the other, even though the Mahasabha was defying Congress resolutions. Instead they chose to shelve the main problems by appointing committees to examine them in detail, one to discover whether it was financially feasible to separate Sind from Bombay and the other to examine proportional representation as a means of safeguarding Muslim majorities.[77] From Jinnah's point of view, this was extremely unsatisfactory. His League was already very isolated and it began to appear

[73] Ibid. p. 123.

[74] Ibid., p. 119.

[75] Halifax papers, 4: Irwin to Birkenhead, 23 Feb. 1928.

[76] *Statement Exhibiting the Moral and Material Progress and Condition of India during the year 1927-28* (London 1929), pp. 24-5.

[77] For the early history of the all-parties conference, see *All Parties Conference 1928, Report of the Committee* (Allahabad 1929), p. 21-2; Khaliquzzaman, op. cit., pp. 93-4; Motilal Nehru papers (Nehru Memorial Museum, New Delhi): Motilal to Tej Bahadur Sapru, 26 Feb. 1928.

as if he had taken a stand for boycott at the expense of his entire political following. So back he went to the Viceroy's House and urged Irwin once more to make a change in the arrangements for the Statutory Commission.[78] Either appoint a mixed Commission, he said, or failing that, a body of Indian Commissioners with twin powers and responsibilities. Not surprisingly, his appeals were disregarded. Irwin saw that Jinnah's influence was on the wane and he had no intention of conciliating him. So what was Jinnah to do? He had failed to get a seat on the Commission and he had also failed to find a platform for boycott which would command even minimal Muslim approval. If he participated further in the all-parties conference he was merely inviting political humiliation. The only sensible alternative was retreat. On 17 March, he withdrew the Muslim League delegation from the conference and by May he was in England licking his wounds.

The withdrawal of the League and Jinnah's departure for Europe had a depressing effect on the all-parties conference. For most Congressmen, Jinnah was 'the only man to deliver the goods on behalf of the Muslim League'.[79] 'Jinnah's absence from the country is most unfortunate', wrote Motilal Nehru. 'I can think of no other responsible Muslim to take his place.'[80] Srinivasa Iyengar, Sarojini Naidu and Shanmukhan Chetty, all advocated postponing the conference till Jinnah returned from Europe in August,[81] and Motilal himself, fearing that the next session might even undo some of the work done at Delhi, inclined to a similar view.[82] Others, however, believing that the conference had degenerated into a slanging match between extremists, felt it useless to wait on Jinnah, or even on the subcommittees set up in March. 'We must decide', Shuaib Qureshi wrote to Dr Ansari, 'to stand by the Congress resolution [passed at Madras] which is based on or embodying the Delhi proposals ..., hold the conference ... adopt the Congress resolution and shape the programme of political activities on that basis.'[83] Jawaharlal showed a similar

[78] Halifax papers, 4: Irwin to Birkenhead, 8 and 15 March 1928.

[79] AICC papers, G 60: Ansari to Jawaharlal Nehru, 29 March 1928.

[80] Purushotamdas Thakurdas papers, 40: Motilal to Thakurdas, 28 April 1928.

[81] Ansari papers: Tgm Srinivasa Iyengar to Ansari, 5 May 1928; Shuaib Qureshi to Ansari, 7 May 1928.

[82] Ibid., Thakurdas to Ansari, 3 May 1928; Purushotamadas Thakurdas papers, 40: Motilal to Thakurdas, 28 April 1929.

[83] Ansari papers: Shuaib Qureshi to Ansari, 7 May 1928.

impatience,[84] though he was less bothered about adhering to the Congress resolution. At a time when his father's faith in settlement by conference was on the wane, he appears to have seized the initiative and to have pressed Motilal into actions which had the effect of alienating the Muslims still further. In a letter written in his capacity as Secretary to other members of the Congress working committee, the younger Nehru said the idea of postponing the all-parties conference had been firmly rejected. It was better, he said, to face the trouble and overcome it than to shirk the issue. What the President had decided, he said, was that the Congress must pursue its own programme despite all defections:

> In the main [he continued] this programme will be naturally based on [the] resolution of the Congress but of course it is open to the Committee to make such alterations in it without going [against] the Congress mandate as it desires to do. We have seen, for instance, the All India Liberal Federation, the Home Rule League, the South India Liberal Federation, Bengal Liberal League, and various other organisation [are in sub] stantial agreement. It should not be difficult if we have the support of most of the organisations [mentioned to win over the] conference to any reasonable plan which pr[ovides something] for all interests.[85]

Even for Congress Muslims, Nehru was advocating a distressing amount of flexibility, and his seizure of the initiative at this time did not augur well for the future of communal unity.

At the meeting called at Bombay on 19 May, Dr Ansari, the conference President, had bad news for his listeners. His endeavours to persuade Muslim League members to attend in an individual capacity had in most cases been fruitless,[86] and the sub-committees set up at Delhi had not produced their reports. The conference decided, nonetheless, 'that a small committee, viewing the communal problem as a whole in relation to the constitution, might succeed in finding a way out'.[87] Motilal Nehru was appointed Chairman and there were nine other members, Shuaib Qureshi and Sir Ali Imam to represent the Muslims, M.R. Jayakar and M.S. Aney for the Mahasabha, Sardar

[84] See, for example, Syed Mahmud papers (Nehru Memorial Museum, New Delhi): Jawaharlal to Syed Mahmud, 17 March 1928.

[85] AICC papers, G 63: circular letter, 3 May 1928 (motheaten).

[86] See Ansari papers: Nawab Ismail Khan to Ansari, 10 May 1928: Mahommed Yakub to Ansari, 9 May 1928.

[87] *All Parties Conference 1928, Report*, p. 23.

Mangal Singh for the Sikhs, G.R. Pradhan for the non-Brahmins, T.B. Sapru, the liberal leader, N.M. Joshi, the trade unionist, and Subhas Chandra Bose from Bengal. Of these, Jayakar took no part at all, and Sir Ali Imam,[88] N.M. Joshi, G.R. Pradhan and Subhas Bose only made limited contributions. The bulk of the work fell on five men, Motilal Nehru, Shuaib Qureshi, Mangal Singh, Aney and Sapru, though Jawaharlal Nehru also attended many of the later and more important meetings.

Between 5 June and 22 June, the committee met for several hours each day in Motilal's house at Allahabad. It made good progress on the general outlines of the constitution but the communal question remained intractable. After a number of deadlocks, Nehru persuaded Mangal Singh and Aney to accept the separation of Sind and equal status for the Frontier, but even then Shuaib Qureshi remained adamant about reservation for majorities, and ultimately Sapru supported him. In the hope of extricating the committee from this impasse, Nehru then called on Ansari, who suggested tailoring the franchise to give each community a voting strength commensurate with its population.[89] On 22 June, however, this suggestion was also rejected and dissentient reports seemed inevitable. Nehru and a close circle of colleagues decided nonetheless to make one further attempt to secure a unanimous report. They called a final meeting at Allahabad on 6 and 7 July and issued additional invitations, chiefly to Mahasabhites and nationalist Muslims.[90]

On 7 July, somewhat surprisingly, this conference adopted a compromise formula, subject to a note by Sardar Mangal Singh. According to this formula, all members of the conference were opposed to reservation of seats, whether for majorities or minorities. 'But', it went on, 'if this recommendation is not accepted and an agreement can be arrived at only on the population basis, we recommend that

[88] As a former Prime Minister of Hyderabad, Ali Imam was keeping out of British Indian politics to avoid prejudicing the Nizam's demand for the restoration of the Berars. The report gives 'ill health' as the main reason for his non-attendance, but there is no mention of ill-health in a letter from Nehru urging him to attend the important meeting of 6 July. See Ali Imam papers (Karachi University Library): Ali Imam to the Nizam, 5 Jan. 1928: Motilal to Ali Imam, 28 June 1928.

[89] AICC papers, AP 2/1928; Minutes of 18th sitting, 22 June.

[90] For details of the progress of these discussions, see AICC papers, AP 2/1928; Mahommed Ali papers (a fuller record); and Motilal Nehru papers: Motilal to Gandhi, 27 June 1928.

such reservation be made for majorities or minorities without any weightage and with a clear provision that it shall automatically cease at the expiry of 10 years, or earlier by consent of the parties concerned.'[91] Far from really solving the problem, this formula merely pandered to all interests without deciding anything. Some accepted it as a statement of principle, while others only supported the principle because they were confident that it would never form the basis of an agreement. Those who fell into this second group subsequently discovered, however, that they had made a serious miscalculation, for by this stage, the committee organizers were more concerned to produce a unanimous report than an agreement which would secure wider acceptance.

On 20 July, in the middle of drafting his report, Motilal wrote a letter to members of the committee which indirectly put a new interpretation on the formula of 7 July.[92] The bulk of the letter referred to a meeting of the committee on 8 July at which the previous day's formula had been modified to allow for reservation of seats according to population for minorities in the Central Legislature and the provinces.[93] Nehru pointed out that these changes had been intended to refer only to Muslim minorities and he wanted permission to make this clear in his report. Both the length of the letter and some of its arguments, however, suggest that he had other intentions as well. There was no need, he said, to make any provision for the Sikhs, for they only wanted reservation if other communities in Punjab were granted reservation. This was the first argument to make Muslims feel uncomfortable for it appeared to close the door on the second part of the original formula. The second was to be found in his conclusion.

We have already arrived at a common understanding to do away with separate electorates, reservation of seats for Muslim majorities and weightage for other minorities, the three greatest obstacles in the way of our political advancement. We should not risk this great

[91] All Parties Conference 1928, Report, p. 50. In his note, Sardar Mangal Singh expressed his opposition to reservation for majorities 'under all circumstances'. If this was found to be the only basis for agreement, he gave notice that the Sikhs would require weightage 'far in excess of their numerical strength'.

[92] Ansari papers: circular letter from Motilal to members of the all-parties conference committee, 20 July 1928.

[93] For the 'official' account of these meetings, see Note on the Informal Conference and After, *All Parties Conference 1928, Report,* pp. 125-6.

achievement by taking a narrow view on the question of Muslim minorities in the provincial councils.

Couched in these terms, this argument seems to be an appeal for compassion towards minority-province Muslims. In effect, however, it required all those who had attended the conference of 7 July to modify their position. They had not agreed to do away with reservation of seats for Muslim majorities. They had merely declared their opposition to reservation, whilst making provision for it in both majority and minority provinces if its abolition was not generally accepted. This, at any rate, was the view of Shuaib Qureshi, who,on receiving Motilal's letter, complained that the original agreement had been altered.[94] Motilal did not accept this, and Sherwani supported Motilal, but Shuaib continued to be dissatisfied and when Motilal's interpretation was enshrined in the report, Shuaib wrote a minute of dissent.

In his minute of dissent, Shuaib does not refer in detail to the proceedings of the Nehru committee. Instead, he harks back to the Congress resolutions passed at Bombay and Madras in May and December 1927.

Is it open to Congress [he asks] to denounce an agreement while the other party to it, the League, stands by it and specially when it has driven one section of it out of its fold on that particular issue? I maintain that it is too late in the day for political explorers to equip expeditions to pick holes in the agreement.

There was an obvious reason for Shuaib's reversion to the *status quo ante:* he was anxious to secure for Muslim majorities in Punjab and Bengal those concessions which had been granted both by Congress and Mahasabha in 1927 but retracted by the Nehru committee following its meeting on 7 July. This is clear both from the fact that he devotes a substantial part of his minute to justifying reservation for majorities and from his willingness to limit such reservations to a period of ten

[94] At the informal conference of 8 July, Shuaib Qureshi had been alone in objecting to the decision to allow reservation of seats for minority province Muslims. He probably feared then that this concession would undermine the second part of the formula agreed the day before. For evidence of Shuaib's indignation on receiving Nehru's letter, see Khaliquzzaman, op. cit., pp. 94-6. Khaliq's memory of these events is faulty in detail. Both he and Shuaib were present on 8 May, and he supported reservation for minorities.

years, the precise stipulation of the second part of the 7 July formula.[95] Shuaib had obviously voted for that formula in the confidence that abolition would not be accepted when the all-parties conference considered the report, and he clearly considered himself the victim of a political manoeuvre when the whole matter was prejudged by other members of the committee before the conference met.

The circumstances in which the Nehru committee took this direction suggest that Jawaharlal was chiefly responsible. During the committee itself, though not officially a member, he had played a part in several of the more important sessions,[96] and after the meetings of 6 and 7 July, by his father's own admission, he was one of the chief architects of the report.[97] Sapru was responsible for the sections on the Indian states and on Dominion Status and responsible government,[98] but Motilal wrote the sections dealing with the communal question and Jawaharlal prepared much of this material himself.[99] It is admitted in the report, for example, that Jawaharlal was responsible for the statistical tables on Punjab and Bengal, which were collated after 7 July and designed specifically to show that Muslims of those provinces would be better off without reservation.[100] It also seems likely, however, from the tone of the report on this issue, that Jawaharlal actually wrote this part himself. The determination of the author to face the problem and solve it, his condemnation of communal organizations for not wanting to change the existing structure of society, and his faith that in a free India political parties would be formed on an economic basis, all smack strongly of Jawaharlal and not his father.[101]

Supporting evidence for this interpretation is also provided by

[95]Shuaib Qureshi, confidential minute on the draft constitution prepared by the Nehru committee (copy provided by Syed Sharifuddin Pirzada).

[96]It is indicative of Jawaharlal's influence that Shuaib Qureshi dissuaded Khaliquzzaman from staying with him when in Allahabad for the meetings of 6 and 7 July. See Khaliquzzaman, op. cit., p. 94.

[97] *A Bunch of Old Letters*, p. 60-1: Motilal to Gandhi, 11 July 1928, 'The members have all gone to their respective homes, leaving Jawahar and myself to prepare the report and we are now hard at work at it.'

[98] Nanda, *op.cit.*, pp. 289-90.

[99] *A Bunch of Old Letters*, p. 65: Motilal to Gandhi, 19 July 1928. 'Jawaharlal has left copious notes for me but points not foreseen by him or me are arising at every step as I dictate the report.'

[100]*All Parties Conference 1928, Report*, pp. 43-4, appendices A and B, p. 137-53.

[101] Ibid., pp. 48-9.

Motilal's depressed state of mind. Before the meetings of 6 and 7 July, he had confided to Gandhi that he had no hopes of a successful boycott of the Simon Commission and only slender ones of a productive conclusion to his committee's endeavours. Indeed such were his feelings that he had already agreed to visit Canada in the autumn and had no intention of changing his mind unless a unanimous report materialised.[102] After the meeting of 7 July, this mood does not appear to have changed. He informed Gandhi that some kind of unanimity had been achieved. It was sufficient to stand by at the all-parties conference and he had therefore cancelled his passage to Canada. But it was neither complete nor of a genuine type; nor was it sufficient to make him yield to Gandhi's suggestion that he should become Congress President. In his view, the first choice was Vallabhbhai Patel, and failing him, Jawaharlal. 'Our race', he wrote, 'is fast dying out and the struggle will sooner or later have to be continued by men of Jawahar's type. The sooner they begin the better.' 'As for myself,' he continued, 'I feel I have lost much of the confidence I had in myself and am more or less a spent force.'[103]

It was in these circumstances that the younger Nehru acquired the ascendancy over his father and pressed him into a brittle defiance of the political system which he had tried so hard to work. How this actually happened is perhaps more a subject for the psychologist than for the historian. Suffice it to say, however, that just six days after describing himself as a spent force, Motilal was displaying a significant change of mood. He told Purushotamdas Thakurdas that he was 'entirely wrong' in thinking that the committee would not be unanimous. 'I like your way of putting it', he wrote, 'when you say that it is disconcerting to find that I have differed from men like Ansari and Shuaib Qureshi, instead of saying that it is unfortunate that Dr Ansari and Shuaib Qureshi should differ from a man like me. How could they dare?'[104] The political implications of this change of mood are made clear in another letter written shortly afterwards to Sen Gupta and Bose in Bengal. In this letter, Nehru again refuses to accept the Congress Presidency. 'My own opinion,' he writes, 'is that the occasion requires a strong go-ahead party in the country prepared to go the whole hog at all costs and that this party should have the further direction of the campaign in its own

[102]Motilal Nehru papers: Motilal to Gandhi, 27 June 1928.
[103]*A Bunch of Old Letters*, pp. 60-1: Motilal to Gandhi, 11 July 1928.
[104]Purshotamadas Thakurdas papers, 71: Motilal to Thakurdas, 17 July 1928.

hands. A quiet climb down from Independence to Dominion Status will bring the Congress into ridicule.'[105] Such was, of course, the logic of the situation, for as Nehru had always known, communal harmony did not only depend on satisfying Shuaib Qureshi. It also depended on the virtually impossible task of winning over those provincial Muslim interests who had never taken part in any national discussions and who, even as the Nehru committee was doing its work, were voting one by one to co-operate with the Simon Commission. Granted, however, that the younger Nehru's impatience of all-parties conferences and his desire (in the words of the report) to get going were justifiable,[106] the method of settling the communal issue employed by the committee nonetheless marked a very serious break with Congress tradition. In effect, it had given up negotiating and begun steamrolling instead.

The emergence of the All India Muslim Conference

The Nehru report was first published on 21 August, and it immediately aroused tremendous interest. Even before the all-parties conference met, a second edition had to be run off, and by the end of September, 12,000 copies had reached the market. The constitution which the report put forward was the most coherent and radical ever framed by a group of Indian politicians, and though its communal provisions have since received most attention, its political provisions were equally controversial and undoubtedly contributed to the welter of communal dissension in which it was soon submerged. All departments of the Central government, including Defence, Finance and relations with the States, were to be transferred to the control of a responsible Indian legislature, and though Dominion Status was the goal, it was demanded as the next immediate step in India's political evolution. The Central Government was to consist of a Governor-General appointed by the King, a Prime Minister appointed by the Governor-General, and six Ministers, appointed by the Governor-General on the Prime Minister's advice. The appointment of a provincial government was to follow a similar pattern. In both cases, Cabinets were to be jointly responsible to their respective legislatures, and the powers of both Governor-

[105] *A Bunch of Old Letters*, p. 64: Motilal to Bose and Sen Gupta, 19 July 1928.
[106] *All Parties Committee 1928, report*, p. 49.

General and Governor reduced to a bare minimum. The lower house of the central legislature and all provincial legislatures were to be elected on an adult franchise. There was also to be a Supreme Court, a Committee for Defence, and a Public Services Commission. Relations between the central government and the provincial governments were not discussed in detail. But it is clear from the schedules of subjects under their charge the the national government was to be of a unitary rather than a federal type, with residuary powers in the hands of the central government. This was subsequently to be a bone of contention with many opponents of the Congress point of view. In the communal sphere, the report recommended the abolition of separate electorates and of weightage for minorities, and it also rejected the Muslim demand for reservation for majorities and for thirty-three per cent at the Centre. Only those Muslims from the North-West had reason to be pleased, for the separation of Sind was supported, as was equal status for the Frontier.

The all-parties conference to consider the report was convened at Lucknow on 28 August. The Raja of Mahmudabad, Sarojini Naidu and Dr Ansari, all urged the Nehrus to postpone it so that Jinnah could attend,[107] but though they secured a token postponement of one day,[108] the indications are that the Nehrus were not anxious to be conciliatory. All 'religious' bodies, including two influential Sikh organizations, the Akali Dal and the Siromani Gurdwara Prabhandhak Committee, were excluded,[109] and the attendance was kept down to about a hundred people.[110] Special passes were issued for the press, and at least one prominent journalist, Syed Habib Shah of the Lahore *Siyasat,* was kept out of the meeting.[111] Such being the case, it was not surprising that the meeting produced a happy result. On 30 August,

[107]Jawaharlal Nehru papers (Nehru Memorial Museum, New Delhi): Dr Ansari to Jawaharlal, 27 July 1928; AICC papers, 2/1928: Sarojini Naidu to Motilal, 26 July 1928; Dr Ansari to Motilal, 25 July 1928; Raja Mahmudabad to Motilal, 23 July 1928.

[108]AICC papers, 2/1928:, Motilal to Sarojini Naidu, 28 July 1928.

[109] Ibid., Jawaharlal to Secretary, All India Aryan League, 21 Aug. 1928.

[110]Ibid., Jawaharlal to Mohanlal Saxena, 3 Aug. 1928. When Saxena asked for a list of persons to be accommodated, Jawaharlal told him it would be impossible to provide one. They were only expecting a hundred people and names would not be known till the last minute.

[111] Firoz Khan Noon, *Dominion Status or Autonomous Province?* (Lahore 1928), p.ii.

it was unanimously agreed that 'simultaneously with the establishment of a constitution in accordance with the Nehru committee's report', Sind should be constituted a separate province, provided that it was found to be financially self-supporting, or failing that, provided that a majority of the inhabitants favoured the scheme. And on the following day, amid much public enthusiasm, the Punjab Khilafatists and Lajpat Rai's party agreed to accept joint electorates without reservation of seats, provided that the franchise was based on adult suffrage and that the question could be reconsidered after ten years. Several other amendments were also passed, including one giving Baluchistan the same treatment as the Frontier, and the conference concluded with a resolution adopting the report in principle and reappointing Nehru's committee with powers of co-option to give its recommendations the shape of a Parliamentary Bill.[112]

As the various agreements were reached, the only murmur of dissent came from Shaukat Ali, who fell out with the Punjabi Khilafatists over the abolition of reservation for majorities, stating that the Central Khilafat Committee still stood by its original resolution on this question.[113] This provoked an angry response from the Punjabis, who held that they had been authorized to come to an agreement on the majority provinces and that therefore the agreement had the blessing of the entire organization.[114] Strictly speaking, the Punjabis were right, for after a nine-hour meeting, the Central Khilafat Committee had agreed to delegate powers for this purpose.[115] The length of time taken to reach this decision, however, suggests that many concurred reluctantly, and amongst them, undoubtedly, was Shaukat Ali. For him, as for his brother, the secession of the Punjabi and Bengali Khilafatists was a bitter blow. Even by 1925, their standing with their own community had been very much in decline, and if Congress now struck bargains independently with different Khilafat factions, their only remaining political asset, control of the all-India organization, would also be in jeopardy. Following the Lucknow conference, therefore, Shaukat girded up his loins for action. He broke with Motilal Nehru, denouncing him for making concessions

[112] *All Parties Conference 1928, Report,* p. 159-68: summary of proceedings of Lucknow Conference.

[113] This was precisely the same question over which Shuaib Qureshi had quarrelled with Motilal.

[114] *All Parties Conference 1928, Report,* p. 164-5.

[115] *Searchlight,* 29 Aug. 1928.

to the Mahasabha, and he also broke with the Muslims who supported Motilal, chief among whom was Ansari, denouncing them as Congress stooges.[116]

Shaukat Ali's repudiation of the Nehru report was a considerable embarrassment to Congress. But a more serious challenge to the report came from those provincial forces on whom the government had relied from the beginning. In the government's view, these interests were the key to the success of the Statutory Commission, and as early as March, even before Nehru's committee was appointed, the Viceroy had been confident that they would come round.[117] As might have been expected, the province which took the lead was Hailey's Punjab. On 14 March, the Punjab Legislative Council voted without a division to appoint a committee to co-operate with the Commission, and on 11 May the committee was set up.[118] Other provinces responded more slowly, but despite early setbacks in the Central Provinces, Madras and the U.P.,[119] these also fulfilled the Viceroy's expectations. By the time the Nehru report was published, three other provinces had voted for co-operation (Assam on 3 April, Bengal on 10 July and Bombay on 3 August) and soon afterwards, Bihar and Orissa, U.P. and Madras followed suit. In this process the Muslims played a crucial part. The earliest councils to vote for co-operation were those with the largest Muslim membership (Punjab, Bengal and Assam),[120] and the last ones, those with the smallest (Madras, U.P. and Bihar and Orissa). Even in the minority provinces, however, it was Muslim co-operation with nominated and official members which enabled the government to carry its point,[121] and only in the Central Provinces,

[116] GI Home Poll. File 1/1928: FR Delhi I Sept; Shaukat Ali papers: Shaukat Ali to Mahommed Ali, 13 Oct. 1928.

[117] Halifax papers. 4: Irwin to Birkenhead, 8 March 1928.

[118] *PLC progs.*, vol. xi, pp. 716-59. In anticipation of this success, Hailey was recommended for the GCIE in February.

[119] The C.P. Council voted against co-operation on 20 Jan., the Madras Council on 24 Jan., and the U.P. Council on 25 Feb.

[120] In the Bengal Council, 72 voted for co-operation (including 32 Muslims) and 50 against (including two Muslims). In the Assam Council, 31 voted for co-operation (including 10 Muslims) and 15 against (no Muslims). See *Bengal LC Progs.*, vol. 29, pp. 181-2; *Assam LC Progs.*, vol. viii, pp. 256-75.

[121] In the U.P., the precise extent of government reliance on the Muslims cannot be quantified because the opposition walked out. In Bihar and Orissa, where a committee was appointed by a majority of six, 19 Muslims supported government and four opposed it.

where the constitution did not provide for government rule by means of such combinations, was no co-operating committee ever elected.

Those who already found themselves in the separatist lobby could look to leadership chiefly from two sources, the Punjab and the United Provinces. In the Punjab, it was Fazli Husain's Unionist party which gave the lead, and in the U.P. a group of Muslim members of the Legislative Council, chiefly from the western divisions of the province, who were co-ordinated by Professor Shafaat Ahmed Khan of Allahabad University and financed by Sir Mahommed Yusuf, the Minister of Local Self-Government. The views of the first group are most succinctly expressed in the majority report of the Punjab Legislative Council co-operating committee set up in May 1928 under the chairmanship of Sikunder Hayat Khan,[122] and those of the second in the *Representation of the Muslims of the United Provinces (India) to the Indian Statutory Commission.*[123]

In many respects, the views of these two groups were diametrically opposed to each other. The Unionist party in the Punjab was confident that any further devolution of power at the provincial level would be to its advantage, and Sikunder's committee reflected this confidence in the outlines of its scheme. It suggested that the Muslims be given a majority of one seat by separate electorates in a house of 165,[124] and it sought to minimise the importance of communal tension in order to secure the widest and most unfettered devolution possible.[125] Within the provincial council, it proposed to abolish the official element, special constituencies and nominated seats,[126] and it rejected anything

[122]*Indian Statutory Commission* vol. iii, *Reports of the Committees appointed by the provincial legislative councils to cooperate with the Indian Statutory Commission* (London 1930), *Cmd. 3572,* pp. 389-508. In the foreword to the Punjab report, it is acknowledged that its preparation was largely Sikunder's work. Zafrullah, Owen Roberts and Chothu Ram praise his efforts to reconcile 'conflicting claims'. But the Hindu and Sikh representatives, Gokul Chand Narang, Raja Narendra Nath and Sardar Ujjal Singh, all submit notes of dissent.

[123]This representation was dispatched to the Simon Commission in July 1928. Besides Shafaat, the main contributors were Sheikh Zahur Ahmed, the Secretary; Hafiz Hidayat Hussain, who wrote the sections on the provincial government and the judiciary; and K.B. Masud ul Hassan, a former Chairman of the Moradabad Muncipal Board, who advised on local government affairs. Nawab Yusuf's financial support is acknowleded in the preface.

[124]*ISC,* vol. iii, p. 418.

[125]Ibid., pp. 397-400.

[126] Ibid. pp. 408, 418, 420.

but the most elementary safeguards for minorities and vested interests. It was not in favour of a second chamber, it was not prepared to allow reservation of Cabinet posts for minorities and it proposed to make the High Court and the provincial services the responsibility of the provincial government.[127] The U.P. Muslims, on the other hand, fearing that in the prevailing communal atmosphere of their province a further devolution of power would merely usher in 'a Brahmin or a Kayasth domination',[128] declared their opposition to all forms of provincial advance if their position was not safeguarded. They favoured a continuation of Dyarchy, with Law and Order and Revenue remaining reserved subjects.[129] They were opposed to the abolition of the nominated element and special constituencies.[130] They demanded a second chamber and they required that thirty three per cent of all Cabinet posts should be allocated to their community. These U.P. Muslim demands were, in fact, the most far-reaching ever put forward by a minority community. They also demanded separate electorates with weightage at every level of government, effective representation on all autonomous institutions created by the legislatures, safeguards for Urdu, adequate safeguards for the exercise of Muslim religious rights, due allocation of grants in aid by government and local bodies, and a share of the services according to their representative proportion in any given body.[131] In short, no body of demands further removed from those of the Punjab Unionists could possibly have been envisaged.

Outside the sphere of provincial devolution, however, the two groups shared similar views. Not only did they both support the separation of Sind, reforms for the Frontier and Baluchistan, a thirty-three per cent Muslim share in the Central Legislature and the

[127]Ibid., pp. 421-3, 439. The report particularly condemned the existing Punjab government practice of appointing ministers to represent communal interests. If adopted, it said, such a practice 'would cut at the very roots of the principle of responsible government. It is inconceivable that a Cabinet constituted on the lines suggested would survive even a day.'

[128]*Representation of the Muslims of the United Provinces (India) to the Indian Statutory Commission* (Allahabad 1928). p. 149.

[129]Ibid., p. 16.

[130]Ibid., p. 12. They proposed that in a council of 200, non-Muslims should account for 100 seats, Muslims for 50, nominated officials and non-officials for 30, and special interests for 20.

[131] Ibid., pp. 16-18, 284.

continuation of separate electorates;[132] they also showed a common opposition to control of the central government by the majority community, though for different reasons in each case. The Unionists were not opposed in principle to full responsible government at the Centre, though for fifteen or twenty years they envisaged some form of Dyarchy. It was their considered opinion, however, that any further advance at the Centre should follow and not precede or synchronise with the establishment of autonomy in the provinces.[133] This was a clear indication of their suspicion of central government control, which was also evident in their rejection of a unitary system of government at the national level. 'In our opinion,' they said, 'the adoption of the proposal that the central government should be vested with unlimited powers of interference with and control over the provincial governments would mean merely the substitution of one oligarchy for another.'[134] What they wanted (and here they were supported by the official members of the Punjab government, Hailey and de Montmorency), was a federal system in which power would devolve directly from Parliament to the provinces and not from Parliament to the provinces through the central government.[135] In their scheme, the central government was to be confined to those spheres of activity which were specifically allocated to it, and residuary powers were to rest with the provinces. This stipulation, which had been made in embryo at the Lahore League of 1924, was to assume great importance as the revision of the constitution progressed.

The U.P. Muslims adopted a very different attitude. The Unionists envisaged the establishment of responsible government at the Centre, and made provision in their recommendations to restrict such a government's control over the provinces. The U.P. Muslims, on the other hand, were scarcely prepared to envisage such a development. In their view, the existence of communal mistrust was a sufficient reason for the maintenance of the *status quo:*

We are of the opinion that the relationship between the Governor-

[132]*ISC*, vol. iii, pp. 407, 411-13, 418-19, 434; *Representation of the Muslims of the United Provinces*, pp. 11,18,137.

[133]*ISC*, vol. iii, pp. 432-3.

[134]Ibid., p. 430.

[135]Ibid., p. 430-1. Hailey and de Montmorency had made this suggestion in a memorandum submitted to the Statutory Commission in 1928. See *ISC* vol. x (London 1930), part iii, p. 26.

General and his Executive Council which now subsists be maintained ... We feel that a strong central government, which is able and willing to pursue a policy that is not coloured by communal, racial, local, provincial or economic prejudices is necessary at the present juncture, and is essential in a country where conflict of interest necessitates absolute impartiality and prompt action.[136]

The U.P. Muslims wanted a strong central government—and this involved vesting residuary powers at the Centre—because they envisaged the continuance of British control. In the words of Masud ul Hassan, they wanted 'fundamental safeguards which nobody in India can touch,'[137] and this was only possible if the British Parliament retained the right to interfere in the provinces on behalf of the minorities. 'We are strongly opposed', wrote Shafaat Ahmed, to vesting the Central Government with the power of amending any constitution that is granted to it by the British parliament'.[138] In their different ways, therefore, both the Unionists and the U.P. Muslims were opposed to what Jinnah and the Congress were campaigning for. Neither wanted to be subjected to a national government at the Centre.

Among the Muslims of these two groups, the publication of the Nehru report did not produce any major changes of political orientation. Most of them had always believed that they would get a better hearing from government than from Congress, and before the report was published, most of them had already decided to co-operate with the Simon Commission.[139] As had been the case with the publication of the Congress-League scheme in 1916, however, the Nehru report immediately made the running politically, and forced even those politicians who were opposed to Congress to define their attitudes to the political future which it outlined. For both the U.P. separatists and the Punjab Unionists, the report posed the question: 'What is your attitude to the prospect of an effective British withdrawal from the central government'?

Among the Unionists, the most systematic response came from

[136] *Representation of the Muslims of the United Provinces,* p. 135.

[137] Ibid., P. 132.

[138] Ibid., p. 134.

[139] An exception was Sheikh Habibullah, a member of the U.P. council, who confessed that the report had made him a supporter of co-operation. He was alienated, however, not so much by the report's communal provisions as by its 'absurd' proposals for the franchise and by its failure to provide special representation for landlords. See *UPLC Progs.,* vol. xxxix, no. 2,18 Sept. 1928, pp. 173-4.

Firoz Khan Noon, the Minister for Local Self-Government, who in October 1928, published a pamphlet with the significant title *Dominion Status* or *Autonomous Provinces.* This pamphlet, which, in the author's words, was 'nothing short of the Nehru Committee's report shorn of its Hindu clothes and centralisation structure and placed into Muslim garb and shaped into a provincial figure', provides a powerful indication of the increasing importance of Centre-Province relations in determining attitudes towards Reform. 'Why do Muslims fear over-centralisation?' asked Firoz. 'It is because in the Central legislature the Hindus will always be in an overwhelming majority and if they have the power to legislate for the provinces also, then the Muslim majorities in Bengal, Punjab, North West Frontier Province, Sind and Baluchistan will be entirely imaginary.'[140] Firoz's answer was to draw up a constitution in which the powers of the central government were even more severely restricted than in the proposals of the Sikunder Committee. Complete responsibility was rejected in favour of a form of Dyarchy. Of nine ministers, four were to be nominated and irremovable by vote (Ministers for Foreign Affairs, Political Relations, Defence and Law), and of the five elected ministers, who were to hold office on the basis of joint responsibility, two were always to be Muslims, and the representation of other minorities was to be encouraged in the Governor-General's Instrument of Instructions.[141] The same restrictions were also applied to the Executive and Judiciary. Officers of the all-India and provincial services, and of the Defence services, were to be paid from a consolidated fund over which the legislatures were to have no control,[142] and the Governor-General was to be empowered 'to enforce representation of all classes and communities of His Majesty's subjects in all departments of the Central Government.'[143] High Court judges were to be appointed by Governors on the advice of their Cabinets,[144] and in the Supreme Court, thirtythree per cent of the judges were to be Muslim and 'there must always be some Europeans....'[145] In effect, the proposals were designed to prevent the majority community from exercising any real power.

In the U.P., where Muslim demands for all manner of separate

[140]Firoz Khan Noon, *Dominion Status or Autonomous Provinces* (Lahore 1928), p.v.

[141]Ibid., pp. 10-11.

[142]Ibid., p. 14

[143]Ibid., P. 11.

[144]Ibid., p. 18.

[145]Ibid., p. 15.

representation had met with a hammer blow from Nehru and his colleagues, those who had been responsible for the Statutory Commission Memorandum convened an all-parties Muslim conference at Kanpur on 4 November. Hafiz Hidayat Hussain, Masud ul Hassan and Sheikh Zahur Ahmed, all three of them important contributors to the memorandum, now figured prominently on the platform and reiterated the demands which they had earlier submitted to the Commission. By November 1928, however, one additional and more extreme demand had emerged—for a fifty per cent share in the provincial government. This demand, which appears initially to be just another indication of Muslim nervousness, may well have been the result of a change of attitude towards the prospect of a national government at the Centre. Hafiz Hidayat Hussain, the Chairman of the Reception Committee, told his audience that the Nehru report's greatest drawback was that it concentrated power in the central government where Muslims would always remain in a minority. The solution, he said, was a federal system of government which would provide for provinces where the Muslim majority could retaliate the treatment [*sic*] meted out to their community in the Hindu provinces.[146] This statement reflects a considerable change in perspective since the submission of U.P. Muslim memorandum to Simon, and it suggests that Nehru's recommendations had forced Hidayat Hussain and his friends to face the question: 'How are we to protect ourselves if we cannot rely on the Raj'? It suggests, moreover, that their answer to this question was to put their faith in a system of 'retaliation', which depended for its effectiveness on a maximum degree of provincial autonomy for the majority-province Muslims. By November, therefore, the political future of the U.P. Muslims was seen to be far more interlocked with that of their Punjabi co-religionists than had been the case in July.

The Kanpur conference was also significant because it witnessed an important accession of strength to the minority-province separatists from those 'nationalist' Muslims who had been alienated by the Nehru report. The President of the session was no less a person than Shaukat Ali, who now established himself in the separatist camp. In the future he was to make occasional forays into 'nationalist' politics, drawn by his personal indications and his lengthy acquaintance with Congress

[146] For an account of the Muslim meeting at Kanpur, *see Indian Quarterly Register*, 1928, vol. ii, pp. 421-5.

leaders. Yet just as the constraints of the system had forced him into the separatist camp, so they continued to keep him there. The same was also true of his brother, Mahommed, who following his return from Europe in October, took up an identical position. Not only did he support the demands of the U.P. Muslims for safeguards: he also campaigned for a loose federation with maximum provincial autonomy. At the Bihar all-parties Muslim conference early in December, he condemned the Nehru report for favouring the Hindu Mahasabha. 'Even in the provinces where Muslims had a majority,' he said, 'the Nehru report was so planned as to counteract the influence of that Muslim majority by having too dominant a central government at Delhi.'[147] It was not to be long before he was to find himself on the same platform as Fazli Husain and Sir Mahommed Shafi.

The Congress response to these developments was to support those Muslims who subscribed to the Nehru report—the Delhi group under Dr Ansari's leadership, including Asaf Ali and Dr Zakir Hussain, the Bengalis, with whom Abul Kalam Azad was the chief Congress link, and the Punjabi Khilafatists led by Zafar Ali, Dr Kitchlew, Mahommed Alam and Habib ur Rahman. Congress support was given chiefly in cash, and for this purpose collections were made both in Bombay and Calcutta. In the first three weeks of October, 25,000 rupees were collected, 16,000 coming through G.D. Birla, and the rest, with the exception of 1,000 rupees each from Sir Ali Imam and the AICC, from Bombay and Ahmedabad. Of this, 5,000 rupees went to Abul Kalam Azad, 3,000 to Lajpat Rai and 1,000 to Sardar Mangal Singh. Most of the rest went to pay Rafi Ahmed Kidwai's salary and expenses and for editions of the Nehru report in various Indian languages.[148] The success of the campaign was limited, particularly in Delhi, where Dr Ansari, despite help from the Punjab, found himself severely taxed both on the platform and in the press by Shaukat Ali.[149] But in the Punjab and Bengal, where Jinnah's League had set

[147]*Indian Quarterly Register, 1928, vol. ii, p. 426.*

[148]Shaukat Ali wrote to his brother about this campaign: 'Hindus want to kill the Muslim opposition [to the Nehru report] by sheer force or propaganda. Birla and others have subscribed 1½ lakhs for this purpose. Abul Kalam, as usual, will get a share of the loot.... Zafar Ali is also hovering about for carrion.' See Shaukat Ali papers: Shaukat to Mahommed, 13 Oct. 1928. For details of the all-parties conference fund, see AICC papers, 16/1928

[149]GI Home Poll.,File I/1928: Delhi FR I Sept, I and II Oct. 1928.

up 'nationalist' branches in December 1927,[150] it was sufficient for resolutions supporting the Nehru report to be passed by both these bodies, and by November, Motilal was clearly basing the success of his propaganda operation on the continued adherence of these two provinces.[151]

The most important personality in Motilal's calculations, however, was Mahommed Ali Jinnah, who returned to India some months later than expected as a result of his wife's illness in Paris. If Jinnah could be won over, the Nehru report would acquire added prestige, and Motilal therefore deputed Purushotamdas Thakurdas to 'rope in Jinnah' before Shaukat Ali got to him.

So much depends on Jinnah [he wrote] that I have a mind to go to Bombay to receive him. If I have the necessary funds within the next few days I hope to create a strong opinion amongst the Mussulmans to greet Jinnah on his arrival. Therefore please lose no time to raise as much money as you can for this great enterprise.[152]

When Jinnah arrived, however, he did not immediately proclaim his support for Nehru's recommendations but characteristically chose to sound out Muslim opinion first. Nehru, who wrote to him from Ahmedabad the day after he arrived, urged him to attend the all-parties committee meeting at Delhi on 5 November, assuring him that members of the committee were not representatives of the organizations to which they belonged and that his presence would not commit the Muslim League to any decision reached. All such decisions, he said, would be open to alteration at the all-parties convention at Calcutta on 17 December.[153] But Jinnah was too experienced a politician to put his head in such a noose. He was not

[150]The new Punjab Muslim League was chiefly composed of the Khilafatists who came to agreement with Nehru's committee at Lucknow. See Rafiq Afzal, *Malik Barkat Ali, His Life and Writings* (Lahore 1969), part i, pp. 22-3. Also GI Home Poll., File 1/1928: Punjab FR I Sept. 1928.

[151]The outlines of this policy had already been formed in Sept., when Nehru told Mrs Besant that the most effective answer to the minority province Muslims who championed the rights of the majority provinces 'would be that the Punjab and Bengal have accepted the Lucknow resolutions and do not need the other provinces to champion their cause'. But by Nov., after the Punjab and Bengal Muslim Leagues had passed their resolutions, Nehru could write to Gandhi that Punjab and Bengal were 'the only two provinces that matter. . . The provinces where the Muslims are in minorities have really no say in the matter'. See *A Bunch of Old Letters,* p. 65-9: Motilal to Mrs Besant, 30 Sept. 1928; Motilal Nehru papers: Motilal to Gandhi, 24 Nov. 1928.

[152]Purushotamdas Thakurdas papers, 71: Motilal to Thakurdas, 20 Sept. 1928.

[153]Ibid: Motilal to Jinnah, 28 Oct. 1928.

prepared to attend any all-parties conference until he knew his brief, and though he sent Nehru a letter to be read out at the Delhi meeting, he waited to see what would happen at the Muslim League council meeting which he had called at Lucknow on 11 November.[154]

The Lucknow Muslim League council meeting was less conclusive than Jinnah would have liked. Three different schools were present (the Independents, the Congress Muslims and the U.P. separatists) and no decision was reached by a substantial majority. A resolution thanking the Nehru committee for its report (but not committing the League to accepting its provisions) was carried by only four votes, and the Raja of Mahmudabad was elected President of the annual session by a majority of two.[155] From Jinnah's point of view, this absence of unanimity made it impolitic for him to open negotiations with the Congress. He ensured that the two organizations met in the same city but he was not prepared to attend the all-parties convention until a full session of the League had met. This attitude forced him into disagreement with Motilal who wished the League to meet after the convention so that it could ratify its decisions. Jinnah was adamant, however, that authorization to attend the convention could not come from the council alone; and he also held that subsequent ratification by the League would not be necessary if adequate authorization was forthcoming in the first place. This difference of opinion caused some ill-feeling between the two men and the air was only cleared when Sir Ali Imam helped them to come to a compromise. The all-parties convention was to begin on 22 December, as Nehru had planned, but its open session was to be held on 27 and 28 December, to allow the League to send accredited representatives. The open session of the Congress was to start on the 29th.[156]

Before the League met at Calcutta, a powerful section of support had seceded from it. This was the Khilafat section which had repudiated

[154] Ibid., Thakurdas to Motilal, 30 Oct. 1928. Thakurdas tells Nehru that Jinnah 'does not wish to prejudice the prospect of bringing the two sides together by joining your committee at this stage before he has roped in his side (*sic*)'. But he obviously feels uneasy for he adds: 'I wish that you could have come to Bombay instead of returning to Allahabad ...'

[155] GI Home Poll, File 1/1928: U.P. FR I Nov. 1928.

[156] AICC papers, AP 35/1928: Confidential note by Motilal Nehru on the timing of the Congress, League and all-parties convention at Calcutta, 14 Nov.; Motilal Nehru papers: Motilal to Gandhi, 24 Nov. 1928. Motilal told Gandhi that Jinnah's 'game' was to postpone ratification. This would mean a protracted controversy in 1929 and it would be impossible 'to keep the Muslims in hand all this time'.

the Nehru report—Shaukat Ali, Mahommed Ali, Shafi Daudi, Hasrat Mohani, Azad Sobhani and a section of the *Jumiat ul Ulema i Hind* under the leadership of Mufti Kifayatullah. The confrontation between these men and the 'nationalist' Khilafatists, which had been on the cards since the Lucknow session of the all-parties conference, came to a head during the Christmas week. By that stage, Punjabi and Bengali opposition had convinced the Ali brothers that bold tactics were necessary to retain control of the organization. Mahommed Ali and H.S. Suhrawardy, the Calcutta Khilafat leader, broke up the Bengal Provincial Khilafat Committee meeting and overruled the election of delegates from the districts to the annual session. Instead, quite unconstitutionally, they enrolled their own delegates from Calcutta itself.[157] The Ali brothers also succeeded in banning the attendance of North West Frontier delegates elected by the Punjab Khilafat Committee, and they outraged the Bihar delegation, led by Shah Mahommed Zubair and Dr Mahmud, by siding with Shafi Daudi's rival organization.[158] These tactics gave them a majority in the annual session but only at the cost of a split in the party. Dr Ansari and his followers broke with the Ali brothers and called their bluff by electing their own delegation to the all-parties convention. The Ali brothers responded by withdrawing from the convention entirely.[159]

The Muslim League meeting at Calcutta was attended by Jinnah, the Raja of Mahmudabad and Sir Ali Imam, the old Independent trio, and by Ansari's Khilafatists. The session began with a note of warning from the Chairman of the reception committee, Maulvi Abdul Karim, who argued that some form of special representation was essential for the protection of Muslim interests, and it continued with a plea for 'sweet reasonableness' by the Raja, who made a strong case for Dominion Status rather than Independence and urged his audience to elect a delegation to the all-parties convention to settle outstanding communal issues on that basis 'in the spirit of broad-mindedness.'[160] On the second day, following a meeting of the

[157] *Indian Quarterly Register*, 1928, vol. ii, pp. 406-8.

[158] *Proceedings of the All Parties National Convention* (Allahabad 1929) pp. 124-8: statement made on behalf of the Hon'ble Shah Mahommed Zubair and other members of the Central Khilafat Committee. Of the 45 Muslims who withdrew from the C.K.C., 28 came from Punjab.

[159] *Proceedings of the All Parties National Convention*, pp. 128-32: letter from the Secretary, CKC (Shaukat Ali), to the President of 'the so-called all parties convention' (Ansari).

[160] Pirzada, op.cit., vol. ii, pp. 139-43.

Subjects Committee on the previous afternoon, Mr. M.C. Chagla, Jinnah's disciple and friend, proposed a delegation to the all-parties convention consisting of twenty persons, ten of whom had seceded from the Khilafat Committee with Dr. Ansari. Haji Abdullah Haroon, the Karachi businessman, objected that the delegation only consisted of members of one party but he was called 'toady' by Zafar Ali and no major changes were made. Two additional delegates were added, however, to give representation to the Frontier and Assam.[161]

The same afternoon, these Muslim League and Khilafat delegates met a sub-committee of the all-parties convention. The demands which they put forward had not been discussed at the open session of either organization, and it is therefore difficult to decide who was responsible for which demand and whether both organizations subscribed to all of them. They were put forward jointly by Jinnah and T.A.K. Sherwani, however, and it must be assumed that they decided to stand together. The demands were as folows:[162]

1. That one-third of the elected representatives of both the Houses of the Central Legislature should be Mussulmans.
2. That in the Punjab and Bengal, in the event of adult suffrage not being established, there should be reservation of seats for the Mussulmans on the population basis for ten years subject to a re-examination after that period, but they shall have no right to contest additional seats.
3. (a) That residuary powers should be left to the provinces and should not rest with the Central Legislature.
   (b) That clause 13A embodied in the Supplementary report be deleted.
   (c) That the division of subjects in the Schedule I and II be revised.
4. That the constitution shall not be amended or altered unless the amendment or alteration is passed first by both the Houses of Parliament separately by a majority of four-fifths of those present and then by both the Houses in a joint sitting by a majority of four-fifths.
5. Article V—Communal representation. . . . . Delete the words 'Simultaneously with the establishment of Government under this constitution.
6. Embody the Pact regarding Communal representation in Punjab in full in the Nehru report.

161 Ibid., pp. 145-8.

162 *Proceedings of the All Parties National Convention*, pp. 76-8.

In all probability, Jinnah was responsible for the demand for thirty-three per cent at the Centre. This had been one of his four proposals in March 1927 and he had every reason to stick to it rigorously, because his Muslim followers in the Central Assembly, and particularly those from the minority provinces, had been very critical of the Nehru report on precisely this point.[163] Jinnah's insistence, in defence of this demand, that the extra seats should be distributed to give weightage to the minority provinces, is probably a reflection of his awareness of this situation.[164] Such men as Nawab Ismail Khan, Mahommed Yakub, Sarfaraz Hussain Khan, Abdul Matin Chaudhuri and Fazl Ibrahimtoolah, were all members of the Legislative Assembly from the minority provinces, as were Shafi Daudi and Syed Murtuza, both former Swarajists who were in the process of taking up a more central position. Nor is it impossible that Sherwani subscribed to similar views, for it was he who raised the question of reservation of seats for minorities both in the provinces and at the Centre during the Nehru committee proceedings, and he himself had been a member of the Central Assembly since the 1926 election. Similar 'Central Assembly' considerations may also have been influential in the framing of the demand relating to Sind, which was designed to allow it to achieve separate status before the Nehru constitution was implemented. The fact that Haji Abdullah Haroon, the wealthy businessman, was both a member of the Assembly and the foremost protagonist of separation cannot be overlooked. At least three of the demands, however, appear to have come chiefly from the Punjab Khilafatists. This group had clearly been put out when the Nehru committee supplementary report made no reference to adult suffrage as a precondition for the introduction of joint electorates in their province.[165] This had been agreed at Lucknow and they wanted that agreement to be incorporated into the Nehru report in full.[166] The demand that reservation of seats should

[163] In his letter to Gandhi of 24 Nov., in which he discussed Jinnah's attitude towards the all parties convention, Motilal attributes Jinnach's prevarication to Central Assembly considerations. '...the Muslim members of the Assembly belonging to Jinnah's party... are one and all bitterly opposed to the Report and the Lucknow decisions. All told they number 8 or 9 and with the addition of Sir Purushotamadas constitute the whole of Jinnah's party. In his anxiety to keep his hold on these people, Jinnah is playing into their hands.'

[164] *Proceedings of the All Parties National Convention*, pp. 79-80.

[165] *All Parties Conference 1928, Supplementary Report of the Committee* (Allahabad 1928), p. 50.

[166] *Proceedings of the All Parties National Convention*, pp. 80-1.

be on a population basis if adult suffrage was not introduced also seems likely to have come from them, though Jinnah may have prompted them to be realistic. Finally, the demand that residuary powers should rest in the provinces certainly did come from them, as it was put forward first in a letter from Ansari's Khilafat faction to the all parties convention.[167] Jinnah, for his part, supported this demand, but more out of necessity than of choice. Being intent on ministerial power at the Centre, he did not wish the Centre's powers to be eroded before he could enjoy them, and he only bowed to the Punjabi Khilafatists, as they had bowed before public opinion in their own province, because he had no alternative.

The reception given to these demands by the all-parties convention sub-committee could have been safely predicted after a perusal of its personnel. Of its thirty-seven members, eleven were Hindus, Sikhs and Christians of the Punjab, one was a leading opponent of the separation of Sind, and six were leading lights of the Hindu Mahasabha.[168] The demand for thirty-three per cent at the Centre was supported by Gandhi and by Sapru, but opposed by the Hindu Mahasabha and the Sikhs. The demand that residuary powers should rest with the provinces was opposed by both the Mahasabha and the Liberal Federation, though both Sapru and Chintamani were prepared to re-examine the schedules of subjects. Neither Gandhi nor Motilal Nehru intervened during the discussion of this most important point. The demand for reservation on a population basis in Bengal and Punjab if adult suffrage was not adopted was skirted by means of the formula: 'We do not contemplate any such contingency.' The demand regarding Sind was rejected on the grounds that it involved altering the agreement reached at Lucknow.[169] In the open session, Jinnah tried to change the verdict of the committee. He told his audience that the modifications required were fair and reasonable; that no country had succeeded in establishing its independence without making provision for its minorities; and that a Hindu-Muslim settlement was essential for the political progress of the country.[170] Yet though

[167] Ibid., p. 127: statement on behalf of the Hon. Shah Mahommed Zubair and other members of the CKC.

[168] Ibid. pp. 73-4. Members of the sub-committee included Malaviya, Moonji, Jayakar, Aney, Chintamani, Harbilas Sarda and Gulshan Rai.

[169] Ibid., pp. 76-7; Ansari papers: a note in pencil headed 'Modifications in the Nehru report', setting out the reactions of the various groups within the sub-committee.

[170] *Proceedings of the All Parties National Convention* pp. 78-82.

he was supported by Dr Sapru, he met with a highly reasoned opposition from Jayakar, who told the convention that Jinnah only represented a small minority of Muslims and that it was not worthwile making concessions because it would make no difference to the Muslim community as a whole. Besides, he said, Jinnah was on their side anyway, and would do his best to bring the Muslim League with him.[171] Jinnah's reply shows how clearly he realized the isolation of his position:

> It is essential that you must get not only the Muslim League but the Musulmans of India and here I am not speaking as a Musulman but as an Indian. And it is my desire to see that we get seven crores of Musulmans to march along with us in the struggle for freedom. Would you be content if I were to say, I am with you? Do you want or do you not want Muslim India to go along with you?[172]

It was a good question. But Jayakar had already answered it. The convention rejected Jinnah's offer and brought him to 'the parting of the ways'.

The circumstances responsible for forcing Jinnah into the wilderness were extremely complex. They went far beyond the individual attitudes of Mahasabha politicians. They reflected the working of the political system itself. In the early 1920s, though the forces of provincialism did occasionally impinge on the all-India scene, the real conflict of interest between the 'nationalist' politician and the provincial politician working the Reforms was obscured by the absence of points of friction. Only when the Montagu-Chelmsford Reforms come under the hammer does this conflict of interest become explicit; and the fascination of studying this period is that one can observe political reactions as the constraints of the system make themselves felt. Jinnah's main difficulty was that he had no solid political base. He was a 'consultative' politician in an age of political responsibility. Consequently, however sincere his 'nationalism', he could only survive by acting as a broker between Muslim politicians in the provinces and his Congress colleagues at the Centre. He was not himself engaged in provincial politics. He merely attempted to fashion the provincial clay at his disposal into a shape suited to his all-India purposes. His task, however, was like that of a sculptor required to work in materials which constantly change their texture. As the provinces threw up new provincial

[171]Ibid. pp. 86-92.

[172]Ibid., p. 93.

demands, so, ineluctably, Jinnah was obliged to change his political objectives. In 1927, he put forward four proposals; in 1928, they became six; and in 1929, fourteen.

Ultimately, negotiation between Jinnah and the Congress was no longer productive. Jinnah was looking over his shoulder at the provinces so much that he was no longer actively engaged in the same battle as the Congress. He was not prepared to accede to the Congress programme merely as an individual. He wanted to take a large body of Muslims with him. Yet those Muslims whose activities forced Jinnah to alter his all-India negotiating position were the provincial opponents of the very men who swelled the ranks of the Congress. Here was the heart of Jinnah's dilemma. It had ceased to be possible to occupy a central position in Indian politics. One either had to be in the Congress camp or the Muslim camp. It was this logic which ultimately turned Jinnah into the *Quaid i Azam* of Pakistan.

But Jinnah's discomfiture at Calcutta was not the end of the story. Just as the rise of provincial Muslim separatism had cut the ground from under the feet of the 'all-India' politician, so was the Calcutta convention followed by the emergence of the All India Muslim Conference. Just as those Congressmen favouring 'Independence' and non-co-operation were beginning to replace the Nehrus and Saprus so the Muslims of the various legislatures gathered at Delhi to declare their allegiance to the King Emperor and their respect for constitutional norms. The Indian body politic was being divided, government and Muslims on one side, Hindus on the other, and as the Congress embarked on the road to Dandi, the beneficiaries of the system rallied to its defence.

The idea of a conference of Muslim legislators was first mooted by the Aga Khan in December 1927.[173] But it was not taken up enthusiastically until after the publication of the Nehru report, at which stage certain of Jinnah's colleagues in the Central Assembly, notably Sir Mahommed Yakub and Mr Fazl Rahimtoolah, brought the scheme

173 GI Home Poll. 32/12/1927: Bombay FR II Dec. 1927, appendix B. In a manifesto issued in that month, the Aga Khan appealed to all Muslim members of the central and provincial legislatures: 'I urge them with all the force at my command to meet and constitute a permanent Muslim governing political body which shall absorb into itself the political activities of the community as a whole and also finally absorb such antiquated political bodies as at present exist.... The need for an authoritative body of this character is great at a time when our constitution is in the melting pot.'

to fruition.[174] They invited members of the legislatures and other prominent men to a conference at Delhi on 31 December and they persuaded the Aga Khan to deliver the presidential address. The reasons for their initiative have already been touched on in discussing Jinnah's own dilemma. The Nehru report had made it clear that Muslims in the Central Assembly could no longer maintain an 'Independent' position. By advocating joint electorates and abolishing weightage it had reduced Muslim representation in the minority provinces and made it almost certain that minority-province Muslim representation in the Central Assembly would also be reduced. These were sufficient reasons for such men to want to make common cause with their provincial colleagues. Those who responded most readily to their invitation, however, were either those who were highly organized already, the Punjab Unionists under the leadership of Firoz Khan Noon and the U.P. Muslims under Shafaat Ahmed Khan and Hafiz Hidayat Hussain, or those who had become disillusioned with the politics of confrontation once it became clear that Jinnah's negotiations with the Congress would be fruitless—the Frontiersmen, the Punjabi and Bengali urban constitutionalists, the minority-province Khilafatists and Sindhis. The appearance of all these different schools on the same platform was the most remarkable feature of the first meeting of the Conference. That Mahommed Ali should sit beside Sir Mahommed Shafi, whom he had so often derided as a government stooge, and that the Aga Khan should be cheered by Azad Sobhani, whose vitriolic speeches at Kanpur in 1913 had forced him to wash his hands of the Muslim League, were amongst the most delicious ironies of the Montagu-Chelmsford Reforms.

The terms put forward by the All India Muslim Conference were a combination of Unionist and U.P. Muslim demands:

1. Federal system with complete autonomy and residuary powers vested in the constituent states.
2. No bill to be passed if ¾ of the affected community is against it.
3. Separate electorates to be retained until Muslims decide to give them up.

[174]See K.K. Aziz, *The All India Muslim Conference, 1928-35, a Documentary Record* (Karachi 1972), pp. 44-7: Statement on the origins of the Conference by Fazl Rahimtoolah, the Secretary; see also GI Home Poll., File 1/1928: Delhi FR I Oct. 1928. This second source attributes a leading role to Mahommed Yakub.

4. Fair Muslim share in the cabinets of provinces and the Centre.
5. Where Muslims constitute a majority of the population, their ascendancy may not be undermined by electoral reorganisation.
6. Where Muslims were in a minority, they shall have no less representation than they do at present.
7. 33% representation in the Central Legislature.
8. Separation of Sind.
9. Reforms in the North-West Frontier Province and Baluchistan.
10. Same safeguards for Hindu minorities in Muslim provinces as for Muslim minorities in Hindu majority ones.
11. Adequate share for Muslims in the services.
12. Safeguards for the protection of Muslim culture and education, language, religion and personal law.
13. No change in the constitution except with the assent of the federal legislatures.

Of these demands, (1) and (5) clearly came from the Unionists, whereas (2), (4), (6), (11), (12) and (13) came from the U.P. Muslims. (3), (7), (8) and (9) were commonly demanded by both groups, (7) gaining added urgency as a result of the presence of several 'all-India' groups. As the Unionists contemplated having a free hand in the Punjab, it is not surprising that only two of the demands can be attributed to them. It is significant, however, that their first demand became the first demand of the Muslim Conference, and that it was given an even higher place than the demand for the continuance of separate electorates. It is also significant that the U.P. Muslim demands, though covering the same ground as those put forward at Kanpur, were shorn of the hysterical percentages which were a feature of that occasion and given a more balanced and deliberate look. Both these facts show clearly which faction was in the driving seat. In the difficult years of constitutional revision which lay ahead, it was the Punjabis who drove the Muslim Indian bus and the other provinces who sat behind.

CHAPTER 4

The Muslim Conference and the Reforms

By the end of 1928, with the formation of the All India Muslim Conference at Delhi, the main Muslim negotiating position for the complex constitutional negotiations which were to follow had been established:

> The principles which we had enunciated [wrote the Aga Khan] were to be our guiding light henceforward in all our encounters with British or Hindu representatives and negotiators, with the Government of India or with the Congress party, in every discussion of schemes of Reform or new projects for the administration of the country . . . If India's political and constitutional evolution could be likened to a protracted and hard fought chess contest (the analogy is imperfect, I know, for there were always at least three players in the game), then it may be said that the board had now been set for an especially crucial game, the pieces were all in place, and there was a considerable lull while everyone thought out his next move.[1]

In this hard-fought contest, as the Aga Khan's analogy implies, the All India Muslim Conference found itself on the government's side and the Congress found itself on the other. Those politicians who dominated the Conference were chiefly men who had worked the Reforms and realized the importance of co-operating with the British in order to secure the concessions they required. Those who dominated the Congress were men who had given up hope of persuading the government to allow them a share of power by constitutional means. The Conference worked by pressurizing the government from within. The Congress embarked on a policy of non-constitutional agitation.

The government had its firmest ties with the organizers of the Conference. It had relied principally on their support in planning its strategy for the Statutory Commission, and this reliance did not diminish in the constitutional negotiations which were to follow. However the Government could not rule India on the backs of the

[1] *The Memoirs of the Aga Khan: World Enough and Time* (London 1954) p. 210.

Muslims, and as Congress influence increased, so did the government's need to be conciliatory. It may not have thought it possible to win over the Jawaharlal Nehrus and the Subhas Boses, but it could not afford to alienate the bulk of educated Hindu opinion, for under those conditions no constitution would be workable. For these reasons, even in 1929, Irwin attempted to persuade Congress to take part in the process of constitutional reform, first by the offer of a round-table conference, and subsequently, on the eve of the Lahore Congress, by a meeting with Gandhi, Motilal Nehru, Sapru and Jinnah. Yet despite these efforts, the one-year ultimatum issued at Calcutta became the Independence resolution passed at Lahore. Congress initiated a boycott of the councils and of the round table conference; and in April 1930, with Gandhi's march to Dandi, the civil disobedience movement began. At first, the government tried to kill the movement with kindness, but when this proved ineffective, the gloves came off. Congress leaders were imprisoned and government began to rule by ordinance. As the revision of the constitution proceeded, however, the government's tough posture in India was found to be increasingly at odds with the need for Congress involvement in the constitution-making process. The importance of Congress had been made apparent by the success of civil disobedience; it commanded not a little respect in Labour circles in England; and in the aftermath of the first round-table conference, the government was obliged to turn once more to conciliation. In March 1931, the Gandhi-Irwin Pact was signed: the government suspended rule by ordinance and released its political prisoners, and in exchange the Congress agreed to accept Dominion Status as its goal, to give up civil disobedience and to attend the second round-table conference.

From the point of view of the Muslim Conference, the most disturbing feature of these developments was that they coincided with the main phase of negotiations regarding the future constitution. The Conference was not a homogeneous body. It consisted of a very large number of Muslim interests, all of which considered it worthwhile at the end of 1928 to group together. They all felt at that stage that they were more likely to get what they wanted from government than from Congress. But as Congress prestige rose, and as government's slow and grudging plans for Reform unfolded themselves, it became an open question for many of these interests whether their original decision had been the correct one. Might not alliance with Congress produce a better deal for the Frontier? Might not Sind be separated at an earlier date? Might not the Bengali Muslims enjoy a greater share of power on Congress terms? This kind of reassessment threatened to weaken the Conference, to undermine its right to speak for the Muslims of the subcontinent as a whole, indeed to jeopardize the Muslim claim for special treatment everywhere.

For the Conference organizers, therefore, being on the government's side of the chessboard did not guarantee favourable treatment. Their alliance with government was subject to the same pressures as the government's confrontation with the Congress, and in order to maintain the credibility of the Conference, they had got to provide their supporters with a better deal than they were promised by other political organisations; and not in the future but as frustration came to a head. This task required great political skill, a high degree of organization, and above all the ability to force the government—and not only the government of India but the British government as well—into concessions which they were very often reluctant to make.

The Muslim Conference: leadership, support and resources

The chief architect of Conference policy during this period was Mian Fazli Husain, the founder of the Punjab Unionist party, who in 1930 was appointed member of the Viceroy's Council with special responsibility for Education, Health and Lands. Fazli's elevation to the Council at this time was certainly not fortuitous. It was a recognition both of his rare political gifts and of the paramount importance of Punjab Muslim support for the government's political strategy. Yet in picking Fazli, the Raj had not obtained a sleeping partner. He knew his own value to government[2] and he was not afraid to sell his support at a high price.

Throughout the period of constitutional reform, Fazli worked at two distinct but related levels. The first was as a member of the Viceroy's

[2]An interesting example of Fazli's confidence on this point is provided by his difference with Hailey over the appointment of the Simon Commission. When the Commission was first announced, Fazli was representing India at the League of Nations. But on his return to Bombay, he told a correspondent of the *Herald* that he objected to the exclusion of Indians and would advocate boycott by the Muslims if the Hindu Mahasabha also supported boycott. When Hailey pulled him up for this, Fazli immediately offered his resignation, and Hailey climbed down. See Hailey papers, 11B: Hailey to Fazli, 24 Nov. and 7 Dec. 1927; Fazli to Hailey, 6 Dec. 1927.

Council, cogently putting forward his views, both in minutes and in personal meetings with other councillors, and the second was as the co-ordinator of Conference activity in the country as a whole. In the first capacity, he made sure that the Muslim point of view never went by default in the council, and in the second that he was never short of a credible sanction outside the council when he met with opposition from his colleagues. For both these roles he was well endowed. He always prepared his brief thoroughly; he made his points directly and well, both on paper and in person; he understood the value of persuasion and organization; and he had a very excellent sense of when to compromise and when to stand firm.

But in keeping the Muslim Conference together, Fazli was dealing with a very mixed bag. Firstly, and most importantly, there were the provincial interests, those who had worked the Reforms in the provinecs, chiefly the Muslim landlords, whose degree of organization varied enormously from province to province. Where the two majority provinces were concerned, Fazli was chiefly interested in securing a better deal for the Punjab, and though his colleagues and followers in the Punjab council were not averse to quarrelling among themselves, he could generally rely on them to back him up. Firoz Khan Noon, Sikunder Hayat, Ahmed Yar Khan Daultana and Nawab Muzaffar Khan—these men knew how to organize the press, they had a virtual majority in the legislature, they had the sympathetic ear of government, and they had an overwhelming interest in keeping the Unionist party together until provincial autonomy had been granted on their terms. In Bengal, on the other hand, though the prospect of provincial autonomy put a premium on united action, the divisions within the community made it difficult to achieve. Abdur Rahim's party was organized separately from Fazlul Haq's, whilst the Nawabs of Dacca and Mymensingh maintained their distance from both. Fazli does not appear to have been on close terms with Sir Abdur Rahim. He had no contacts with Fazlul Haq. If he had any allies, it was the Nawabi party—Nazimuddin, A.H. Ghuznavi and Syed Abdul Hafiz. But though he did his best to cajole them into action, he found them generally unresponsive. On the whole, Fazli expected little from the Bengalis:

> The masses have hardly any feeling except one of misery, now approaching the verge of exasperation. The middle class Muslims go their own way trying to make some sort of living.... As regards the upper

educated people, their very position has made them intensely selfish, trying to gain something from both sides. It is perhaps uncharitable but it is not altogether incorrect'.[3]

Amongst the minority provinces, there were similar discrepancies. The most organised was the United Provinces, where the Nawab of Chhatari, Sir Mahommed Yusuf, the Raja of Salempur, Dr Shafaat Ahmed Khan, Sir Mahommed Yakub and Hafiz Hidayat Hussain all realized the need to keep the community united under the Conference banner. They may not have relished an alliance with the Punjabis but it made sound tactical sense. It was advocated vociferously by Shafaat Ahmed, Shafi's relation, and no less effectively behind the scenes by the Governor of the province, that most eminent of Punjabis, Sir Malcolm Hailey. In Bihar, the Conference possessed one of its most energetic workers, Maulana Shafi Daudi, who in 1928 was elected working secretary of the entire organization. But though Daudi was ably assisted at Patna by Zamiruddin Ahmed, his impact in Bihar was limited. Coming from north of the river, he did not find an open welcome in the salons of Patna and Bankipore, and even in the service of a wider cause,the barriers of parochialism did not come down. In Bihar, as in the other minority provinces, the Central Provinces, Madras and Bombay, the Conference relied chiefly on the passive support of local interests. In all these provinces, almost all Muslim members of council subscribed to the Conference,[4] but they did not throw up any provincial leaders of all-India stature. They relied on their case being put forward by the North Indians. For Fazli Husain, this passivity had its dangers, for where support was passive, inroads into Muslim unity could more easily be made. He made sure, therefore, that the demands of the minority provinces, like the demands of the Bengalis, were kept in the forefront of the Conference programme. Throughout the period of constitutional revision, in all public negotiations, whether with government or with other political parties, he insisted that the demands of the minority provinces and of the Bengalis be settled first. He made the Punjab the sheepdog of Muslim India and pushed the more timid brethren into the front line.[5]

[3]See Fazli Husain papers: undated note 'Bengal and its problems'.

[4].See *List of Members of the Working Committee, the Executive Board and the General Body of the All India Muslim Conference* (Patna 1932).

[5] See, for example, Fazli Husain papers: Fazli Husain to Iqbal, 30 May 1931; Fazli Husain to the Nawab of Chhatari, 5 Sept. 1931.

A second group of importance consisted of the urban constitutionalists—men like Jinnah, Shafi, Shah Nawaz and Abdullah Suhrawardy, who had been thwarted in their political ambitions by the nature of the Montagu-Chelmsford Reforms and who had attempted in the late 1920s to do a deal with the Congress at the all-India level in order to improve their own position. These men had been forced to take sides with their provincial brethren by the growth of communalism in the provinces and the subsequent polarization of all-India politics. But their ambitions remained distinct, particularly with regard to devolution at the Centre, and they were less sturdy than the provincial interests in their support for separate electorates.[6]

Thirdly, there were the minority-province Khilafatists, men like the Ali brothers, Hasrat Mohani and Azad Sobhani, whose importance had declined with the abolition of the Khilafat and whose increasingly fragile relationship with the Congress was disrupted by the Nehru report. Like the urban constitutionalists, these men had gravitated towards the Conference. But they sat uncomfortably on the same platform as Firoz Khan Noon and the Nawab of Chhatari. Not only were their political methods different—sometimes embarrassingly different—but also, by dint of their previous association with such Congress Muslims as Ansari, Khaliquzzaman and Sherwani, they possessed a sympathy for the 'nationalist' school which made them unreliable allies. There was always the danger that they would repudiate the Conference programme in some new all-India agreement with the Congress.

Lastly, there were the Frontiersmen and the Sindhis. In both these areas, the fact that no concessions had been made to the political ambitions of the inhabitants meant that those who favoured a policy

[6]Jinnah did not attend the Muslim Conference at Delhi in Dec. 1928, but in March 1929, after a meeting with Conference representatives, he drew up his famous 14 points, which were virtually identical to the Conference demands of 1 Jan. 1929. Technically he remained open to negotiation on the question of electorates, providing the 14 points were accepted. But if Motilal Nehru is to be believed, such an offer did not belong to the realm of practical politics: 'He is simply trying to reinstate himself with his followers', he wrote to Gandhi in Aug. 1929, 'by making preposterous demands.... I am quite clear in my own mind that the only way to reach a compromise with the truly nationalist Muslims is to ignore Mr. Jinnah and the Ali brothers altogether.' See Motilal Nehru papers: Nehru to Gandhi, 14 Aug. 1929. I am indebted to Mr V.C. Joshi of the Nehru Memorial Museum for this reference.

of quiet, firm pressure within the system were easily outrun in the race for popular support. Even before Fazli was appointed to the Viceroy's Council, the Pathans of Peshawar and Mardan had worsted the administration, and had embarrassed the Conference by openly declaring their allegiance to the Congress; and in Sind, though matters had not yet come to a head, those who were in the vanguard of the separation movement were already showing signs of impatience. Such men as Haji Abdullah Haroon, the Memon merchant prince, and Sheikh Abdul Majid Sindhi, Mahommed Ali's old Khilafat colleague, were not committed to the Conference irretrievably and if the Conference wanted to retain their support it had to deliver the goods faster than its opponents.

What advantages beyond his personal ability did Fazli Husain possess in keeping these interests together? Within the Imperial machine, his main advantage was the presence of officials who understood and sympathized with his point of view. Hailey and de Montmorency, the Governors of the U.P. and the Punjab, Herbert Emerson, the Home Secretary, and James Dunnett, the Reforms Commissioner, were all Punjab civilians, men who saw the essentials of the Indian problem from the same viewpoint. They were not always responsive to Fazli's opinions. Dunnett was often too 'original'[7] particularly where the issue of central responsibility was concerned; Hailey and de Montmorency were disinclined to give away as much as Fazli wanted in the Punjab. But in the last resort, they realized that they and Fazli stood or fell together, and in Fazli's dealings with the government of India that was a considerable advantage.

Outside the Council, Fazli was poorly served. Unlike the Congress, the Conference did not have the backing of wealthy industrialists. There were no Birlas, no Ambalal Sarabhais, no Jamnalal Bajajes. Nobody contributed in lakhs. The nearest equivalent was Haji Abdullah Haroon and he was a small man by comparison. The Conference was backed primarily by the princely states and the landed interest. The Nizam of Hyderabad made at least one substantial donation.[8] The Nawabs of Bhopal and Rampur were more regular supporters.[9] The Aga Khan gave generously and regularly; and

[7] Fazli Husain papers, Diary, 21 May 1930: 'Dunnett is inclined to be original, while I wish him to be only imitative.'

[8] Ibid., Sir Akbar Hydari, Prime Minister of Hyderabad, to Fazli Husain, 29 July 1931.

[9] Interview with Syed Hussain Imam of Gaya, Karachi, April 1970.

paid out bonuses when his horses won the Derby.[10] In the U.P., the Raja of Salempur rose to political prominence by financing the Conference. According to one source, he gave more money to the Conference than anybody except the Aga Khan.[11] In the Punjab, Firoz Khan Noon organized collections amongst the Unionists. but for the most part, the Conference was financed by small monthly subscriptions.[12] It had no substantial reserves. The money was spent as it was collected, and the working secretary, Shafi Daudi finished his association with the Conference deeply in debt.[13]

Partly as a result of these financial problems, the Conference did not have a newspaper to match the big Congress organs. There was no *Tribune*, no *Leader*, no *Hindu*. To reach that kind of audience, it had to rely on the sympathy of the British-owned papers, the *Civil and Military Gazette*, the *Pioneer*, the *Statesman*, the *Madras Mail* and the *Times of India*. But there were a number of lesser local papers, both in English and Urdu, which served the Conference well. In the Punjab, there was the *Muslim Outlook* which had been founded by Shafi, Abdul Quadir and Fazli Husain in 1924; there was *Siyasat*, edited by Syed Habib Shah: and there was the more distinctly pro-Unionist paper, *Inquilab*, edited by Ghulam Rasool Mihr. In the U.P., there was Hafiz ur Rahman's *Aligarh Mail*; there was the Allahabad *Star*; and there was Abdullah Khan's *Hamdam*, which the Government assisted by the establishment of a special post office.[14] At Delhi, there was *Millat*. In Bihar, there was Shafi Daudi's *Ittehad*. But what the Conference lacked was an efficient news agency to ensure that its position was reported without bias in the British press. In 1931, efforts were made to remedy this defect, but the five lakhs required for the project do not appear to have been collected.[15]

[10]Fazli Husain papers, Shafi Daudi to Fazli Husain, 17 Aug. 1931; see also Azim Husain, ***Fazli Husain, a political Biography*** (Bombay 1946), p. 312.

[11]Fazli Husain papers: Mushir Hussain Kidwai to Fazli Husain, 18 May 1930.

[12]Ibid., circular letter to Fazli Husain requesting 30-rupee subscription of the month of July 1931, enclosed, Shafi Daudi to Fazli Husain, 17 Aug. 1931.

[13]Ibid. By Aug. 1931, Daudi had loaned nearly 1,500 rupees to the Conference to keep the central office running. See also Shafi Daudi papers: Shafi Daudi to his bank manager, 3 March, 1939 (Nehru Memorial Museum, New Delhi).

[14]Fazli Husain papers: Abdullah Khan to Fazli Husain, 4 Dec. 1932.

[15]For a discussion of the Muslim Conference and the press, see Fazli Husain papers: Fazli to the Raja of Salempur, 3 May 1931. See also Mihr collection, 454: Progs. of the All India Muslim Conference Working Committee, Lahore, 24 May 1931, resolution 1.

Fazli's main advantage was a thoroughly conscientious Conference working secretary, Maulana Shafi Daudi, a man of great experience in many different political spheres, in local, provincial and national politics. As a former Khilafatist, Daudi was well acquainted with the politics of religion; as a non-co-operator, he had learnt how to give a programme mass appeal; as Motilal's lieutenant in Bihar, he had acquired the techniques of provincial organization; as a member of the Central Assembly, he was well aware of what was at stake in all-India terms; as a national politician, he had innumerable contacts in many different provinces. For all these reasons, he was an ideal man for the job. He may not have spoken very good English, and a certain class of Muslim has neglected to give him his due for this reason,[16] but he was an extremely devoted and selfless worker in the Conference cause and to him undoubtedly goes much of the credit for the success of the organization.

From his newspaper office at Bankipore, the *Quaumi* press, Daudi corresponded with Muslim leaders throughout India. He was responsible for much of the Conference publicity; for the organization of deputations to the Viceroy; for the running of the Executive Board; for sending telegrams to Britain during all stages of the process of constitutional reform; for relations with the press; for the collection of subscriptions; for touring on behalf of the Conference in Bihar, U.P. and Bengal; and for trouble-shooting in difficult areas, in Alwar and on the Frontier. In short, he did the work of several men, and for nearly five years was scarcely ever at home[17] With this man, Fazli Husain had what has been described as 'a perfect liaison'[18]; and thanks to this liaison the Muslim Conference became the organizational arm of his work in the council. When the government appeared to be making too many concessions to Congress or too few to the Muslim community, it was Shafi Daudi on whom Fazli relied for a public statement, a Conference resolution or a deputation in support of his point of view. But even with Shafi Daudi, Fazli had his problems, for as an old Khilafatist and non-co-operator, he was inclined to favour agitation when the going was rough.

[16]See, for example, Mahommed Mujib, *The Indian Muslims* (London 1967), p. 443. Rafi Ahmed Kidwai apparently poked fun at Daudi on these grounds.

[17]Shafi Daudi's diary, though reticent like the man himself, tells its own tale of endless travelling, meetings and organization. I am indebted to his son Mr. Ata ur Rahman Daudi of Muzaffurpur, for translating many passages into English.

[18]Interview with Syed Hussain Imam of Gaya, Karachi, April 1970.

The Simon Commission report and the Government of India dispatch

The Muslim Conference met its first serious challenge with the publication of the Simon Commission report in May 1930. Already by that stage, the report had been deprived of any degree of finality by the Viceroy's offer of a round-table conference, but the fact that the Commission had been appointed by Parliament, the co-operation which it had received from the provincial wings of the Conference, and the enormous amount of work which had gone into producing its report, all gave it a degree of authority which, in view of its findings, was highly dangerous to Conference interests.

From the Unionist point of view, the report was not an unadulterated disaster. It put greater powers into the hands of the Governor than Fazli would have liked, but it did concede a full measure of provincial autonomy. There were to be no official ministers, there was to be joint responsibility, and all government departments were to be transferred.[19] Nor did the report subject the provinces to a responsible centre. It rejected the idea of an immediate federation of British Indian provinces, instead introducing a proposal for an all-Indian federation of British India and the States at some future, unspecified date.[20] This was clearly to be a very conservative body, designed primarily to uphold British control at the Centre, and it was only to be brought into being once the new provincial governments had established themselves. '...the nature of the constituents themselves', ran the report, 'has a great influence on the form which federation takes.' This recommendation was very much to Fazli's liking, for it was tantamount to giving the provinces a veto on the form of the federal government. Moreover, it was clear, as the report admitted, that such a federation, consisting of both autocratic and democratic governments, would only be possible if 'the greatest possible internal freedom' was given to each of the constituent units.[21] This was also to Fazli's liking.

But the merits of the report stopped there. In the first place, the writers of the report did not think that the existing provinces were ideal units for federation. They made 'a definite recommendation for reviewing, and if possible for resettling the provincial boundaries

[19]*Report of the Indian Statutory Commission* vol. ii, *Recommendations Cmd. 3569,* presented to Parliament, May 1930, pp. 16-17, 33-4. 44-8.

[20]Ibid., pp. 9-14.

[21]Ibid., pp. 18-19.

of India at as early a date as possible.'[22] Muslim majorities were not mentioned specifically but the possibility of redistribution affecting those majorities was not ruled out. Nor was the separation of Sind granted in principle. There would first have to be 'a close and detailed enquiry into the financial consequences which would follow such a step.'[23] This was not heartening news for the Sindhis. The Frontier's demand for equal status was also neglected. 'The inherent right of a man to smoke a cigarette', said the report, 'must necessarily be curtailed if he lives in a powder magazine.' The military importance of the Frontier made it necessary that 'executive responsibilities should, as at present, rest with the Chief Commissioner'. The Commission recommended the formation of an irresponsible legislature along the lines of the Morley-Minto Reforms.[24] In Baluchistan, the report envisaged no change at all. The authors believed that the demand for representative insitutions of a western type did not come from the Baluch but had been foisted on them from outside.[25]

The report also displayed an unsympathetic attitude towards separate representation. In the light of the virtually unanimous recommendations of all provincial governments and provincial committees, it grudgingly admitted that in default of a new agreement between Hindus and Muslims, 'Mahommedan voters should not be deprived of this special protection until a substantial majority of Muslim representatives in the provincial legislatures declare themselves in favour of a change.' But it did not confine itself to recommending a continuation of the same system of separate communal electorates. It examined a number of alternatives, including proportional representation, and ultimately recommended a scheme of its own whereby Muslims would be returned by a system of reservation within joint electorates provided that they polled forty percent of the votes of their own community.[26] In the Central Legislature, moreover, it recommended the abolition of separate representation and the introduction of a system of indirect election by proportional representation, calculating, though with what validity is uncertain, that the

[22]Ibid., p. 16.

[23]Ibid. p. 25. In the meantime, as a palliative, the Commission recommended the establishment of a special legislative committee within the Bombay Council.

[24]Ibid., p. 103.

[25]Ibid., p. 106.

[26]Ibid., pp. 60-3.

Muslims would win thirty per cent of the seats by this method.[27] The report's biggest bombshell, however, was its hostility to the Muslim demand for majorities by separate electorates in Punjab and Bengal. The Commission approached this question from the standpoint of the Lucknow Pact. As regards weightage for the minority provinces, it agreed that it should not be withdrawn without the consent of the Muslims. But it was not prepared to countenance majorities by separate electorates for the Punjab and Bengal at the same time:

It would be unfair that Mahommedans should retain the very considerable weightage they now enjoy in the six provinces, and that there should at the same time be imposed, in the face of Hindu and Sikh opposition, a definite Muslim majority in the Punjab and Bengal, unalterable by any appeal to the electorate.

In so many words, the authors laid down that if the Punjabis and Bengalis wanted majorities they would have to fight for them within joint electorates.[28]

The Muslim response to the publication of the report was one of annoyance and exasperation. The Conference supporters had taken no part in the non-co-operation movement – Muslims in general had held aloof from it – and their support for government had been an important factor in the preservation of law and order. But they appeared to be getting nothing for their pains; indeed to many of them, the Simon Commission report seemed like an open invitation to throw in their lot with the Congress. This was particularly the case at Lahore, where the Conference organizers had difficulty restraining their supporters. Nawab Muzaffar Khan, the Unionist party trouble-shooter, held meetings both with the publicists and the politicians to try to reverse the trend towards despair. But he had a hard row to hoe.[29] The editors of the *Inquilab, Siyasat, Muslim Outlook,* and other Muslim papers told him frankly that the scheme of provincial autonomy suggested by the report was entirely unsatisfactory. They alleged that the report 'had practically established Hindu Raj, under British protection, in all provinces throughout India, including the

[27]Ibid. pp. 118-21.

[28]Ibid., pp. 71-2.

[29]The following account of Nawab Muzaffar's meetings with Muslim politicians and journalists at Lahore is based on his secret note, which was forwarded by the Punjab Government Chief Secretary to Herbert Emerson, Government of India Home Secretary, on 4 July 1930 (GI Home Poll., 346/1930).

two provinces of Bengal and Punjab where the Muslims were in a majority'. 'What was the use of the Commission and its long enquiry', they asked, 'if they had to settle the question themselves with the Hindus?' Dr Iqbal, Chaudhuri Afzal Haq and Malik Barkat Ali were no less scathing. According to Iqbal:

A death blow had been struck at the Muslim majority in the Punjab. He was for starting a very strong and effective agitation against the report and was prepared for every sacrifice. Chaudhuri Afzal Haq was of the same view and said that he and other Congressites like Alam, Zafar Ali and Abdul Qadir Qasuri were all for the Muslim majority in the Punjab. They would like to make a common cause, go to [the] villages and set up an unprecedented agitation.

Muzaffar did his best to reassure them. He drew particular attention to the Commission's federal scheme 'which prevented Hindus becoming powerful in the Central Government', to its concession that separate electorates should continue while the Muslims wanted them, and to the 'inclination of the Commission' regarding the demands of the Sindhis and Frontiersmen. But he had difficulty meeting their point that the Muslim position in the Punjab was in jeopardy; indeed, he was of the same opinion himself:

Up till now the Muslim majority in the Punjab has been maintained with the help of official votes. If the Simon suggestions are followed and the official element removed, the present strength of the Muslims will be gone and they will be at the mercy of the Hindus. I personally would prefer hundred times real British Raj to this sort of self-government.

As a temporary expedient to win over the discontented, he suggested that Iqbal be given a seat on the round-table conference, but he made it clear that more drastic measures were required if a situation, 'neither in the interests of the Muslims nor of the British Government' was to be avoided.[30]

On 5 July 1930 at Simla, the Executive Board of the Muslim

[30]Prominent Bengali Muslims were no less displeased. Sir Abdur Rahim complained that the advance outlined by the report was unsatisfactory. Communal divisions had been used at every stage as an argument against making substantial concessions. No real effort had been made to provide a viable framework for Federation, nor to deal with the question of Defence. 'It is now for the Mussulmans of Bengal to consider seriously', he said, 'whether they should or should not discard separate electorates and take their chance in a common electorate according to the extended franchise.' See *Indian Annual Register,* 1930, vol. ii, pp. 351-54.

Conference passed detailed resolutions on the report. While appreciating the fact that the future constitution was to be organized on a federal basis and that the provinces were to be given a substantial degree of autonomy, the Board described the report as 'unacceptable to the Mussulmans of India' and 'retrograde and reactionary in spirit'. It demanded that the community be guaranteed 'a clear majority in Bengal and Punjab', that Sind be separated, that the Frontier and Baluchistan be given equal status, that the community be guaranteed 'adequate and effective representation in the cabinets and public services of the country', that election to the Federal Assembly be by separate electorates, that the army and navy be speedily Indianized and that an element of responsibility be introduced in the federal government.[31] The meeting was most notable, however, for the spirit of defiance lent to its proceedings by the President, Maulana Shaukat Ali:

> The Maulana said that they would wait for four or five months for their demands to be conceded after which he and his workers would not keep to non-violence. The Maulana said that they got too involved these days in section 144 and the Indian penal code. They had lost their historical sense, the kind of sense which Bacha Saqqao showed in capturing Kabul with 27 horsemen....[32]

With such plentiful evidence of Muslim disillusionment, Fazli had a strong hand to play in dealing with his colleagues in the council. His basic argument was that the Indian Muslims 'would prefer the present position and no political advance to the political advance outlined in the Simon report.'[33] In other words, if government was to press forward with its plans for Reform (and by 1930 it had very little alternative), it would have to make more substantial concessions to the Muslims. In general terms, the government acknowledged this necessity. It was too committed to the Muslims to alienate them, and if concessions had to be made to retain their support, it was prepared in the last resort to make them. This attitude gave Fazli considerable

[31]Mihr collection, 454: *Resolutions of the All India Muslim Conference, the Executive Board and the Working Committee, from September 1929 to March 1932.* The demand for an element of responsibility at the Centre reflects the presence of all-India politicians on the Executive Board. One of the difficulties faced by those provincial politicians who dominated the Conference was in keeping these men under control.

[32]For an account of the Simla meeting, see *Indian Annual Register,* 1930, vol. ii, pp. 325-8.

[33]Halifax papers, 6: Note by Fazli Husain, enclosed, Irwin to Wedgwood Benn, 28 Aug. 1930.

powers of leverage within the council, and a study of the formulation of the government's response to the Simon proposals, the government of India dispatch of 20 September 1930, illustrates how he was able to use this leverage to improve the Muslim position.

Even before the Simon Commission report was published, Fazli realized the importance for the Conference of winning over the Frontier Muslims. But the mutiny of the Gurhwalis at Peshawar in April and the subsequent imposition of martial law made his task difficult. Members of council believed that the primary need was to restore government prestige and they were not initially receptive to his suggestions for Reform. By degrees, however, he won them over to his point of view. Early in May, he made initial approaches to Haig, the acting Home Member, and to Schuster, the Finance Member, and finding them sympathetic, put up a note for Haig to lay before the Viceroy.[34] After this, the council appears to have listened carefully to Fazli's advice. They appointed a Muslim High Court Judge to the enquiry committee set up to investigate the Peshawar troubles,[35] and they allowed Fazli to organize two deputations, one to the Governor of the Punjab and the other to the Viceroy, so that government could publicly reassure the Muslims, both with regard to the position on the Frontier and to the position of the community as a whole under the reformed constitution.[36]

In his plans for Reform, however, Fazli got most support from Howell, the Foreign Secretary, and Emerson, the Home Secretary. Howell believed that the Frontier administration had been culpably inefficient and considered a new deal necessary to improve government's image.[37] Emerson agreed with Howell. In his view, the introduction of Reforms was 'by far the most promising method of providing a rallying post for the well-disposed'. Emerson's main point, however, was that the Frontier question had an important bearing on government's relations with the Muslims generally:

In the older provinces, Mahommedans have the majority in the Punjab and Bengal only, and in both these provinces the majority is a small one. Hence they naturally wish to strengthen their position *vis a vis* the Hindus by bringing within the orbit of the Reforms the N.W.F.P

[34]Fazli Husain papers: Diary, 6 and 8 May 1930.

[35]Ibid., Diary, 14 May 1930.

[36]Ibid. Diary, 31 May 1930 and 4 June 1930.

[37]GI Home Poll, 206/1930: Note by Howell, 24 May 1930.

where their community is in an overwhelming majority. Not only do they feel that there is insufficient reason for withholding the Reforms but they believe that ultimate self-government in the N.W.F.P. will be of great value to them in the future political game. The movement for constitutional reform in that province has therefore received a strong and perfectly legitimate impetus from outside with the result that it is impracticable to regard the problem as a parochial one[38]

By the beginning of June, the Viceroy had agreed to let Fazli go to the Frontier to see the situation for himself,[39] and on his return he wrote a memorandum making a strong case for Reform. It was not possible, he said, for the Frontier to continue any longer with a different scheme of government from all the other provinces. The Frontier people were aware that the Punjabis had benefited from the Reforms—particularly in the field of education and local self-government—and from the other side of the Frontier, reports were also filtering into the Peshawar bazaars about the 'socialist and democratic' measures being carried out in the Soviet Union. Already, he said, the Frontier people, and particularly the educated, were feeling a sense of inferiority, not only *vis-a-vis* the Europeans, but also *vis-a-vis* the Punjabis, and it was highly desirable that Reforms should be granted promptly and their co-operation enlisted in uplift work before they became 'thoroughly discontented, disgusted and disappointed.'[40] These views carried weight within the council, and a sub-committee was set up under Fazli's presidency, to draft a new constitution. This constitution gave the Frontier a unitary system of government, a legislature with a majority of elected members, and two responsible ministers. The Chief Commissioner still retained considerable powers (forty-nine per cent of the seats were to be filled by nomination) but the constitution conformed in type with those of other provinces, a point on which Fazli insisted, and it contained within itself the seeds of future liberalization. During the drafting of the government of India dispatch, Fazli piloted this scheme through the council, and persuaded his colleagues to finance the province's anticipated deficit by means of a central subvention.[41] But he continued to feel that a more liberal constitution was necessary if the atmosphere in the province was to

[38]Ibid., Note by Emerson, 26 May 1930.

[39]Fazli Husain papers: Diary, 30 June 1930.

[40]Ibid. Memorandum on Reforms for the Frontier, 5 July 1930.

[41]GI Reforms Office, 67/v/1930: Minutes of informal discussion in council on the government of India's proposals for Reform, 12th meeting, 19 July 1930.

be changed, and during the first round-table conference he tried to improve the scheme by bringing pressure to bear on the government in Britain. In a brief to Sir Mahommed Shafi, one of the Muslim delegates to the Conference, he wrote:

It is up to you to get this province into line with other provinces if you can, or at all events, to get the very best for the province. The important point concerning this matter is that if that province is not given a really good constitution, it will always be ready to play into the hands of the Congress and therefore the position of the Indian Mussulmans will be very much weakened. Political wisdom lies in doing the province well, and I trust British statesmanship will not fail to grasp this point.[42]

Once he had improved the position on the Frontier, Fazli endeavoured to get the council to make a decision in principle on the separation of Sind. He submitted to the Viceroy a pamphlet by Mahommed Ayub Khuhro in favour of separation,[43] and at Irwin's instigation, Haig examined the question in some detail. Haig came to the conclusion that there was 'a strong prima facie case in favour of separation'. He held that Sind was quite distinct from the rest of Bombay presidency, geographically, racially, linguistically and administratively, and he recommended that separation should be carried out if it really was a practical proposition. On that point, however, he held that there was no evidence on which to make a decision. He considered that the Bombay government had based its case against separation on poorly analysed statistics and he recommended that the whole matter should be examined by a special committee.[44] Sir George Schuster, the Finance Member, agreed. The existence within the territory of Sind of the vast Sukkur Barrage Irrigation Scheme, for the Bombay government one of the principle arguments against separation, was for Schuster an argument in its favour. He had a poor opinion of the Bombay Finance Department and felt certain that 'full advantage will not be taken of this project, the success or failure of which may have results which affect the whole of India, so long as it remains under the Bombay Government.' For financial reasons, therefore, he was prepared to support separation, providing that the government of India's interest in the Barrage

[42]Fazli Husain papers: Fazli to Shafi, 1 Dec. 1930.

[43]GI Reforms Office, 126/1930: Note by Fazli Husain, 23 Aug. 1930.

[44]Ibid., Note by Haig, 27 Aug. 1930.

could be recognized.[45] With the exception of Birdwood, the Commander in Chief, who had a scheme of his own for amalgamating Sind and the Punjab, other members of council followed Haig and Schuster, and the result was that the government of India dispatch was modified to provide for a speedy enquiry into the financial aspects of separation.[46] The government recommended that the enquiry should be completed within six months, and that a decision on separation should be taken on the basis of its findings. This was a considerable improvement on Simon's recommendation for a Boundary Commission, which, as Fazli pointed out, was 'next door to shelving the question.'[47]

But Fazli's most strenuous efforts were devoted to securing the Muslim position in the majority provinces, and more especially in the Punjab. He pursued this objective in two ways: firstly, by working for maximum provincial autonomy on terms which were favourable to Muslim control; and secondly, by working for a central government which would exercise minimum control over the provinces.

In the pursuit of maximum provincial autonomy, Fazli argued strongly against vesting the Governor with unspecified powers of 'supervision, direction and control'. He dissented from the view supported in the government of India dispatch that the Governor should have a discretionary power to appoint an official minister,[48] and he also opposed giving the Governor overriding powers, even in the interests of 'safety and tranquillity' and 'the protection of minorities'.

> 'Safety and tranquillity' will not do because it has been argued often enough that 'safety and tranquillity may be endangered by wrong action in almost any department.... I am quite clear that what is needed is specification of the departments in which overriding powers of the Governor are desired to be secured.[49]

Similarly, with regard to the protection of minorities, he pointed out that they were not only interested in questions of religion and

[45]Ibid., Note by Schuster, 2 Sept. 1930.

[46]Ibid. Note by W.H. Lewis, Assistant Reforms Commissioner, 6 Sept. 1930. See also *Government of India Dispatch on Proposals for Constitutional Reform, 20 September 1930*, presented to Parliament, Nov. 1930, *Cmd. 3700*, pp. 16-17.

[47]Ibid., Note by Fazli Husain, 23 Aug. 1930.

[48]GI Reforms Office, 67/v/1930: Minutes of informal discussion in council on government proposals for Reform, 21st Meeting, 3 Sept. 1930: see also *Government of India Dispatch*, p. 38.

[49]GI Reforms Office, 67/x/1930: Note by Fazli Husain, 18 Aug. 1930.

culture, but also in representation in local bodies and services. In both these spheres, he argued, overriding powers would involve 'a very serious encroachment on the responsibility of the ministry to the legislature'.[50]

At the same time, he endeavoured to secure for the Muslims of Punjab and Bengal a majority of seats by separate electorates. This was a difficult task. There were some Governors, in all probability Hailey and de Montmorency, who believed that 'political considerations' might require that the Muslims be given majorities in these two provinces while retaining their weightage in the minority provinces.[51] But most members of council were more circumspect. To show public approval for a system which put minorities at the mercy of an unalterable communal majority was likely to make government a number of powerful enemies and to be a source of incessant agitation. Moreover, it was so obviously 'undemocratic' that it would certainly not meet with parliamentary approval in Britain.[52]

Fazli's main argument was that the Simon Commission had done a great injustice to the majority provinces by making its recommendations on the basis of the Lucknow Pact. That understanding had been repudiated both by the Congress and by the Conference and formed no basis for a discussion of the problem. Recognition of Muslim majorities in Punjab and Bengal should not be made dependent on the surrendering of weightage in the minority provinces. The question

[50]Ibid. Fazli's views on these questions show how far his interests were removed from those of the minority-province Muslims. He made no effort to support statutory safeguards for minorities in cabinets and services, even though the Muslim Conference was putting this demand forward vociferously on their behalf. Indeed, he appears to have argued against statutory representation in Cabinets, and to have concurred with the general council view that for the services a negative formula was the best answer. It is clear that in his scheme of provincial autonomy, the minority would have to accept the arbitration of the majority. In his view, even giving the Governor overriding powers would be an insufficient guarantee: 'Personally', he wrote, 'I think the Governor will not be able to do much, for the reason, among others, that he would not consider it worth his while to pick a quarrel with his Cabinet for the sake of any minority.' See Minutes of informal discussion.., loc. cit., 3rd meeting, 27 June, 1930; Fazli Husain papers: Fazli Husain to Mahommed Shafi, 1 Dec. 1930.

[51]GI Reforms Office, 65R/1930 (Secret): Proceedings of the Governors' Conference, 1st meeting, 21 July 1930.

[52]GI Reforms Office, 67/x/1930: Minutes of informal discussion in council, 1st meeting, 25 June 1930.

of Muslim representation in Punjab and Bengal should be treated on its own merits and not from an all-India point of view. Fazli appears to have carried the day on this issue. It was recognized that 'the Muslims both in the United Provinces and in Bihar and Orissa would react sharply against any decision to deprive them of their present weightage'[53] and no attempt was made to do so. But where the granting of a communal majority to the Punjabis and Bengalis was concerned, Fazli found his colleagues far less tractable. They were prepared to concede separate electorates so long as majority-province Muslims desired them, but they were very reluctant to make precise recommendations regarding the distribution of seats. Indeed, they were inclined to postpone consideration of the problem until the 1931 census was published.

Fazli made it plain that this was not satisfactory to Muslim opinion. Whatever the figures for the 1931 census might be, he said, the main question was whether the issue should be decided on a population basis, or on the basis of voting strength or some other criterion:

> Muslims attach a great deal of importance to an expression of opinion on this matter. The Simon Commission has practically decided that distribution on population basis should not decide the matter, but it has not decided whether a bare majority should to given to Muslims or not. The draft also shelves this question. The way it will strike the Indian Mussulmans is that the Labour Government has been believed to have expressed itself in the past against Muslim claims; and, therefore, if neither the Commission nor the Government of India support their claim, they cannot expect the Labour Government to support them. The alternative is that the Muslims in these two provinces should rely on their own strength, work toward the lowering of the franchise (against which the draft has expressed dissent from the view of the Commission) and abandon their present attitude in Indian politics.[54]

This was strong talk. But Fazli backed it up with two suggestions for solving the question which were designed to meet the 'technical' objection to a communal majority. The first provided for a small number of nominated seats and the second for a small number of special constituencies. The Muslims were to be given a virtual majority of the elected seats and to pick up the extra votes they needed from nominated or special members: 'It should be noted', he wrote, 'that

[53]Proceedings of the Governors' Conference loc.cit. 1st meeting, 21 July 1930.
[54]GI Reforms Office, 67/X/1930: Note by Fazli Ḥusain, 1 Sept. 1930.

where special constituencies exist and the number of electorates which the Muslims have is less than half the total number of seats, it is not open to the criticism that a communal majority has been set up.[55]

At a result of Fazli's pressure, the council was persuaded to modify its draft dispatch. 'It was decided that Council might definitely express an opinion that they would not consider it right to penalise Muslim majorities in the Punjab and Bengal because of weightage given to that community elsewhere.'[56] This was an important concession. But the council went further. Though they did not recommend Fazli's scheme for solving the problem, they did recommend a scheme put forward by the Punjab government which was very similar in principle. In that scheme, the Muslims were to have sixty-six seats out of 134, and the balance of power was to lie with two Europeans. Fazli would obviously have liked the Muslims to be more self-reliant. But he was not dissatisfied. The Punjab scheme gave the Muslims a virtual majority by separate electorates and it was an offer which might be improved in subsequent negotiations.[57]

Fazli fought his most difficult battle, however, over the relations between the provinces and the Centre. He anticipated that the Muslims would secure control of the Punjab under the reformed constitution and he wished to exercise that control free of central interference. But on this question, he met with determined opposition within the government of India. In the strategy of the Raj, the devolution of power to the provinces under the Montagu-Chelmsford constitution had worked as a successful counterweight to the nationalist challenge at the Centre. But with provincial autonomy about to be introduced, a new danger emerged, which Dunnett, the Reforms Commissioner, labelled 'extreme provincialism'. Dunnett argued that if provincial autonomy was introduced without any change at the Centre there was a danger of the government of India falling to the provinces.[58]

[55]Ibid.

[56]Minutes of informal discussion in council, loc. cit., 20th meeting, 2 Sept. 1930.

[57]*Government of India Dispatch*, p. 28: 'The scheme satisfies neither the Muslim, nor the Hindu, nor the Sikh members of the government, but in our view merits consideration.'

[58]It was on this question that Dunnett found the Simon Commission report most unsatisfactory. 'One of the greatest failures of the report is its blindness to the dependence of central administration in almost all departments on provincial co-operation. A system of self-sufficient federal agencies is impossible. This is one reason why there cannot be full responsibility in the provinces and full irresponsibility at the Centre.' GI Reforms Office, 67/vi/1930: Note by Dunnett, 10 July 1930.

It is difficult to examine this question independently of the challenge which the Raj was facing from the Congress. Some members of council felt that a concession at the Centre should be made as a positive response to that challenge. The Viceroy himself was of this view, and amongst the Indian members, the case for responsibility at the Centre was put forward very strenuously by Sir Joseph Bhore, the Member for Industry and Labour. Moreover, those who took the opposite view, the advocates of 'extreme provincialism', the Punjab and Madras governments and the Punjab Unionist party, who argued that the Raj should stand fast at the Centre, these interests were equally influenced in the formation of their political views by the likelihood of Congress domination at the Centre. Dunnett's contribution, however, was to point out that what was at stake was not who should control the central government but whether there should be a central government at all. Dunnett argued that it would be unwise to appease Muslim fears of a Hindu Centre if the price was loss of British control over the provinces.

The question first came up when the Simon report's recommendations for the central government were being discussed. The council agreed that 'it would not be right to commit the future and that to try to develop the Centre along the same lines as the provinces might be a serious political mistake'. But though they agreed with the report's long-term recommendations for an all-India Federation, they felt that dealing with the central government over the interim period presented difficulties, and they recommended that 'the constitutional problem of British India should be considered on its own merits'.[59] The main question was: how was the central government to ensure compliance with its wishes in the period between the establishment of provincial autonomy and the eventual establishment of the all-India Federation? In a note on the scope of the central government's powers of supervision, direction and control, Dunnett argued that these powers would be more effective if they were exercised, at least to some extent, in association with the Central Legislature. He considered it impracticable to place them solely in the hands of the agents of the Crown, and he argued that it would be better 'to give the Centre powers so obviously effective that their exercise will be obviated by their mere existence than to require the Centre to fall back on the Secretary of State for the assertion of its legislative

[59]GI Reforms Office, 67/v/1930: Minutes of informal discussion in council on Government proposals for Reform, 5th meeting, 2 July 1930.

authority'.[60] This note produced a very strong counter-attack from Fazli Husain. He informed the council 'that unless the Assembly were wholly excluded from the use of this power, provincial opinion would reject any reforms'. In his view, 'the provincial electorate would derive its sovereignty from Parliament and it would be inappropriate that the Assembly should be set up in a position to dominate the provinces'.[61] But though his point was taken, Dunnett's argument clearly carried more weight. It was recognized that the central government did require a measure of popular support in its dealings with the provinces, and as an initial step the council decided not to exclude the Assembly from an interest either in the supervision of central subjects or in the raising of loans for provincial purposes.[62]

The chasm widened when discussion turned to the question of introducing responsibility in the Central Executive. The Viceroy favoured a unitary scheme because this would ensure legislative support for unpopular measures.[63] But Sir George Schuster was rigorously opposed to the transfer of Finance, at least until a Reserve Bank had been set up, and it was generally recognized that the India Office would not stand for it.[64] On these grounds, the unitary scheme was talked out almost as soon as it was suggested, and when Sir Joseph Bhore reintroduced it, complete with official advisers on the Egyptian model, it met with the same fate.[65]

Fazli's view was that no change should be made at the Centre until the provinces had established themselves.[66] But once a decision had been made in principle that certain subjects should be transferred, he endeavoured to limit them to the bare minimum. He was prepared to see the transfer of those subjects which already fell within the portfolios of the three Indian members of council, but he strongly rejected Dunnett's contention that if some form of Dyarchy was introduced, the Home portfolio should also be transferred:

[60]GI Reforms Office, 67/vi/1930: Note by Dunnett, 10 July 1930.

[61]Minutes of informal discussion in council...,loc. cit., 11th meeting, 18 July 1930.

[62]Ibid.

[63]Ibid., 13th meeting, 28 July 1930.

[64]Ibid., 13th and 17th meetings, 28 July and 16 Aug. 1930.

[65]Ibid., 17th and 18th meetings, 16 and 18 Aug. 1930.

[66]In a note of 18 Aug. 1930, Fazli associated himself with those provincial ministers who felt that 'the proposed provincial autonomy should have a chance for the next ten years or so to get established before an all grasping Central Legislature begins to encroach upon them'. GI Reforms office, 67/x/1930.

Provincial Governments would prefer being under an irresponsible Home Department at the Centre .... An irresponsible Home Department cannot set itself against the responsible Home Department in the province; but a responsible Home Department at the Centre can claim to represent the Legislature, and through the Legislature, the country, quite as much as, if not to a larger extent than the provincial government. Again there is a tendency in all deliberative bodies of an all Indian nature to kill provincial bodies. That is the reason why the All India Congress Committee prospers; while the provincial Congress Committees, are except in a few cases, inert; and, in some cases, not even alive.[67]

The nature of Fazli's argument against the transfer of the Home Department suggests that Dunnett's reasoning was sound. But Fazli's colleagues preferred the devil they knew. Feelings in favour of responsibility in the Central Executive were tempered by the likelihood of a Congress majority in the Central Legislature. Dunnett himself estimated that if the Congress entered the provincial councils to the full extent of its strength it could be expected 'to establish a very strong position in the three presidencies, Bihar and Orissa, the Central Provinces, and possibly Assam, and to be far from negligible in the United Provinces'. And on these grounds, he argued against Simon's recommendation for indirect election to the Assembly. Such a system, he said, would throw power into the hands of the dominant provincial caucus and would probably 'put Congress in a dominating position in the Legislative Assembly threatening the power of the Central Government'.

We may have to lay our plans with a Congress which will capture and work the provincial constitutions, but will retain their creed of Independence and seek to destroy the Central Constitution from within. Indirect elections will help them. Independence should be a clear-cut issue and the best safeguard against it is direct election.[68]

But if Congress could capture the provincial councils, would it have difficulty capturing the Assembly, even if there were direct election? The use of such arguments encouraged parsimony. Fazli's colleagues decided it would be better to retain control of the Home Department. Sir James Crerar, the Home Member, argued that 'all those activities ... which are effectively related to law and order must remain in official hands',[69] and it was decided ultimately that 'the close connection

[67] Ibid.

[68] GI Reforms Office, 67/vi/1930: Note by Dunnett, 30 July 1930.

[69] GI Reforms Office, 67/v/1930: Minutes of informal discussion in council.. 17th meeting, 16 Aug. 1930.

of this problem with internal security and defence' made it impossible to state conditions for its transference :

In the search for some source of definition of what those conditions might be it was suggested that the transfer of Home Affairs at the Centre must necessarily depend more or less directly on the success or failure of the transfer in the provinces of Law and Order to responsible Ministers.[70]

But though Fazli scored a notable victory over Dunnett on this question, he remained apprehensive that the form of Dyarchy suggested by the government would be considered transitional and encourage agitation :

Sir Fazli Husain expressed his personal opinion that the scheme put up by the Government of India would mean, within the next ten years, either the surrender of the whole position, or a going-back on the Reforms entirely. It might be more graceful to make the surrender now and to give over all departments to popular control.... If this was more than British opinion would concede, then in his opinion, the alternative was to stand fast at the Centre.[71]

On this issue, Fazli was not appeased. In its dispatch on the Reforms, the government of India recommended that the functions of the central government should be divided into three categories: those like Defence, Foreign Relations, Financial Stability and Responsibility for Peace and Tranquillity, over which Parliament should continue to exercise control; those like Taxation, Commercial Policy and Railways, over which it would need to exercise occasional control; and those like General Economic Development, Labour, Posts, Telegraphs, Communications, Customs, Education, Health, Agriculture and Social Reform, over which it could safely relinquish control to the Indian Legislature.[72] These last subjects were to be transferred to elected members of the legislature who would hold office within a unitary form of government and who would be *responsive* to the legislature (but not *responsible* to it) in certain specified areas.[73] It was to be the most diluted form of Dyarchy, but in that the door had opened even a crack, Fazli continued to be fearful, and it was only when this scheme for a British Indian Federation was replaced at the first round-table

[70]Ibid. 18th meeting, 18 Aug. 1930.

[71]Ibid., 23 rd meeting, 5 Sept. 1930.

[72]*Government of India Dispatch*, pp. 14-15.

[73]Ibid., pp. 106-11.

conference by a new scheme for an all-India Federation involving the Princes that these fears subsided.

The first round-table conference: the Liberal challenge fails

With the beginning of the first round-table conference, the constitution-making process entered a new and important phase. The focus of political attention shifted from India to Britain, and all those claims which had previously been argued before the government of India were subjected to direct British government arbitration. This had a profound impact on Indian politics. It subjected the claims of the government's allies to fresh discussion in a new environment and it gave to those dissatisfied with the *status quo* the hope that they might obtain in London what they had been denied in New Delhi. Behind the scenes, of course, the government of India continued to exercise considerable influence. But with claims and counterclaims now being made in London, outward and visible signs of support became more necessary. Public relations became a vital aspect of any party's programme, and with the civil disobedience movement raging in India and demonstrating to the British government that the Congress did have mass support, it soon became necessary for parties opposed to the Congress to develop sanctions of their own.

For Fazli Husain, one of the main problems was a shortage of qualified personnel to put the Muslim Conference case effectively in these new surroundings. Men like Jinnah, and even Shafi, were chiefly interested in responsibility at the Centre, and the danger was that the provincial Muslim case would go by default. 'Frankly', Fazli wrote to Sir Malcolm Hailey, 'I do not like the idea of Jinnah doing all the talking and of there being no-one strongminded enough to make a protest in case Jinnah starts expressing his views when those views are not the acceptable Indian Muslim view.'[74] But finding such people presented problems, for Jinnah and Shafi were among the most fluent lawyers in India. They were well acquainted with political debate at the highest level and they would make a good showing in London. Fazli's main counterbalance to these men was Zafrullah Khan, an Ahmadi whom he had brought into politics in the face of much orthodox criticism. Zafrullah was an advocate of exceptional ability, Fazli's successor in the government of India,

[74]Fazli Husain papers: Fazli Husain to Hailey, 10 May 1930: also Azim Husain, op. cit., pp. 250-1.

and subsequently Pakistan's Foreign Minister and the President of the International Court of Justice at the Hague. But even Zafrullah could not hold the fort alone. So Fazli persuaded Hailey to allow Shafaat Ahmed to go from the United Provinces. He recognized Shafaat's shortcomings: he was inclined to spoil a point by pushing it too far and he was obsessed with constitutional safeguards for minorities.[75] But he was by far the keenest U.P. Muslim both in debate and organization, and he also had the advantage of a special relationship with Shafi which might be useful to Fazli in keeping Shafi under control. Hailey had originally favoured Hafiz Hidayat Hussain, whom he believed to command more 'all round support in point of character'. But under pressure from Fazli he conceded that Shafaat would provide 'a somewhat effective counteraction to Jinnah', and the two men ultimately agreed that Shafaat should go with the Nawab of Chhatari.[76]

But despite these precautions, the round-table conference gave Fazli an uneasy time, and for the very reasons which he had anticipated. The conflict between those politicians intent on securing all-India concessions and those whose future lay in the consolidation of provincial gains had never come to a head in India. Both groups had lobbied the government of India independently, and in its assessment of their representativeness, the government had thrown its weight behind the provinces.In London, however, both groups gathered round the same table, and put their cases to a new arbiter, the Labour government. The pressures for a settlement were strongest on the all-India politicians. The Hindu 'liberals' who gathered in London—men like Sapru, Sethna, Sastri and Setalvad—all realized that the continuation of non-co-operation posed a serious threat to their political future, and they were anxious to return to India with positive proof of their effectiveness as an inducement to Congress to return to the conciliar fold.[77] Their main aim was to achieve a measure of responsibility at the Centre, and in furtherance of this aim they put forward the idea of a Federation of British India and the princely states. They

[75]Shafaat had written a lengthy note on this question as a member of the U.P. co-operating committee. See *ISC,* vol. iii, pp. 281-381.

[76]Fazli Husain papers; Hailey to Fazli, 24 May 1930; Fazli to Hailey, 29 May 1930.

[77]For an account of the Liberal strategy at this time, see D.A. Low, 'Sir Tej Bahadur Sapru and the first round table conference' in D.A. Low, (ed.), *Soundings in Modern Asian History* (London 1968), pp. 294-329; also Sir Chimanlal Setalvad, *Recollections and Reflections, an Autobiography* (Bombay 1947), p. 357 *et seq.*

knew how reluctant all British political parties were to part with the reality of political power, and the Federal idea offered the most credible means of reassuring them that devolution at the Centre was feasible without surrendering to the 'Independence' school. In order to set the seal on the idea, however, the communal question had to be settled, and to this end they adopted a generous attitude to Muslim demands. This, in its turn, acted as a spur to Muslim involvement in negotiations on this question. Such men as Jinnah and Shafi were equally anxious to rehabilitate themselves as national leaders, and the atmosphere of the conference—the sympathetic impression created by Ramsay Macdonald, the feeling that far-reaching concessions were possible, and the absence of pressure from their Indian followers—encouraged a similar spirit of generosity on their side. For those whose interest lay in the provinces, however, this quest for all-India agreement had distinct dangers, and this was particularly so for the Punjabi Muslims, who were seeking very specific concessions in the face of well-organized Hindu and Sikh opposition. The Hindus, represented by Narendra Nath, and the Sikhs, represented by Sardar Ujjal Singh and Sardar Sampuran Singh, were strongly opposed to subordination to a communal Muslim majority, and in the Mahasabha leaders, Moonji and Jayakar, they had firm allies. The danger of the Punjabi Muslims being sacrificed to 'national' advantage were consequently very real, and all the more so in view of the historical sympathy of the Labour party for the 'national' school.

In the initial stages of the Conference, when discussions were proceeding informally, the Muslim delegation, under the leadership of the Aga Khan, appears to have worked cohesively and to have stuck rigidly to the Muslim Conference demands. The Hindus showed every desire to win over the Muslims, being prepared, according to one report, 'to concede the substance of Jinnah's 14 points, except that they are sticky on the subject of residuary powers and relations between the Centre and the provinces'.[78] But the Muslims showed no inclination to compromise,[79] and the Hindu party then became split between the Liberals, led by Sapru, who were prepared to pay a high price for a settlement in order to push through their demand for Federation, and the Mahasabhites, led by Jayakar and Moonji, who were not prepared to surrender important points without knowing what they would receive in return.[80] By the middle of November,

[78] GI Reforms Office, 173/1930R: W.H. Lewis to Dunnett, 31 Oct. 1930.

[79] Ibid., V.P. Menon to Dunnett, 7 Nov. 1930.

[80] GI Reforms Office 147/1930R: Tgm Secretary of State to Viceroy, Reforms Office (Haig to Dunnett), 13 Nov. 1930.

however, even Sapru's negotiations had become deadlocked over the question of electorates;[81] and though differences of opinion over the allocation of residuary powers and Muslim representation at the Centre continued to be explored, the situation did not materially improve over the next three weeks.[82]

At this stage, the Prime Minister himself intervened, and negotiations were resumed under his chairmanship, first in London and subsequently at Chequers. During these negotiations, the Punjab clearly emerged as the main stumbling block to an agreement. The Punjab Muslims demanded a majority by separate electorates. The Sikhs and Hindus held that such a concession was undemocratic. Ramsay Macdonald, for his part, inclined to favour the minorities. He told the Muslims that it would be impossible to talk of democracy 'if all the seats were fixed and reserved', and he suggested a scheme of his own 'reserving in a mixed electorate 80% of the seats and leaving 20% to go to anyone.'[83] This was well received by Moonji, Narendra Nath and Jayakar, but it was opposed by Mahommed Ali; and ultimately he was supported by Sapru. Mahommed Ali told the Prime Minister that he was prepared to discuss a solution 'on the basis of a mixed electorate' but he was adamant that the Muslim majority in the Punjab should be recognized. The Hindus, however, were not prepared to make this concession and the talks broke up.

For Fazli Hussain, observing these developments from India, the attitude of the Prime Minister, the willingness of Mahommed Ali to consider a solution based on joint electorates, and the continued quest for an agreement by both Hindu and Muslim Liberals,[84] were all subjects of intense concern. On 21 December, he wrote in his diary: 'The Muslim position at the round table conference is deteriorating and I must do something to put it right. I cannot let my life's work be spoiled. I must think hard and plan out a course of action

[81]Ibid., Tgm Secretary of State to Viceroy, Reforms Office (Haig to Dunnett), 18 Nov. 1930.

[82]Ibid. V.P. Menon to Dunnett, 5 Dec. 1930. In Menon's view, the Muslims were less anxious to compromise than the Liberals. They knew, he said, 'that their political position is not a stake and in the event of the failure of the Conference, the Government is bound to protect their interests'.

[83]This account of the negotiations at Chequers is based on Mahommed Ali's letter to Nawab Ismail Khan, 19 Dec. 1930 (Mahommed Ali papers).

[84]Negotiations between Hindu and Muslim Liberals were still in progress when the Minorities Committee was first convened on 23 Dec. See GI Reforms Office, 147/193OR: Tgm Secretary of State to Viceroy, Reforms Office (Haig to Dunnett), 23 Dec. 1930.

which will answer the purpose.'[85] Fazli attributed most of the trouble on the British side to the Labour party and its 'theories', and on the Indian side, to Bhopal, Shafi, Fazlul Haq, Sultan Ahmed and Jinnah. What he feared most was that the Muslims would give up separate electorates in order to strengthen the case for devolution at the Centre, and that as a result, the Punjab would be relegated 'to the position of a backward province tied to the chariot wheels of Hindu India.'[86]

Now, who will benefit more by responsibility being introduced at the Centre at this stage, Hindus or Muslims? Undoubtedly the Hindus. Therefore who should be anxious to settle communal differences in order to secure the promised gain? Naturally, the Hindus. Then why should Muslims, who are politically, educationally and economically weaker in the country, pretend that by ousting the British power from India, and by introducing responsibility, they stand to gain so much that for it they are prepared to sacrifice communal interests? .. Is the Indian Muslim community to be ruined by the Muslim delegates to the Round Table Conference?[87]

But Fazli did not only remonstrate with individuals. He organized the press in India, he arranged for an emergency meeting of the Muslim Conference working committee,[88] and he put pressure on the Viceroy to make it clear to the authorities in England that any discussion on the basis of joint electorates did not have the support of the community. In a very strong note to the Viceroy's Secretary, he deplored the Labour government's insistence that the Muslims should not have a majority, and he made it plain that the Muslims of Punjab and Bengal considered it 'an act of treachery on the part of the Government in as much as the Government encouraged the Muslims to oppose the civil disobedience movement and for their pains are now siding with the Hindus'.

As a matter of fact [he wrote] if separate electorates were taken away, I and with me a large number of Muslims will feel called upon to try our luck in the political reconstruction of India through the Congress rather than submit to gradual obliteration through the proposed reformed constitution.'[89]

[85]Fazli Husain papers: Diary, 21 Dec. 1930.

[86]Ibid., Fazli Husain to Sikunder Hayat Khan, 26 Dec. 1930 and 12 Jan. 1931.

[87]Ibid., Fazli Husain to Shafaat Ahmed, 20 Dec. 1930, quoted in Azim Husain, *op, cit.,* pp. 255-6.

[88]This meeting took place at Lucknow on 21 Dec.

[89]Fazli Husain papers: Fazli Husain to George Cunningham, 23 Dec. 1930.

At the same time, in the Secretary of State's Council, the Punjabi Muslim case was being pressed by the Muslim member, Umar Hayat Khan Tiwana. In a note which emphasized the military importance of Muslim support for government, Umar Hayat gave his opinion that the Punjabis had a very special claim to consideration.[90] In his view, weightage was of little avail to minority-province Muslims 'because they would remain in a minority in any case'. In Bengal, 'voting Mahommedans' were in a majority, but 'such a class could not help the British Empire or India with a single recruit...' In Sind, 'those who were recruited and sent to Karachi for training, deserted and tracked back on foot to their homes... The only province of significance for the Mahommedans is the Punjab.' Even within the Punjab, however, Umar Hayat made important distinctions. The two Punjabi Muslim representatives at the round-table conference, Shafi and Zafrullah, came from the Sikh Punjab:

One has got half a dozen near relations as barristers who cannot say a word against the High Court or the Hindus... . If they are boycotted by them, they will starve, as they have got no other income to fall back upon; while the other barrister from Sialkot is not a proper Mahommedan as he belongs to the Ahmedia sect.

The only significant class of Muslims were those from the West Punjab, and particularly those from the Rawalpindi division:

It is the Rawalpindi division which is full of soldiers which predominate in the Army; and they are the people who have served the Government since Punjab was annexed. They fought on the side of the Government during the Sikh wars and were instrumental in suppressing the Mutiny. My home is in the middle of this division .... I am the biggest landed proprietor in the province and even the children know my name. I know the feelings of the inhabitants of this tract in particular and other Mahommedans in general.

In this very representative capacity, Umar Hayat proceeded to criticize the influence of the Hindu moneylender, which he held responsible for the indebtedness of the Muslim agriculturalist, and the ascendancy of the Hindu money-lending class within the Punjab High Court, which he alleged had undermined the privileged position given to the agricultural classes by the Land Alienation Act.

[90] IOR/L/PO 48: Confidential note by Umar Hayat Khan Tiwana. The note is not dated, but it was seen by Wedgwood Benn on 22 (? Dec.).

Whole of Mahommedan Punjab is sick of all this and there have been periodical outbursts when the agricultural Mahommedans have burnt the houses of the moneylenders along with their account books ....: So the only remedy for the Mahommedan agriculturalists is firstly, separate electorates, so that they may be able to send their representatives who do not belong to this class; and secondly, that they have a clear majority to safeguard their interests and get certain amendments passed to some Acts which were originally passed for their salvation and have since been misinterpreted.

Within the minorities subcommittee, the Muslims did initially stick to separate electorates: Shafi's speech of 1 January 1931 was very strong on this point.[91] But only five days later, Shafi went back on this position and offered to accept joint electorates on the basis of Mahommed Ali's formula,[92] provided that the Punjabis and Bengalis got representation according to population, and the minority-province Muslims retained their weightage.[93] Shafi clearly had hopes that this offer would be accepted, because it was virtually identical to a solution proposed earlier by Sir Chimanlal Setalvad. On this occasion, however, Moonji dominated the proceedings. If the Hindus were generous enough to agree to Muslim demands, he said, they would be reduced to a minority in almost every province in India. The Muslims had no right to special treatment, either on account of their historical importance, or because of the part they played in the existing Imperial machine. Historically, there was no continuity between the mass of the Muslims and the Moghuls. They were merely Hindus converted to Islam. And if they did play an important part in the Army, it was only because of the recruitment policy of the Raj. When pressed, Moonji agreed that the minorities might be given weightage, but he rejected Mahommed Ali's formula, which he held to be a form of separatism, and he refused to accept the principle that representation in Punjab and Bengal should be according to population.[94] In this, he was supported by the Punjabi Hindus and Sikhs; and on these grounds Shafi's suggestion was talked out. On 14 January, however,

[91] *Round Table Conference, First Session, Proceedings of the Sub-Committees,* (London 1931), part ii, p. 102.

[92] According to Mahommed Ali's formula, for a Muslim candidate to be returned, he had to obtain at least 40 per cent of his votes from his own community, and 10 per cent from other communities.

[93] *Round Table Conference, First Session, Proceedings of the Sub-Committees,* part ii, pp. 115-16.

[94] Ibid., pp. 116-21.

when discussion was resumed, Shafi made yet another attempt to produce a settlement; this time by offering terms very similar to those suggested in the government of India dispatch. The Punjabi Muslims were to be given forty-nine per cent by separate electorates, and the Bengali Muslims forty-six per cent; and both were to have the opportunity to increase this percentage by contesting special constituencies. Neither the Sikhs nor the Punjabi Hindus showed much interest in this offer. But both Moonji and Ramsay Macdonald thought it worth pursuing, and the committee was adjourned so that discussions could be resumed in private.[95] During these discussions, differences were fined down to a matter of one seat in a house of 134. But even then the Sikhs refused to budge, and it is difficult to avoid the conclusion that this one seat had a strong symbolic significance.[96] Despite Fazli's efforts to strengthen Muslim determination in London, it was in reality the polarization of political feeling in India which prevented the conference from coming to an agreement.

In the aftermath of the deadlock, the Muslim delegation dissociated itself from all previous conference discussions on the constitutional question. Participation in such discussions, Fazlul Haq told the conference, had been conditional on the settlement of the communal question, and in the absence of such a settlement, the Muslims were not prepared to see any changes in the constitution whatsoever.[97] This was an understandable bargaining position. But though the Muslims had not got what they wanted in the minorities sub-committee, they had no reason to be displeased with the work of the other committees. The Provincial Constitution Committee had accepted the recommendations of the government of India's dispatch, almost without alteration. All subjects were to be transferred, and there was to be joint responsibility and a unitary executive. Only where the powers of the Governor were concerned, were the delegates dissatisfied.[98] The Sind and Frontier Committees also produced satisfactory

[95]Ibid., pp. 127-9.

[96]During the proceedings of the conference, Sampuran Singh referred to 'letters flooding into London from the Punjab'. If Muslim government was introduced, he said, 'there might be a civil war and we might be annihilated and washed off the face of the earth'. Ibid., p.86. Other observers testify to the reluctance of the Sikh delegates to come to terms for fear of retribution on their return to Punjab. See Jehanara Begum Shah Nawaz, op. cit., pp. 113-14; Interview, Sir Francis Mudie, Dundee, July 1969.

[97]*Round Table Conference,* first session, Proceedings (London 1931) *Cmd 3778,* p. 245.

[98]Ibid., pp. 301-4.

results. The Sind Committee, while reserving judgement on the financial aspects of separation, recommended that the principle should be accepted.[99] And the Frontier Committee even went beyond the government's dispatch, suggesting a council with a larger elected element.[100]

For Fazli, however, it was the work of the Federal Structure Committee which proved most satisfactory. On the eve of the conference, when the All India Federation scheme was first published in London, Fazli had welcomed it:

Personally, I am for it [he wrote in his diary], because it means movement towards Federation and the British Government will supply the power at the Centre, so that disruptive tendencies have no chance of success .... It really comes to Dyarchy and nothing else and only means decentralisation, greater autonomy for provinces and less scope for parliamentary interference. British public don't know enough to see change of these laws.[101]

This essentially provincial view of the likely impact of the Federal idea proved even truer than Fazli could have imagined. With Sapru at the helm, the idea was launched at the first plenary session of the conference of 17 November, and as arranged on board the *Viceroy of India* as the various delegates travelled to England, it met with a cordial reception from both the Muslims and the Princes. British parliamentarians responded less rapidly, but before long, even the Conservatives had heralded the idea as the answer to India's constitutional dilemma, and had agreed to the introduction of central responsibility if an all-India Federation was set up.[102] As negotiations proceeded upon the form of the Federation, however, it became apparent that the princes and the politicians had very different aims. Whereas the politicians had supported Federation to pave the way for central responsibility, the princes had seen it chiefly as a mechanism for restricting central government interference in the states. Some feared that the powers of paramountcy might be exercised by a responsible British Indian Centre and wished to influence the shape of the Central Executive. Others feared an extension of influence by

[99]Ibid., pp. 412-13.

[100]Ibid., pp. 378-80.

[101]Fazli Husain papers: Diary, 14 and 15 Nov, 1930.

[102]A detailed account of the acceptance of the Federal Idea by the British political parties is to be found in R.J. Moore. *The Making of India's Paper Federation 1927-35,* in Philips and Wainwright, *The Partition of India: Policies and Perspectives, 1935-47* (London 1970).

the Imperial power itself. Both these fears were assuaged by the adoption of the all-India federal idea. But once advance at the Centre had been made dependent on the establishment of such a Federation, the princes found themselves in possession of an even more valuable bargaining counter – a virtual veto on constitutional advance. And once that situation developed, their enthusiasm for federation began to wane. Firstly, when it became plain that the politicians were not prepared to grant them any special position in the lower house of the legislature, they began to talk less of acceding to the Federation as an order, and more of the rights of individual princes to decide the question for themselves.[103] And secondly, on the very important procedural point of how the Federation was to be formed, they declared themselves unwilling to federate with a unified British India. They were only prepared, they said, to federate with a British Indian Federation.[104] Whilst they had acquired a veto on the form of the central goverment, therefore, the formation of that government depended no less than before on the settlement of the British Indian issue. In short, a policy had been initiated which could only serve to hamper the eventual development of a responsible centre. Where Fazli Husain was concerned, however, the emergence of this problem was very welcome, for it made it likely that the first stage in the reform of the existing constitution would be the establishment of provincial autonomy unfettered by responsible central control. This prize, for which Fazli had campaigned unsuccessfully during the drafting of the government of India dispatch, was now delivered into his hands as a result of Liberal ambition and princely manoeuvre.

The Gandhi-Irwin Pact and after: a disturbing diplomatic interlude

At the closure of the first round-table conference, the Prime Minister, Ramsay Macdonald, announced that the government was prepared to accept devolution of power at the Centre if a legislature could be constituted on a Federal basis. This was a powerful bargaining counter for the Liberals – even though the communal problem had not been settled – and they returned to India intent on using it to lever the

[103]Round Table Conference, First Session, Proceedings of the Sub-Committees, part i, pp. 46-7: Speeches to the Federal Structure Sub-committee by the Maharajah of Bikaner and the Nawab of Bhopal, 5 Dec. 1930.

[104]Ibid., pp. 17 and 48: Speeches by the Nawab of Bhopal (2 Dec. 1930) and by Sir Akbar Hydari, the Prime Minister of Hyderabad (5 Dec. 1930).

Congress into the constitution-making process. In this, they were assisted by the government of India, which released the leading members of Congress so that they could reconsider their position in the light of the progress made in London. There then followed a fortnight of hectic negotiations and consultations, first between Congress and the Liberals, and then between Gandhi and the Viceroy, and the result was the Delhi Pact of 5 March 1931. The government agreed to suspend rule by ordinance and to release its political prisoners, and Congress agreed to suspend civil disobedience, to accept Dominion Status as its objective, and to attend the second round-table conference.

It would be wrong, however, to mistake the process of conciliation for the prospect of agreement. Though the government of India wished to recapture the middle ground of Indian politics and was prepared to make concessions to get Congress back into the constitution-making process, it was still firmly committed to its provincial allies and well aware of the importance of keeping them on its side. Similarly, though Congress did not wish to appear totally inflexible to those who were deciding India's future in London, it had little hope of achieving its objectives at a conference attended by those it was committed to supplanting. The reasons which had provoked the civil disobedience movement still held good; and it was primarily in order to convince British opinion of the validity of their respective interpretations of Indian politics that the two sides came together.

As soon as the Pact had been signed, however, it appeared that Congress had gained a good deal more than the government. The Viceroy may have been astonished 'that Gandhi should have been so far persuaded to come in line',[105] but the message which reached the villages was that Congress had won a great victory and that *Ram Raj* was just round the corner. Before the Pact was signed, the government had virtually brought civil disobedience to an end by the use of extraordinary powers. But with the suspension of those powers and the relaxation of administrative control, the way was clear for the reassertion of Congress influence. It was an opportunity which many leading Congressmen seized with both hands. In a circular to local Congress committees written on 10 March, Jawaharlal Nehru indicated that he saw the Pact as 'a truce only and no final peace'. 'That peace can only come', he wrote, 'when we have gained our objective in its

[105]Halifax papers, 6: Irwin to Wedgwood Benn, 9 March. 1931.

entirety.' In the meantime, Congressmen were to establish definite centres of work and strengthen Congress organization in the rural areas so that they could meet 'any contigency that might arise'.[106] In Jawaharlal's own district, moreover, even the truce was not being observed.

Just before the truce [wrote the Collector of Allahabad], things were improving and rent was beginning to come in; and it looked as if the no-rent campaign was shortly to be broken. The release of the prisoners, however, had an extremely bad effect. They went back to their villages proclaiming their victory—and victory for the tenant means non-payment of rent. Rental payments fell off at once and have got steadily worse .... The Congress undertook effectively to discontinue the no-rent campaign. But actually, they have effectively continued it.[107]

The government's apparent capitulation to the Congress inevitably raised questions about its capacity to protect its friends. In the Punjab, as far north as Jhelum, Muslims began debating whether a Congress government would repeal the Land Alienation Act.[108] In Bengal, the prospect of civil war between Congress and government left the Muslims uncertain as to how to safeguard their own position.[109] And in the U.P., where the re-assertion of Congress authority was most marked, fuel was added to the fires of suspicion by an outbreak of very serious communal rioting. At Benares, on 11 February, a Muslim shopkeeper, returning home after a clash with Congress pickets, was murdered in a narrow lane near the bazaar. This incident was followed by a riot in which three died and seventy-seven were injured. The position grew worse after the Gandhi-Irwin Pact, when Congress policy appears to have assumed a more communal guise, particularly in Allahabad and Muttra.[110] But it deteriorated irretrievably on 24 March at Kanpur, when a riot broke out in which ninety-nine Muslims and forty-nine Hindus lost their lives; 500 houses, forty-two temples

[106]GI Home Poll. 33/xi/1931: AICC circular no. 12, 10 March, 1931.

[107]Ibid., R.F. Mudie to Commissioner, Allahabad Division, 25 March 1931.

[108]GI home Poll. 5/45/1931 Extract from tour report of officers of the third batallion, the Baluch regiment, Camp Jhelum, 21 March, 1931. For a full account of the nervousness produced among the Muslims in the Punjab, see GI Home Poll. 33/vii/1931: de Montmorency to Emerson, 13 May 1931.

[109]Ibid., Reid to Emerson, 11 May 1931.

[110]See GI Home Poll. 33/xi/1931: Marsh Smith's confidential report on the rural areas of Allahabad district, 28 March 1931; Collector of Muttra to Commissioner of Agra, 27 March 1931.

and eighteen mosques were burnt or damaged; and whole areas of the city were reduced to smouldering wreckage.[114] As at Benares, this incident was sparked off by Congress attempts to enforce a hartal on Muslim shopkeepers, on this occasion as a sign of mourning at the execution of Bhagat Singh, but as a result of administrative negligence, the riot was not contained at the crucial time, and the results were disastrous. A Commission of Enquiry was immediately set up, and this eventually showed that individual Hindus and Muslims had made heroic efforts to save members of the other community from the outrages of the mob.[112] But even the death of so prominent a Congressman as Ganesh Shankar Vidyarthi, who was killed by a Hindu mob while protecting his Muslim neighbours, did little to modify the traumatic effect of this riot on the North Indian Muslim psyche. Never before in living memory had a riot of such proportions taken place, and Muslims were quick to reach the conclusion that they were experiencing the first fruits of the Congress victory. 'The riots in the U.P. have been simply dreadful...', Shafaat Ahmed wrote to Jinnah. 'The Hindus are so puffed up with what they call their victory over the British Government that they wish to dispose of the Muslims like so much cucumber.'[113]

The Muslim Conference response to these developments was to become more strident in its demands. A special session of the organization, held on 5 April at Delhi, was highly critical of both Congress and government, and many of the demands first voiced at Delhi in 1928 were pushed even further. Moving the first resolution, Zahur Ahmed of Allahabad condemned 'the so-called non-violence of the Congress satyagrahis' as being 'little short of an unclean political stratagem adopted in the face of the superior organised force of the state and cast off in dealings between the communities'.

> This Conference [ran the resolution] warns the Governments in England and this country that their spineless handling of the situation due to their continued pandering to the Congress will create a condition of things in India which will spell the complete ruin of this unfortunate country.

The U.P. Muslims were undoubtedly worried; and they reacted as

[111]The *Leader* of 18 April 1931 carries pictures of the devastation.

[112]See GI Home Poll. 215/1931: a copy of the report and details of the government's action upon it.

[113]Mukhtar Masood, ed., *Eye Witnesses of History, a Collection of Letters Addressed to Quaid-i-Azam* (Karachi 1968), p.66: Shafaat Ahmed Khan to Jinnah, 26 March 1931.

worried men. On the one hand they rattled the sabre: 'Why not test our metal today?', asked Zahur Ahmed. On the other, they called for further safeguards. In addition to demands made on previous occasions, they demanded for the first time that fundamental rights should be made justiciable, that Muslims should be subject 'only to their own personal law in all matters related to religious observance', and that no government should at any time have the power to alter this law. These were significant developments. All three demands demonstrate the anxiety of the minority-province Muslims at the prospect of Congress rule, and the last two illustrate a growing convergence of political and religious themes.[114]

Hand in hand with these resolutions went others designed to maximize provincial autonomy. In part, these were sponsored by the minority-province Muslims. For as their future appeared more insecure, so the 'hostage' argument grew in strength. Many of them thought that a strong Punjab was their best guarantee of even-handed treatment within their own provinces; and such men were apprehensive lest the ascendancy of Gandhi deprive them of this protective shield.

> The feeling among Muslims here [wrote one such politician] is that Gandhi will support the demand for Unitary Government. If this is done, the Muslim provinces will be like clay in the hands of the potter. The Hindu majority in the Centre and the Hindu government will make short work of the Punjab and Sind.[115]

Those most apprehensive at such a development, however, were the Punjabis themselves, for they stood to be deprived not of a protective shield but of the chief prize for which they had been working—provincial autonomy. Significantly, therefore, their terms for joining an all-India Federation are raised at this time. Not only do they demand that the provinces should enter such a Federation as sovereign units on virtually the same terms as the states. They also demand that there shall be no change in the Federal constitution unless all the constituent units agree.[116] The most striking indication of this change of mood, however, was a proposal put forward by Firoz Khan Noon for the provincialization of the Army. This was not embodied in a

[114]Mihr Collection, 254: Resolution of the All India Muslim Conference, New Delhi, 5 April 1931; *The Leader*, 8 April 1931.

[115]Mukhtar Masood, op. cit., pp. 66-7: Shafaat Ahmed Khan to Jinnah, 26 March 1931.

[116]*The Leader*, 8 April 1931.

formal resolution, though it was much ventilated in Delhi when the Conference met.

> If the Army were at a later stage handed over to Indian control [Firoz told the Viceroy] it would be at the beck and call of the Hindus. What then would happen, he asked, if communal disorders started? His solution was that the control of the Army should pass not to the Centre but to the provinces.[117]

The Viceroy told Firoz that such a proposal was impracticable; and Firoz is reported to have agreed. But while it was not formally advocated, it illustrates the strength of the centrifugal forces at work. The Punjab Unionist party, which was heavily dependent on the soldier's vote and heavily involved in recruitment for the Army, was beginning to see devolution at the Centre as a threat not only to its political interests, but also to its privileged position within the Imperial military machine.

At the same time, however, just as the government had made conciliatory gestures to the Congress, so the Congress began to make conciliatory gestures to the Muslims. By the terms of the Delhi Pact, Gandhi had committed himself to attending the round-table conference, and he realized that his position would be enormously strengthened if he arrived in London as the purveyor of a united demand. No sooner was the pact signed, therefore, than he began to say that it would be useless to go to London without a settlement of the communal question, and even that he would be prepared to give the Muslims all they wanted as the price of agreement.[118] As in his negotiations with Irwin, however, it may be doubted whether Gandhi ever thought agreement possible on the basic constitutional issues. The Congress decision to start non-co-operation had itself been an acknowledgement that a joint demand by both communities was no longer a feasible method of securing political reform; and the movement itself had done nothing to change this estimate of the situation. The Congress had strengthened its position and made it imperative for government to take it into account. But Muslim support for non-co-operation had been negligible; and Muslims working the Reforms had been alienated still further.

Gandhi's conciliatory gestures to the Muslims are best seen as part of his diplomatic tussle with the government of India. The government

[117]Halifax papers, 6: Irwin to Wedgwood Benn, 2 April 1931.

[118]GI Home Poll. 136/1931: Williamson's note on the Karachi session of the Congress, 7 April 1931.

wanted to shoehorn him into the company of those whose claims the Congress had consistently refused to recognize. Congress wanted to lend weight to its claim to represent the Indian people as a whole. On both sides, the important thing was not actually to make concessions but to appear willing to do so. It was noticeable, for example, that there was no sign of Gandhi's 'blank cheque' when he and Vallabhbhai Patel met members of the Muslim Conference working committee at Delhi early in April. As in London, negotiations became deadlocked over the question of electorates.[119] But Gandhi did not even make concessions on points on which Conference Muslims and Nationalist Muslims were in agreement. Rather he used the fact that differences existed within the Conference, and between the Conference and the Nationalist Muslims, as a reason for making no concessions at all. If a settlement was to be 'frankly based on communalism', he said, then there must be unanimity. 'My own personal position is quite clear. It is that of full surrender to any unanimously expressed wish of the Mussulmans and Sikhs. I would like the Hindus to see the beauty of this solution. It can only come out of the consciousness of moral strength.'[120]

Gandhi might also have added: 'and out of an understanding of the divided nature of Indian politics'. For as Emerson made clear during discussions with Gandhi in May, if Reform had to wait for communal agreement, there never would be any Reform. Moreover, even if Gandhi took that view, Government could not accept it.

> Government had often been accused of Machiavellian methods, and if it adopted the line taken by Mr Gandhi, there would be an immediate outcry accompanied by political agitation on an intense scale. This must therefore be ruled out, and Government must pursue the policy of constitutional advance even if no agreed settlement were reached. Why should Mr Gandhi take in this matter a more reactionary attitude than Government?[121]

The answer was simple: for diplomatic reasons. Gandhi knew that with or without agreement Reform would come, and despite his insistence that the Indians should settle the communal question themselves, he also knew that the government would eventually have

[119] *The Leader*, 6 April 1931.

[120] Ibid., 8 April 1931.

[121] GI Home Poll. 33/ix/1931: Note by Emerson on his talks with Gandhi, 13-16 May 1931.

to settle it. Indeed, by May, he was himself suggesting that Lord Irwin should be asked to arbitrate.[122] The real 'beauty' of his 'solution' was that it preserved the Congress claim to represent India as a whole without involving it in negotiations with other parties to find a settlement. If Congress were to shut the door on negotiations, it would suffer diplomatically in London. But if it actually got involved in negotiations, it would divide its own supporters and lose the momentum which it had already generated. Gandhi's formula was an attempt to get the best of both worlds.

Even so, there were Muslims both within the Conference and the Congress who were prepared to try their hands at a settlement. The Conference Khilafatists had been reluctant converts to the Conference platform, and when the faith of their leaders in government promises appeared ill-founded, as it did after the Gandhi-Irwin Pact, it was natural for them to doubt the wisdom of their conversion. Would it not be better, they asked themselves, to try again for a settlement with the Congress? The urban constitutionalists of Punjab asked themselves the same question. Shafi's efforts at the round-table conference had not won him any popularity among the Unionists.[123] But their ascendancy in 1920 had not benefited him; and the same logic which had made him a party to Jinnah's four proposals in 1927 continued to make him sympathetic to the prospect of a negotiated settlement. To some extent, Iqbal fell into the same category. True, by the time of his speech to the Allahabad Muslim League in 1930, his spiritual and cultural ideology had acquired a distinct territorial dimension.[124] But Iqbal was an urban Muslim of Kashmiri descent and as yet his ideology appealed only to a restricted audience within Punjab—the Arains, the Kashmiris, the urban intelligentsia and the products of Islamia college. He had little in common with the bulk of the Unionists and he was prepared to consider a settlement with Congress if it secured advantages to his class. Unlike Shafi, however, Iqbal was amenable to Fazli Husain's influence, and this was to be an important factor in the negotiations ahead.[125]

[122]Ibid.

[123]See Halifax papers, 6: de Montmorency to Irwin, 6 Feb. 1931, enclosed, Irwin to Wedgwood Benn, 16 Feb. 1931.

[124]See Pirzada, op. cit., vol. ii, p. 153-71.

[125]Iqbal and Fazli Husain both had links with Sialkot. They had also studied in the same class at Government College, Lahore. For an interesting account of Fazli Husain's efforts to 'help' Iqbal, see Azim Husain, op. cit., pp. 318-21.

Those keenest for a settlement, however, were the Congress Muslims —Ansari, Khaliquzzaman and Sherwani. For these men, the period after the Calcutta convention had been difficult. They had refused to be browbeaten by the Ali brothers, and they had continued to work within the Congress. But the Lahore session of 1929 had left them very disillusioned. The Nehru report, over which they had broken with so many of their friends, had been thrown into the Ravi, and the Congress had decided that negotiations for a communal settlement would have to be suspended until *purna swaraj* was achieved. This was distinctly unpalatable to them. *Swaraj* was to be achieved by civil disobedience, a movement in which the Muslims were not likely to figure prominently, and even if it were achieved by that method, it was unlikely that it would result in a communal settlement to their advantage. Consequently, early in 1930, Ansari, Khaliquzzaman and Sherwani resigned their various offices in the Congress, remaining only four anna members;[126] and Sherwani even made attempts to come to terms with the Muslim League.[127] These attitudes softened when government began to deal firmly with Congress. At that stage, Ansari broke his silence and denounced the Government's 'black and tan' methods;[128] and Khaliquzzaman even served for a while, though somewhat half-heartedly, as Congress dictator.[129] But throughout this period their underlying aim was to get Congress back to conciliar politics, and they welcomed the Gandhi-Irwin Pact for this reason.[130]

These Congress Muslims took the lead in proposing terms for a settlement at a well-attended meeting of nationalist Muslims at Lucknow on 18 and 19 April. They offered a provision to protect Muslim culture, language, education and religion; a guarantee that appointments to

[126]The conflict of loyalties and of political interpretation brought to a head by the Lahore Congress is best seen in Ansari's letter to Gandhi of 13 Feb., and in Motilal's reply to Ansari of 17 Feb. 1930 (Ansari papers: Jamia Millia Islamia, New Delhi). See also Khaliquzzaman, op. cit., p. 104.

[127]Ansari papers: Sherwani to Ansari, 3 March 1930.

[128]Ibid., undated draft of Ansari's letter to the press (July? 1930).

[129]Khaliquzzaman, op. cit., p. 107; Halifax papers, 6: Irwin to Wedgwood Benn, 30 Oct. 1930.

[130]Ansari continued to favour a conciliar policy until his death in 1936. In 1934, he and Dr B.C. Roy were amongst the first to call for the return of Congress to the legislatures. This nationalist Muslim preference for conciliar politics is a significant indicator of the extent to which they relied, consciously or unconsciously, on British arbitration in their hopes of a fair deal.

the services would be according to a minimum standard of efficiency with no community being allowed to predominate; a promise of separation for Sind and of equal status for the Frontier and Baluchistan; and a Federal constitution in which residuary powers would reside with the provinces. On the question of electorates, however, they remained adamant. Ali Imam, the President, confessed to a feeling of remorse for his part in the drafting of the Simla manifesto of 1906. Separate electorates, he said, had poisoned the relations between the communities and should be abolished. If they could not stand on their own feet, why not frankly say that they depended on the British and that they did not want freedom? Ansari was less outspoken. The Nationalist Muslims recognized, he said, that the Muslim demand for safeguards was genuine, and he promised that they would 'do their best to press all such genuine demands and secure their acceptance by all concerned'. But Ansari, too, refused to countenance separate electorates. The measure and method of representation in the Federal and provincial legislatures should be settled, he said, on the basis of joint electorates and adult suffrage. And he suggested that a round-table conference of Muslim organizations be convened for this purpose.[131]

For the organizers of the Muslim Conference, this initiative was potentially very dangerous. For if members of the Conference became involved in discussing such terms, existing Conference demands would appear questionable. Fazli Husain did his best to close Conference ranks on this issue. Adult suffrage was not practical politics, he told Mushir Hussain Kidwai, and to consider joint electorates on such terms was merely to give away a substantial advantage without being sure of any substantial return. The first essential was to secure Congress acceptance of the Conference demands for continued weightage in the minority provinces and for the recognition of Muslim majorities in Bengal and Punjab. If these demands were accepted in principle, he said, then discussion might be started on the question of electorates. In the meantime, the best policy was to stick to separate electorates and to show no inclination to give them up unilaterally.[132] For the same reasons, Fazli also dissuaded Iqbal from calling a meeting of the Muslim Conference to consider the nationalist Muslim offer. There was no need for further meetings, he told him, because the

[131]*The Leader*, 19, 20, 22 and 23 April 1931.

[132]Fazli Husain papers: Fazli Husain to Mushir Hussain Kidwai, 27 April 1931.

Muslim Conference programme was already decided. Any meetings to discuss the programmes of other organizations, he said, would be likely to impair the representative standing of the Conference itself. The point to emphasize was that there was almost no difference between the demands of the nationalists and of the Conference. The Punjab press, he said, should be urged to make the most of this.[133] Fazli also discouraged Iqbal from considering certain other terms for settlement which were being canvassed in Lahore by Sir Mahommed Shafi. Fazli told Iqbal that these terms fell short of the Conference demands and should not be put forward by the Conference Muslims themselves. Shafi's terms were almost identical to those put forward in the government of India's dispatch, and the Conference had nothing to gain by offering to accept what the government had already recommended. If the Hindus chose to make such an offer, it would be up to the Muslims to consider it. But it was not up to the Muslims to make offers themselves.[134]

But despite this advice, Iqbal, Shafi, Shaukat Ali and Nawab Ismail met Ansari, Khaliquzzaman and Sherwani at Bhopal in the middle of May to see if they could reach a compromise. During the two days they spent together, discussion appears to have been thorough and long. But no definite agreement emerged; only two sets of suggestions regarding the introduction of joint electorates on which both sides agreed to consult their individual organizations. Ansari's suggestions, which were the more radical, were designed to commit the Muslims to some form of joint electorate, at least for an experimental period, either by introducing them first partially and then more substantially, or by alternating them with separate electorates and providing for a referendum once the trial period was over.[135] Shafi's suggestions were to have a less immediate impact. One provided for the introduction of joint electorates with adult suffrage after ten years, though with the provision that they could be introduced earlier if a majority of Muslim councillors so desired. The other provided for five years of separate electorates with a referendum on joint electorates at the beginning of the fifth year. But even Shafi's suggestions failed to meet with Fazli's approval. He told Iqbal that the first committed the

[133]Ibid., Fazli Husain to Sir Mahommed Iqbal, 30 April 1931.

[134]Fazli Husain papers: Fazli Husain to Sir Mahommed Iqbal, 1 May 1931.

[135]*The Leader*, 25 June 1931: Statement by Dr Ansari on the breakdown of negotiations.

community irreversibly to joint electorates, albeit after ten years, and so gave away their main bargaining counter, while the second did not make it clear who was to take part in the referendum.

> The only position which Muslims can take up is that the first election under the new constitution be held on the basis of separate electorates and that it should be open to Muslim members of any legislature to pass a resolution by a majority that the next election be held through joint electorates and that in future that shall be acted upon.[136]

With a little help from Firoz Khan Noon, who arrived in Lahore at Fazli's instigation to assist with the drafting of a Conference response,[137] this advice appears to have been taken. At a meeting of the Conference working committee at Shafi's house on 25 May, a formula very similar to Fazli's was agreed upon,[138] and when this was put to a meeting with the Nationalists at New Delhi on 19 June, it effectively brought negotiations to an end.[139]

After the breakdown of negotiations, Ansari became far more critical of the the Conference, seeking to undermine its all-India position by a direct appeal to the Muslims of Bengal. This was shrewd tactics. For the Muslim Conference was dominated by Punjabi and U.P. Muslims, and despite the adherence of the Nawabi party and a section of the Calcutta intelligentsia, the problems of Bengal had never received priority. At the round-table conference, for example, when Shafi put forward his second offer of terms for a settlement, it was noticeable that the Bengalis were to get the poorer deal—forty-six per cent compared with forty-nine per cent for the Punjabis. At a Muslim Nationalist meeting at Faridpur on 27 June, Ansari made the most of these indications of neglect. He denounced the Conference leadership—'the benighted knights of Bengal and the Punjab'—and he told his audience that adherence to the Conference was likely to place the Bengali Muslims in a permanent position of inferiority. It was time, he said, that the Muslims of India returned their verdict on the futility of separate electorates. The Bengali Muslims had been successful under joint electorates in local elections and they could make the same impact on provincial

[136]Fazli Husain papers: Fazli Husain to Iqbal, 14 May 1931.

[137]Ibid., Fazli to Shafi Daudi, 16 May 1931.

[138]Ibid., Fazli to Iqbal, 30 May 1931.

[139]*The Leader*, 25 June 1931: Statements by Dr Ansari and Shafi Daudi on the breakdown of negotiations.

elections if only they developed the will to work and the courage to be independent. At the same time, Ansari put forward more detailed terms for an all-India settlement. These terms, he claimed, had been part of the original package, but had not been divulged at Lucknow for fear of prejudicing negotiations. They included reservation of seats for minorities of less than twentyfive per cent (and weightage for Muslim minorities if others also received it); reservation according to population in Punjab and Bengal if adult suffrage was not introduced; an embargo on constitutional change unless eighty per cent of both federal Houses approved it; and thirty-three per cent at the Centre. No more far-reaching terms had ever been put forward by a nationalist Muslim organization.[140]

But even to these terms, the Congress response fell short of 'full surrender'. At Bombay in the second week of July, after a lengthy but fruitless attempt to win Shaukat Ali's support for an agreement based on joint electorates,[141] the working committee adopted proposals which only improved marginally on the Nehru report.[142] It accepted joint electorates and adult suffrage, with reservation for minorities of less than twenty-five per cent. It agreed to equal status for the Frontier and Baluchistan. It accepted the need for a convention to safeguard Muslim rights in cabinets, and for a special provision to protect Muslim personal law It also agreed that population should be reflected in the legislatures if adult suffrage was not introduced. But it only adopted the other Faridpur proposals subject to qualification. Sind was to be separated 'if the Sindhis will bear the financial burden'. Residuary powers were to rest with the provinces 'unless it is found to be against the best interests of India'.[143] And two of Ansari's proposals were rejected—the first for thirty-three per cent at the Centre, and the second making changes in the Federal constitution dependent on eighty per cent approval by both houses.

The Muslim Conference was not impressed. At Allahabad on 9 August, the Executive Board ruled that the Congress resolutions, far from solving the communal question, sought to deprive the Muslims of almost all their safeguards without offering them any advantage

[140]*The Leader*, 29 June 1931; *Indian Annual Register*, 1931, vol. ii, pp. 311-16.

[141]*The Leader*, 11 and 12 July 1931.

[142]Ibid., 15 July 1931.

[143]Jawaharlal Nehru believed it was. See Syed Mahmud papers: Jawaharlal to Syed Mahmud, 30 April 1931. 'About the residuary powers vesting in the provinces, I do not agree. This is bound to encourage provincialism and this is even now a bane of India.'

in return. They were to sacrifice separate electorates and weightage in minority provinces. But they were not even assured of majorities in Punjab and Bengal. The question of Sind's separation, already ceded in principle in London, had been reopened. And the demand that residuary powers should rest with the units of the all-India Federation had been 'qualified by a condition which makes that recognition unreal as well as changeable'.[144]

Hostility increased when Gandhi tried to take Ali Imam and Ansari to London with him as Congress nominees. This seemed a deliberate attempt to undermine the Conference claim to speak for the Muslims as a whole, and it brought home the dangers of the parleys which had taken place earlier. In Fazli's view, Gandhi was out to get 'the position of dictator' and did not mind too much how he went about it. 'This is to be the reality', Fazli wrote to Lord Irwin, 'but he is ready to clothe this reality in the apparel of negotiation, discussion, argumentation, controversy, anything you like.'[145] The Muslims had said that they wanted safeguards. What was the Congress reply?

> To confuse the issues, to indulge in irrelevance and to begin to talk of Muslim demands, and then begin to talk of Congress Muslims, of Dr. Ansari and so on. These are all devices with which Hindus as well as Muslims are quite familiar. Gandhi's insistence upon Dr. Ansari's inclusion and his parading readiness for complete surrender in case complete Muslim unity is forthcoming have nothing new about them. They are the very old devices which the Congress, Gandhi and the Indian Hindus have been condemning in the British Government and the British statesmen. They are doing now exactly what they alleged Lord Birkenhead was doing—asking for complete unanimity and resorting to the well known principle of Divide and Rule.[146]

But despite the fears generated by the activities of the Congress—fears which led to talk of boycotting the round-table conference[147] and which gave Fazli the necessary leverage to secure the exclusion of

[144]Mihr collection, 254: Resolutions passed by the Conference Executive Board, 9 Aug. 1931.

[145]Fazli Husain papers: Fazli to Lord Irwin, 24 Aug. 1931. Though Lord Irwin was succeeded as Viceroy by Lord Willingdon in April 1931, Fazli Husain continued to correspond with him in England.

[146]Ibid., Fazli to Maswood Ahmed, Syed Abdul Hafiz, and Syed Hussain Imam, 1 Oct. 1931.

[147]See Ibid., Fazli to Shafi Daudi, 31 July 1931. Shafi Daudi canvassed round-table delegates about the possibility of boycott. But Fazli advised caution.

Ansari from Gandhi's party[148]—the round table conference did not produce many surprises. For with Gandhi refusing to take part in discussions on the communal question except as a mediator, the situation was only marginally different from what it had been in 1930. As on the previous occasion, the Hindu Liberals found members of the Muslim delegation who were prepared to come to terms. But once again the Punjab proved an insuperable barrier to general agreement. The Muslims wanted a statutory majority, in fact if not in name, but neither the Sikhs nor the Hindus were prepared to accept it, and the Sikhs took the lead in resisting it by demanding terms for themselves which were so plainly unjust to the Hindus that they could not be accepted. If Begum Shah Nawaz is to be believed, however, there was a time, after the Muslims and Liberals had agreed among themselves, when a settlement did seem possible. Shafi ordered sweets and drinks and 'with joy and happiness', the Muslim delegates assembled in the Aga Khan's rooms at the Ritz to celebrate the great occasion. But the party failed to start. For the chief guest, Gandhi, who had gone to secure the agreement of the Sikhs and the Mahasabha, came back without it. Gandhi said: 'Gentlemen, I am sorry to report that I have failed in my efforts for settlement. The Sikhs and the Mahasabhites are not prepared to accept the terms devised by us.' 'There was a hush in the room', recalls Begum Shah Nawaz,'...and most of us felt like shedding bitter tears.' Shafi, however, had an alternative proposal. He said to Gandhi: 'Let us, the Muslims and the Congress come to a settlement tonight on those very terms.' Gandhi replied: 'Shafi, I know my limitations and I cannot do it.' And so the party broke up, Shafi and his daughter returned home, 'and when we reached our flat, Father broke down completely and fainted.'[149]

Gandhi's refusal to commit himself to terms which the Mahasabha and Sikhs would not accept was part and parcel of the same policy which he had enunciated in India in the summer. He was prepared to be a mediator, but he was not prepared to take sides. Publicly, this

[148]Ibid., Note by Fazli Husain on Secretary of State's telegram of 13 June 1931. Fazli also tried to get Sir Ali Imam excluded. But his arguments were not accepted. Ali Imam was not a member of Congress, and he was ultimately selected to replace Mahmudabad. Mahmudabad had been invited to the first session but ill-health kept him in India. He died on 23 May 1931. See Ibid., Fazli Husain to Eric Mieville, 27 July 1931.

[149]Jehanara Begum op. cit., pp. 127-31.

was explained in ideological terms. The nature of the Congress position as the representative of the people precluded it from being party to an agreement. All the Congress could do was to accept what was acceptable to all the other parties. As in so much of Gandhi's politics, however, ideology and political self-interest went hand in hand. Gandhi knew the power of the communal appeal, and he knew what it would mean for Congress if he committed himself publicly to stand against communal Hindu demands. Within the existing electoral system, until such time as it became clear what concessions were forthcoming, it could only mean a communal backlash and loss of support. It was far better to let government make the decisions and bear the unpopularity that they would bring. And so, having been through the ordeal of negotiations with the other delegates, Gandhi put the ball firmly back into the government's court. In the Minorities Sub-Committee, he confessed himself saddened and humiliated by his failure to produce a settlement. But he attributed it to the fact that the delegation had been selected by the government.[150] The argument, in short, moves back into a well-worn groove. The government was demanding communal agreement as the price of discussing political concession. But agreement would only be possible if the government first agreed to make the concessions. 'If we knew in a definite manner that we are going to get the thing we wanted', he said, 'we should hesitate fifty times before we threw it away in a sinful wrangle.' The Congress would accept any agreement accepted by all the parties. But in the meanwhile it was incumbent on the government not to hold up constitutional progress. For there would be no progress at all if unanimity was demanded, whereas 'the iceberg of communal difference will melt under the warmth of the sun of freedom'.

Not long after the round-table conference ended, the Congress resumed civil disobedience. It was part of the logic of the situation. Despite the outward show of conciliation, the polarization of political forces at the provincial level, which by 1928 had divided Indian politics into communal camps, had remained in essence unchanged. For a brief period, after the Gandhi-Irwin Pact, both Congress and government adopted more flexible positions for the sake of the political public in Britain. But this was merely war by other means, a diplomatic interlude which lapsed into war again when the diplomacy was over.

[150]*Indian Round Table Conference, Second Session, Proceedings of the Federal Structure Committee and Minorities Committee* (London 1931), p. 530.

Who won the diplomatic contest? In India, before the round-table conference, Congress undoubtedly gained more. But in London, the advantage lay with the government. It succeeded in making Congress look like one force among many, and this strengthened its hand in Britain when the next period of repression began. For the government's allies, however, and particularly for the Muslims, this was a disturbing period. It was difficult for the leaders of the Muslim Conference, let alone the rank and file, to distinguish between appearances and reality, and as government conciliated Congress, and Congress prestige rose, there seemed a real possibility that Conference interests would be sacrificed. As Congress and Government played out their various roles, therefore, the Muslim Conference began to adopt a more independent position. This had been apparent before the round-table conference, when fears that government would give way to Congress provoked talk of boycott; and when the round-table conference did nothing to safeguard the Muslim position, this trend became more marked. Though the government had won a position of strength *vis-a-vis* the Congress, therefore, in the same process it had impaired the confidence of its most important allies. In the absence of a communal settlement, it had obtained the responsibility for deciding the issue itself. But the Muslims were no longer sure that the decision would be in their favour, and as the Communal Award approached, they became increasingly belligerent.

The Communal Award: a triumph for Muslim provincialism

One of the chief factors accounting for Muslim belligerence was the fear that central responsibility would be conceded on terms favouring the Congress. In June 1931, commenting to Irwin on the negotiations which had taken place at Bhopal, Fazli Husain gave his opinion that Congress unwillingness to safeguard the Muslim position was based on its confidence that central responsibility was assured. According to Fazli, the Congress argued as follows: 'If we let the Muslims have weightage and majorities now under separate electorates, we shall not be able to get rid of them later, but if the British Government imposes them on us, we shall be justified in throwing them overboard at the earliest possible opportunity.'[151] As the second round-table conference approached, this fear of central responsibility on Congress

[151]Fazli Husain papers: Fazli to Irwin, 8 June 1931.

terms prompted the Conference to insist that the Minorities Committee should meet before the Federal Structure Committee.[152] The Conference was not prepared, it said, to discuss central responsibility until after the Muslim position had been safeguarded—or, in other words, until the forces of Muslim provincialism had been fortified against that very contingency. 'As you can well understand', the Aga Khan wrote to Sir Sam Hoare, 'this central responsibility is a leap in the dark, and before my people are ready to put their necks in the noose, they must know whether it can be tightened or not.'[153]

On this point, the round-table conference did little to reassure them. No communal settlement was reached and no safeguards were provided. Indeed the willingness of Muslim delegates to negotiate with Gandhi on terms inferior to Conference demands, and their participation in the work of the Federal Structure Committee contrary to Conference injunctions, caused considerable uneasiness.[154] The fact that Jinnah and Shafi had been prepared to discuss vital issues relating to the powers of the central government, and their declaration at the close of the committee's proceedings that 'the better mind of India' would not be satisfied unless provincial autonomy and central responsibility were introduced simultaneously,[155] appeared to have given the Muslim case away.

At the Conference itself, the Aga Khan did his best to counter the effects of these developments by the formation of a 'Minorities Pact' between the Muslims, the Anglo-Indians, the Indian Christians, the Europeans and the Depressed Classes.[156] This Pact, which was inspired by Fazli Husain and the Punjabis,[157] united the majorities in Bengal and Punjab with the minorities in other provinces and made it more difficult, particularly by its generous treatment of the Depressed Classes, for the government to throw over the Muslims. The government estimated that the organizations subscribing to the Pact rep-

[152]Mihr collection 454: Progs. of Muslim Conference Executive Board, Allahabad, 9 Aug. 1931, resolution 4; Progs. of Muslim Conference Working Committee, Simla, 13 Sep. 1931, resolution 3.

[153]IOR/L/PO 48: Aga Khan to Hoare, 30 Aug. 1931.

[154]Mihr collection 454: Progs. of Muslim Conference Working Committee, Delhi, 18 Nov. 1931, resolutions 1 and 2.

[155]*Indian Round Table Conference, Proceedings of the Federal Structure Committee and Minorities Committee,* pp. 464-5. Jinnah also made a final plea for the construction of a British Indian Federation.

[156]Ibid., appendix iii, pp. 550-5.

[157]Fazli Husain papers: Fazli to Alma Latifi, 6 Oct. 1931.

resented 120 million people, and with Congress resuming civil disobedience, it had no wish to lose this substantial body of support.[158]

The Aga Khan also materially assisted the Conference by securing the exclusion of Shafi and Sultan Ahmed from the work of the committees set up to continue the work of the round-table conference. He told Hoare that they had a leg in the Hindu Liberal camp and he appealed to him 'in the name of the large, loyal, law-abiding Muslim population ... to get the proper kind of men nominated at this time of life and death'.[159] For the main committee—the Consultative Committee—he suggested Shafaat Ahmed, Zafrullah and Hafiz Hidayat Hussain. The government appointed Shafaat, Zafrullah and A.H. Ghuznavi. This strengthened Conference powers of leverage in the difficult months ahead.

But in India, Conference supporters were no longer satisfied with manoeuvres. They were impatient for results. When Haji Abdullah Haroon, acting on instructions from the Aga Khan, attempted to organize a deputation to the Viceroy to elicit a reassuring statement of the government's position, he met with a poor response, even from leading members of the working committee. Iqbal, the President elect, confessed that while in London, he had been 'very pessimistic about Muslim demands'. But he did not feel that another deputation was the answer. He preferred to reserve his views for expression on the Conference platform.[160] Nawab Ismail felt even more strongly. In his view, the policy of the Conference was counterproductive, and he resigned his membership.

> The indifference displayed by the British Government to Muslim demands convinces me that we can gain nothing by supporting the Government at this stage .... The Conference is at present dominated by persons who fight shy of exercising any compulsion on the Government for the acceptance of Muslim demands.[161]

Nor was Ismail Khan an isolated individual. Others who shared his views, notably the old Khilafat faction, were already beginning to pressurize the dominant interests. A resolution of the working

[158] IOR/L/PO 48: Cabinet Minute RTC (31) 11, 9 Nov. 1931.

[159] Ibid., Aga Khan to Hoare, 17 Dec. 1931; Note by Hoare, 19 Dec. 1931.

[160] *Haji Sir Abdoola Haroon,* a biography by Alhaj Mian Ahmad Shafi of Lahore (Karachi, n.d.), pp. 99-100: Iqbal to Haroon, 16 Jan. 1932.

[161] Ibid., pp. 97-8: Nawab Ismail to Haroon, 14 Jan. 1932.

committee, held at Delhi on 4 January, mentioned the possibility of 'political crisis'. It noted 'the general tendency of the Muslim public to take active part in the political struggle', and it considered it 'absolutely necessary to decide as soon as possible ... the proper course of action for the grave contingency which has now arisen'.[162] On 31 January, again at Delhi, the same committee moved one stage further towards non-co-operation. A resolution was brought forward calling upon Muslim members of the round-table conference to non-co-operate with the committees set up by it. This resolution was only kept in abeyance 'after a long discussion'. But the Khilafat faction was reluctant to accept the decision, and Hazrat Mohani and Ghulam Rasool Mihr dissented.[163]

This spirit of defiance was intensified by two developments in India. The first was the emergence of a confrontation between the Maharaja of Kashmir and his Muslim subjects, and the second was the harsh treatment meted out to Ghaffar Khan and the Redshirts when the government reimposed rule by ordinance to combat the resumption of civil disobedience.

Kashmiri Muslim opposition to the Maharaja first attracted attention in British India in July 1931.[164] But it intensified considerably in September, when a number of demonstrations in the Kashmir valley were put down with considerable brutality.[165] Resentment was greatest in the urban areas of Central and Eastern Punjab, where many Kashmiri Muslims had settled, but within a matter of weeks the Kashmir issue was causing concern as far away as Bengal.[166] An All India Kashmir Committee was set up, supported by Sir Mahommed Iqbal and the Quadiani Ahmadis; and the old Punjab Khilafat Committee, by this stage refurbished as the *Majlis-i-Ahrar-i-Islam,* began sending *jathas* across the border into Kashmir. The main demand of these pressure groups was that the government should take over the state, institute

[162]Mihr collection 454: Progs. of Muslim Conference Working Committee, Delhi, 4 Jan. 1932, resolution 2.

[163]Ibid., Progs. of Muslim Conference Working Committee, Delhi, 31 Jan. 1932.

[164]See Rafiq Afzal, *Malik Barkat Ali, His Life and Writings,* part i, pp. 30-2.

[165]For a summary of the Middleton Enquiry into these disturbances, see Indian Annual Register, 1932, i, pp. 472-4.

[166]In London in November, Fazlul Haq received telegrams from Bengal urging him to withdraw from the round-table conference if Kashmir Muslim grievances were not remedied. See IOR/L/PO 48: Transcript of the deputation which met the permanent secretary at the India Office, 9 Nov. 1931.

enquiries, and if necessary, depose the Maharaja. But the government did not accede to this demand and so drew upon itself the anger of the Muslim community. By the end of 1931, the Muslim Conference had become a vehicle for the expression of this anger. Partly, this was because Conference organizers felt a genuine sympathy for the Kashmiri Muslims; partly because they realized the importance of keeping the *Ahrars* under the Conference umbrella. These urban activists had a value to the Conference as the shock troops of the politics of Reform, and if they were not appeased, there was a danger that they might secede from the Muslim camp and regroup with the Congress. In large measure, however, the agitation was encouraged because it offered a means of increasing pressure on Government to satisfy Muslim demands in the constitutional field. In November 1931, the New Viceroy, Lord Willingdon, told the Secretary of State that 'the Mahommedan community—I am rather afraid with the support and approval of my Mahommedan Honourable Colleague—are keeping up the agitation . . .until they see whether they get satisfactory terms as a result of your discussions in London.'[167]

The reimposition of rule by ordinance in the Frontier provoked a similar response. A Conference resolution was passed sympathizing with the Frontier Muslims in their distress, and Shafi Daudi and Maulana Mazharuddin were deputed to visit the province to see the situation for themselves.[168] The main fear was that the Redshirts would be thrown further into the arms of the Congress at a time when the imminence of a new constitution offered hopes that the Frontier would draw into line with the rest of Muslim India.[169] As the same resolution put it: 'The sudden promulgation of the terrible ordinances ...[will] have no other effect than to banish the idea of cooperation with the Government in the general mass of the people.' The government of India did not wish to alienate the Conference and the way was cleared for the mission. It was arranged that Daudi and Mazharuddin should meet the Governor, the Inspector-General of Police, and other officials, and that they should be free to go wherever they pleased. But the result of the mission was not to the government's liking. The government had hoped that its hand would be strengthened

[167]Templewood papers (IOL MSS Eur. E 240) 5: Willingdon to Hoare, 22 Nov. 1931.

[168]Mihr collection 454: Progs. of Muslim Conference Working Committee, Delhi, 4 Jan. 1932, resolution 1.

[169]Fazli Husain papers: Diary, 3 Jan. 1932. At this time, Fazli was leadinga delegation to South Africa. He returned to India on 26 Feb.

against Muslim criticism. But Daudi and Mazharuddin came to the conclusion that the Ordinance should be repealed, that Frontier officials responsible for acts of repression should be transferred, and that internees not convicted of acts of violence should be released.[170] Both before and after the mission, moreover, the two men were in regular contact with prominent Congress ulema and with the Ahrars,[171] and this prompted fears that a common front might be produced between Muslim activists in both organizations.[172] These fears were increased when the Conference called on Muslims to observe 'Frontier Day' on 5 February, and the government had to issue special instructions to prevent any unnecessary confrontations from taking place.[173]

Such being the Muslim mood, it was not surprising that the committees set up to continue the work of the round-table conference met with difficulties. Willingdon smoothed over Muslim doubts about participating in the Consultative Committee late in January,[174] but even though they served, they refused to discuss any question relating to devolution of power at the Centre unless Muslim demands were met. By the end of February, this effectively brought the Committee's work to a halt, and Willingdon had no alternative but to adjourn its proceedings.[175] The other committees were similarly affected. The Franchise Committee did not actually have to stop work. But, as Lord Lothian, its chairman, confided to Hoare, this was only because the communal question did not come within its brief. 'If would have torn my committee to pieces', he said, 'if I had admitted it.'[176] Even Lord Eustace Percy's Federal Finance Committee found it difficult to make helpful recommendations because of the fluidity of the situation. 'Eustace Percy tells me', Willingdon confided to an old friend, 'that they have collected all their facts and don't know what the devil to do with them. And that is much what we all feel.'[177]

[170]Mihr collection 454: Progs. of Muslim Conference Working Committee, Delhi 31 Jan. 1932, resolution 5.

[171]Shafi Daudi papers: Diary, 4-20 Jan. 1932.

[172]GI Home Poll. 123/1932: Note by Howell, 15 Jan 1932; circular letter to all local governments, 16 Jan. 1932.

[173]GI Home Poll. 14/ix/1932: Circular letter to all local governments, 1 Feb. 1932.

[174]Templewood papers, 5: Willingdon to Hoare, 25 Jan. 1932.

[175]Ibid., Willingdon to Hoare, 22 Feb. and 6 March 1932.

[176]IOR/L/PO/ 48: Lothian to Hoare, 4 March 1932.

[177]Harcourt Butler papers (IOL MSS Eur. F 116) 54: Willingdon to Harcourt Butler, 14 Feb. 1932.

By this stage, Willingdon was seriously worried: delay was encouraging dissaffection, and the government was running short of allies. The Princes showed no signs of coming into Federation,[178] and the problem of running the central government without British Indian allies, which Dunnett had elucidated during the drafting of the government of India dispatch, was turning him into 'a sort of Mussolini'.[179] The Budget of November 1931 and the various ordinances to deal with the Congress were all rejected by the Assembly and had to be certified. Willingdon called it 'a hopelessly Gilbertian state of things'.[180] 'How on earth Edwin Montagu ever got himself to put forward, and Parliament to pass, such a strange form of legislative life, I really fail to understand.'[181] But what was the answer? Again in line with Dunnett's original analysis, Willingdon considered that the only practical solution was to strengthen the central government by introducing a greater degree of responsibility. This is a constant theme of his correspondence with Hoare from November 1931 to March 1932. Indeed, when Hoare wrote to him in January that the all-India Federation must come first, Willingdon replied that this was the best way of forcing every all-India politician into the Congress.[182] Both from the point of view of reassuring the all-India politician, and in order to force the Princes to be more realistic, Willingdon considered that determination to press on with a British Indian Federation was the best method of procedure. If necessary, he said, he would come home to explain the idea personally to the Conservatives.[183] But the idea was rejected outright. The Conservatives had only agreed to concede responsibility at the Centre if the Princes were brought in, and Hoare knew that any talk of a British Indian Federation would provoke a full-scale revolt in the party at Westminster.

Willingdon does not in the least realise [he wrote to Lothian] the almost insuperable difficulty of the kind of piecemeal proposals that he and his Council have been making. I go constantly on worrying him with the urgent necessity of getting something out of the Princes.

[178]Templewood papers, 5: Willingdon to Hoare, 1 Feb. 1932.
[179]Ibid., Willingdon to Hoare, 20 Dec. 1931.
[180]Ibid., Willingdon to Hoare, 1 Feb. 1932.
[181]Ibid., Willingdon to Hoare, 17 Jan. 1932.
[182]Ibid., Willingdon to Hoare, 8 Feb. 1932.
[183]Ibid., Willingdon to Hoare, 22 Feb. and 14 March 1932.

On no account must the Princes be allowed to give a negative to All-India Federation ... If they say 'No', all the fat in the world will be in the fire here. Nine out of ten members of the House of Commons will then go straight back to unadulterated Simon Report.[184]

If Willingdon's efforts to strengthen the Centre illustrate one side of the Imperial dilemma, his determination to win back Muslim support illustrates the other. The government had encouraged provincialism to offset challenges to its authority at the Centre. But in the process it had become dependent on provincial allies. By March 1932, Fazli-Husain had the Raj over a barrel, and the Viceroy was crying for help. Early that month, when Willingdon met the Muslim members of the Consultative Committee and other Conference leaders in deputation, and learnt from them of the prospect of non-co-operation, he speedily relayed his fears to the India Office:

These gentlemen are most anxious to support us, but are seriously disturbed at the unsettled frame of mind of their followers and are doubtful if they can control them. Many influences are at work and very important decisions are likely to be reached at the Muslim Conference to be held at Lahore on 21 March. It is very desirable that a decision as to whether HMG now accept responsibility for settling communal problems should be arrived at with as little delay as possible.[185]

But the British government was reluctant to accept the responsibility for making any decision, let alone the kind of decision which Willingdon envisaged—a 'hookum' which would take the whole question out of the sphere of controversy. Hoare told Willingdon that any decision by the British government would have to be essentially 'provisional' in character, in line with the Prime Minister's speech at the close of the round-table conference. It should be open to revision if Indian political parties came to an agreement of their own.[186] This attitude conflicted markedly with Willingdon's desire for a statement of intention to quieten Muslim fears. Ultimately, however, Willingdon did score a minor victory. The British government was persuaded to publish a statement in which it accepted responsibility for making the decision and promised to discharge it without unavoidable delay. Willingdon was delighted. The statement

[184]Lothian papers (Scottish Record Office, Edinburgh) GD 40/17/152: Hoare to Lothian, 3 March 1932.

[185]IOR/L/PO 48: Tgm Viceroy to Secretary of State, 9 March 1932.

[186]IOR/L/PO 48: Tgm Secretary of State to Viceroy, 14 March 1932.

was in time for the Lahore session of the Conference and it averted an open breach between the government and its allies.

Even so, the Lahore session of the Conference was far from being a gathering of loyalists. Indeed, in his presidential address, Iqbal encouraged members of the audience to put their religion and culture before their citizenship of India. The British government, he said, could no longer be relied on to hold the balance impartially between the communities. Hindus and Muslims were being driven indirectly 'into a kind of civil war'. The situation was one in which every community would have to look to its own strength. The Muslims must not be found wanting. Mussolini's maxim was: 'He who has steel has bread. Iqbal modified it: 'He who is steel has everything.'[187] The Conference resolutions reflected the same spirit. The main one, which dealt with the constitutional question, expressed dissatisfaction with the round-table conference and declared that the organization could take no further part in the process of Reform. The British government's undertaking was welcomed. But a decision was demanded 'at the earliest opportunity', so that the community could know where it stood. In the meantime, the working committee was to draw up a programme of direct action, branches were to be established in all parts of the country, and volunteers enrolled and prepared to make'all possible sacrifices'. The government was given till the end of June to announce its decision. Failing that, the Executive Board was to meet to launch the direct action programme.[188] This threat hung over Willingdon as he pushed the British government into making out a programme for Reform. He realized the dangers of delay and he asked for an early decision. If it could be made by July, he told Hoare, 'it would have an enormously good effect here, and I think would completely satisfy the Muslims, who have given us until the beginning of July for a decision to be made'.[189] By this stage, the Muslims were making the running.

The British government accepted that the matter would have to be settled. No further constitutional progress was possible without a

[187]*Indian Annual Register,* 1932, i, pp. 301-8.

[188]Mihr collection, 455: Resolutions passed at the Lahore session of the All-India Muslim Conference (Delhi 1932). Another resolution, proposed by Shafi Daudi and seconded by Ahmed Yar Khan Daultana, demanded the immediate introduction of provincial autonomy 'while details of the Federation scheme are being explored and worked out'.

[189]Templewood papers, 5: Willingdon to Hoare, 1 May 1932.

settlement, and constitutional progress was essential, for as Hoare told the Cabinet: 'We cannot go on indefinitely ruling by Ordinances'.[190] But the task was unenviable in the extreme. For whatever was decided, the Raj was bound to be weaker. The constitution itself had set up a tension between centrifugal and centripetal forces which could only be resolved to the Raj's disadvantage. Between the all-parties conference of 1925 and the round-table conference of 1931, Indian politicians of both communities had tried unsuccessfully to reach agreement. Now the Raj was forced to tackle the problem itself. Was Muslim provincialism to be encouraged further? Or was the trend already established to be reversed? In many ways, the decision had already been made. Strengthening the Centre had been rejected. The only alternative was to strengthen the provinces. It was a victory for the strategy of the Punjab civilians.

The main problem was representation in Punjab and Bengal, and the main question : how far should the Muslims be strengthened? It was uncertainty on this point, Hoare told his Cabinet colleagues, which more than anything else was holding up the evolution of a new constitution.[191] In making detailed recommendations to decide the issue, Hoare was guided by the government of India dispatch. He had accepted it as a basis for settlement in November 1931, and in March 1932, when pressing his colleagues for a decision early in the summer, he relied on statistics drawn up on that earlier occasion. In the Punjab, he favoured giving the Muslims 48.8 per cent by separate electorates, to be made up to fifty-one per cent from the special constituencies. This was the device originally recommended by Fazli Husain and Hoare preferred it to the official Punjab scheme which would have left the balance of power with two Europeans. 'In the Punjab...', he wrote, 'I myself do not think it is any good talking of less than 51%.' Whether the Muslims got a majority or not depended on how generously the Sikhs were treated. But Hoare believed the Sikhs incapable of satisfaction, and he favoured giving them only eighteen per cent to make the Muslim majority possible. In Bengal on the other hand, Hoare's recommendations were to leave the Muslims in a very definite minority. Special electorates were to continue to

[190]IOR/L/PO 48: Secret Cabinet Minute, C.I. 32 (2), 11 March 1932.

[191]Ibid., Hoare opposed extending the range of the Award beyond representation in the legislatures. To do so, he believed, would be to abandon the concept of evolving a constitution by free mutual discussion.

account for twenty per cent of the seats (though Hoare admitted that the Minorities Pact might make it difficult to keep this figure so high), and the rest were to be divided among the communities according to population. This would give the Muslims 41.4 per cent and the Hindus 40.4 per cent. The balance of power was to be held by the Europeans. Both in the majority provinces and in the minority provinces, Hoare recommended that separate electorates should continue, and in the minority provinces, Muslims were to continue to enjoy the same weightage. It was also anticipated that separate representation would be extended to the Depressed Classes 'from among the seats allotted to the non-Muslims or Hindus'.[192]

The provincial governments were in broad agreement with these suggestions, though in many cases they voiced fears which reflected the political uncertainties of the Raj's position. Sykes, the governor of Bombay, would have preferred the decision to be included in the final bill. In his view, an early decision made it likely that the prospective Federation would be ruined by the establishment of 'a congerie of provincially autonomous governments'. But he recognized the necessity for it, and he thought if it favoured the minorities, they might organize on the government's side.[193] The governor of the Central Provinces agreed that the Muslims should continue to enjoy separate electorates. But as the head of a province where Muslim support for government had been insufficient to prevent serious disruption, he warned against building too much on the existing strategy. The support of the Muslims had secured 'certain temporary advantages, but it raised their hopes unduly, consolidated the Hindus against us and made suspect our impartiality'.[194] In the Punjab, Hoare's suggestions were accepted with fewer qualifications. But even there, increasing militancy among the Sikhs was causing concern, and de Montmorency suggested that the range of the decision should be extended to include minority representation in Cabinets. If the Sikhs and Hindus were satisfied on this question, it might offset the effect of a decision in favour of the Muslims.[195] Hailey, the Governor of the U.P., the original architect of government strategy, appears to have felt by this stage that the government of India was inclined to go too far in buying off the

[192]Ibid.

[193]IOR/L/PO 48: Sykes to Willingdon, 11 April 1932.

[194]Templewood papers, 65: Extracts from Governor's letters on the communal problem.

[195]IOR/L/PO 49: de Montmorency to Willingdon, 29 April 1932.

Muslims, and for this reason he welcomed Hoare's decision to limit the range of the decision to representation in the legislatures. He did not undervalue Muslim support, but he warned against making wholesale concessions in their favour. This would force all the Hindus into non-co-operation and it would leave the Muslims with nothing to agitate for. This was also the view of the Chief Commissioner of Delhi. As to the effect of the decision, Hailey believed it would depend on whether the Punjabi and Bengali Muslims were satisfied. But the Punjab was the crucial province. 'So far as our local opinion is concerned', he wrote, 'Muslims appear to attach less importance to a statutory majority in Bengal than in the case of Punjab.'[196]

But it was over Bengal that the main conflict of opinion arose. Anderson, the new Governor, recommended that the Muslims should have 44.4 per cent and the Hindus 42.8 per cent.[197] This was in line with Hoare's own recommendations, merely taking into account the number of seats conceded by the Europeans in the Minorities Pact. But Willingdon, who was under pressure from Fazli Husain, considered this unsatisfactory from the all-India point of view. Fazli told Willingdon that if the Bengali Muslims did not get their majority, there was a danger that they would go over to Congress, and in order to offset the effect of such a development, he urged him to increase Muslim representation throughout the minority provinces -- by three seats in Madras, two in the Central Provinces, and by one seat in both U.P. and Bihar and Orissa. 'The loss of a Muslim majority in Bengal is a very important matter and I want to use all these palliatives so as to keep politics undisturbed.'[198] These views forced the council's arm. On 14 June, the government of India recommended that Anderson's offer be revised. The Bengali Muslims should get 48.4 per cent and the Hindus only 39.2 per cent.[199] Hoare objected. Such a concession was unfair to the Hindus. But Willingdon remained adamant.

Do please visualise the political situation out here. The Congress are against us, the Moderates are not cooperating, and remember that these two bodies are nearly all Hindus ... The Muslims, who, on

[196]IOR/L/PO 48: Hailey to Willingdon, 7 April 1932.

[197] IOR/L/PO 49: Tgm Anderson to Hoare, 7 June 1932.

[198]Fazli Husain papers: Fazli Husain to Eric Mieville, Private Secretary to Viceroy 14 June 1932. In this letter, Fazli expands on views put forward the previous day at a meeting of council.

[199]IOR/L/Po 49: Tgm Willingdon to Hoare, 14 June 1932.

the whole, have generally supported Government, are, with the Princes, at present on our side. But if you give them less than de Montmorency proposes for Punjab and I propose for Bengal, I am quite certain that they will non-cooperate too. You may say that in Bengal, you must consider the Governor's views. My answer is that he is only looking at Bengal ... and that I have to look at the country as a whole .... What we propose is, I think, fair and equitable. Anything else would spell disaster and I can only add that if owing to your decision I lost their support as well, I should probably have to ask you to send out someone else to take up the role of Akbar....[200]

Under this pressure, the British government gave way. On 4 August, the Cabinet agreed to the Viceroy's terms, and on 16 August, the Communal Award was published.

The publication of the Award was a crucial event in the history of Muslim separatism. For it gave to the Muslims of Punjab and Bengal the possibility of dominance in their own provinces. This was the objective for which Fazli had worked throughout the period of constitutional reform, and in August 1932 his efforts were crowned with success. From the beginning, he had realized that only the British government would give him the substance of this concession, and he had successfully prevented others from surrendering this demand in negotiations with other bodies. This policy paid off handsomely. The government was made to pay the full price for the support on which it had come to rely.

But the Communal Award was not only significant because it made Muslim control possible in two substantial Indian provinces. It was also significant for the future of the government of India. The Award was the price the Imperial power had to pay for continued control at the Centre. But the Muslims who triumphed by the Award were not enamoured of any other kind of Centre but a British Centre. As the constitutional negotiations proceeded and the central responsibility issue was increasingly discussed, Conference demands became more and more separatist in their orientation. By March 1932, the Aga Khan was telling the Secretary of State that the community's survival depended not only on the substance of the fourteen points but also on 'the permanence of the real authority of the Imperial crown throughout India'.[201] By the same date, moreover, for Fazli Hussain, the architect of Conference policy, even the all-India Federation no

[200]Templewood papers, 5: Willingdon to Hoare, 10 July 1932.

[201]IOR/L/PO 48: Aga Khan to Hoare, memorandum 2 March 1932.

longer offered the prospect of security. Late in February, on his return from South Africa, Fazli landed at Porbander, Gandhi's birthplace, in the princely state of Rajkot. He was greeted by a Congress demonstration and by shouts of 'British Government *Murdabad*' and '*Inquilab Zindabad*'.

What struck me [he wrote in his diary] was that in an Indian State, which are believed to be so non-political, there should be so much agitation of an anti-British character. It appears that whenever a town is practically Hindu, anti-British feeling is very strong, and the fact that it is an Indian state makes no difference. The longer Federation is put off the better for the country as a whole.[202]

Whilst the Communal Award had made continued Imperial control possible, therefore, it had also fortified the Punjabi and Bengali Muslims against any other kind of centre. In terms of the structure of the system of Imperial control, this was a crucial milestone on the road to Pakistan.

[202] Fazli Husain papers: Diary, 26 Feb. 1932.

Conclusion

The period of operation of the Montagu-Chelmsford constitution produced developments of great significance for the future of Muslim India. It was during this period that political interests were consolidated around communal issues, and that Muslim attitudes were framed both towards the emergence of provincial autonomy and towards the eventual withdrawal of Imperial control. These attitudes, though subsequently developed and refined under the impact of provincial autonomy, continued to govern Muslim thinking in the remaining years of Empire.

In existing studies of Partition, the period from 1937 to 1947 commands more attention. It was then that the Pakistan movement gathered momentum and that the Muslim League began to command a substantial mass following. It was only then—though there were rumblings earlier—that the political and religious themes of modern Pakistan fused together. But though the ideology of Muslim separatism emerged more strongly later, the structure of power within the community created during these years remained in essence unchanged. Though the Pakistan movement initially obtained more adherents in the minority provinces, it was only when the League had captured Bengal and Punjab that Pakistan became a possibility; and when the lines of Partition were drawn and the Imperial power withdrew, it was chiefly the Muslims of those provinces who found themselves on the Pakistani side of the line. Hitherto, studies of the later years have seen the conversion of Bengal and Punjab as a reluctant concession to the demands of a 'national' movement. This study suggests that it may be valuable to re-examine those years from a more purely provincial point of view. To those provincial interests which campaigned from the late 1920s against the introduction of a responsible government at New Delhi, the Pakistan movement offered a chance to create a centre of their own.

Within Pakistan, it was the Punjab which emerged as the dominant provincial interest, and the military machine created by the British, and manned chiefly by Punjabis. which was to loom large in the political complexion of the state. This was also foreshadowed in the period under study. It was at this time that the Raj transformed its military alliance with the Punjabi Muslims into an electoral alliance, and that the Punjabi Muslims, from a consolidated base in their own province, assumed the political leadership of Muslim India. It was also in these years, as a result of Punjab civilian advice, that the Raj adopted a strategy for dealing with the growth of nationalism which made it heavily dependent on Punjabi Muslim support. By the end of this period, moreover, it had already paid a significant price for it. By the terms of the Communal Award, the Punjabi Muslims were granted the prize for which they had been campaigning—control of their own province under the new constitution. Finally, as the Montagu-Chelmsford constitution was being revised, it was the Punjabis who took the lead in working against responsible government at the Centre. From as early as 1928, their inclination was to pull out of British India and develop a relationship with the Crown, and under their leadership this attitude was adopted by the All India Muslim Conference. This also was to be significant for the future.

In the consolidation of political interests around communal issues, the Imperial power played an important role. By treating the Muslims as a separate group, it divided them from other Indians. By granting them separate electorates, it institutionalized that division. This was one of the most crucial factors in the development of communal politics. Muslim politicians did not have to appeal to non-Muslims; non-Muslims did not have to appeal to Muslims. This made it very difficult for a genuine Indian nationalism to emerge. In the years before 1920, cross-communal alliances did take place in the interests of Reform at the provincial level. But after 1920, with the introduction of Dyarchy, communal antagonism became a permanent feature of provincial politics, and the formation of all-India cross-communal alliances became first difficult and then impossible. In this period, the effects of the working of separate electorates were compounded by the balancing of communal interests within provincial councils. By the end of the 1920s, all-India Muslim politics had become in essence the sum of the politics of Muslim provincialism, and the all-India Muslim politician without a provincial base had either to withdraw from politics or to submit to these forces. Jinnah's retirement to England provides the most striking example of the working of these constraints. The alliance of the main Khilafat faction with the forces of Muslim provincialism provides another.

In the years after 1920, Congress efforts to abolish separate electorates reflect the working of these factors. Separate electorates provided the government with communal allies, and in many provinces enabled it to run the system of control without Congress co-operation. Consequently, the Congress could not condone their continuance without jeopardizing its coherence as an all-India organization. This was part of the logic of the working of the system. For Muslim interests in most provinces, the way forward was by accepting the government's categories and working the system. For the Congress, it was by opposing those categories and rejecting the system. When government resisted devolution at the Centre in 1920, the Congress strengthened its own centre. When separate electorates began to work effectively to the government's advantage, the Congress campaigned for their abolition. Where the Raj exploited the particular, the Congress built on the general, and where strategies were reversed, so were reactions. But Congress itself was affected by the developments it refused to condone. As the main opposition party, it relied on the support of those excluded from the rewards of the existing system, and with political relations in the provinces polarized along communal lines, the sources of opposition were also affected. In this situation, the Congress as a conciliar party came to depend increasingly on communal Hindu support, and in those circumstances, an all-India communal settlement was no longer possible.

By the end of the 1920s, all-India politics had become deadlocked, and the Congress had no alternative but to broaden and extend its popular appeal. By this stage even the most constitutional Congressman realized that it was no good opposing the system on its own terms. The only way forward was to challenge the social and economic forces which the constitution had been designed to reinforce. It was at this time that the Congress began to work systematically in the countryside and to bracket the landlord with the government.

By this stage, however, Muslim provincialism was in the ascendant, and the new orientation of Congress policy only added a fresh dimension of uneasiness to an already tense communal situation. The majority-province Muslims had little to fear from an extension of the franchise or from a broadening and deepening of political mobilization, but for them 'Congress' already meant 'Hindu', and Congress control at the Centre threatened to limit their capacity for manoeuvre. In the minority provinces, and particularly in the United Provinces, Muslims had a great deal to fear, because their social and economic importance, which had made them so valuable to the system of control, was brought under fire. For these reasons, by the early 1930s, for both majority and minority-province Muslims, the political future lay in co-operation at the all-India level. By this stage, an important section of U.P. Muslims had accepted the need for a strong Punjab, and Muslim politics had assumed a distinct centrifugal tendency. As the Congress began to undermine the foundations of the Raj, the Muslims began to leave by the back door.

The Imperial answer to this dilemma was the All India Federation. It was never wholly approved in New Delhi, and it was accepted in Britain for reasons which had more to do with British political problems than with the reality of power in the subcontinent. But by 1931 it had become the cornerstone of a new Imperial strategy. The theory was that with the bulk of the politically active Hindu community against continued British control at the Centre, the only way forward was by the construction of a new Centre as a rallying point for the well-disposed. Within the British Indian context, even the united support of the Muslims was inadequate for this purpose. But it was hoped that by bringing in the Princes, a stable Centre might be possible. This turned out to be a bankrupt notion. In the first place, even if the Princes had come in, the areas of common concern would necessarily have been extremely limited, and the provinces would have exercised very substantial powers of leverage against the Centre. This was a point continually stressed by the Reforms Commissioner but it was never fully appreciated in London. More importantly, however, the acceptance of the idea of an all-India Centre did not solve the vital problem of how British India was to be governed in the interim. Indeed in many ways it made it more acute, for it increased pressure on the Raj from those who would lose by its inauguration. In the short term, of course, there were expedients. Until 1937, the Raj still held control of all the vital departments not only at the Centre but also in the provinces, and by an act of will it could continue to exercise control through its administrative and military machine. But with provincial autonomy in the offing, this was no long-term solution. Politically, even by 1932, the Raj had become a victim of its own system of control.

The system of control which the Imperial power built up in India reflected the nature of the Imperial presence. For a few thousand

Europeans to rule the vast subcontinent, it was necessary to build on the existing social and political structure; to recognize the realities of power and influence in Indian India. More than this, it was necessary to categorize and to classify; to organize Indian society, albeit largely on its own terms, so that the Imperial system was subsumed and validated by Indian society at large. From the man who waited in the Collector's office, sitting or standing according to status, to the nine or eleven-gun Raja or Nawab, Indians were separated from each other and given a place in the hierarchy of Empire.

Until electoral institutions were introduced and political responsibility devolved to Indian hands, this system worked satisfactorily. True, it was cumbrous, often long-winded; but it was not inflexible, and however slowly it worked, it was capable of modification and adjustment to meet changing realities. With the introduction of electoral institutions, however, a chink appeared in the armour of autocracy; for however restricted the franchise, electoral institutions offered to the opponents of the Imperial system an opportunity to secure by organization what they could not achieve by deputation and petition.

The Raj itself attempted to contain such developments by constitutional manipulation It attempted within the conciliar sphere to reproduce the system of control which had served it well outside it. In the days of consultative politics, representation was by interest. In the days of political responsibility, the same system continued. The rural areas were favoured; the Muslims were given separate electorates; seats were allotted to special interests; and the Depressed Classes were granted the same privileges, though they subsequently gave them up. But these expedients failed to provide the Raj with a viable means of control. Political realities began to change too fast. As the localities were drawn into the orbit of provincial politics, and the provinces into the orbit of national politics, categories broadened and the Raj's capacity for manoeuvre was seriously reduced. By the time the Montagu-Chelmsford constitution was revised, the management of Indian politics was no longer conducted at the local level. It was no longer a question of district officials, with the authority of the Imperial system behind them, balancing the claims of Hindu and Muslim in some village or district town. The Raj was called to balance the U.P. Muslims against the U.P. Hindus, the Punjabi Muslims against the Punjabi Hindus, and ultimately, the Muslims of India against the Hindus of India.

The working of the electoral system forced the Raj to the wall. Imperialism and Democracy were incompatible bedfellows. In Britain, political reform strengthened the existing social and economic system by absorbing and accommodating its political opponents. In India, no such absorption was possible. The Europeans who ruled the Empire were themselves a socially and culturally discrete community, meeting and working with Indians only on their own terms. In the days of autocracy, this was their strength. In the days of electoral politics, it became their undoing. With each stage of devolution, Indian was set against Indian, caste against caste, community against community. But as each area of government and administration was ceded to Indian control, it was followed by demands for more concessions. Ultimately, even the Raj's closest allies were only allies for a purpose.

In 1947, the Raj withdrew, ceding its dominant position to those who had triumphed in the electoral arena. But the final act of devolution was also a final act of division. It was the system which won in the end.

Glossary

Alim	A Muslim religious scholar; pl. ulema.
Ahmadi	A follower of Ghulam Ahmed of Qadian, a nineteenth-century religious leader whose followers have been declared non-Muslims in Pakistan.
Anjuman	Association.
Arain	A caste of market-gardeners from Central Punjab.
Arti	A ceremony, involving the lighting of a flame and the singing of songs, associated with Hindu prayers.
Arya Samaj	A reformist Hindu sect founded by Dayananda Saraswati.
Azan	Summons to Muslim prayer.
Bania	A caste of Hindu moneylenders.
Chamar	A Hindu of low caste whose business is working in hides and leather.
Chela	Disciple, pupil.
Crore	Ten million, a hundred lakhs.
Dar ul Harb	A country under a government that does not recognize Muslim law.
Dar ul Islam	A country under a government which recognizes Muslim law.
Dharamsala	A charitable institution provided as a rest place for Hindu pilgrims.
Dusehra	A ten-day Hindu festival, held in October and dedicated to the worship of Rama.
Goonda	A hooligan or thug.
Gurdwara	A Sikh temple.
Haj	The Muslim pilgrimage to Mecca.
Haji	One who has performed the Haj.
Hakim	A Muslim physician.
Haram	Forbidden, prohibited.
Hartal	A strike.
Hijrat	Migration or departure from one's own country. One of the options enjoined upon Muslims under a government which does not recognize Muslim law. Originally the name given to the flight of the Prophet Mahommed from Mecca to Medina which marks the beginning of the Muslim era.
Hookum	An order.
Jamaat or Jamiat	Association, organization, party.
Jat	A caste of peasant farmers found in Eastern Punjab and Western U.P.
Jatha	An organized band or group.

Jihad	A holy war waged by Muslims against unbelievers.
Kayasth	A caste of Hindu scribes or accountants, found mainly in U.P.
Khaddar	Homespun cloth.
Khoja	A Muslim sect, originally from Western India.
Kotwal	The chief police officer for a city or town.
Lakh	One hundred thousand.
Lambardar	A village headman in Punjab.
Majlis	An assembly.
Maulana	A title given to eminent Muslim religious scholars.
Maulvi	A Muslim teacher or learned man.
Mofussil	Country districts, particularly in Bengal.
Mohalla	A quarter of a town or city.
Moharram	The first month of the Muslim calendar, of which the first ten days are specially dedicated to the memory of Hussain, the grandson of the Prophet, who was martyred at Kerbela.
Mukhya	A village headman.
Mulla	Originally a judge or magistrate; more colloquially used for a Muslim schoolmaster or village priest.
Naib	
Tehsildar	Assistant Tehsildar, a land Revenue official in charge of part of a tehsil.
Namaz	Prayer, obligatory for Muslims five times a day.
Nawab	A noble, title denoting nobility.
Pargannah	A subdivision of a district, particularly in Bengal.
Pukka	Real, genuine.
Puja	Ritual of Hindu worship.
Rais	A gentleman of respectable position.
Raiyat	Cultivator, farmer, peasant, tenant.
Raja	Originally a King or Prince; awarded as a title of rank by the Government of India.
Rajput	Warrior caste from Rajputana.
Ram	One of the ten Avatars.
Ram Dol	Krishna's cradle, which is taken in procession to celebrate his birthday.
Ram Lila	A Hindu religious festival, culminating in Dusehra.
Ram Raj	A Hindu utopia.
Sabha	An association (usually Hindu).
Sangathan	Organization; one plank of an Arya Samaj campaign to revitalize Hindu society.
Sankh	A conch shell blown at Hindu prayers.
Satyagraha	Commitment to the truth force, the use of moral pressure for political purposes as pioneered by Gandhi.
Shia	A major sect of Islam, which regards the first three Caliphs as usurpers and recognizes Ali, the son-in-law of the Prophet, as the only rightful Caliph.

Shuddhi	A movement for the purification of Hindu society and the reconversion of Muslims.
Sunni	The main sect of Islam; a follower of the Prophet and the first four Caliphs.
Swadeshi	Made at home; a movement to support Indian industry.
Swaraj	Freedom, self-government.
Tabligh	The preaching of Islam.
Taluqdar	A landed aristocrat in Oudh.
Tanzim	Organization; the name given to a reform movement among the Indian Muslims.
Tazia	A float taken in procession by Shia Muslims during Moharram.
Tehsil	Subdivision of a district, in the charge of a tehsildar.
Vakil	A lawyer or pleader.
Wahabi	A puritanical sect of Islam founded by the Arabian reformer, Sheikh Abdul Wahab.
Zemindar	A landowner.

Bibliography

UNPUBLISHED SOURCES

OFFICIAL

Records of the Government of India, Home Department, Political and Public branches, National Archives of India, New Delhi.

Records of the Government of India, Reforms Office.

Records of the Government of the United Provinces, General Administration Department, U.P. Government Secretariat, Lucknow.

India Office Records, Public and Judicial Department.

India Office Records, Parliamentary Department.

India Office Records, Private Office papers.

UNOFFICIAL

1. *Collections of papers*

Ali Imam papers, Karachi University Library.

All India Congress Committee papers, Nehru Memorial Museum and Library, New Delhi.

Ansari papers, Jamia Millia Islamia, New Delhi.

Birkenhead papers, IOL MSS Eur. D 703.

Chelmsford papers, IOL MSS Eur. E 264.

Fazli Husain papers, by courtesy of Mr. Azim Husain.

Gandhi papers, Gandhi Smarak Nidhi, Delhi (microfilm copy, Trinity College, Cambridge).

Hailey papers, IOL MSS Eur. E 220.

Halifax papers, IOL MSS Eur. C 152.

Harcourt Butler papers, IOL MSS Eur. F 116.

Lothian papers, Scottish Record Office, Edinburgh.

Mahommed Ali papers, Jamia Millia Islamia, New Delhi.

Meston papers, IOL MSS Eur. F 136.

Montagu papers, IOL MSS Eur. D 523.

Nehru papers, Nehru Memorial Museum and Library.

Purushotamdas Thakurdas papers, Nehru Memorial Museum and Library.

Reading papers, IOL MSS Eur. E 238

Shafi Daudi papers, by courtesy Mr Ata ur Rahman Daudi, Muzaffarpur.

Shaukat Ali papers, Jamia Millia Islamia, New Delhi.

Shuaib Qureshi's minute of dissent to the Nehru report, by courtesy of Syed Sharifuddin Pirzada.

Syed Mahmud papers, Nehru Memorial Museum and Library.

Templewood papers, IOL MSS Eur. E 240.

Thompson papers, IOL MSS Eur. F 137.

2. *Interviews*

Azim Husain, Berne, April 1969.
Sir James Penny, Oxford, June 1969.
Sir Francis Mudie, Dundee, July 1969.
The Nawab of Chhatari, New Delhi, September 1969.
Syed Mahommed Jaffri (formerly Sub-Editor of *Hamdard*), Delhi, September 1969.
Aruna Asaf Ali, New Delhi, November 1969.
Ata ur Rahman Daudi (son of Shafi Daudi), Muzaffarpur, January 1970.
Lady Imam, Bankipore, January 1970.
Zamiruddin Ahmed (Assistant Secretary of the Muslim Conference), Patna, January 1970.
Dr Azimuddin Ahmed (son of Sir Sultan Ahmed), Patna, January 1970.
The Maharajkumar of Mahmudabad, Lucknow, February 1970.
General Habibullah, Lucknow, February 1970.
K.L. Gauba, New Delhi, March 1970.
Sardar Shaukat Hayat, Lahore, March 1970.
Mazhar Ali Khan, Lahore, March 1970.
Begum Shah Nawaz, Lahore, March 1970.
Malik Lal Khan, Lahore, March 1970.
Begum Viquarunissa Noon, Lahore, March 1970.
Ghulam Rasool Mihr, Lahore, March 1970.
Dr Niaz Ahmed, Lahore, March 1970.
Malik Shaukat Ali (son of Malik Barkat Ali), Lahore, March 1970.
Chaudhuri Khaliquzzaman, Karachi, April 1970.
Syed Hussain Imam of Gaya, Karachi, April 1970.
Lady Haroon, Karachi, April 1970.
G.M. Madeni, Karachi, April 1970.
Nawab Siddiq Ali Khan, Karachi, April 1970.
M.A.H. Ispahani, Karachi, April 1970.
Syed Hamza Ali (son of Syed Raza Ali), Karachi, 1970.
Mahommed Ali Chaiwallah (Jinnah's solicitor), Bombay, September 1970.
Akbar Peerbhoy, Bombay, September 1970.
Rasoolbhai Rangoonwallah, Bombay, September 1970.
Fazl Rahimtoolah, Bombay, September 1970.

3. *Unpublished theses and dissertations*

Bayly, C.A. 'The development of political organisation in the Allahabad locality 1880-1925', unpublished D.Phil. thesis, Oxford, 1970.

Gordon, R.A. 'Aspects in the history of the Indian National Congress, with special reference to the Swarajya party, 1919-1927', D. Phil. thesis, Oxford, 1970.

Reeves, P.D. 'The Landlords: response to political change in the United Provinces of Agra and Oudh, India, 1921-31, Ph.D. thesis, Australian National University, 1963 (microfilm copy in the India office Library).

Robinson, F.C.R. 'The two nations', fellowship dissertation, Trinity College, Cambridge, 1969.

PUBLISHED SOURCES

OFFICIAL

U.P. District Gazetteers.

Punjab District Gazetteers.

British Parliamentary Debates.

Proceedings of the Imperial Legislative Council (1909-20).

Proceedings of the Imperial Legislative Assembly (1921-36).

Proceedings of the U.P. Legislative Council (1909-36).

Proceedings of the Punjab Legislative Council (1921-36).

Proceedings of the Bombay Legislative Council (1921-36).

Proceedings of the Bihar and Orissa Legislative Council (1921-36).

Proceedings of the Assam Legislative Council (1921-36).

Proceedings of the Bengal Legislative Council (1921-36).

Census of India (1901, 1911, 1921, 1931).

India Office List (1900-35).

Punjab Civil List (1920-35).

United Provinces Civil List (1920-35).

Moral and Material Progress of India (1908-9 to 1934-5), from 1929-30 published as *'India in...'*.

India's Contribution to the Great War (Calcutta 1923).

Report of the Public Services Commission 1886-7, with appendices (Calcutta 1888).

Report of the Royal Commission on the Public Services in India, vols. 1-20 (London 1913-1917).

Ritchie, J.A. *The Progress of Education in India 1917-22* (Calcutta 1923).

Littlehailes, R. *The Progress of Education in India 1922-27* (Calcutta 1929).

Parliamentary Papers and HMSO publications

Cmd. 4635 (1909). Progress of Education in India, Fifth Quinquennial Report, 1902-1907.

Cmd. 7485 (1914). Progress of Education in India, Sixth Quinquennial Report, 1907-1912.

Cmd. 9109 (1918). Report on Indian Constitutional Reforms (Montagu-Chelmsford report).

Cmd. 9190 (1918). Report of the Indian Sedition Committee (Rowlatt Committee report).

Cmd. 256 (1919). Progress of Education in India, Seventh Quinquennial Report, 1912-1917.

H.C. 203 (1919). Joint Select Committee on the Government of India Bill, Vol. i, Report vol. ii, Minutes of Evidence.

Cmd. 681 (1920). Report of the Committee Appointed to Investigate Disturbances in thePunjab (Hunter Committee report).

Cmd. 1251 (1921). Return Showing the Results of Elections in India.

Cmd. 2154 (1924). Return Showing the Results of Elections in India.

Cmd. 2360 (1925). Reforms Enquiry Committee (Muddiman Committee) Report.

Cmd. 2361 (1925). Views of the Local Governments on the Working of the Reforms, 1923.

Cmd. 2362 (1925). Views of the Local Governments on the Working of the Reforms, 1924: Reforms Enquiry Committee, appendix 5, Written Evidence (London 1925); Reforms Enquiry Committee, appendix 6, parts i and ii (London 1925). 1925.

Cmd. 2923 (1927). Return Showing the Results of Elections in India.

Cmd. 2986 (1927). Indian Statutory Commission. Statement Published on 8 November 1927 by the Governor-General in India.

Cmd. 3302 (1928-29). Report of the Indian States Committee.

Cmd. 3451 (1929). Report of the Indian Central Committee.

Cmd. 3525 (1930). Supplementary Note by Dr. A. Suhrawardy to the Report of the Indian Central Committee.

Cmd. 3568 (1930). Report of the Indian Statutory Commission (Simon Commission), vol. i, Survey.

Cmd. 3569 (1930). Report of the Indian Statutory Commission, vol. ii, Recommendations.

Cmd. 3572 (1930). Indian Statutory Commission, vol. iii, Reports of the Committees Appointed by the Provincial Legislative Councils to Co-operate with the Indian Statutory Commission.

Report of the Indian Statutory Commission, vols. iv-xiv. Memoranda Submitted by the government of India and the India Office and by provincial Governments (London 1930).

Cmd. 3700 (1930). Government of India Despatch on Proposals for Constitutional Reform.

Cmd. 3738 (1931). Proceedings of the Indian Round Table Conference, First Session.

Cmd 3891 (1931). Cawnpore Riot Enquiry Commission Report.

Cmd. 3922 (1931). Return Showing the Results of Elections in India.

Cmd. 3997 (1932). Proceedings of the Indian Round Table Conference, Second Session.

Indian Round Table Conference, Second Session: proceedings of the Federal Structure Committee and the Minorities Committee (London 1932).

Cmd. 4086 (1932). Report of the Indian Franchise Committee.

Cmd. 4147 (1932). East India (Constitutional reforms): Communal Decision.

Cmd. 4238 (1933). Reports and Proceedings of the Indian Round Table Conference, Third Session.

UNOFFICIAL

1. *Material published by Indian political organizations*

Annual Reports of the Indian National Congress.

All Parties Conference 1928, Report of the Committee Appointed by the Conference to Determine the Principles of the Constitution for India (Allahabad 1929)

Proceedings of the All Parties National Convention (Allahabad 1929).

All Parties Conference 1928, Supplementary Report of the Committee (Allahabad 1928).

Representation of the Muslims of the United Provinces (India) to the Indian Statutory Commission (Allahabad 1928).

Speeches Delivered at the Chashi given by Ch. Chothu Ram to meet Sir Fazli Husain (Lahore. 1932).

For information on the Muslim League, I have relied on S.S. Pirzada's *Foundations of Pakistan, All India Muslim League Documents, 1906-47*, 2 vols, (Karachi 1969-70).

For the Muslim Conference, there is K.K. Aziz's *All India Muslim Conference, a Documentary Record* (Karachi 1972), but I have chiefly relied on the material available in the Mihr collection at the Research Society of Pakistan, Lahore.

Presidential Address (by the Aga Khan) to the Muslim Conference, Delhi, December 1928 (Bombay 1928).

Report of the All India Muslim Conference, Lucknow (Aligarh 1930).

Presidential Address by Sir Mahommed Iqbal, All India Muslim Conference, Lahore, March 1932 (Lahore 1932).

Resolutions of the All India Muslim Conference, the Executive Board and the Working Committee, from January 1929 to March 1932 (Lahore 1932).

Resolutions Passed at the Lahore Session of the All India Muslim Conference, March 1932 (Delhi 1932).

List of Members of the Working Committee, the Executive Board, the General Body of the All India Muslim Conference Elected on 24 August 1932 (Patna 1932).

Resolutions Passed at the Special Session of the All India Muslim Conference, Calcutta, December 1932 (Calcutta 1932).

Copies of Letters to Maulana Mahommed Shafee Daoodi, 1932 (? Patna 1932).

Prominent Men Elected by the Working Committee of the All Indian Muslim Conference (?Patna 1932).

Speech by Sir Fazli Husain at the Opening of the Punjab Unionist Party Headquarters (Lahore 1936).

2. *Newspapers, journals, periodicals and annuals*

Bombay Chronicle.

Civil and Military Gazette (Lahore).

Comrade (Delhi).

Indian Annual Register 1923-32 (Calcutta), published as the *Indian Quarterly Register 1924-29.*

Indian Daily Telegraph (Lucknow).

Indian Social Reformer.

The Leader (Allahabad).

Moslem Outlook (Lahore).

Pioneer (Allahabad).

Searchlight (Patna).

The Times (London).

Times of India (Bombay).

Tribune (Lahore).

3. *Articles*

Barrier, N.G. 'The Arya Samaj and Congress Politics in the Punjab 1894-1908'. *Journal of Asian Studies* (*JAS*), xxvi, no. 3 (May 1967), pp. 363-79.

Bayly, C.A. 'Local Control in Indian Towns: the Case of Allahabad, 1880-1920' *Modern Asian Studies* (*MAS*), 5 (1971), pp. 289-311.

Brass, P.R. 'Muslim Separatism in the United Provinces: Social Context and political Strategy before Partition', *Economic and Political Weekly*, v, nos. 3, 4 and 5 (annual number 1970), pp. 167-86.

Danzig, R. 'The Announcement of August 20th, 1917', *JAS,* xxviii, no. 1 (November 1968), pp. 19-37.

Gopal krishna. 'The Development of the Indian National Congress as a Mass Organisation', *JAS,* xxv, no. 3 (May 1966), pp. 413-30.

Gordon, R.A. 'The Hindu Mahasabha, and the' Indian National Congress 1915-26, (MAS), 9,2, (1975).

Heeger, G.A. 'The Growth of the Congress Movement in Punjab, 1920-1940', *JAS,* xxxi, no. 1 (Nov. 1972), pp. 39-51.

Islam, Zafar ul and Jensen, R. 'Indian Muslims in the Public Services 1871-1915, *Journal of the Asiatic Society of Pakistan,* iv (1964), pp. 85-93.

Jones, K.W. 'Communalism in the Punjab: the Arya Samaj Contribution', *JAS,* xxviii, no. 1 (Nov. 1968), pp. 39-54.

Minault, G, and Lelyveld,D, The Campaign for a Muslim University 1898-1920, *Modern Asian Studies,* 8,2 (1974), pp. 145-189.

Moore, R.J. 'The Demission of Empire in South Asia: Some Perspectives', *Journal of Imperial and Commonwealth History,* xx no. 1 (Oct. 1973), pp. 79-94.

Owen, H.F. 'Negotiating the Lucknow Pact', *JAS,* xxxi, no. 3 (May 1972), pp. 561-87.

Robinson, F.C.R. 'Consultation and Control: the United Provinces' Government and its Allies, 1860-1906', *MAS, 5 (1971), pp. 313-36.*

Rothermund, D. 'Constitutional Reform versus National Agitation in India 1900-1950', *JAS,* xxi, no. 4 (Aug. 1962), pp. 505-22.

4. *Printed books and pamphlets*

Afzal, M. Rafiq (ed.). *Selected Speeches and Statements of Quaid-i-Azam Mahommed Ali Jinnah* (1911-34 and 1947-48) (Lahore 1966).

———————————————. *Malik Barkat Ali, His Life and Writings* (Lahore 1969).

Aga Khan. *Memoirs, World Enough and Time* (London 1954).

Ahmed, Aziz. *Studies in Islamic Culture in the Indian Environment* (Oxford 1964).

————————. *Islamic Modrnism in India and Pakistan* (London 1967).

Ahmed, Jamal Mahommed. *The Intellectual Origins of Egyptian Nationalism* (London 1968).

Ahmed, Nafis. *An Economic Geography of East Pakistan* (2nd edn, Oxford 1968).

Ahmed, Shafaat. *Presidential Address to the Punjab Muslim Educational Conference* (Allahabad 1929).

Allana, G. *Quaid-i-Azam Jinnah, the Story of a Nation* (Lahore 1967).

Ambedkar, B.R. *Pakistan or the Partition of India* (Bombay 1946).

Azad. Maulana Abul Kalam, *India Wins Freedom* (Calcutta 1959).

Aziz, K.K. *Britain and Modern India, 1857-1947* (London 1963).

———.*The Making of Pakistan, a Study in Nationalism* (London 1967).

———. *The All India Muslim Conference 1928-1935, a Documentary Record* (Karachi 1972).

Banerjea, S.N. *A Nation in Making, Being Reminiscences of Fifty Years of Public Life* (London 1925).

Barrier, N.G. *The Punjab Alienation of Land Bill of 1900* (Durham, North Carolina 1966).

——————(ed). Roots of Communal Politics (Delhi 1976)

Bayly, C.A., *The Local Roots of Indian Nationalism. Allahabad 1880-1920* (Oxford 1975)

Beteille, A. *Castes: Old and New. Eassays in Social Status and Social Stratification* (Bombay 1969).

Bhatnagar, S.K. *History of M.A.O. College, Aligarh* (New Delhi 1969).

Binder, L. *Religion and Politics in Pakistan* (Berkeley 1961).

Birkenhead, 2nd earl of. *F.E., the Life of F. E. Smith, First Earl of Birkenhead, by His Son* (London 1965).

Birla, G.D. *In the Shadow of the Mahatma: a Perzonal Memoir* (Bombay 1953).

Bolitho, Hector. *Jinnah: Creator of Pakistan* (London 1954).

Bose, S.C. *The Indian Struggle 1920-42* (London 1964).

Brass, P.R. *Language, Religion and Politics in North India* (Cambridge 1974).

Brecher, Michael, *Nehru; a Political Biography* (London 1959).

Broomfield, J.H. *Elite Conflict in a Plural Society, 20th Century Bengal* (Berkeley and Los Angeles 1968).

Brown, J.M. *Gandhi's Rise to Power: Indian Politics 1915-22* (Cambridge 1972).

Butler, Sir Spencer Harcourt. *India Insistent* (London 1931).

Callard, K. *Pakistan, a Political Study* (London 1968).

Chaudhuri, N.C. *The Autobiography of an Unknown Indian* (London 1951).

Chintamani, C.Y. *Indian Politics since the Mutiny* (London 1939).

Chirol, V. *Indian Unrest* (London 1910).

————. *India* (London 1926).

Chopra, P.N. *Rafi Ahmed Kidwai* (Agra 1959).

Coatman, J. *Years of Destiny: India 1926-32* (London 1932).

Coupland, R. *The Indian Problem 1833-1935* (Oxford 1968).

Dani, Ahmed Hassan. *Peshawar, Historic City of the Frontier* (Peshawar 1969).

Darling, Sir M.L. *The Punjab Peasant in Prosperity and Debt* (3rd ed, Oxford 1932).

———————.*Wisdom and Waste in the Punjab Village* (Oxford 1934)

——————————.*Apprentice to Power, India 1904-1908* (London 1966).

Das, M.N. *India under Morley and Minto* (London 1964).

Desai, A.R. *Social Background to Indian Nationalism* (Bombay 1948).

Dichter, David, *The North West Frontier of Pakistan, a Study in Regional Geography* (Oxford) 1967).

Dwarkadas, Kanji, *Ruttie Jinnah. The Story of a Great Friendship* (Bombay 1962).

————————————. *India's Fight for Freedom 1913-1937, an Eye-witness Story* (Bombay 1966).

Dumont, L.C.J. *Religion, Politics and History in India: Collected Papers in Indian Sociology* (Paris 1970).

Dungen, P.H.M. van den. *The Punjab Tradition: Influence and Authority in 19th-century India* (London 1972).

Farquhar, J.N. *Modern Religious Movements in India* (London 1929).

Faruqui, Zia ul Hassan. *The Deoband School and the Demand for Pakistan* (London 1963).

The Frontier Question in the Assembly, being the Statements of Pandit Motilal Nehru, Maulvi Shafi Daudi and Syed Murtuza (Delhi 1926).

Frykenberg, R.E. *Land Control and Social Structure in Indian History* (Madison, Wisconsin 1969).

Gallagher, J., Johnson, G. and Seal, A. (eds.). *Locality, Province and Nation, Essays on Indian Politics 1870-1940* (Cambridge 1973).

Gandhi, M.K. *Communal Unity* (Ahmedabad 1949).

——————*An Autobiography, the Story of My Experiments with Truth,* translated from Gujerati by Mahadev Desai (London 1966).

——————.*Collected Works of Gandhi,* vols. xiii-xlvi (Ahmedabad 1964-71).

Gopal, Ram. *Indian Muslims, a Political History, 1858-1947* (Bombay 1959).

Gopal, S. *British Policy in India, 1858-1905* (Cambridge 1905).

———.*The Viceroyalty of Lord Irwin* (Oxford 1957).

Griffin, Sir Lepel. *Chiefs and Families of Note in the Punjab,* Vols. i-iii (rev., Lahore 1940).

Gwyer, M. and Appadorai, A. (eds.). *Speeches and Documents on the Indian Constitution, 1921-47,* vols. i-ii (London 1957).

Halifax, Earl of. *Fulness of Days* (London 1957).

Hamid, A. *A Brief Survey of Muslim Separatism in India* (London 1968).

Hardinge, Lord. *My Indian Years 1910-1916* (London 1948).

Hardy, P. *The Muslims of British India* (Cambridge 1972).

Hayat, Abul. *Mussulmans of Bengal* (Calcutta 1966).

Heimsath, C.H. *Indian Nationalism and Hindu Social Reform* (Princeton 1964).

Hodson, H.V. *The Great Divide, Britain-India-Pakistan* (London 1969).

Husain, Azim. *Fazli Husain, a Political Biography* (Bombay 1946).

Husain, Sir Fazli, *Our Political Programme* (Lahore 1930).

Hussain, Mahmud and others (ed.) *A History of the Freedom Movement,* vols. ii-iv (Karachi 1961-70).

Hussain, Syed Abid. *Indian Culture* (Bombay 1963).

Ibbetson, Sir Denzil. *Punjab Castes* (A Punjab Government reprint, Delhi 1970).

Ikram, S.M. *Modern Muslim India and the Birth of Pakistan* (Lahore 1965).

Ikramullah, Begum Shaista. *From Purdah to Parliament* (London 1963).

Iqbal. Afzal (ed.) *Select Speeches and Writings of Maulana Mahommed Ali,* First edition (Lahore 1944) Second edition, vols. i-ii (Lahore 1963).

——————————.*My Life: a Fragment, an Autobiographical Sketch of Maulana Mahommed Ali* (Lahore 1946).

Ismail, Sir Mahommed. *My Public Life* (London 1954).

Ispahani, M.A.H. *Quaid-i-Azam Jinnah as I Knew Him* (Karachi 1967).

Jambunathan, M.R. (ed.). *Swami Shraddhanand, an Autobiography* (Bombay 1961).

Jayakar, M.R. *The Story of My Life,* vol. i (Bombay 1958); vol. ii (Bombay 1959).

Johnson, G. *Provincial Politics and Indian Nationalism: Bombay and the Indian National Congress 1880-1915* (Cambridge 1974).

Joshi, V.C. (ed.) *Lala Lajpat Rai, His Writing and Speeches,* vols. i-ii (Delhi 1966).

Kabir, H. *Muslim Politics, 1906-42* (Calcutta 1943).

Karim, Maulvi Abdul. *Letters on Hindu-Muslim Pact* (Calcutta 1924).

Khaliquzzaman, Chaudhuri. *Pathway to Pakistan* (Lahore 1961).

Kidwai, Mushir Hussain. *Swaraj and How to Obtain it* (Lucknow 1924).

—————————*Panislamism and Bolshevism* (London 1938).

Kumar, R. (ed.) *Essays on Gandhian Politics, the Rowlatt Satyagraha of 1919* (Oxford 1971).

Lambrick, H.T. *Sind, a General Introduction* (Hyderabad 1964).

Lawrence, W.R. *The Valley of Kashmir* (reprint, Srinagar 1967).

Leach, E. and Mukherjee, S.N. (eds.). *Elites in South Asia* (Cambridge 1970).

Lewis, B. *The Emergence of Modern Turkey* (London 1961).

Low, D.A. (ed.) *Soundings in Modern South Asian History* (London 1968).

———————. (ed). *Congress and the Raj* (London 1977).

Lytton, Lord. *Pandits and Elephants* (London 1942).

Malik, Hafiz. *Muslim Nationalism in India and Pakistan* (Washington 1963).

Masood. Mukhtar (ed.). *Eye-witnesses of History, A collection of Letters Addressed to Quaid-i-Azam* (Karachi 1968).

Mayo, Katherine. *Mother India* (London 1927).

Mehrotra, S.R. *India and the Commonwealth 1885-1929* (London 1965).

———————.*The Emergence of the Indian National Congress (London 1971).*

Mehta, A. and Patwardhan, A. *The Communal Triangle in India* (Allahabad 1942)

Mehtar, M.A. *Whys of the Great Indian Conflict* (Lahore 1947).

Meston, Lord. *Nationhood for India* (London 1931).

Minto, Mary, Countess of. *India, Minto and Morley, 1905-1910* (London 1934).

Montagu, Edwin Samuel. *My Indian Diary* (London 1930).

Moon, Sir Penderel. *Divide and Quit* (London 1961).

Mujeeb, Mahommed. *The Indian Muslims* (London 1967).

Mukherjee, S.N. (ed.). *The Movement for National Freedom in India*, St Anthony's papers, no. 18 (Oxford 1966).

Naidu, Sarojini. *Mahommed Ali Jinnah, an Ambassador of Unity: His Speeches and Wrintings 1912-1917* (Madras 1917).

Nanda, B.R. *Mahatma Gandhi* (London 1958).

———————.*The Nehrus, Motilal and Jawaharlal* (London 1965).

Nehru, J. *An Autobiography, with Musings on Recent Events in India* (London 1936).

—————.*The Discovery of India* (London 1946).

—————.*A Bunch of Old Letters, Written Mostly to Jawaharlal Nehru and Some Written by Him* (London 1960).

Noman, Mahommed.*Muslim India* (Allahabad 1942).

Noon, Firoz Khan. *Dominion Status or Autonomous Provinces?* (Lahore 1928).

———————. *From Memory* (Lahore 1966).

O'Dwyer, Sir Michael.*India as I Knew it 1885-1925* (London 1925).

Pandey, G, *The Ascendancy of the Congress in Uttar Pradesh 1926—34* (Delhi 1978).

Parikh, Narhari, D. *Sardar Vallabhai Patel*, vol. i (Ahmedabad 1953); vol. ii (Ahmedabd 1956)

Patel, G.I. *Vithalbhai Patel, Life and Times*, vol. i-ii (Bombay 1950).

Philips, C.H. (ed.) *Politics and Society in India* (London 1963).

————————————.*The Evolution of India and Pakistan 1857-1947, Select Documents* (London 1964).

Philips, C.H. and Wainwright, M.D. (eds.) *The Partition of India, Policies and Perspectives 1935-1947* (London 1970).

Pirzada, Syed Sharifuddin (ed.) *Foundations of Pakistan, All India Muslim League Documents, 1906-47*, vol. i (Karachi 1969); vol. ii (Karachi 1970).

Prasad, Rajendra. *India Divided* (Bombay 1947).

————————*Autobiography* (Bombay 1957).

Rahman, Matiur. *From Consultation to Confrontation, A study of the Muslim League in British Indian politics, 1906-1912* (London 1970).

Rashiduzzaman, M. *The Central Legislature in British India, 1921-47* (Dacca 1965).

Reed, Sir Stanley. *The India I Knew, 1897-1947* (London 1952).

Reid, Sir Robert. *Years of Change in Bengal and Assam* (London 1966).

Robinson, F.C.R., *Separatism among Indian Muslims. The politics of the United Provinces Muslims 1860–1923* (Cambridge 1974).
Ronaldshay, Lord. *India, a Bird's Eye View* (London 1924).
— — — — — — — —.*'Essayez'* (London 1956).
Saiyid, Matlub ul Hassan. *Mahommed Ali Jinnah, a Political Study* (Lahore 1945).
Sampurnanand. *Memories and Reflections* (Bombay 1962).
Sarda, Harbilas. *Recollections and Reminiscences* (Ajmer 1951).
Sarkar, S. *The Swadeshi movement in Bengal, 1903-1908* (New Delhi 1973)
Sayeed, Khalid bin. *Pakistan, the Formative Phase, 1857-1948* (2nd ed. London 1968).
Schuster, Sir George, and Wint, Guy. *India and Democracy* (London 1941).
Seal, Anil, *The Emergence of Indian Nationalism, Competition and Collaboration in the later Nineteenth Century* (Cambridge 1968).
Sen, N.B. *Punjab's Eminent Hindus* (Lahore 1943).
Setalvad, Sir Chimanlal. *Recollections and Reflections, an Autobiography* (Bombay 1947).
Shafi, Alhaj Mian Ahmed. *Haji Abdullah Haroon, a Biography* (Karachi, n.d.)
Shafi, Sir Mahommed. *Some Important Indian Problems* (Lahore 1930).
Shah Nawaz, Jehanara Begum. *Father and Daughter* (Lahore 1971).
Siddiqui, N.H. *Landlords of Agra and Avadh* (Allahabad and Lucknow 1950).
Sitaramayya, P. *The History of the Indian National Congress*, vols. i-ii (Bombay 1946-47).
Smith, W.C. *Modern Islam in India* (Lahore 1954).
Tandon, Prakash. *Punjabi Century, 1857-1947* (London 1963).
Tara Chand, Dr. *Influence of Islam on Indian Culture* (Allahabad 1963).
Taylor, A.J.P. *English History 1914-1945* (Oxford 1965).
Templewood, Lord. *Nine Troubled years* (London 1954).
Tendulkar, D.G. *Abdul Gaffar Khan* (New Delhi 1967).
Tinker. H. *The Foundations of Local Self-Government in India Pakistan and Burma* (London 1954).
Tomlinson, B.R. *The Indian National Congress and the Raj, 1929–42* (London 1976).
Trevaskis, H.K. *The End of an Era: Memories of the British Raj in India, 1905-1928* (Shoreham on Sea 1973).
Tyabji, H.B. *Badruddin Tyabji: a Biography* (Bombay 1952).
Wasti, Syed Razi. *Lord Minto and the Indian Nationalist Movement 1905-10* (Oxford 1964).
Zakaria, Rafiq. *Rise of Muslims in Indian Politics* (Bombay 1970).

Index